The story of

How
We
Became
one

*From Bill Penzey
and the Penzeys One staff*

Our four decades of selling spices have taught us that cooking is not a one size fits all world: far from it. We've learned the true beauty of cooking lies in the incredible diversity of the people who cook, and in the incredible variety of the food they cook. Those years have also taught us for all the diversity, for all the variety, people who cook have something in common. They care enough to make the lives of those around them better. The research shows that people who share dinner together at the kitchen table go on to share a brighter future. A brighter future made possible by people with the spirit to build it one meal at a time. It is this spirit we celebrate, this spirit we hope to spread, this spirit that makes all who cook ONE. We think you will find that Diversity, Variety, Caring and Actual Cooks make for a really worthwhile magazine. Come along and join us.

Be **one**

contents

Ahe, there be dinner afoot

PENZEYS Presents
THE
JOHNNY CASH PARTY
JUNE **11** 2005
WISCONSIN
SATURDAY
7:30 P.M.

RESERVE SEAT
JUNE 11, 2005
ADMIT ONE THIS DATE ONLY

PENZEY HOUSE
BE THERE OR
SPEND ALL
IN A BURNING
RING OF FIRE.

1 ADULT
JUNE 11, 2005

Love to Cook

Cook
to
Love

volume one, issue one, 2005
$4.95

Penzeys
one
The food magazine by & for everyone

one TOWN -- Birmingham
20 pages of recipes & people

WEEKNIGHT PIRATES
The Adventure Begins

2x4=
8 Great Soup Recipes

INSIDE SCOOP
Tips from the Crossroads of Cooking

PLUS: one LOVE - Children, The Creative Cook, one WORLD - Turkey, and so much more.

And
so it
begins.

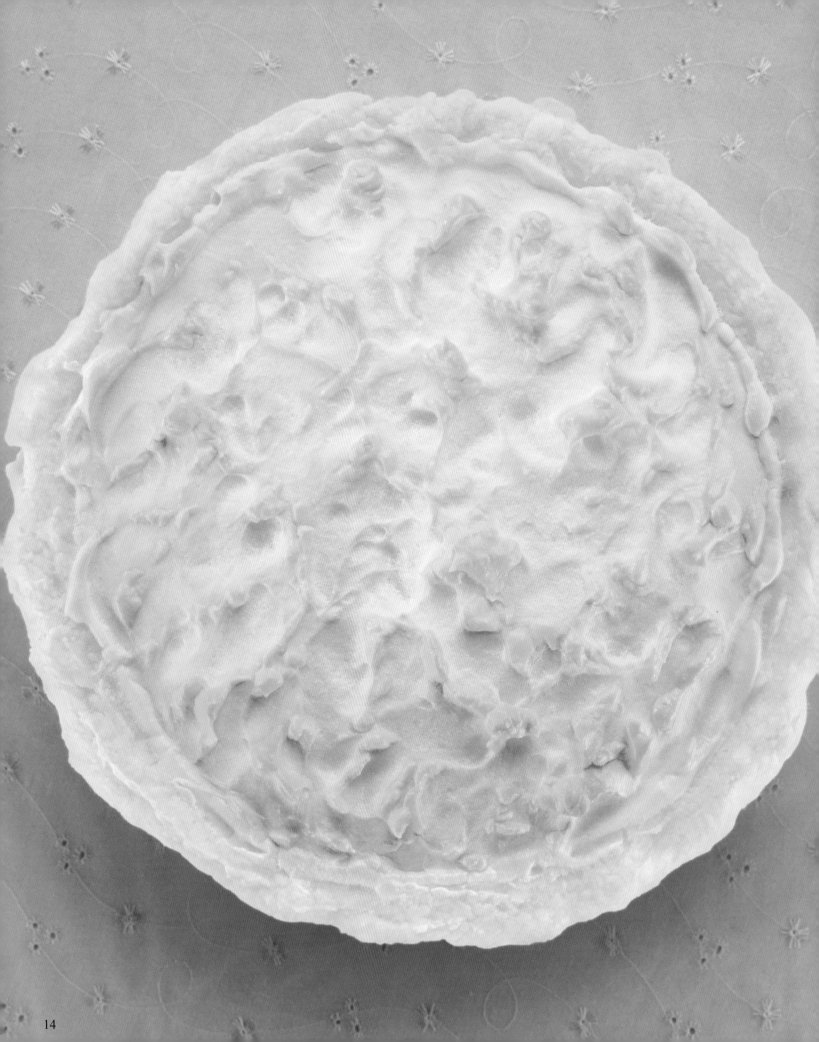

a letter from the editor

Welcome to our magazine. In so many
ways it's a tribute to all the food magazines that have
come before us and the many fine people who produce them.
We can't take credit for the idea of combining great recipes, beautiful
food photos and clever writing. Still I hope you like what we've done with the
format, that you find the recipes useful, the photos appealing and that once or twice
as you read your way through our magazine you find a smile upon your lips. In many ways we
are like the magazines that have come before us, but there are two ways that we hope you will
find us different. Two ways that we think are important.

First, is the people we feature, whose recipes inspire our photos and whose lives inspire our words.
Hard to say if it is all the media mergers, or if it is simply easier to write about people who have already been
written about, but it seems the magazines that do a nice job with photography and writing keep featuring
the same group of people over and over again. We are not saying that recipes from people with cookbooks
or television shows to promote or recipes from chefs at expensive restaurants in large cities are any less valid than
recipes from the rest of us. What we are saying is that there is so very much more to the world of food. Our decades
in the spice trade have taught us the incredible value of variety. It may be painfully sappy to call everyone who cooks
as unique as a freshly fallen snowflake, but you are.

All of us are born into a unique style of cooking that is the sum of the generations of family members who've preceded
us. As we grow we reach out and discover our own individual likes and dislikes while at the same time being influenced by those
around us. If you are like me, the day you think you have yourself figured out, fate magically brings some wonderful soul with their
own food story into your life. If you are very lucky they will be willing to share your dinner table for the rest of your life. Of course
when two people love each other very much, suddenly there are children about and the whole cycle starts over again. This is
the process of life that, when it comes to what we cook and how we cook it, produces infinite variety. To us the idea that there is
only one right way to cook anything is not only wrong, but downright antisocial. So if you let us, we are going to pretty much skip
the narrow slice of cooks that are so well covered elsewhere and instead sing the praises of the cooks that make up the rest of
the pie. In this way we hope to not only introduce you to some good recipes you might have otherwise missed, but some good
people as well.

Which brings up our other difference. Somewhere over the decades of talking face to face with the people who came
out of their way to buy spices and seasonings, it hit us why people actually make the effort to cook. People aren't cooking to
become rich, or powerful, or famous. People go to the effort of cooking to make the lives around them better. Cooking is
ultimately an act of kindness. It may seem like a small thing, but I have come to believe that it really is one of the biggest
things out there. People everywhere making an effort to do nice things for others is an idea the media does not have
time for. Understanding that for every act of meanness on the nightly news there are thousands or maybe even
millions of acts of kindness puts it all in perspective. As hard as it is to believe from what we are all being told
every day, humans are actually for the most part pretty nice people.

And the wonderful thing is that this desire to do for others is not in the sole possession of any one
group or organization. The kindness of cooking transcends all. It is not found in only one region of
the country or even one country for that matter. It does not happen in just one race, one
religion, one orientation, one political party or even one shoe size. Yes, the desire to
make an effort to improve the lives around you does not yet live in everyone,
but it does live in everyone who cooks. As wide a group of people that
we who cook are, it is the desire to do for those around us
that binds us together, it is the piece we share
that makes us one.

Bill

Making a magazine, you
don't get much time to
admire the fruits of your work;
the next deadline is always
looming. But four years ago
I promised many of you a
book of the thoughts behind
the first issue of our magazine,
an editor's cut. Looking back
at this first issue I can't help
but feel proud about what
we were able to accomplish.
Proud of what we did with
the pages that were so totally

blank when we started. It took great effort by both the people featured in the magazine and the people working on the magazine and to all I am deeply grateful.

Our goal from the start has been to create a magazine that loves cooks just the way cooks love the people they cook for; to do our part to keep cooking alive by shining a light on how much goodness cooking brings to our lives. The

motto: Love to Cook—Cook to Love really is the feeling that cooks share in common, the same feeling that brings our customers into our stores. Penzeys Spices now has over a million customers, and I can tell you from first hand experience people who cook are a pretty wonderful bunch, and a pretty diverse bunch as well. They are the variety that spices our life. In many ways the magazine is our attempt

to bring these cooks and their recipes into your home, much the way they come into our stores. To bring the smiles into your life that we are lucky enough to get every day from spending time with people who cook.

We started Penzeys One before we were really ready. It would have been great to have a few more years to build up the staff and money needed to launch a

magazine, but with all that was going on at the time I felt we needed to bring to the world the goodness of hanging out with people who cook. The year 2003 for most was not the best of times. The excitement of the turn of the millennium had been replaced with something darker. Events had gotten the best of us.

There is no better cure for darkness than love, or if you

don't feel entirely comfortable with the word love, maybe the word kindness instead. I felt if only we could open people's eyes to what cooking really is, an act of kindness, we could change the equation of how we see the world. To see each meal cooked, each dinner served, as a gift that comes from the kindness of someone's heart is to see millions and millions more acts of goodness to weigh against

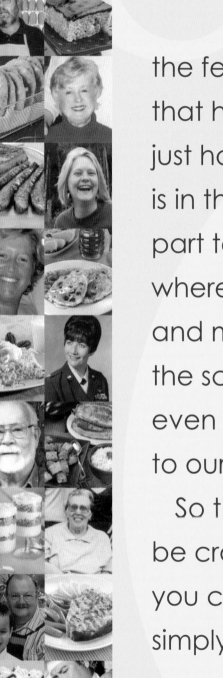

the few acts of unkindness that had us reeling. By showing just how much kindness there is in this world we could do our part to tip the scales back to where they once had been, and maybe over time push the scales further, creating an even better world to pass on to our children.

So there you have it. I might be crazy, but I actually believe you can change the world simply by showing cooking

for what it is: an act of love. Will we succeed? Only time will tell, but at least I can say we've gotten to share in some very tasty recipes along the way. Right from the beginning I knew if we were going to have any chance of building a better world with a cooking magazine the recipes would have to be really good. By reaching out to our customers, people who actually spend their nights home cooking for

the people they care about, I think I can say we have already succeeded in getting really, really good recipes onto our pages.

We could not have done any of this without the cooks who have graced our pages. My hope is they have helped on many a night answer the question of what's for dinner, that a few of the recipes on these pages have found their way onto your list of favorites,

and that maybe you actually feel a connection to the people on these pages. And I also hope by reading their stories, by seeing how cooking has surrounded their lives with richness, your eyes have been opened a little more to the richness you bring to the lives around you each and every time you cook.

Thank you for cooking,

Bill

Jerry Bojarski   Caroline Brown   David Carter   Lynn Enk   Eva Erato-Rudek   Dan Gronitz

Lani Haag   Mary Henneman   Carrie Jebe   Ben Johnson   Keith Kucharski   Judi Larkin

Dave Laschen   Matt Milanowski   Aneh Mundi   Jenna Murack   Kevin Murack   Scott Nelson

Jack Nichols   Robert O'Brien   Sarah Pehowski   Bill Penzey   Jeri Penzey   Pam Penzey

Kathy Pohl   Colin Radcliffe   Fiona Richard   Jeff Scheibe   Lorene Sommario   Patrick Spencer

John Tillison   Jon Truelove   George Van Valkenburgh   Jack Weissmann   Deb Westmaas

We know our magazine is at its very best when our readers feel they have personally met the people featured on our pages. With this in mind our goal is to have *Penzeys One* be merely a piece of glass between the people inside and the people who are reading. A lot of work goes into keeping the glass clean.

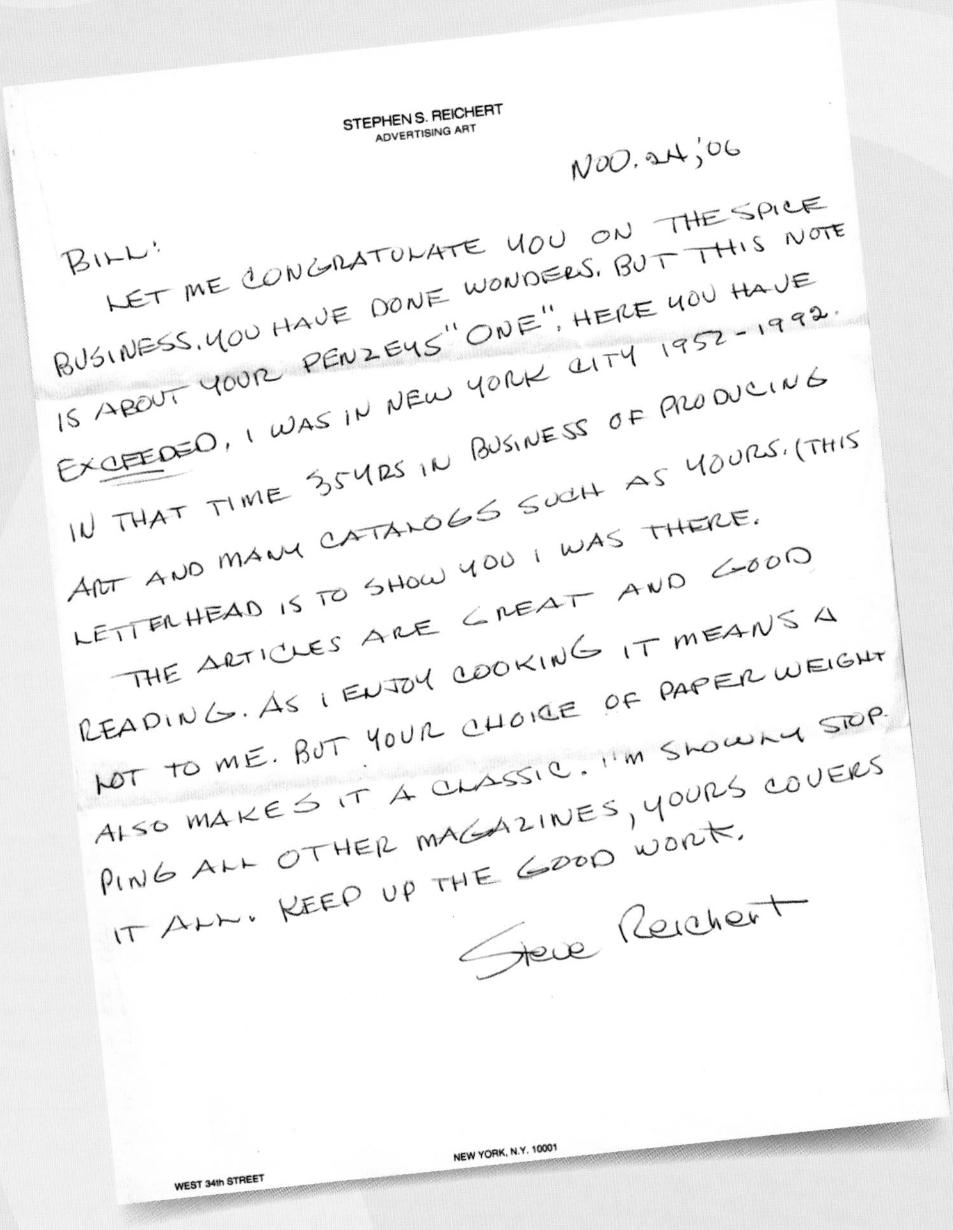

STEPHEN S. REICHERT
ADVERTISING ART

Nov. 24, '06

BILL:
LET ME CONGRATULATE YOU ON THE SPICE BUSINESS, YOU HAVE DONE WONDERS, BUT THIS NOTE IS ABOUT YOUR "PENZEYS" ONE", HERE YOU HAVE EXCEEDED, I WAS IN NEW YORK CITY 1952-1992. IN THAT TIME 35 YRS IN BUSINESS OF PRODUCING ART AND MANY CATALOGS SUCH AS YOURS, (THIS LETTERHEAD IS TO SHOW YOU I WAS THERE.

THE ARTICLES ARE GREAT AND GOOD READING. AS I ENJOY COOKING IT MEANS A LOT TO ME. BUT YOUR CHOICE OF PAPER WEIGHT ALSO MAKES IT A CLASSIC. I'M SLOWLY STOPPING ALL OTHER MAGAZINES, YOURS COVERS IT ALL. KEEP UP THE GOOD WORK.

Steve Reichert

WEST 34th STREET   NEW YORK, N.Y. 10001

With us starting what we hoped would be a very different food magazine we originally used the letters to the editor section to highlight the excitement of our readers. Now that you have a sense of what we are up to, we really would like to hear your ideas and thoughts. We know that in our readership, there is tremendous diversity of backgrounds and wealth of experience, but there is something more as well—wisdom, I believe a great pool of it.

We really do want to gain from your wisdom, and use it to help us grow. Maybe in your experiences you've learned something that you could share with us to help us on our path. Or possibly you have ideas for people or story topics we could include to strengthen what it is we are. If you have thoughts, please send them.

Thanks, bill@penzeysone.com

A Note on Hope

We love this note, hastily scrawled on the back of a receipt. It's good to hear from our readers, no matter what form. Thanks, Nancie.

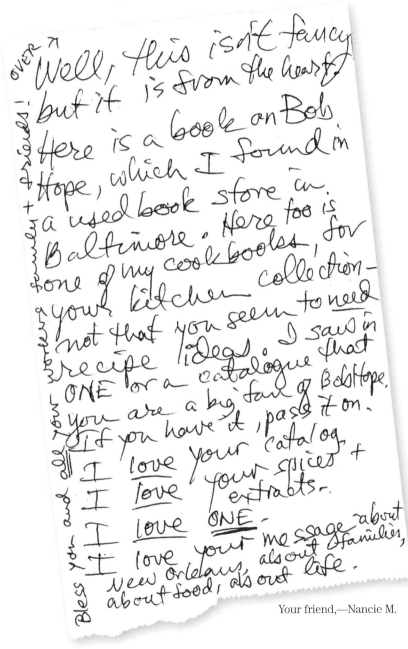

Your friend,—Nancie M.

Kudos from the Cook

NUTS!

As a 75 year old caregiver who cooks only for two oldsters who don't need any extra calories in their life, I have been making a concentrated effort to get rid of a bookcase of cookbooks and collected recipes for at least a year. So when your magazine arrived today, my first impulse was to pitch it unread. Then I decided to look at it while having lunch, THEN I would pitch it. I regret to say I spent the next 1½ hours engrossed in *One*. Not the way I intended to spend my afternoon!

Kudos to all who put the magazine together. I enjoyed reading about the people you wrote about and there were a number of recipes I will try. I had a good laugh from "The Creative Cook" and really enjoyed One World. I look forward to trying Hazim's Chicken and Pasta.

So, you've hooked me for a year. (At my age, I never think beyond a year!) Keep on track.—Jean S.

From the Heart

I must admit, when I first caught your new magazine I groaned and thought, "Not another cooking magazine!" But, I'm very happy to admit I was wrong; (bet you don't hear that too often—at least my husband doesn't!). Last night I began skimming through the issue you sent and found myself completely mesmerized. Not only were the recipes interesting and useful, but the personal stories and pictures were captivating. Never have I seen a publication that really touches the heart as yours does. As a former editor and now marketing manager, I have a little bit of an idea of the effort it takes to get something like this pulled together—let me compliment you on the outstanding layout and design, and wonderful writing. I hesitated before about subscribing; now it is a "no-brainer." Thanks to the *One* team and you for all the great work. I look forward to many more wonderful issues.—Nancy R.

Lost…and Found

Just a note to thank you for sending the issue that was lost. It came today and after showing it to a friend she is also putting in a subscription. I'm hoping our new Barnes & Noble will start carrying it—I would hate for 61,000 people here to miss out on your great *One*. Thank you again.—Lois B.

Keep the Kindness

I just received the new issue of *One*, and something amazing happened: I actually took the time, right then, to read through it!

In the past, it's been beautiful, informative, valuable, and formidable. Overwhelming, actually. There was so much to it that I felt I had to have a big block of free time to read it. After I did, I seldom retained much. Today, I saw several ideas that I can do easily, and will do. That's not different from before. It's just the old less-is-more thing.

For me, you've done the right thing to increase its value. Don't lose the kindness, however, as you focus on flavor. That's a big part of what I love about Penzeys and why I patronize you rather than other merchants. In my opinion, we all need to start loving one another and taking much better care of one another, or we aren't going to make it as a nation, or as a species.— Sue K.

A Different Kind of Magazine

I have just renewed my subscription. It's not because I need more recipes; I certainly don't! It's because I like the inclusivity, the diversity, shown in your magazine—covering cuisines of many different ethnicities, highlighting people with many different lifestyles, etc. Keep up the good work!—Patricia B.

Back-issues available

Dear Penzeys,

I just now subscribed to *One* after seeing the Cash and Curry edition, which I bought at a local Penzeys. I really want a copy of the Gulf Coast issue. How can I order that back-issue?—Cindy F.

EDITOR'S NOTE: Cindy, thank you for your interest in our magazine! Back-issues are available on our website, www.penzeysone.com.

Soup's on!

I have thoroughly enjoyed my subscription to *One* magazine! The pages of some of my issues are grease-splattered and rumpled. Certain issues of mine will fall open to certain newly-found favorites (ie. Chocolate Soup— see recipe on p.40). I have been touched by the stories. I have shared dinner ideas with my neighbors on the playground as we watch our children play. I take current issues with me to the grocery store when I do my shopping. I have even impressed my in-laws with my cooking. Best of all, I can find answers to one of Life's persistent questions: What shall I make for dinner?

I love what you are doing with this wonderful magazine. Cooking is personal. I do it because I love those I am cooking for, and simply because I love the art of food. Your magazine has opened up a wealth of ideas to me. Thanks—Jan Marie

Chocolate Soup

A Kinder, Gentler World

Thank you for making it possible for us, the cooks, to have a place where we can convey our shared vision of a better, kinder and gentler world that we can leave for our children and our children's children when we are gone to Our Father's kingdom. With love. —Jesus and Roberta Beltran

EDITOR'S NOTE: Jesus's recipe for Chilaquiles was featured in Volume 3, Issue 1. He and Roberta appeared as extras in the HBO television series "John from Cincinnati," which was filmed in Imperial Beach, California, by writer/producer David Milch.

Do You *Get* It?

I'm sure you know that every issue is being read by people new to Penzeys as well as those familiar with the concept of *One*. New subscribers don't, at this stage, begin with Issue #1. I, myself began with Issue #2 and only yesterday did I get Issue #1 (which I ordered from your website just so I wouldn't be missing one). I have always enjoyed the magazine, the features, the recipes, the people, but I really didn't *get* it. As soon as I opened issue #1 and read Bill's 'Welcome Letter,' I *got* it. Reading the welcome letter which explained the philosophy without assuming I already knew, made me suddenly a part of *One* as opposed to just reading a magazine. I strongly recommend inserting a copy of this 'Welcome Letter' into the first issue that every new subscriber receives. Don't change a word. I think you will find that instead of new subscribers you will have new family members who love to cook. Best Wishes from one who cooks, too.—Theresa C.

EDITOR'S NOTE: Great idea. In fact, after reading your letter we've incorporated it into our magazine. Our "philosophy" will now be a recurring item on page 2, so everyone can "get it" from day one. Thanks Theresa.

Our four decades of selling spices have taught us that cooking is not a one size fits all world: far from it. We've learned the true beauty of cooking lies in the incredible diversity of the people who cook, and in the incredible variety of the food they cook. Those years have also taught us for all the diversity, for all the variety, people who cook have something in common. They care enough to make the lives of those around them better. The research shows that people who share dinner together at the kitchen table go on to share a brighter future. A brighter future made possible by people with the spirit to build it one meal at a time. It is this spirit we celebrate, this spirit we hope to spread, this spirit that makes all who cook ONE. We think you will find that Diversity, Variety, Caring and Actual Cooks make for a really worthwhile magazine. Come along and join us.

Be **one**

Real Recipes from Real People

I was recently married and my new husband, Chris, loves reading *One* before I even get to look at it. He's a great cook and likes to experiment and has tried several recipes from past issues. No doubt he'll try at least one from this one.

I love your magazine—it's real people—real recipes from families, some handed down through the generations. I love the personal stories about the people, no matter what "group" they belong to. People need to realize we're all one big family and we should be helping each other in times of need.

Thanks for a great magazine. I'm a charter member—I'm one of those who took a chance and got a 3 year subscription, and I have no regrets! Keep up the good work Bill and the rest of the staff.—Ramona P.

Stories of Katrina

I have read many a food magazine, but never one that brought tears to my eyes. Thank you for bringing these stories of hope, strength and love to our attention. I lived through the Northridge earthquake in 1994, my most vivid memory was how wonderfully normal it felt to be back in my slightly disheveled kitchen surrounded by family and food. Again, thank you, I have been purchasing your wonderful products for years and will continue to renew my subscription to your magazine as well.—Susan W.

Regarding Issue 3,

I have never enjoyed or wept so much reading a magazine in my life! As a resident of Covington, Louisiana who has had to deal with the repercussions of Katrina, every story touched my heart. We sustained minimal damage to our home, moderate damage to our yard and neighborhood. We relied on our generator to power our home for weeks, had no phone or cable for months. But we had nothing to endure that comes close to what the true survivors in your magazine have gone through. We housed and fed friends and neighbors who were less fortunate than us. We had "clean out the freezer" barbecues; everyone spread the word when a grocery store re-opened, or someone saw a gasoline tank truck at the station up the street. People picked up "FEMA ice and water" for everyone. We survived by helping each other … and, I hope, are better people for it. Thank you for your wonderful magazine, for this very special issue, for spreading the word so well that we still need SO MUCH HELP, and for caring. Bill, I "get it."—Georgia Y.

Three Time's the Charm

Just received issue 3—was certain you could not continue to make each issue better—glad to say I was wrong. Great magazine!!! —Linda S.

Flavored with Human Interest

Just wanted to send a quick note to tell you that yours is the first food magazine I read from cover to cover and can't put down. I loved the first issue, in fact, that was what caused me to subscribe. Every issue since then has had wonderful human interest stories in them about individuals who also cook, and what makes their recipes special. Many times, their lives and what they have experienced are what makes their recipes and their stories so special. Keep up the good work. Also, any thoughts of a central Florida Penzeys in the future?—Wendy

EDITOR'S NOTE: We're always looking for new locations, so don't worry, eventually we'll be everywhere! Thanks for writing.—Bill

It's All About People

I just wanted to let you know how much I enjoy your magazine. I have loved your spices since my grandmother-in-law introduced me to them, and was excited to hear about your new magazine.

Even though I liked your catalog and thought I would like this magazine, I have been pleasantly surprised by how much I love each issue. The recipes are wonderful but I thoroughly enjoy the articles as well. Thank you for featuring people from all walks of life and for treating them with such respect.—Jennifer C.

Magazine Is Number ONE!

Yesterday morning I awoke very early and was unable to go back to sleep. I went and got all my issues of *One*; I have every issue as an original subscriber. For the next hour or so I enjoyed each issue just as much as the numerous times I've gone through them. This is a magazine that I will never tire of reading. The recipes are wonderful, the stories inspiring, and the ideas I come up with after reading about the spices are always fun. Thank you for such a great publication. Thank you for a fantastic product and a magazine that is number ONE!—Elizabeth G.

Curry Queries

Yes, I love your magazine, just like everybody else. I wonder, though, why in the Curry section of the last issue (Vol. 1, Issue 4, p.59) you are showing people how to make Garam Masala and telling them it is available in supermarkets when you sell it yourselves? I love your recipes, and have gotten more useful ones and tips out of the few issues you have published than out of a whole shelf of cookbooks. Thank you!—Judy G.

Dear Penzeys,

I love your magazine but I was disappointed in the last issue. Why did you complicate the curry recipes so?? You have that wonderful Rogan Josh blend that I use on leg of lamb steaks with sauteed onions and thick European yogurt—delicious. And I do a shrimp curry with your Maharajah blend. And your Garam Masala … no one beats your curries.—Loris Z.

EDITOR'S NOTE: Yes I know. I believe in our spices (great quality, great prices) but I also believe that the value that cooking brings to life is more important than where you buy your spices. We want the magazine's message of people cooking and caring to work for everyone, not just our spice customers. At times this is going to lead to a long list of spices where a single blend would work. Sorry about this, but you should always feel free to substitute whatever you have on hand. Thanks for writing.—Bill.

One Thing in Common

I know by now you probably receive hundreds of letters from subscribers who tell you how wonderful your magazine is and how much they enjoy it. I have been a subscriber since your first issue, and it only took the first one to become a favorite. Your store is a regular shopping trip for me, and *Penzeys One* recipes regularly appear on our dinner table (one of my all-time favorites is the Chicken Biryani Curry, Vol. 1, Issue 4). Please keep up the good work. I love the stories and the fact that you have the courage and humanity to include such diversity in your articles. Cooking and food are one thing that most all of us have in common, and it's nice to be reminded of that in each issue of *One*. Thank you again!—Pam M.

I really like fennel. Anything with oregano, garlic and basil gets a little bit of fennel as well. I have a mortar and pestle that I got years back from somewhere, probably my father, that I keep next to the stove to lightly crush the whole seeds. Fennel is great for pasta sauces, Italian dressings, even frozen pizza. You don't need a lot, maybe ¼ tsp per serving.

the inside scoop

At Penzeys we sit at the crossroads of cooks. Every day we talk to over a thousand cooks in our mail order call center and our 40+ stores. We are always on the lookout for useful ideas and it only seems right to give our magazine readers the inside scoop on what we are hearing at the crossroads.

Shingletown, CA is home to Berta and her easy **hummus dip** recipe. In a food processor add a 15 oz. can of garbanzo beans (a.k.a. chick peas), 1 TB lemon juice, 4 TB olive oil, 3 to 4 cloves of garlic, 1/2 tsp. **chipotle pepper**, and 1/4 tsp. salt. Puree until smooth and serve with toasted pita bread or crackers. Makes about 1 cup.

Jane in Hendersonville, TN gave us a tip for Baked Potatoes. Rub potatoes with olive oil and sprinkle with **seasoned salt.** Wrap in foil and bake at 350° for 1 to 1-1/2 hours. Carefully open the foil during the last 10 minutes to crisp up the skins. If your kids don't eat the skins you'll be stealing them.

Seasoned Baked Potatoes

Janet from Portales, NM makes poppy seed butter by mixing 1 TB prepared yellow mustard and 1 TB **blue poppy seeds** with 1 stick softened butter. Great on sandwiches, especially ham and cheese wrapped in foil and baked. Her husband bought her a tiara for this recipe. Wonderful with brown mustard, too.

Poppy Seed Butter

Sausage Rolls

These sausage rolls come from Sandra of Long Lake, NY. She dips them in steak sauce, but we thought they were delicious without dipping. This recipe will make 8 larger rolls for lunch or dinner. Smaller rolls make great appetizers. Substitute grated potato for the turnips if desired. We were happy to see a recipe that actually used turnips, which are quite delicious.

1/2 cup grated turnip (1 small turnip)
1 lb. Breakfast Sausage
1/2 tsp. ground **mace**
2 cloves fresh garlic or 1/2 tsp.
  granulated garlic
1/2 cup onion, minced or chopped

Mix together, brown and drain.
Roll up cooked mixture in crescent rolls (you will need 2 - 8 oz. packages) or puff pastry. Bake at 350° until golden brown, about 10-15 minutes.

Penelope of Vancouver, WA makes her own baking powder. Her recipe is 2 TB **cream of tartar**, 1 TB baking soda and 1 TB cornstarch. At first we thought this would be nice to know if you happen to be baking in the middle of the night and run out of baking powder. We discovered that our baked goods rose higher, were lighter and just generally better. Thanks, Penelope.

Cheese Scones

CHEESE SCONES
2 Cups flour
1 tsp. baking powder
1/4 tsp. mustard powder
1/2 tsp. salt
1/2 Cup softened butter (1 stick)
1/2 Cup milk, plus 1 TB for brushing
1/2 Cup shredded cheddar cheese

Mix together the flour, baking powder, mustard powder and salt. Rub butter into the flour until the consistency of breadcrumbs. Make a well in the middle, add the milk and cheese. Knead gently, roll out to 1" thick. Cut into triangles, place on an un-greased pan in a pie pattern. Brush with milk and bake at 400° for 15 minutes. Cool, split and serve with butter.

Cheesy Toast Points are from Olivia in Double Oak, TX. Mix together 4 oz. Roquefort cheese, 4 oz. cream cheese (1/2 package), 1 TB lemon juice, and 1 tsp. **black sesame seeds.** Toast 10-12 slices of bread, remove crusts and cut into bite size triangles. Place mixture into a sandwich bag and cut off one corner to make a mini-piping bag. Pipe onto the toast points. Top with a tiny piece of plain cream cheese and a piece of walnut.

Cheesy Toast Points

Here's something different for fish: Emily of Golden Valley, MN suggests rubbing salmon, swordfish, or tuna with a little olive oil then sprinkling with **ground sumac** before grilling. The sumac adds a nice tartness. Salt and pepper to taste.

Inge of White Plains, NY makes a quick horseradish sauce for roast beef. Mix 1 TB **horseradish powder** with 2 TB water and set aside. In a saucepan melt 1 TB butter and mix in 1 TB flour. Cook gently, stirring, to make a roux, about 3 minutes. Add 1/2 cup milk and whisk until smooth. Add the horseradish mixture along with 1 tsp. balsamic vinegar, 1 tsp. chicken soup base, or 1 bouillon cube. Serve warm.

Grilled Swordfish

Delicious Saltines

We don't even know what to call this other than delicious. Line a rimmed baking pan with parchment paper (lightly oil the pan so the paper sticks). Place saltine crackers side by side on the parchment until it's covered. In a sauce pan melt $1^1/2$ sticks of butter with $1/2$ cup sugar. Pour over the saltines evenly. Bake in a 350° oven for 10 minutes. Remove from oven and sprinkle on 2 cups (12 oz.) chocolate chips. Return to the oven for a minute or so to get the chips to stick to the saltines. Refrigerate for two hours then cut or break into pieces. Ellen from Somerville, NJ got this recipe from her friend Diane who got it from a friend of hers. Good news travels.

For an easy Mexican Bean Dip all you need is a 14 oz. can of refried beans, 1 cup of salsa, 1 cup of your favorite shredded cheese, 1 TB **chili powder** and 1 tsp. **granulated garlic**. Spread the beans in the bottom of an 8x8 casserole dish then spread the salsa over the beans. Sprinkle the chili powder and garlic evenly over the salsa then top with the cheese. Bake in a 350° oven for 20-25 minutes until the cheese is bubbly. Serve warm with tortilla chips. Thanks to Anne of Hopkinton, MA.

Mexican Bean Dip

Gingered Carrot Salad

Not eating enough vegetables? Try this Ginger Carrot Salad from Marion of Calimesa, CA. Start by shredding 4 large carrots. Add 1/2 Cup golden or mixed raisins and 1 TB finely chopped **crystallized ginger**. Slowly add 2-3 TB of rice vinegar until salad is well moistened. Toss and refrigerate, covered, until ready to serve. It will get better overnight.

Teresa from Whitesburg, GA calls this recipe "chocolate soup" because it's so good her family eats it by the spoonful before it ever makes it to ice cream. Slowly melt 1 stick of butter over medium-low heat. Add 2 heaping TB **cocoa powder** and whisk about a minute until smooth. Add 1/2 cup half & half and 3/4 cup sugar, then stir for about 2 more minutes. Remove from heat and add 1 tsp. **vanilla extract**. Makes a great dip for fruit. Hide your spoons.

Chocolate Soup

Spiced Baked Squash

Pumpkin Pie spice with baked squash? Kind of makes sense when you think about it. Cut an acorn or Hubbard squash in half and scoop out the seeds. Add to each cavity 2 TB pineapple juice and 1/8 to 1/4 tsp. **pumpkin pie spice**. Wrap in foil and bake at 350° for 1 hour. Add brown sugar to taste if you like a sweeter flavor. Mary - Shelter Island, NY

here's one from us:

When cooking frozen or canned corn, add a pinch of **rubbed sage**. Use about 1/4 tsp. per pound of corn. Don't overdo it. Too much sage can be too much of a good thing. No sage in the house? Use **poultry seasoning**.

Herbed Corn

Seasoned Dumplings

Joyce of St. Louis, MO adds cumin to her dumplings. Try adding 1/2 tsp. to your favorite dumpling recipe or try ours. Mix together 1 cup flour, 2 tsp. baking powder, 6 TB milk, 1 egg, 1/2 tsp. **ground cumin**, and 1/2 tsp. salt. Drop TB size or larger dollops into boiling water or soup, especially homemade chicken soup. Simmer 10 to 15 minutes. Makes 6 large or 12 little dumplings.

For our first Weeknight Pirates article Jack drew a very charming shark. But we felt he wasn't exactly "food grade."

So then Jack cleaned him up a bit. But what's a shark without teeth?

Ah, finally. The shark of our dreams. Lots of teeth, and "food grade" to boot!

We take seriously the One thing that all Cooks share: the wonderfulness that cooking brings to our lives.

Everything else about cooking to us is just plain fun.

WEEKNIGHT PIRATES

On weeknights we still appreciate the finer things in life, but like pirates, we're not willing to spend much time or go to much effort to get them.

Gingered Tuna Salad

Ahoy there—tuna again? Sure it's healthy, but this recipe will be a hit with everyone—even the land lubbers will ask for your recipe, and leftovers make a great sandwich.

1 12 oz. can chunk white tuna in spring water
2 tsp. curry powder
1 TB olive oil
1/4 Cup minced red onion (1/2 small onion)
3 TB crystallized ginger chunks
1/3-1/2 Cup mayonnaise (1/2 Cup will be more moist, but 1/3 cup will have fewer calories and less fat)
1 TB rice vinegar (or 1 tsp. white vinegar and 2 tsp. water)
1 tsp. prepared Dijon style mustard
1/4 Cup chopped pecans
1/4 tsp. salt
1 dash cayenne pepper (to taste)

Drain the tuna and set aside. In a small saucepan over low heat, saute curry powder in olive oil for 5 minutes, stirring every so often. While curry powder is cooking, mince the onion. Chop the crystallized ginger into small pieces, about the size of the minced onion. In a medium sized bowl, whisk to combine mayonnaise, rice vinegar and Dijon style mustard. Add cooked curry powder mixture (make sure to scrape it all in), crystallized ginger, onion, chopped pecans, salt, and a dash of cayenne pepper. Whisk again. Add tuna, mix with a fork until the tuna is well blended and coated with the dressing. To serve, line 4 plates with a cup or so of chopped lettuce, top with tuna salad and ring with rounds of crusty bread, quartered cherry tomatoes and baby carrots if desired. This salad is excellent served chilled or at room temperature.
Yield: 3 Cups salad (serves 4 or so).
Prep. time: 20 minutes. Cooking time: 5 minutes to saute the curry in oil.

Chicken & Salad Wraps

Just the kind of meal you can eat on the run with one hand on the tiller—flavorful, healthy, incredibly tasty and sure to be a bang-up success with the whole family.

Chicken:
- 4 boneless/skinless chicken breast pieces (a 1 lb. package)
- 1 TB oregano
- 1 tsp. granulated garlic
- 1 tsp. salt
- 1 tsp. black pepper
- 2 TB water
- 2 TB lemon juice–juice of 1 lemon
- 1 TB prepared Dijon mustard
- 1 TB honey
- 1/4 Cup vegetable oil

Salad:
- 1 head romaine/iceberg lettuce (about 1 lb.)
- 1 Cup Creamy Salad Dressing (oil and vinegar dressings make the wrap soggy)

Creamy peppercorn dressing (feel free to use another creamy dressing of your choice):
- 1 TB cracked black pepper
- 1-2 tsp. salt
- 1 tsp. thyme
- 1/2 tsp. granulated garlic
- 1 TB water
- 1/2 Cup sour cream
- 1/2 Cup light (low-fat) mayonnaise
- 1 TB honey
- 2 tsp. balsamic or red wine vinegar

Wraps:
- 6 large flour tortillas

Rinse chicken, pat dry. In a bowl big enough to hold the chicken, mix the seasonings with water, let stand a few minutes. Add lemon juice, mustard, honey and vegetable oil, whisk to combine. Add chicken, toss to coat, cover and set aside a few minutes while cleaning and chopping the lettuce. To cook the chicken, use a grill top or heavy pan on medium heat, about 6 minutes per side. Prepare the dressing, but don't coat the lettuce until the chicken comes off the grill. To prepare the dressing, mix pepper, salt, thyme and garlic in water, let stand 2 minutes. Add sour cream, mayonnaise, vinegar and honey, whisk to combine. Set aside. Once the chicken has cooked, let it rest 5 minutes before cutting. Use this time to dress the lettuce. Cut the chicken lengthwise into long thin strips. Lay the 6 tortilla shells out flat, layer on chicken and top with lettuce. Fold the bottom few inches of the tortilla up over the chicken, and wrap the sides over each other. If it insists on opening up, turn the wrap over on the plate. Serve and enjoy.

Serves: 4-6. Prep. time: 15 minutes plus marinade time. Cooking time: 12 minutes.

Pillaging, plundering, and adventuring can be exhausting. Add to that hornswaggling scallawags and oiling the blunderbuss and the life of a pirate can get pretty crazy, which is why we offer these Weeknight Pirate recipes. They're easy, delicious, and quick, because as any Weeknight Pirate worth his salt knows, the less time spent in the galley, the more time there is for treasure hunting.

Aye, there be dinner afoot

Steak Tacos

Hearty beef in a flash—great for a weeknight, and the salsa adds a spicy flavor perfect for pleasing the whole crew.

1	lb. round or sirloin steak
1-2	TB lime juice (2 limes)
1	TB corn oil
1/2	tsp. cumin
1/2	tsp. granulated garlic
1/4	tsp. Mexican oregano
1/4	tsp. cayenne pepper (optional)
1/4	tsp. black pepper
1/4	tsp. salt
8-12	soft flour tacos

Toppings: use some or all

1	Cup shredded lettuce
1/2	Cup shredded cheese (cheddar or Parmesan)
1/2	Cup sour cream

Salsa:

1	ripe avocado
2	ripe medium tomatoes, chopped
1	medium red onion or 1 bunch green onions, finely minced
1	TB fresh cilantro leaves, chopped (1 tsp. dried, but we prefer fresh for salsa)
1	TB lime juice (juice of 1 lime)
1/4	tsp. granulated garlic
1/4	tsp. cumin
1/4	tsp. salt
1/4	tsp. Mexican oregano
1/4	tsp. cayenne pepper (optional)

Thinly slice the round steak, toss with lime juice, corn oil, spices and salt. Cover and set aside while preparing salsa and toppings. The longer the steak has to marinate, the better the flavor; if you have a chance, season the steak in the morning and refrigerate the covered bowl. If there isn't time for that, even the few minutes it takes to make the salsa will give the steak great flavor. To make the salsa, place the chopped tomatoes, minced onion, cilantro, lime juice and seasonings in a medium glass or china bowl. Stir well to mix the flavors. Cut the avocado in half, carefully remove the skin, and chop into small pieces. Add to the bowl, stir gently to combine. Place a layer of plastic wrap on top of the bowl, patting on top of the salsa. This helps keep the avocado green.

Heat a large pan over high heat. When hot, add steak, cook, stirring frequently, for about five minutes, until steak is crispy brown. Serve on flour tortillas with salsa and any other toppings you desire. Have hot sauce on the table, as these tacos are spicy but not hot. Flour tortillas taste even better if they are warmed for about 3 minutes in a 325° oven (10-20 seconds in a microwave works fine, especially in the summer).

Serves: 6.
Prep. time: 15 minutes.
Cooking time: 5 minutes.

Bill's Spaghetti and Chicken

Quick, easy, healthy spaghetti sauce that can be on the table in half an hour. Great with any combination of veggies a pirate can get their hands on.

Arrr, this be lookin' good

Sauce:

- 2 boneless/skinless chicken breast pieces, cubed
- 1 TB canola oil, divided
- 1 medium onion, minced
- 8 oz. fresh mushrooms, sliced
- 1 red bell pepper, cored and minced, optional
- 1-2 TB oregano
- 1 tsp. fennel seed
- ¼ tsp. cayenne pepper or crushed red peppers
- 2 TB balsamic or red wine vinegar
- 1 15 oz. can whole tomatoes
- 1 15 oz. can chopped tomatoes
- 8-12 oz. broccoli, cut into florets

Pasta:

- 8-10 oz. thin spaghetti noodles (dry)
- 2 tsp. basil
- ½ tsp. granulated garlic
- ¼ Cup shredded Parmesan cheese, optional

Heat a large pan over medium-high heat, add 2 tsp. oil. When hot, add chicken, cook 3-5 minutes per side. The key to lower fat cooking is in good browning, so don't rush or put too much meat in the pan or it will steam, not brown.

Remove the chicken from the pan. Add the last teaspoon of oil, then add the onions, mushrooms and bell pepper. Cook 3-5 minutes, stirring, until starting to brown. Add spices. They'll start to stick to the pan, which is fine. Stir them around with the onion-pepper-mushroom mix, then add the balsamic vinegar. The vinegar will bubble up; use it to dislodge the tasty browned bits in the pan. Use a fork to chop the tomatoes a bit while they are still in the can–just move it back and forth vigorously for a moment. Add the tomatoes to the pan, stir, then add the chicken. Reduce heat to simmer. The sauce should cook 20 minutes, which is just enough time to make the spaghetti noodles and broccoli.

To prepare the pasta and broccoli, bring at least three quarts of water to a rolling boil. Add the thin spaghetti noodles, cook until done– usually 7-8 minutes. Place the cut broccoli florets in a steamer and put over the top of the boiling water the pasta is in for the final 5-6 minutes of pasta cooking time. If you don't have a steamer, just cook the broccoli the way you normally would. Drain the pasta, then add the basil and garlic, stir to coat. Divide the pasta and broccoli among 4 plates, place a ladle of sauce on top, sprinkle with Parmesan cheese if desired and enjoy. Make sure to drizzle some of the thinner juices of the sauce over all of the pasta. That way it won't start sticking together while you are eating it.

Serves: 4. Prep. time: 10 minutes. Cooking time: 30 minutes.

AVAST, YE SHRIMP!

Shrimp with Herbs, Tomato and Pasta

A delightful dish from the sea. Herb-crusted shrimp with quickly seasoned pasta that's perfect for a busy week night, even if the busy night includes company, because this is a festive meal that's easy to multiply when guests drop by. Just keep some frozen shrimp in the freezer, and you'll be ready to set sail in a flash.

1/2 lb. package fresh pasta
1 lb. fresh shrimp, medium to large
1 TB olive oil, divided
2 tsp. basil
1 tsp. oregano
2 TB lemon juice, divided (1 small lemon)
2 TB dried shallots (or 1/2 small onion, minced)
1 large ripe tomato, diced
2 tsp. whole fennel seed
1/4 tsp. granulated garlic
1/4 tsp. salt
1/4 tsp. pepper
1/4 Cup Parmesan cheese strands

Have an idea for a Weeknight Pirates recipe? Send it in to us, along with a photo of you dressed up as a pirate. Or... you can let us take care of it for you.

Penzeys ONE
Weeknight Pirates
19300 W. Janacek Ct.
Brookfield, WI
53045

recipes@penzeys.com

Cook the pasta according to the package directions while you are cleaning the shrimp. Drain and toss with 1 tsp. of olive oil, set aside. Peel and de-vein shrimp, rinse well. Pat dry, place on a plate. Press basil and oregano lightly onto both sides of the shrimp. In a large nonstick pan, heat 2 tsp. olive oil over medium-high heat. Add shrimp in a single layer, cook 2-3 minutes per side. Coating should be browned, turn heat down a bit if it gets too dark. Remove the shrimp to a serving plate. Add 1 TB lemon juice to the pan, swirl to coat. Add shallots or onion, cook, stirring, until wilted–about 2 minutes. Add chopped tomato, fennel seed and garlic, raise heat to high, cook, stirring, for 3 minutes. Add freshly cooked pasta to the pan, plus salt and pepper, toss to coat. Arrange pasta with tomato topping in the middle of a large platter, surround with shrimp. Spray the shrimp with the remaining 1 TB lemon juice, sprinkle the shredded Parmesan cheese over the top, and serve.

Yield: 4 servings
Prep. time: 10 minutes
Cook time: 15 minutes

Melty Portobella Sandwiches

A meatless sandwich that'll please the most swashbuckling guy you know. Portobella mushrooms really are as good as steak— try them and see.

- 6 oz. sliced portobella mushrooms
- 1 tsp. your favorite seasoned salt
- 1 1/2 TB olive oil, divided
- 1 small onion, sliced thin
- 2 slices provolone cheese
- 4 thick slices of bread (Texas toast), toasted

Gently rinse and clean the mushrooms, pat dry. Place in a bowl and carefully toss with seasoned salt and 1 TB olive oil. In a large fry pan, sauté onions in 1/2 TB olive oil over medium high heat until brown, about 5 minutes. Remove and set aside. Carefully place the mushrooms in the pan flat side down (start the toast now). Fry for two minutes, then gently turn each piece. Fry for another 30 seconds then arrange the mushrooms into two lots, roughly the shape of the toast. Top with a slice of provolone and cover the pan for about thirty seconds until the cheese is melted. Slide a spatula under the mushrooms, trying to keep the shape, and place on the toast. Top with onions and serve.

Serves: 2
Prep time: 5 minutes
Cook time: 10 minutes

Birmingham really was
just the right spot to start.

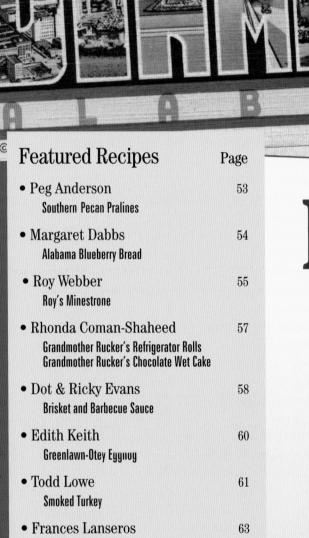

Featured Recipes

Birmingham, a great food town of great food people. We always wanted to be a part of Birmingham's rich food culture, and when we got our chance to open a store there late last year we did not want to just feature our usual store opening recipes. Instead we wanted to feature recipes from Birmingham. Pam Penzey hand addressed and signed letters seeking recipes to all of the regular mail order customers we had in the greater Birmingham area. Within the first few days of receiving replies we knew what we were getting was far too good to only use in Birmingham. When the idea of the magazine came along it seemed a natural fit to feature Birmingham in the very first issue.

We want to thank the people whose recipes are here, not just for the food, but also for being such interesting, thoughtful, cool people. Our original plan for this magazine was to simply have it be a reflection of the people who worked on the magazine. Corresponding with our regulars in Birmingham, hearing their stories, seeing their lives, made us realize that in our customers we had so much more of a tale to tell than just our own. Birmingham opened our eyes to what this magazine could be, and for that we will be forever grateful.

Peg and Kate, one of her twin granddaughters. Though the girls used to try and fool her on occasion, she could always tell them apart by their smiles.

Peg Anderson

Peg Anderson with her Daughters of the American Revolution pins

Peg Anderson's
Southern Pecan Pralines

They take a few minutes of stirring, but these are easy, delicious candies.

2	Cups brown sugar, packed
¾	Cup evaporated milk
2	TB. butter
2	Cups pecan halves

In a heavy saucepan, mix the sugar and milk. Using a candy thermometer, cook, stirring, to 234°. Stir in butter and nuts. Remove from heat, let stand ten minutes. Beat with a wooden spoon about 10 minutes until thick but still glossy. Drop by spoonfuls onto a pan lined with wax paper and allow to cool. Store in a tightly covered can, separating the layers with wax paper.

Yield: 2-3 dozen pralines. Prep. time: 5 minutes. Cooking time: roughly 30 minutes total.

The recipes **PegAnderson** sent us for everything from peach cobbler to sweet potato casserole got our mouths watering. There was something about those crab recipes though – crab imperial, deviled crab, and not one, but two recipes for crab cakes that were the tip-off. Sure enough, Peg's actually from Maryland. As she says, "Unfortunately, I am not a southern-raised girl. The expression for that is "GRITS" - Girls Raised in the South!"

Though Peg spent her girlhood in Maryland, she moved to the South 52 years ago. As Peg says, *"But then, Birmingham is not your true southern city. It was founded by a bunch of Yankees who came here to take advantage of the raw materials for iron and steel industries. Over the recent years there have been many other non-southerners moving here as well."*

Well, we figure 52 years in Alabama is long enough for a great cook to become an old hand with pecans and okra and these pecan pralines (though Peg tried to coach us, we still are having a hard time remembering how to pronounce it in the true southern way - was that pray-leen or praw-leen?).

Anyway, however you say it, this is a delicious and easy candy everyone will love, and we're very happy Peg was gracious enough to share the recipe and her history with us.

Margaret Dabbs,

Jasper attorney, is downright famous for her Alabama Blueberry Bread. The batch makes two, and if we're not mistaken, she said each one of her sons can eat a whole loaf. With bread this good so could we.

Margaret started making the bread in big batches when her in-laws, who farmed, would show up with big buckets of fresh blueberries, and what else are you gonna do, but bake loaf upon loaf of Alabama Blueberry Bread?

We had a little trouble getting hold of Margaret for a bit - which happened to be just the bit when Hurricane Ivan passed through. As you can see, the Dabbs' place did not survive un-scathed. Though it was a scary night, when the worst of it passed over, it wasn't anywhere near

as bad as it could have been. It became pretty obvious to the family sometime during the night that a tree had fallen and hit the house. Luckily, it didn't really break through into the living space. Even luckier it wasn't the big oak, the big over-a-hundred-years-old-oak, which pulled through the storm with flying colors.

The tree that did fall was certainly big enough to cause damage and problems. Due to its tricky placement and the proximity of nearby homes, it had to be removed using ropes, a three day process, but like Margaret said, all in all, they fared pretty well, and consider themselves fortunate.

Thank goodness it wasn't the Century Oak

Margaret Dabbs

The Dabbs boys and their favorite snack

Alabama Blueberry Bread
Really, really tasty, and easy too. Margaret Dabbs makes this bread for the family and friends, who all love it, and we agree. We've made this bread with both large and small blueberries, since they vary about the country, and it was fabulous either way.

3	Cups flour
1	tsp. salt
1	tsp. baking soda
1-2	TB. ground cinnamon (Margaret uses 3 full TB. of cinnamon, but suggested starting with less and building to more as you make the bread again and again)
2	Cups sugar
½-1	tsp. ground cloves
½-1	tsp. ground nutmeg

3	eggs, well beaten
1¼	Cups canola oil
2	pints of blueberries (mash about 1 Cup of these)
2	tsp. lemon extract
1	Cup chopped nuts, optional

Preheat oven to 350°. Grease 2 large (9 inch) loaf pans. Mix ¼ cup of the sugar and half of the cinnamon. Sprinkle pan and top of bread with this mixture. Place flour, salt, baking soda, sugar, cloves, nutmeg and the remaining cinnamon in a large bowl. Make a well in center of dry ingredients. Add eggs, oil, and lemon extract. Stir until dry ingredients are moistened. Stir in blueberries and nuts. Mashing some of the blueberries gives the bread a nice blueberry color. If you use frozen blueberries, make sure they are frozen plain and not sugared. Divide batter between two loaf pans.

Bake 1 hour. To remove the loaves from their pans without losing the sugary topping, try this trick: double a sheet of aluminum foil, cut it to half the width of the pan and place it in the greased bread pan, up and over the edges, then pour in the batter. This will give you a handy way to lift the bread right out of the pan, as in the photo. Let cool before eating. It's really even better the next day, believe it or not. Keep refrigerated.

Yield: 2 loaves. Prep. time: 10 minutes. Baking time: 1 hour

Roy Webber

Roy's Minestrone

This hearty, thick, "vegetable fest" of a soup really is a meal in itself.

½	Cup dried kidney beans (or 15 oz. can)
½	Cup dried white beans (or 15 oz. can cannellini beans)
5	slices bacon (+ olive oil, if necessary)
1	medium onion, diced
¼	small head of cabbage, shredded
2	medium carrots, diced
3	stalks celery, sliced
1	clove garlic
3	small yellow squash or zucchini, sliced
1½	Cups brown stock
½	tsp. parsley flakes
¼	tsp. ground black pepper
1	tsp. basil
¼	tsp. thyme
¼	tsp. Turkish oregano
½	Cup green beans, cut in bite-sized pieces
½	Cup macaroni noodles, uncooked
1	14½ oz. can tomatoes, chopped
2	tomatoes, chopped
8	leaves Swiss chard
	Parmesan cheese, grated, for topping

If you are using dried beans, soak the beans, separately, overnight and cook until tender. Drain and rinse the kidney beans. Puree the white beans. Set the beans aside. Chop the bacon into small pieces and fry gently to release the fat and crisp it up. Remove the bacon from the pan and set on paper toweling, leaving the bacon fat in the pan. Fry the onion in the bacon drippings, adding olive oil if necessary. When the onion is tender, add the cabbage, carrots, celery, garlic, and squash. Fry gently for 20 minutes until the vegetables are softened, then add all the other ingredients except the chard and kidney beans. Simmer for another 20 minutes, then add the kidney beans and chard. Adjust the seasoning. This soup can be left to develop flavors overnight in the fridge or served immediately. To serve, spoon into bowls and sprinkle with Parmesan cheese and bacon bits.

Serves: 8-10

Prep. time: 30 minutes (not including soaking)

Cooking time: 40-45 minutes

Roy Webber has lived in Birmingham for 27 years, and loves to garden. His fabulous minestrone soup uses many of the wonderful vegetables his garden produces, and honestly, his pickled beets sound wonderful too.

Rhonda Coman-Shaheed

The European Vacationers enjoy their time in Paris

A recent shot of Christopher, Rhonda and Antonio looking fabulous.

Rhonda Coman-Shaheed

has lived in the Birmingham area all her life. She met her husband Antonio in high school, and today works as a para-educator in the Birmingham School System, the same system where she went to school. Rhonda mainly works with special needs children who need some extra help to get through the school day, which she finds very rewarding. When she gets home, she loves to cook - and cook and cook, for, as she says, "I've got to feed that boy! He's huge!" That boy is Rhonda and Antonio's only child, Christopher, who at the tender age of 15 dwarfs both his parents - and yes, he does play football. Rhonda figures he gets his size from her Grandfather Rucker, who was All-American at Tennessee State in the '40s. Rhonda's Grandmother Rucker taught her how to cook at an early age, which was a great foundation for all the meals she makes now. She loves Greek and Italian food, particularly since the whole family took a trip over there. By "the whole family" we don't mean just Antonio, Rhonda and Christopher, but 30-60 of their closest relatives as well. Every other year the whole extended group gets together for a huge trip. They've visited Italy, Greece, France and Monaco, took a cruise to Mexico, and are busily planning a trip to Hawaii and Australia. Bet she'll come home with some great ideas for lamb from that trip. Rhonda does figure the travel increases her love of food and ability to cook great authentic meals at home.

We want to especially thank Rhonda's Uncle Sparky and his best friend "Uncle" Ed, both great cooks themselves, for turning Rhonda on to Penzeys, which gave us a chance to meet Rhonda and her mouth-watering chocolate wet cake.

Grandmother Rucker's Refrigerator Rolls

Rhonda always makes these for big family gatherings and holidays. You can also cut the batch size down to serve these delicious airy rolls for a regular Sunday dinner.

56

Antonio and Rhonda's wedding with both the cakes Grandmother Rucker baked

When Antonio and Rhonda were married, Grandmother Rucker made both the wedding cake and the groom's cake, along with creating all the floral arrangements. The groom's cake was a triple layer of luscious chocolate wet cake, one of Rhonda's favorite childhood recipes.

Rhonda grew up spending summers and many a holiday with her Grandmother Rucker in Knoxville, TN. There her love of cooking blossomed. Grandmother Rucker was a magnificent cook, and an even better baker. She took Rhonda under her wing and taught her everything. Southern summers were the perfect time to bond in the kitchen over chocolate wet cake, peach cobbler and homemade rolls. Grandmother Rucker firmly believed the table should always be fully dressed for dinner. She and Grandfather Rucker loved to have the whole family over for holidays with the table – floral arrangements and all – set for a minimum of 30.

1	pkg. or 1 cake yeast
1½	Cups lukewarm water
½	Cup evaporated milk*
¼	Cup sugar
8	Cups plain flour, sifted and divided
1	tsp. salt
3	TB shortening
1	large egg

Soften yeast in a small amount of the lukewarm water. Add yeast and remaining water to evaporated milk. Stir in the sugar. In a roomy bowl, sift 3 Cups flour and salt together. Cut in the shortening until blended to a pebbly consistency. Beat egg slightly and add to yeast/milk/sugar mixture. Add this to flour mixture and beat well. Add the remaining 5 Cups of flour, 1 Cup at a time, to make a soft dough. You may not need the full 5 Cups to get the right consistency—you don't want the dough too hard or dry. Knead by hand on a well-floured board for about 10 minutes. Put into a large greased bowl. Cover and place in the refrigerator and use within 8 hours. When wanted, shape the dough into rolls and let stand in a warm room for 1 hour before baking. If you want to use the dough right away, keep at room temperature, shape into rolls, and let rise for 1 hour before baking. We brushed the rolls with a beaten egg for a glossy finish. Bake in a preheated 375° oven for about 20 minutes.

Yield: about 4 dozen rolls Prep. time: 20 minutes

Rising time: 1 hour Baking time: 20 minutes

* Evaporated milk is liquid condensed unsweetened milk sold in a can. It should not be confused with "condensed milk," which is a very thick, very sweet canned milk product used for desserts.

Grandmother and Grandfather Rucker were married for 60 years, and passed away within 3 weeks of each other after a long and wonderful life together.

Chocolate "Wet" Cake

The cake Grandmother Rucker made for the groom's cake at Rhonda and Antonio's wedding. This is a great snack cake—deliciously fudgy, and the frosting's awesome.

2	Cups sugar
2	Cups flour, sifted
½	Cup butter (one stick)
½	Cup shortening
4	TB cocoa powder
1	Cup water
½	Cup buttermilk
1	tsp. vanilla extract
½ -1	tsp. cinnamon
2	eggs

Frosting:

2	TB cocoa powder
½	Cup (1 stick) butter or margarine
3	TB milk
½	box powdered sugar (enough for spreading consistency), about 2½ Cups
½	Cup chopped nuts, optional

Preheat oven to 400°. It is important the oven is at the proper temperature for this recipe, so do give it enough time to preheat. Grease and flour a 9x13 inch pan. In a roomy mixing bowl, combine the sugar and flour. In a heavy saucepan, bring the butter, shortening, cocoa and water to a boil, then add to the mixing bowl with the flour and sugar. Add the buttermilk, vanilla, cinnamon and eggs and mix well. The batter will be thin and may spatter. Pour into the pan and bake at 400° for about 25 minutes. For the frosting, bring the cocoa, butter or margarine and milk to a boil. Pour into a mixing bowl and add powdered sugar until the frosting is the desired consistency. Stir in the chopped nuts if using. Spread over the cooled cake and enjoy.

Yield: 24 small pieces (9x13" pan). Prep. time: 10 minutes. Cooking time: 25 minutes.

Dot & Ricky

Brisket and Barbecue Sauce

This is a great smoker recipe, but if you live in an area where sometimes it is just too cold to fire up the smoker, we've found that roasting the brisket in a slow oven (60 minutes per pound at 275°), produces mouthwatering brisket especially with the fabulous sauce.

| 8-12 | lbs. beef brisket |
| 2 | tsp. of your favorite southern-style seasoning per pound |

Rinse the roast and pat dry. Sprinkle both sides with seasoning. Place in a plastic bag and marinate in the refrigerator overnight. The next morning, start a charcoal fire in a smoker (we use a big barrel smoker with offside fire box). Pre-soak hickory chips or chunks in water. Once the coals are hot, place the brisket, fat side up, in a disposable aluminum pan large enough to accommodate the roast and place it on the grill. Cover the smoker. Add several soaked hickory chips directly on the coals. Replenish the coals and the chips periodically. Baste meat occasionally with fat from cooking. Cook for 6-8 hours. The meat should pull apart easily. An alternative is to cook it about 5 hours and then finish it off in a 250° oven, covering the meat with aluminum foil. Pour off fat before serving. Slice thinly across the grain. Serve with barbecue sauce.

Barbecue Sauce:

1	Cup ketchup
$\frac{1}{3}$	Cup soy sauce
2	TB shallots
$\frac{1}{4}$	tsp. ginger
$\frac{1}{4}$	tsp. granulated garlic
$\frac{1}{4}$	Cup sugar
$\frac{1}{4}$	Cup white vinegar

Mix all the ingredients in a heavy bottom pan and bring to the boil to dissolve the sugar. Lower the heat and simmer until thick, about 10 minutes.

Serves: 30-50

Prep. time: 2 minutes

Cooking time: 6-8 hours

Dot and Ricky Evans

sent us this wonderful recipe for brisket - true southern style brisket from the smoker. They're a match made in heaven, these two, as Dot does the prep work and Ricky mans the grill. The end result? One of the best sandwiches we've ever had the privilege to eat. Dot moved down from New York City 35 years ago, and married native Alabaman Ricky who grew up just 70 miles north of Birmingham. Dot and Ricky love gardening on their shady acre, which can be a challenge. The dwarf hostas they love do grow profusely, in fact they've become kind of famous for them. Their special joy is bass fishing on the Tennessee River, which produces some fine eating. Dot and Ricky tent camp along the banks of the river. That would be considered rigorous in Wisconsin, but with the remarkably active 80-somethings we've gotten to know in Birmingham, Dot and Ricky will probably be camping in the wild for another few decades at least.

Isn't this a darling bean pot? It was in the photo Dot sent us, and we can't help but think "Dot and Ricky's Baked Beans" might be just as delicious as their brisket.

Edith and Bill Keith, married 55 years, play Ring around the Ghosties with their little granddaughters

Edith Keith

All of us at Penzeys say "Here's to you Edith." Clink!

Edith Keith was one of the very last people to respond to our call for recipes from the Birmingham area. After reading her letter, we knew we had to include her and her recipe, even if it did have a quart of hard liquor. See for yourself...

Dear Pam,

It gives me great pleasure to answer your letter requesting a family favorite recipe. I have an outstanding family recipe, but it may not be suitable for Penzeys in that it does not call for any spices or special flavorings. This recipe originated at my mother's family plantation home, Greenlawn, in Meridianville, Alabama. Greenlawn, the house, still stands. It was built between 1850-1855. There was little cash in circulation in the rural south following the war between the states. Recipes used were combinations of ingredients that could be raised or grown at home. This recipe uses only four ingredients. Its quality depends heavily on the freshness of those ingredients and the quality of the bourbon.

Sincerely,

Edith Keith

(Mrs. William A. Keith)

Birmingham, Alabama

We had a lot of fun testing this recipe. We asked Edith if it could be made without the bourbon, and after a moment of shocked silence, the response, **"Oh, honey... No!"** delivered in the best southern accent possible, pretty much sums it up. As Edith said, this is a treat for a very special holiday occasion. Back in the day it was created, everyone around was poor in a way we would find hard to imagine these days. Anything the family had came from what they could grow and make themselves. Looking forward to holiday eggnog could pretty much keep you going for a whole year.

Greenlawn-Otey Eggnog

This recipe uses only four ingredients, so make sure they are all fresh and high quality. Traditionally made at Christmas and New Year's. Serve with a spoon to get every drop!

1	dozen pasteurized eggs
2	Cups sugar, divided
2	Cups bourbon (1 pint)
4	Cups whipping cream (1 quart)

Have ready:

1	large punch bowl
2	large mixing bowls
1	small dividing cup or dish

The key to this recipe is the careful separation of the eggs. Break and separate the egg whites, placing the whites in one large bowl, yolks in the other. Separate each egg individually before adding to the bowl, so that if one yolk breaks you don't have to start over.

Mix the egg whites on high speed until the egg whites are stiff, about 5-8 minutes. Add 2 TB. of the sugar and whip briefly into the whites to stabilize. Without washing the beaters, beat the egg yolks until light and lemon colored. Add the sugar, beat briefly, then add the bourbon and beat to a pale, creamy consistency, until all the graininess of the sugar has disappeared. Pour this mixture into the large punch bowl. At this point whip the whipping cream to soft peaks, 3-5 minutes. Add this to the punch bowl but don't stir yet. Place the whites on top of the other ingredients, and, using a wire whisk, carefully and gently fold and incorporate all ingredients. Do not stir or whip, just fold down and over, turning bowl and going down, across, up and over.

Best served right away, though it will hold pretty well for an hour or two in the fridge. Top with a dash of freshly grated nutmeg as desired.

Yield: 1 large punch bowl of eggnog.
Prep. time: 30 minutes.

Todd Lowe

Todd Lowe is the kind of man you want around in times of trouble; chances are he'll show up on your doorstep with a big old smoked turkey and some loaves of homemade bread. "Turkeys are my mission," he said. Whether it is a birth or death in his close-knit community, to Todd that means it's time to fire up the smoker.

When Todd sent us his succulent turkey recipe, he also included a very spicy and delicious recipe for grilled chicken called "Hazim's Chicken." It didn't seem a particularly Southern recipe, and sure enough, Todd Lowe's friend Hazim is from Turkey. It turns out that when Hazim first visited friends in the Birmingham area, Todd and his wife Barbara invited them all out for a boat ride, as they live on the lake in Tuscaloosa, which Todd said is pretty much heaven. The Lowes spent years being transferred around the country during his days at Midwest Steel, so they had a pretty good idea that if they ever had a chance to put down roots, Birmingham would be just the spot to do it. Now that they have their own business and all they need is a late postal pickup, their lake home near Birmingham is the perfect spot. It's also a lot warmer than Todd remembers it being growing up in Minnesota. Anyway, Hazim had such a wonderful time with the Lowes he cooked dinner to return their hospitality. Everyone loved his spicy tender chicken and pasta so much Todd made sure to get the recipe. It's been a favorite of theirs ever since.

If you'd like to make Hazim's Chicken and Pasta, and we highly recommend you do, you'll find it in the "One World" section. Even though Hazim travelled here to our country to share his recipe, and Bill travelled to Turkey and came home to write about his trip, we think it all comes together nicely.

We're so smart, this is what happens. We simply have to accept that it is sometimes just too cold and windy in Wisconsin to use a smoker. We set up a cardboard windbreak, but we didn't think about what would happen when the blustery wind started gusting, and the windbreak fell on the smoker...

Todd Lowe's Smoked Turkey

Todd Lowe is a big fan of a small company in Wisconsin that sells a little seasoning called Bicentennial Rub, which he always uses for his smoked turkeys.

We here at Penzeys are not experts in the smoking department (see photo of our smoker after the "cardboard windbreak of flames" episode), but we are doing our best to learn, and following Mr. Lowe's excellent instructions, we were able to make this delicious turkey on only our second try. We've left this recipe pretty much just as Mr. Todd Lowe wrote it, because we are very comfortable with the thought that he, indeed, is an expert smoker.

Equipment:
Water smoker consisting of a base with charcoal pan and a lift off body with water pan and two grills ("smoker body").

Charcoal chimney to start coals with newspaper rather than lighter fluid.

Fuel:
Mesquite charcoal and mesquite chips. Chips should be soaked in water for at least 24 hours. I keep a bucket on my deck for this.

1	turkey, 16 - 22 pounds
2	oranges
3-4	TB. seasoning, divided
2	oz. olive oil plus a few drops

Start two chimneys of charcoal for smoker. Put large pan of water on stove and boil. Slice oranges in half then place flat side down and slice as thin as you can. Place oranges and juice in microwave safe bowl, sprinkle with 2 tablespoons seasoning and add 2 oz. of olive oil. Heat in microwave for 5 minutes at 50% power. Thoroughly clean turkey inside and out then pat dry with paper towel. Cut skin between thighs and breast then spread legs out from body. Place on broiler pan breast up for transport to smoker. Put a few drops of olive oil on turkey and rub with paper towel then heavily rub with seasoning - using 1-2 TB. Fill body cavity with oranges and drizzle remaining juice and oil over turkey. Lightly rub water pan and grill with oil. When charcoal at top of chimneys is burning, dump chimneys into charcoal pan. Do not place smoker body on base. Place water pan in smoker body and fill with boiling water. Insert grill in body at the lower position and place turkey breast side down. Pour any excess oil and juice over back of turkey and sprinkle with seasoning. Put several large mesquite chips on coals and lift smoker body onto base and add smoker top. Check water every 2 hours and add chips. When water must be added, lift body from base. Additional charcoal may be needed after 4 - 6 hours. After approximately 5 hours, remove smoker body from base and turn turkey to breast side up. Cooking time will be from $5\frac{1}{2}$ to 11 hours depending on size of turkey, outside temperature, and wind. Turkey is done when juices run clear.

We often smoke turkeys a day ahead when we are feeding a large group. For day ahead preparation, slice the turkey after it has cooled and place in storage bags. To bring up to serving temperature, the turkey is steamed in a vegetable steamer. The benefits of smoking a turkey are that the water pan provides high humidity so that the turkey does not dry out and the smoke not only provides exceptional flavor but also is a preservative. A smoked turkey will last significantly longer in the refrigerator than a baked turkey.

Frances Lanseros

"This is the latest picture of me, taken at my grandson's wedding. My oldest daughter Jennifer Weber and her youngest son Albert (the groom).

How white my hair is getting - has gotten?! No matter. There's a lot of spirit in the old gal yet!!"

The captions on the back of the photos Frances sent really were a snapshot of her life, so we've included them verbatim...

Frances Lanseros is a difficult person to fit into a four page spread. She does so much. She's in her mid-80s, chops wood, has a huge organic garden where she grows plant dyes to color the wool she spins herself, plays the piano, writes poetry, and in general just keeps a schedule that would have any normal person exhausted by noon.

Frances grew up on a working farm in Upstate New York. She fell in love with the soil the moment she could walk, and has wonderful memories of her favorite childhood job, driving the tractor. She has been in the Birmingham area for many years now, and enjoys teaching the school groups who come by all about her garden and the process of taking wool from fleece to finished sweater.

When we first started talking with Frances, Hurricane Ivan had just been through, and we asked her if she'd left during the storm. She just laughed and said she wouldn't think of leaving. She had canned 18 chickens prior to the storm, and made sure she'd chopped enough wood to see herself through in case the power was out for a week.

Did we mention Frances has a wolf? Nineteen years ago, she came across an orphaned wolf pup on a trip out West. On the strength of her experience raising wolf-dog hybrids as a girl, she was able to save her new pal Meeza from a dire fate. Meeza loves Frances, and though she has no such love for the tabby cat, she still lets it sit on Frances's lap. Meeza is very gentle and watchful, and when Frances has school children over to learn about organic gardening or yarn-making, Meeza sits right at Frances's side. Sometimes the children are allowed to touch Meeza's luxurious, silky soft coat with Frances's hand right over theirs. We would love to pet Meeza also. How beautiful her eyes and markings are...

Frances Lanseros's
Sweet Potato Soup

This soup is thick and delicious like split pea, but with a beautiful golden color kids love. Great on a rainy day.

2 medium sweet potatoes (yams), peeled and cut into 1 inch cubes
1 large onion
2 cloves garlic (or ½ tsp. granulated garlic)
1 bay leaf
   salt to taste
1 tsp. thyme
⅛ tsp. cayenne pepper
2 Cups chicken broth (or 2 tsp. chicken soup base in 2 Cups hot water)
1 Cup low fat buttermilk
1 Cup skim milk
1 Cup ham, chopped
1 TB. lime juice (½ fresh lime)
3 TB. chopped fresh cilantro (optional)

In a large pot, combine potatoes, onion, garlic, bay leaf, salt, thyme, cayenne and chicken broth. Bring to a boil, reduce heat and simmer, covered, for 15 minutes or until the sweet potatoes are tender. Remove the bay leaf, pour the soup in a blender or food processor and blend until smooth. Return the soup to the pan, add the buttermilk, milk, ham and lime juice and heat gently. Do not boil. Serve once hot, sprinkling each serving with cilantro if desired.

Serves: 6-8. Prep. time: 10 minutes. Cooking time: 25 minutes or so.

"Yes - I went out to forested areas after lumber companies took what they wanted, brought it home, cut (and chopped) and piled it up all by myself! After the storm in '93 that dropped 16" of snow here, making no electricity for a whole week & I had to live in this barn, I told myself "Never again!" So I had a tiny wood cook stove put up in the kitchen. Every winter I use that for heat and cooking now. Wood heat is so cozy! This is also where I dye the wool."

Frances Lanseros

Frances Lanseros's Cucumber Salad
Original Recipe

50	large cucumbers, pared
2	bunches celery
8	large onions
4	sweet red bell peppers

Chop all fine. Cover with brine (enough water to cover plus 1 Cup salt) and leave overnight. Drain in the morning.

2	quarts vinegar
4	Cups sugar
2	small cups flour
2	tsp. turmeric powder
½	Cup mustard powder

Cook and stir until thick–keep stirring so it doesn't burn. Add cucumber mixture and cook about 10 minutes, or until heated through.

Can in hot jars.

5 minute water bath.

Frances Lanseros's Cucumber Salad

The original recipe, which has been in Frances's family for at least 6 generations, is a canning recipe starting with 50 large cucumbers. We decided to also include a smaller non-canned refrigerator pickle batch, for those who'd like to try it but don't can or don't have 50 cucumbers worth of relatives. Frances says cucumber salad is a great addition to tartar sauce and is delicious in sandwiches of any type of meat.

10	large cucumbers
3	stalks celery
1	large onion
½	red bell pepper
1	Cup salt
2	Cups white vinegar
1	Cup sugar
½	tsp. powdered turmeric
2	TB mustard powder
¾	Cup flour

Peel the cucumbers. Finely dice the vegetables and place in a large bowl. Sprinkle with salt and let stand in the refrigerator overnight. Drain the vegetables and pat dry. Make the sauce by heat- ing the vinegar, sugar, turmeric, mustard powder, and flour, stirring frequently. This should thicken and form a thick sauce in 5 or so minutes. Mix the vegetables and sauce together and pack into jars, refrigerate.

Yield: 12 Cups. Prep. time: 20 minutes. Cooking time: 5 minutes.

"Some yarn I prepared from fleece and spun, and dyed making my own dyes from roots, leaves, flowers, etc. Every year dyes from the very same plants etc. are different in color and shades depending on the weather - hot, too dry, too wet or too humid. Fascinating! These were done in the early fall when colors tend to be more warm yellow & gold."

"Meeza at 3 months, such a cuddle-bunny!"

MY BUDDY THE ROCKING CHAIR

Starlit darkness donned the heavens
After the slipping away of the setting sun.
The livestock fed and checked for the night,
And the rocking chair calls, for the day's chores are done. . .
- the day's chores are done.

Wet woolen mittens hang by the fire.
Snowy soaked boots standing in pairs.
Tomorrow's wheat bread rising for morning.
And the rocking chair calls after the day's many cares. . .
- the day's many cares.

The wood box is filled with dried hickory pieces.
An old school wall-clock ticks off the time.
Tabby's stretched out with trusted contentment,
And the rocking chair calls for the hour's now mine. . .
- the hour's now mine.

So with hot tea in cup, these weary bones
Are lowered to the blessed old oaken chair
By the humming banked fire. This lovely day is done.
And the rocking chair rhythmically agrees, "The-day-was-fair. . .
- The-day-was-fair."

Francheska Lanseros

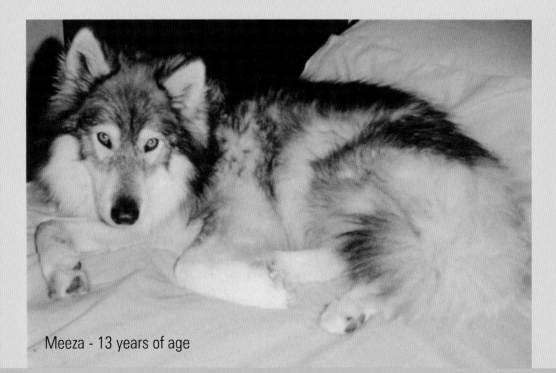

Meeza - 13 years of age

Frances Marie Weyher

is a great cook. Her husband, Richard, cooked in the Navy for many years. He was the one who encouraged Frances to send us her wonderful recipes.

Frances says they make a great team in the kitchen. She loves to bake, and he can make a kitchen "Ship-Shape" – really – in about 10 minutes.

Frances grew up in the Birmingham area, then moved to Norfolk where her husband was stationed while in the U S Navy.

Toward the end of that time, Frances's Daddy started needing help in his advancing years, so they made the decision to move back to Birmingham to help him out. They've never regretted it, as they love their home, church, friends and just the area in general – it really was like coming home.

Here's a quick recipe Frances makes up for Richard and his friend Walter when they go off hunting. After a long day outdoors, it's easy to pop in the oven, or can be cooked over an open fire while camping.

Start with 2 clean potatoes. Cut in quarters, lay on aluminum foil. Put four onion rings, two bell pepper rings and two 1/2 tsp. pats of butter on top, along with a healthy sprinkling of your favorite seasoning. Fold the foil securely on all sides. Bake at 350˚ approximately 30-45 minutes, depending on the size of the potatoes.

Each package serves one hungry guy.

The Weyhers

Frances talks about her husband Richard...

"The snapshot enclosed was taken on vacation. Richard is retired from the U S Navy, and the cap he has on is USS Enterprise C U N 65. Enterprise was the world's first nuclear powered aircraft carrier and Richard is a 'Plank Owner' meaning he was stationed aboard Enterprise when it was commissioned on November 25, 1961. When Enterprise is de-commissioned Richard will receive some sort of remembrance (perhaps a coin after metal from Enterprise has been melted down), as will the other plank owners (original crew members). Richard served 23 years in the US Navy, and we're very proud that he had a small part in our nation's naval history."

Frances Marie and Richard with his plank owner's cap.
Any other plank owners from the USS ENTERPRISE out there? Richard would love to connect up with you again – please drop us a line.

Oatmeal Cake

The Weyhers' daughter always asked for this unassuming little cake for her birthday, and it really is that good. We like to pretend it is a bowl of oatmeal and have it for breakfast.

1¼	Cups boiling water
1	Cup quick cooking oats
½	Cup vegetable shortening
1	Cup brown sugar
1	Cup white sugar
2	eggs, beaten
1	tsp. vanilla extract
1½	Cups flour
⅓	tsp. salt
1	tsp. cinnamon
1	tsp. baking soda

Frosting:

8	oz. cream cheese (we used the lower fat cream cheese known as Neufchatel cheese)
¼	Cup butter (½ a stick)
1	lb. bag of powdered sugar
2	tsp. vanilla extract
2	Cups chopped nuts (we used pecans)

Add the boiling water to the oats and leave to stand for 20 minutes, stirring occasionally. Cream together the shortening and sugars then add the beaten eggs and vanilla. Mix together the dry ingredients and add to the creamed mixture along with the oatmeal mixture. Bake in two 9 inch greased and floured cake pans for 35-40 minutes at 375°.

Turn out and leave to cool before frosting.

To make the frosting, cream together softened (room temperature) cream cheese and butter, then blend in the sugar, vanilla, and nuts. Spread evenly over cake.

Yield: 12 good-sized slices.
Prep. time: 10 minutes (plus 20 for the oatmeal). Baking time: 40 minutes.

This is the Weyhers' daughter's birthday cake - she asked for it every year growing up, and it is that good. One of the great things about getting recipes from other parts of the country is seeing how people who have used a local ingredient for generations work with it, and this is one of the greatest uses of pecans we've ever seen. Yum! And since it has oatmeal in it, it's really good for breakfast.

Pauline Jones

Great Grandma Pauline Stewart Jones with Micah and Maddy Semon, who love their MeMe's cooking.

MeMe's Cream Cheese Pound Cake

We made this delicious old-fashioned cake in a tube pan but a loaf pan would work too. It really doesn't need any topping, but we drizzled it with vanilla icing–fresh sugared berries or peaches would go wonderfully well too...

3   sticks butter, softened
8   oz. cream cheese (we used Neufchatel, the lower fat cream cheese)
3   cups sugar
6   eggs
3   Cups flour
1   TB. pure vanilla extract

Icing:
1/2   Cup powdered sugar
1   TB. softened butter
2-3   TB. milk

Whip butter and cream cheese together. Add sugar and beat well on high speed until light and fluffy. Starting with 2 eggs, then 1 cup flour, alternate adding eggs and flour, mixing well between each addition. Add vanilla extract at the end and mix well. Grease and flour a tube or loaf pan, carefully pour in batter. Place in a cold oven. Turn oven on to 350° and bake cake for 1 1/2 hours. This is a dense, moist cake, so insert a toothpick in the middle to see if the cake is done–it should come out relatively clean. Let cool briefly, carefully turn out of pan. Completely cool before whisking icing ingredients together and drizzling over cake, if desired.

Yield: 16 slices.

Prep time: 10 minutes.

Baking time: 90 minutes.

Pauline Stewart Jones

was born 89 years ago. Married at 18, she had twins at 19 - which her granddaughter Marsha has always felt to be "extremely illustrative of her efficiency." Her husband Jewel was a carpenter and farmer who raised white-faced Herefords while Miss Pauline manned the local Post Office, where she was postmistress for more than 40 years. Their farm was named "DO-TIL-I" . As he always said, "It'll do till I can do better".

MeMe and Popeye, as they became known, loved to bring the family together and meals in the special dining room served on MeMe's fabulous china have become special memories for the kids, grandkids, and now great grandchildren. Whenever the children are coming, she bakes Cream Cheese Pound Cake. It has been the family favorite since MeMe learned how to make it from her own mother nearly 80 years ago.

This cake is delicious, and we want to say thanks to Marsha for sharing MeMe's recipe with all of us.

MeMe's Cream Cheese Pound Cake

Dr. Greg Alexander

Public Health is not really something a lot of us fully understand. It seems to be something we only think about when something goes wrong. As long as everything is running smoothly, it is pretty much invisible. To keep us all feeling like there's nothing to it requires an enormous amount of work by a lot of good folks who truly have the best interests of all of us at heart.

These are people like Dr. Greg - who works on preventing pre-term birth and infant mortality, and his wife, Dr. Donna, who focuses on policy and health care coverage, particularly regarding children with special health care needs. They work with departments full of people to constantly advance our knowledge and better our world.

And they cook dinner every night.

Dr. Greg Alexander,

Professor and Chair of the Department of Maternal and Child Health at the University of Alabama at Birmingham, didn't know what he was getting into when he welcomed us to Birmingham and sent his recipe for Savory Butter Beans.

We just couldn't find fresh butter beans anywhere in Milwaukee, even at the height of summer at the farmer's market. The back and forth dialogue on how we could make the recipe work for everyone was a truly gratifying journey into the world of a really high level and just plain nice guy.

As he said,

"For two decades I have worked closely with several French OB and Pediatric researchers from Paris and Toulouse, who love my butter beans (although they like my lamb shanks more)."

Clearly these are researchers with good taste, and, of course, the first thing was to secure that recipe for lamb shanks too. They are, indeed, melt in your mouth delicious. After that, we worked the butter bean recipe out for dry lima beans, which are always available. However you make this recipe, do give it a try – they're not just Savory Butter beans, they're Awesomely Savory Butter beans...

Thanks Dr. Greg!

DR. GREG AND COOKING:

"How do I find the time? Hmmm. Can't think like that. It is my escape - a research project I can get the results today, make a positive difference for family tonight and unwind. If I didn't cook when I got home I would pull a manuscript or grant out of my briefcase and keep working. Cooking is much better for me and those around me. I can talk with them, let the struggles of the day slip away, and transition from Chair to father/husband/friend."

In 1988, the Institute of Medicine defined the following as the Goals of Public Health:

The air, food, and water supply remain safe.

The medical care system functions efficiently and effectively.

Communities work together to support the optimal growth and development of all children and families and promote equality of life across the life-span.

Workplaces, schools and recreation sites are safe.

People engage in healthy lifestyle choices that prolong a high quality of life.

Appropriate and necessary services and supports are designed and maintained to meet community and individual needs for physical, mental and spiritual health.

Interested in learning more? Pick up a copy of

Needs Assessment in Public Health,

by Donna J. Petersen and her husband Greg R. Alexander

DR. GREG AND DR. DONNA:

"My wife (Dr. Donna Petersen) and I met in graduate school at Johns Hopkins University. Donna and I both like to cook (she had a job as a cook at a diner when she was a student). And, we eat home-cooked dinners with our two daughters (9 and 13 years) at the dining table nearly every night. During the week, I do most of the cooking and Donna attends to the homework. We like to go out to eat but do not go to chains or fast food places. Saturday mornings in the summer are typically started with a trip to the farmers markets to stock up with vegetables for the week. We have written a book together on needs assessment in public health and have worked closely as a team (both as professionals and parents) throughout our careers."

Savory Butter Beans

We made this recipe using dry butter beans (lima beans), since fresh butter beans are not available in Wisconsin. Broad beans work well too. These beans are lusty either way, but according to the Doctor of Butterbeans, fresh ones have great color...

4	Cups fresh butter beans, washed
2	TB butter
1	shallot, finely minced
3	cloves fresh garlic, minced, or ¾ tsp. dry minced garlic covered with 2 tsp. water and rehydrated 5 minutes
½	Cup andouille sausage, chopped (1 sausage)
½	Cup smoked ham, chopped
5	Cups water, approximately
1	tsp. dry savory leaves (1 TB fresh)
8-10	whole green peppercorns
1	tsp. ham soup base
	salt and pepper to taste

If using dry beans, soak ¾ of a 1 lb. bag in a deep bowl covered with cold water overnight. You can also use the whole bag and just increase all the other recipe ingredients by ¼. In a 2-3 quart saucepan, melt the butter and gently saute the shallot and garlic until soft. Add the ham and the sausage and gently saute, adding ½ cup water if necessary to prevent burning. Add the butter beans and enough water to fully cover the beans. We used 5 cups of water total, but it might vary depending on the size of the pan and your beans. Add savory, green peppercorns and ham base. Bring to boil. Reduce heat, cover and simmer 2 to 3 hours, stirring occasionally, until beans are tender and the water is reduced to form a broth. Stir carefully once the beans start getting soft so they don't get broken. About halfway through cooking, taste and add salt and pepper to taste. We added ½ tsp. both salt and ground black pepper. Can be served over rice or as a side dish. Add hot sauce to taste.

Yields: 1 good-sized bowl of beans.

Prep. time: 10 minutes chopping plus soaking time if you use dry beans.

Cooking time: 2-3 hours.

Dr. Greg Alexander

Dr. Greg and Dr. Donna are off on their Continuing Adventures in Public Health. She has accepted a position as Dean of the Department of Public Health at USF, so the whole family is on the move. They are probably toasting each other with a pair of his famous Peach Daiquiris right now. As he said, "I make a memorable Peach Daiquiri which made the winters of Minnesota more acceptable." We wish them all the best of luck, and hope that someday, maybe by the next time winter rolls around, he might send us that recipe too...

Lamb Shanks Toulouse

Dr. Alexander does research with some French doctors, and they love his cooking, too. He wrote this recipe up at the request of his dear friend, Dr. Francois de Caunes, from Toulouse.

4	lamb shanks
2	tsp. sea salt, divided
2	tsp. mignonette pepper (roughly ¾ tsp. each of cracked black and white pepper and coriander)
4	TB flour
⅓	Cup olive oil or ½ stick butter
8-10	cloves garlic
1	large onion
1	shallot
2	leeks
1	turnip
2	carrots
2	stalks of celery
4-8	anchovies (optional, but they add a great depth of flavor without an anchovy taste–give 'em a try)
14	oz. can plum tomatoes
½	6 oz. can tomato paste
2	bay leaves
½	tsp. thyme
1	bottle red wine–Rhone is very good
¼	tsp. white pepper
6	fresh mint leaves for garnish

Rub the shanks with 1 tsp. salt and mignonette pepper and then dust with flour. Chop all the vegetables and put to one side.

Heat olive oil or butter in a large, heavy casserole with a lid. Two at a time over medium heat, brown shanks all over but do not burn. Once browned, remove and set aside. Add garlic, onion, shallot, leeks, turnip, carrots and celery and cook over medium low heat, stirring occasionally to get up any brown bits on the bottom, until tender. Add a bit of butter or olive oil if the vegetables get too dry. After about 10 minutes, the vegetables should be nice and tender. Add anchovies, tomato paste and plum tomatoes, bay leaves and thyme, stir and simmer for

5 minutes. Pour in the bottle of red wine, and stir thoroughly. Season with salt and white pepper to taste–we used ¼ tsp. white pepper and another 1 tsp. salt. Return the lamb shanks to the pot, stir and bring to a boil. Cover, reduce heat and simmer for 2-3 hours until the meat is completely falling off the bone tender. Place the shanks in a deep serving dish. Skim any fat off the sauce and spoon over and around the shanks in the serving dish. Garnish with fresh mint leaves.

Dr. Alexander serves this hearty dish with saffron rice or couscous, a spinach/mandarin orange salad and red wine, with a glass of Armagnac after. When the shanks are very large, it helps to de-bone the meat from the shanks before serving to reduce into smaller portions.

Serves: 4-6. Prep. time: 10 minutes. Cooking time: 3½ hours or so total.

With the first issue I really wanted to touch on how at the very heart of cooking is our desire to nurture and provide for those around us. To shine a light on the goodness within us all that is so important to understanding why we are all here. I still really like this section. It mirrors the changes in my own life at the time with my daughter's birth that seemingly by chance happened at the same time as the birth of *Penzeys One*.

Cooking is all about creating a brighter future, but seeing cooking as an act of kindness can open all of us to seeing our past in a new light as well. No one is self-made; each of us has relied on the kindness of others along our paths to get us to where we are today. To see cooking for what it is, an act of love, is to see just how much love has been given to all of us in our lives. It is a debt we owe to the past that as cooks we repay to the future.

We did make one change to this section for the book from the original magazine version. We added in the Abuela of the Heart story from my niece Caity's IFS trip to Argentina. I had wanted to have an adoptive grandparent story in the first issue but we ran out of time. I understand that sadly not every family situation is healthy. Sometimes there is no other choice than to set yourself adrift, but I wanted to make the point that it is never too late to find or even create a new family to moor yourself to. And yes, page 75 is Jeri's and my daughter Theodora (we call her Teddi) from her first day to her first birthday.

Do what you can to find somewhere to belong.

one love

With this issue being the birth of **one** we thought it would only be right to pay tribute to babies and the desire to have them. Yes, it gives us a chance to show our baby pictures to the world, but it is more than just that. It also gives us a chance to look at the love that whether we admit it or not, is inside of each of us as humans. It is this love that gives us our desire to do for others and leads us out to the kitchen time and again.

You certainly don't have to be a parent to be a good cook or understand our approach to why we cook. Yet we are so lucky to live at the dawn of the time where anyone who really wants kids can have them. If you have the desire, why not make it happen? Even if you are past the age that it makes sense, or you are absolutely one hundred percent convinced that parenthood is not for you, it is never too late to have kids in your life. You can go as far as being an official adoptive grandparent or do as little as just taking your niece or nephew to a movie now and again. Ultimately you will find kids can take a whole bunch out of you, but somehow have a knack for always putting back a little bit more. You might also be surprised to find how much you enjoy giving your time to help someone else. This enjoyment in giving might not be in everyone, but we at **one** believe it's in everyone who cooks.

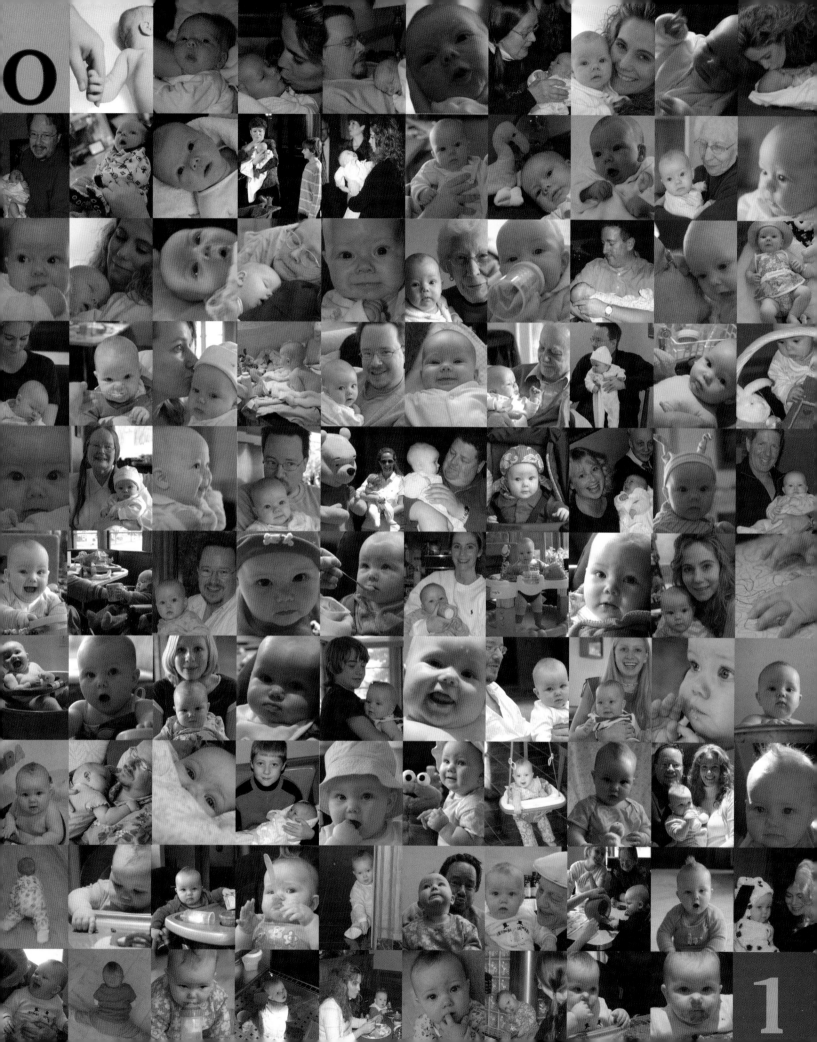

Maria, Kasenia and Emily Olney

6 People.
4 Countries.
1 Family.

It was nine o'clock Monday morning and the FedEx man was knocking. Lisa Olney was jet-lagged as she answered the door having just gotten off a long flight from Russia late Saturday night. She and her husband David had adopted Maria, a beautiful brown-eyed Russian baby girl. As Lisa opened the envelope her mind reeled from shock and joy. Before her eyes were the papers she thought she would never see – signed official adoption papers for Emily. Her baby from India was coming home. Their long struggle had finally paid off. The Olneys needed to find a second crib because in a month's time they would have twins. The difference was that their twins would be from two different countries half a world away.

The Olney Family, joined by David's brother, clockwise from top right; Lisa, David, Kasenia, Maria, Emily, Uncle Bruce and Shawn.

"It's natural to believe families must begin with babies."

Although Lisa Olney worked with adoptions every day, adopting a child themselves was a huge step for her and husband David. While Lisa had no doubts about adopting a child, David was not so sure. They learned of a seminar about adoption given by Families Adopting Children Everywhere (FACE, www.faceadoptioninfo.org). Their goal is to educate families in what to expect when adopting children. Attending that seminar turned David around because as he put it, "For the most part I was lost in the details as far as expense or how much time it takes." He added, "It was easy to lose track of why you are interested in adoption in the first place. It's really about the kids."

They submitted the paperwork to adopt Emily. While it was making its way through the proper channels, the Indian orphanage that was her home was swept up in legal problems. All adoptions from that orphanage were delayed indefinitely. With Emily's adoption in limbo, Lisa continued to work on other cases. One of her tougher placements was three 8-year-old boys from Vietnam. Finding a family for an older child is more difficult. It's natural to believe families must begin with babies. By chance, David picked up the folder containing the boys' dossiers and he started to look through them. He turned to Lisa and said that they should adopt one of the boys. She thought he was kidding since they already had the adoption for Emily in the works. But David was serious. After thinking about it, he was certain he could relate better to an older child than to an infant. At first, Lisa said no but David did not let up. "So for six weeks he bugged me about adopting one of these boys," she said. "Finally I caved in."

Shawn, an 8-year-old Vietnamese boy, was going to join the Olney family. Like his soon-to-be Indian sister's adoption, Shawn's adoption was delayed and months passed. Then, a picture of a little Russian girl came across Lisa's desk. "It was instantaneous. I took one look at those big brown eyes and I knew I wanted this child to be my daughter." They filed the papers and this time the adoption went smoothly. A short time later they held Maria in their arms. Then came the knock of the FedEx man and in less than a month Emily was home. Shawn's paperwork in Vietnam was then sorted out and a few months later he joined them. In less than half a year's time, this loving couple went from a quiet, empty nest, to a house filled with the happy sounds of a family.

French Toast

It's Dad's turn to cook on Saturday mornings in the Olney house. On the menu most Saturdays is French Toast. Simple yet delicious and all the kids get to join in and help. Well, except for Shawn. He'd rather have a bowl of noodles for breakfast.

Recipe by Dave, Lisa, Shawn, Emily, Maria and Kasenia Olney. Quick, easy and delicious, perfect for a special breakfast. The Olneys enjoy a lot of spice - start with half the spices listed, you can always add more...

6 -8   slices of your favorite bread
  6   eggs
  1   tsp. cinnamon
$1/2$ tsp. ground nutmeg
$1/2$ tsp. ground allspice
    butter and maple syrup to taste

In a bowl, beat the eggs well. Add cinnamon, nutmeg and allspice and mix well. Dip both sides of the bread in the egg mixture, letting the eggs soak in for a few seconds before turning. Cook in a hot, lightly oiled skillet 4-6 minutes, turning once when nicely browned. Transfer cooked French toast to a plate, garnish with butter and maple syrup to taste. Serves: 4-6. Prep. time: 5 minutes. Cooking time: 6 minutes.

Shawn makes this tasty meal for the whole family—it's quick and easy too.

2	packages of shrimp flavored ramen noodles
2½	Cups of water
2 TB	Buffalo sauce (Shawn likes Texas Pete Buffalo Sauce, but any kind of thick red hot sauce will do. We used Frank's Hot Sauce and it tasted great)
	aleppo pepper, to taste

Place 2 packages of shrimp ramen noodles in a large bowl with the water and only 1 package of the shrimp flavoring. Place in microwave on high for 3 minutes and 15 seconds. Remove, and in the center of the noodles, pour approximately 2 TB. of sauce. Sprinkle with aleppo pepper to taste. Divide noodles and broth into 4 small bowls to share with sisters. Can be eaten at breakfast, lunch, or dinner.
Serves: 2-4. Prep. time: none. Cooking time: 3 minutes 15 seconds.

Shawn's Noodles

Defending civilization one meal at a time.

Dinner is a daily tradition in the Olney household. It is a time for bonding, for discussing problems and sharing laughs. Both Lisa and David do some cooking, but as David puts it, "The meals that taste good are cooked by Lisa." She tries to put a meal on the table each and every day. She knows if she makes the effort, it is guaranteed that at least once a day, the family will all be together.

David was talking to a friend that had also adopted a boy from Vietnam. She was wondering if it would be so bad to let her son have different meals if he did not like what was being served or even let him eat dinner in his room. David dug in his heels, "You've got to hold your ground. You are a defender of civilization." Melodramatic? Maybe, but to David, sharing food and the companionship that comes with it is the foundation of civilized society. This is why the Olneys feel adoption is so important. Far too many children are being raised in orphanages and they are being turned out into the world without ever being part of a family. How can they ever become parents without ever having parents?

Kasenia takes a break from hunting Easter eggs in the back yard.

years old Kasenia was the size of babies half her age. The doctors

"She is so beautiful!"

painted a bleak picture saying that she would forever be in a wheelchair and they feared she was cognitively disabled. Lisa did not buy that. "I knew that cognitively she was fine. The way she was playing peek-a-boo with me and checking to see if I was looking at her. She was so engaging."

Try as she might, Lisa could not find parents for this little girl. The Olneys were left with a choice. Adopt her themselves or leave her at the Russian orphanage. Even the Russian adoption officials tried to talk them out of it. They said in addition to her poor health, she was undesirable because she was of "mixed" race, part Uzbeki, and part Russian. That for Lisa was the last straw. She could not leave this beautiful little girl with people who thought that way. Despite her grim medical prognosis, Lisa and David brought Kasenia into their family.

Physical therapy has been a big part of Kasenia's life in America. Today she can walk with the help of canes though the experts said she never would. The doctors are now convinced that if she stays

Lisa Olney was in Russia helping a family through an adoption. She decided to videotape children in an orphanage hoping to find families for them. Watching the video, the camera focused on a little girl and Lisa shouted, "She is so beautiful!" By the emotion in her voice, it was obvious the Olney house was not quite full. Lisa called

David from Moscow that night. She could not get this little girl out of her head. Their hands were quite full with three children already so they agreed that she should try to find a family for this girl. "I really did try," Lisa says. She had a family lined up but they backed out after their doctor saw her medical file. Born 13 weeks prematurely, at 2

at her current pace, she will be able to give up her canes by first grade. She is a very determined little girl. While David and Lisa have done a lot for her, she has more than paid them back. "She has the sweetest, kindest, most loving personality that I have ever met in a child." After a pause Lisa adds, "She's like an angel."

Kasenia gets around with the help of what she calls her "sparkle sticks".

Lisa showed her father a picture of Emily before she was adopted. Being from an older generation, he was not prepared for the idea of a granddaughter that was a different color than him. Without thinking he said, "Lisa, she's so... brown." But as the Olneys have found, family doesn't necessarily have to come from babies that look just like you. For Lisa's dad, getting the chance to hold his granddaughter in his arms made him colorblind. Today Emily has Grandpa wrapped around her little finger. He absolutely adores her and Emily feels the same.

Pho (Rice Noodle & Beef Soup)

Simple, traditional Vietnamese soup. It takes a bit more time than seasoned ramen noodles, but not much more effort, and it's really delicious.

Broth:

- 3 lbs. beef spare ribs
- 10 cups water
- 1 large onion, peeled and chopped
- 1 whole star anise (5-7 points)
- 2 cloves garlic, peeled and minced
- 1 whole clove
- 1 2 inch piece fresh ginger root, peeled and sliced
- 1/2 tsp. whole peppercorns, black or white
- 1 TB salt
- 1 TB fish sauce

Soup:

- 2 Cups dry rice noodles (about half of a 1 lb. package)
- 1 small bunch green onions (scallions), circle-cut
- 1 lime, sliced

Wash ribs, pat dry. Put them in a soup pot with water, onion, star anise, garlic, clove, ginger, peppercorns, salt and fish sauce. Bring to a boil, cook 2 hours, skimming off the froth every 20 minutes or so to get a nice clear broth. Strain the broth through cheesecloth, discarding all but the bones. Remove the meat from the beef bones, chop into small bite-sized pieces. The broth and meat can be refrigerated at this point until you're ready to finish the soup by making the noodles.

Cook the rice noodles according to package directions. Generally, water is brought to a boil, the noodles are added, the heat is turned off, and the noodles are steeped 10 or so minutes. Stir frequently so they don't clump. Rinse with fresh water to remove starch. Bring the broth back to a boil, fill soup bowls 2/3 full with noodles, top with a handful of beef bits and circle-cut scallions. Pour hot broth over to fill. Serve with lime slices to season each bowl. Serves: 4-6. Prep. time: 10 minutes. Cooking time: 2+ hours.

Adopting an older child can be more difficult for both the child and the family. Unlike infants, they understand what is happening to them. It's not surprising that many older children have problems adjusting to their new surroundings, even if the situation before their adoption was far from pleasant. Experts call it survivor's guilt and Shawn was no exception. A happy kid by nature, he still had some struggles adjusting to life with his new family. The breakthrough for Shawn came about a year after becoming an Olney. It was Mother's Day and Shawn seemed a little down. Lisa had always been up front with the kids about their adoptions so she asked him if there was something he would like to do for his mom in Vietnam. She was thinking he would like to send her a card or a gift. He told Lisa that he wished he could send her to an eye doctor because she had problems with her vision. Even though Shawn's birth mother gave him up to an orphanage, he still cared for her and wanted to help. Lisa acted immediately.

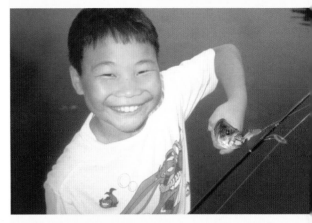

Through some connections in Vietnam, she made arrangements for Shawn's mother to visit an eye doctor. Her vision was worse than expected but the doctor was convinced that surgery would correct her eyesight. The Olneys gave the go ahead and for less than $1000, Shawn's mom could see again. Shawn was so proud that he could help his mom, even from so far away.

Lisa decided early on in life that she wanted to work with children. While in law school she worked on child welfare cases during a summer internship in New York City. Many of the cases she worked on were extremely difficult and heartbreaking. Once she graduated, she landed a job at a respected law firm near her hometown. After her difficult summer in New York she was happy enough practicing general law, but felt unfulfilled. She began to get a few adoption cases and things began to change. Adoption cases were much more satisfying than the typical cases she worked. Then came a case that changed her life. It involved an adoption of a little girl from India. When it was completed, the family sent her a picture of the girl taken in front of the Taj Mahal. She had her arms wide open as if she was welcoming in the whole world. At that very moment, Lisa says, she decided to adopt a baby girl from India and specialize in international adoptions by starting her own agency.

For the *Love* of a Child

She called the agency For the Love of a Child. It grew rapidly as she started programs or worked with foundations in Lithuania, Russia, and Vietnam. The agency clearly filled a need in the community but after she and David adopted four children themselves, she had to turn her focus to her own family, especially little Kasenia. Lisa sold the agency and did not work on any adoptions for a full year. But as Kasenia grew stronger so did Lisa's desire to do adoptions again. As owner of an agency, much of her time was spent on employees, payroll and other details. This time would be different. "If I worked for an agency and did one or two [adoption] programs, I could fulfill within me what I wanted to do and still be a mom and a wife." Lisa now works for a non-profit agency called World Child International (www.worldchild.org). She recently started a program in Guatemala and is very proud of her work.

Delicious Indian food for the whole family—richly flavorful without being hot and spicy. A great recipe for boneless/skinless chicken, and the sauce for the rice is awesome. If you've never cooked Indian rice, give it a try—it's great.

6	boneless, skinless chicken breasts
1	Cup plain yogurt
1/4	Cup lemon juice
2	TB tandoori seasoning

Mix yogurt, lemon juice, and Tandoori seasoning. Spread over chicken breasts and refrigerate overnight. Cook chicken, brushing with marinade, on a hot griddle or under the broiler, about 5 minutes per side depending on the thickness of the breasts. You don't want to fully cook the chicken since it will finish cooking in the sauce. You just want a nice, brown crust. Let the chicken cool slightly and cut into 1-2 inch chunks.

Spicy Red Sauce:

1	29 oz. can of tomato puree
2	tsp. powdered ginger
1/2	tsp. aleppo pepper
1	TB Hungarian sweet paprika
1 1/2	tsp. ground cumin
1 1/2	sticks of butter
1 1/2	Cups whole milk
2	tsp. flake salt or coarse salt
2	tsp. garam masala
2	Cups basmati rice, cooked

Mix the tomato puree, ginger, aleppo pepper, paprika and cumin together in a roomy bowl. Melt the butter over medium heat in a large, non stick pan. Add the chicken and cook for 3 minutes, turning the chicken often. Remove the chicken pieces. Add the tomato mixture to the pan and cook on low heat until the mixture begins to thicken. Add the whole milk, salt, garam masala, and the chicken. Stir to cover the chicken with the sauce. Allow to simmer, uncovered, for 30 minutes. Serve over basmati rice. Prep. time: 5 minutes. Cooking time: 45 minutes. Serves: 8-10.

Tandoori Chicken *with* Spicy Red Sauce

The Kids Are Alright.

Carol Browning and Nancy Maynard are just two of the many people who have been drawn close to the family of Pat Brown and Dennis Kohler. At their Sunday church service, Carol and Nancy first learned Pat and Dennis were being blessed with triplets. It was in the Joys and Concerns segment of the service that Pat stood up and spoke of his excitement that he and Dennis were going to be the parents of triplets. Though she admired his spirit,

Carol turned to her friend Nancy and said, "These guys have no idea what they are getting into." Carol, a retired physician with more than thirty years working in newborn intensive care, knew exactly what they were getting into. As did Nancy, a retired pediatric nurse and nurse educator. Is it luck when you meet exactly the people you need to meet at the exact time you need to meet them, or is it something more?

MONSTER COOKIES

See next page for recipe

MONSTER COOKIES

So much of the story of the triplets, Isabella, Derek and Karissa, has been like that seemingly chance connection at church on that Sunday morning. Theirs is a story of overcoming long odds and obstacles time and again. It is also the story of an incredible outpouring of love. Not only the love of two very caring and committed parents, but also the love of many others who have been drawn in by this plucky trio.

Watch Pat and Dennis for even a brief time with their triplets and it quickly shines through what great parents they are. In Pat there is that all too rare combination of someone who not only has dreams, but also has the determination it takes to make those dreams come true. Before meeting Dennis, Pat felt he had spent as much time as he could searching for the perfect partner. He had come to the conclusion that if he was to

This is a monster simply because of the huge quantities used to make it, though they are so good they would turn any monsters under the bed into pussycats. If you make the whole batch there'll be plenty for the freezer (you will never be short of a cookie with this as a stand-by), but the recipe can be cut in half or even quartered for a more normal-sized batch or if you'd like to bake them all at once.

12	eggs
1	lb. butter, room temperature (4 sticks)
2	lbs. brown sugar
4	Cups white sugar
1/4	Cup vanilla extract
3	lbs. crunchy peanut butter (4 1/2 Cups)
8	tsp. baking soda
18	Cups quick cook oats (a 42 oz. drum plus 3 more Cups!)
1	lb. chocolate chips (2 heaped Cups)
1	lb. M&Ms (2 Cups)

Preheat oven to 350°. In a large bowl (a really large bowl—we had a 13 quart stainless steel bowl that worked fine), cream together eggs, butter, sugars and vanilla extract. Mix in the other ingredients by hand to form a stiff dough. Make sure the oats are the quick cooking variety, as they make the cookies fluffier than regular oats. Bake teaspoons full of dough on a greased cookie sheet for about 10 minutes.

Yield: an enormous number of cookies. Prep. time: 20 minutes to mix everything if making the full batch. Baking time: 10 minutes per sheet.

Dennis holding Karissa, Kati with Derek, and Pat and Isabella.

Spinach & Eggplant Lasagna

This vegetarian dish really is a meal in itself, and it's so tasty you'll never miss the meat or the noodles.

2	medium eggplants
1	15 oz. can chopped tomatoes
1½	tsp. dried basil, divided
½	medium onion, minced
1	Cup Parmesan cheese, divided
15	oz. ricotta cheese
1	large egg
2	cups low fat mozzarella, shredded
1	10 oz. package frozen, chopped spinach, thawed and squeezed
	basil and oregano to taste, about ½ tsp. each

Preheat oven to 350°. Slice the eggplant lengthwise approximately ¼ inch thick and broil on a greased tray until brown on one side. While the eggplant is cooking, simmer the tomatoes with 1 tsp. basil and the minced onion on low. In a roomy bowl, mix together ½ cup Parmesan cheese, the ricotta, egg, and ½ tsp. basil and roughly divide into 3 parts. Assemble the lasagna in a 9x13 pan starting with ¼ of the tomato sauce then ⅓ of the eggplant and ⅓ of the ricotta mixture. Repeat this for the next layer. Use the rest of the eggplant, all of the spinach, and ⅓ of the mozzarella as the next layer. Next, top with ricotta mix, the remaining tomato sauce, basil and oregano. The final layer is the remaining ½ cup Parmesan and the rest of the mozzarella. Bake uncovered for 30-40 minutes at 350°. Leave to cool for 10 minutes before cutting.
Serve with a crispy green salad for a healthy meal.
Serves: 6. Prep. time 10 min. Cooking time: 40-50 minutes total.

ever have a family he would have to do it on his own. After thorough research, he realized his best chance was surrogacy. Talking through it, his friend Erica agreed to act as surrogate and all the arrangements were made.

Before he met Pat, Dennis also wanted to have more kids in his life, but did not think it was in the cards for him. Besides, he had a daughter Kaitlyn and he loved her dearly. After meeting Pat and hearing of his plans, Dennis was skeptical. Owner of a landscaping company, Dennis was a practical man by nature and knew that for a lot of reasons what Pat wanted to do was not going to be easy. As their relationship grew stronger Dennis came to understand Pat did not want easy, Pat wanted family. And a family is just what they would become.

There are no guarantees with surrogacy and often heartbreak is encountered along the way. But after three attempts they over-achieved and three babies were on the way. Things went fine early in the pregnancy but as is common with multiple births, pre-term labor came way too soon. Erica was put on bed rest but still delivered Isabella, Derek, and Karissa almost four months early. It was a very trying time for Pat and Dennis. They spent as much time as

Karissa, Kati, Isabella and Derek.

possible at the hospital with the kids and helped where they could. The babies were well cared for, so Pat and Dennis were able to devote themselves to holding and loving the triplets, sometimes just letting the babies grasp a finger in their tiny hands through an opening in the incubator.

Shortly after the triplets' birth, chance would bring Pat and Dennis face to face with Carol Browning and Nancy Maynard. One of the men's few breaks from the long hours at the hospital was a church dinner hosted by Carol and Nancy. The women, recalling the story they had heard a few months earlier in church, were eager to hear how the triplets were doing. It was then that Pat and Dennis first learned the women's backgrounds. To talk to people with such vast experience with newborns brought much relief to the new fathers. Having seen this situation repeatedly over the years, Carol and Nancy first let the guys know that they were not alone in this experience. In talking with them, Carol found out the hospital where the babies were born could not accept Pat's insurance so they

needed to be moved quickly. Pulling some strings, she was able to help get the babies moved to her former hospital.

Carol and Nancy did not stop there. They knew the kids would not be sent home perfectly healthy. Pat and Dennis would have a myriad of machines, tubes, and wires to manage, along with three tiny babies. Though Pat and Dennis were up to the task, Carol and Nancy wanted to help. They began to gather volunteers, mostly retirees busy with their own lives, yet able to find time to make a difference in someone else's. At first the work was more difficult because the babies were so tiny and fragile. The bigger payoff came as the babies grew older, stronger and more engaging. The hugs, the kisses and the laughs made it all worthwhile.

Carol organized the caregivers. She had someone there to help at least three days a week for a minimum of three hours. If there was a medical appointment for one triplet, a volunteer or two would come to the house so all three kids would not need to go. Additionally they helped out on Sunday afternoons so Pat and

Karissa and Derek at play.

The fax Kaitlyn sent us for her Easy Stir Fry recipe. We particularly enjoy step number 11.

Rice Recipe

No rice yet
Stir so doesn't burn

1. Spoonful of oil
2. Fresh vegetables   lots
   Stir for <u>5 minuets</u> on <u>high</u>
   Remove moisture (boil off)
   Start to turn veggies brown
3. Put some sort of meat in
4. Push veggies to the sides of pan
5. Crack one egg in the middle of pan without touching any veggies   Scramble the egg in the middle of pan
6. Mix
7. Add <u>cooked</u> rice
8. Mix
9. Sesame oil (2-3 table)
10. Mix
11. Sweet soy sauce (Put on like light chocolate on ice cream)
12. Mix well

Kaitlyn's Easy Chicken and Rice Stir Fry

Light, easy stir fry—the flavors of the veggies really shine.

3	TB sesame oil, divided
4	cups fresh veggies, washed and chopped (pea pods, broccoli, peppers, bean sprouts, onion, zucchini are nice, mix and match a cup each of 4 kinds)
2	boneless/skinless chicken breast pieces (half a pound or so)
1	egg
2	Cups cold cooked rice
2-3	TB soy sauce (to taste)

Heat 1 TB of oil in a large, heavy duty pan or wok. Add fresh vegetables and cook, stirring, for 5 minutes on high. Lots of moisture will come out—let it boil off and the veggies will start to brown. Push veggies to side, add 2 TB of sesame oil. Add the chicken breast pieces, cook, stirring, about 5 minutes, mixing the veggies back in as the chicken cooks. Push the veggies and chicken to the sides of the pan, leaving a space in the middle. Break the egg into a small bowl, whisk it until smooth, then pour into the center of the pan, making sure it doesn't touch the veggies. Scramble the egg, stirring until cooked and in small pieces. Add the cold cooked rice, cook, stirring, just until rice is heated through, about 2-3 minutes. Season with soy sauce to taste, stir and serve. We like hot sauce on the side.

Serves: 4.
Prep. time: 10 minutes.
Cooking time: 12 minutes or so.

While the volunteers play a part in helping to raise the triplets, the vast majority of the work falls into Pat and Dennis's hands. Why do we as a society feel the need to question those who do our most important work? One of Dennis's friends innocently asked him what he did at home all day. Dennis made him a list:

What I do all day

- Change 20 diapers
- Keep the kids from permanent harm
- Every other day, give the kids a bath, which includes finding 3 outfits, getting toys, keeping the floor dry and preventing girls from dunking Derek
- Make breakfast, give the kids their medicine, clean up from breakfast, wonder if more food got on the floor than in their stomachs.
- Singing Time: B-I-N-G-O, Row, Row, Row Your Boat, Twinkle, Twinkle Little Star, Alphabet Song, Shoo Fly, and so on...
- Story Time. Exciting stories such as Green Eggs and Ham, Brown Bear, Where's Spot, Barnyard Dance, The Big Red Barn, Oh, Mine? and more...
- Tower Time. Build the towers from blocks so the kids can knock them down. How many times can they do it?
- Chase giggling kids
- Make lunch, clean up from lunch, wonder how so much food can get on the floor
- More story time to calm kids before nap time
- Naptime... Hmm... What to do? Take a nap? A shower? Do laundry? Dust? Wash windows? Work on business things? Return phone calls? Pay bills? Oops, they're up.
- Corral kids and convince them to go downstairs
- More tower building, reading, playing, chasing and cleaning up after them
- Snack time, clean up from snack time, wonder how so much food can get on the floor.
- More fun and games but safety first. Babies yelling, laughing, crying, chasing, banging pots and pans, giggling, hugging, kissing, playing peek-a-boo. Let's go outside. 3 pairs of boots, 3 pairs of snow pants, 3 coats, 3 pairs of mittens, 3 hats. Stay outside for only 10 minutes because it's cold. Take all that stuff off. Wipe 3 noses.
- I haven't even thought about dinner. Oops, we need groceries. Here we go... where are those coats?

Dennis could spend time with their oldest daughter Kaitlyn, who could have felt displaced by suddenly having three new siblings. But Kaitlyn did not feel displaced at all. In fact she is one of the best helpers. With triplets, sometimes it's just a matter of needing someone to hold, rock, or distract one of the babies so you can tend to one of the other babies, or maybe even have your own potty break. Kaitlyn filled the role perfectly. Today she will take them up to her room to dance and play. She enjoys fixing her sisters' hair and has even been known to change a diaper or two. She loves being a big sister.

Pat and Dennis were both home in the early going. Eventually Pat had to return to work but Dennis's work hours were more flexible, which allowed him to be home with the triplets. Dennis had done this before. Back when Kaitlyn was a baby, he was able to work from home and help care for her. Pat says Dennis is a natural with the triplets. Though he was prepared to have children alone, sharing the experience with Dennis has made life so much richer. It is one thing to be so aware of what is going on to be there before trouble happens with one child, or even twins, but the way Dennis does this with triplets is stunning. Carol Browning with her 30 years experience as a doctor in newborn intensive care calls Dennis "absolutely amazing." "Dennis is the ultimate nurturer. I have never seen anyone, male or female, and I have had a lot of experience with parents, who has done a better job than he is doing with these children."

While Carol organized and scheduled the caregivers, Nancy coordinated food deliveries. Nancy arranged for volunteers to deliver three meals a week and asked them to make enough food so the guys would have plenty of leftovers. "All the food was very good," said Dennis. "Some people would even bring four course meals including dessert and something to drink!"

Calling the group that helps out "volunteers" is not exactly accurate. "We consider them extended family," says Pat. They truly are. When multiples are born, volunteer helpers are common in the early going but it usually lasts about six months. Not so for this group. The triplets are nearly two years old now and Carol thinks the volunteers will continue until the kids start school. How important is this extended family? "They may not have a mom but they have twelve grandmas," said Pat. "They are all good people and wonderful female role models."

Today the volunteers come and play with the kids, feed them, change diapers, and help wherever they can. They all feel they get back more from the babies than they give. The food deliveries are no longer needed but Carol still coordinates things, sending the guys a calendar every month mapping out when the caregivers will be there. Asked if she thought the outpouring of support would have been different for a more traditional couple, Carol pondered that for a few seconds. She said, "Perhaps." Then added, "A good bit of it comes from the personal appeal of these guys. Other people, no matter what their orientation, might well not have elicited this response."

Pat's faith and determination helped him fight and overcome many obstacles to bring these kids into the world. Three babies and two parents is a daunting task. Even without the volunteers' help, these strong gentlemen would have prevailed. But the help and kindness of Carol, Nancy and the rest of the volunteers has given Pat and Dennis the chance to raise their triplets as three individuals who each know how very much their parents love them. Their parents and so many more. ❶

The triplets enjoy a meal.

ABUELA CATA

Eva, me, Abuela Cata and Sofia enjoy order-out pizza at Abuela Cata's apartment.

RMANA BERNARDA
<100 RECETAS>

Para que puedas recordar los "sabores argentinos". Con mucho cariños Besos... Cata y Manela

Parana, 22/07/06.

"So you can remember the flavors of Argentina!"

Abuela Cata picks out her favorite recipes from her recipe book which she gave to me on my last day.

La Abuela de La Corazon

"On my last day in Argentina, with my real sister Eva along, we went to visit Abuela Cata," writes Caity PenzeyMoog. "On the first day I met Abuela Cata, Paula described her as a grandmother of the heart. I didn't quite understand what that meant, but correctly figured she wasn't actually related by blood to the Sacripantis. So on that last day, while we ate my favorite empanadas and I reveled in my fluency in the language, I asked Abuela to tell me her story....

"Years and years ago I lived in the same apartment building as Alicia and Daniel, in the city, but I was one floor up. They were newlyweds and we became friends. Alicia was studying to be a lawyer then, and you know, she works very hard - too hard! And I would say, 'Alicia, you need to stop working all the time and have the babies,' and she would just shake her head and smile. Then one day, she came to me with all smiles and said she had something to tell me, and I knew! I said 'You're pregnant, aren't you?' and she just nodded, and that was such a wonderful day. So when Sebastian came, I babysat all the time so she could work, and I was so happy to have a baby to take care of." There she mimed rocking a baby in her arms, and I asked if Sebastian was a naughty baby, since he's a pretty high-spirited teenager, and she laughed and shook her head. "He was a little angel! The sweetest baby. And now he is at the University, and he stills comes to lunch to see his Abuela Cata. And then of course, along came Paula, and Sofia who loves to cook with me, and I loved caring for all the babies. After awhile, Alicia and Daniel moved to a bigger apartment a few blocks away, but then came the time they needed to move to a new smaller city, far away but better for the children. I knew they would be moving soon. Then one day, Alicia came over. She put a key in my hand. I asked, 'What is this?' She said, 'It is your key, to your new apartment in Paraná.' They bought this apartment for me, two blocks away from their new house, just so I could be near them."

"Two Hearts" candy, meant to be shared. Paula or I would buy it then break it in half to share.

I loved these candies. Caramel with liquid chocolate in the middle. I ate so many the last day at Abuela Cata's that Paula called me a "Gordito." So I stopped. Then there was a tap on my knee and a bunch of candy landed in my lap. It was Abuela Cata—sitting next to me.

Empanadas—Beef Stuffed Pastries

One of the great dishes of the world. Sugar-topped empanadas have raisins inside with the meat, plain ones have olive and egg—we've made both.

Filling 1:

1	lb. diced tenderloin or sirloin
2	medium onions, chopped
1	clove garlic, minced
1	TB butter
1	tsp. salt
1/2	tsp. pepper
1	tsp. sweet paprika
1/4-1/2	tsp. crushed red pepper (optional)
1/3	Cup pitted small green olives, halved
1/4	Cup minced green onion
1	hard-boiled egg, chopped

Sauté the onion and garlic in butter until golden. Add diced beef, salt, pepper, and paprika, and crushed red pepper if using and cook until meat is nicely browned. Remove from heat and add the olives, green onion and hard-boiled egg.

Filling 2:

1	lb. diced tenderloin or sirloin
1	medium onion, chopped
1	clove garlic, minced
1	TB butter
1	tsp. salt
1/2	tsp. pepper
1	tsp. sweet paprika
1/4-1/2	tsp. crushed red pepper, (optional)
1/3	Cup raisins
1/4	Cup minced green onion

Sauté the onion and garlic in butter until golden. Add diced tenderloin, salt, pepper, paprika, crushed red pepper if using and cook until meat is nicely browned. Remove from heat and add the raisins and green onion.

Crust:

4	Cups flour
8	TB butter, softened
2	tsp. salt
1	Cup water (approximately)
1	egg, beaten with 2 tsp. water for egg wash

Dissolve salt in water. Combine flour with softened butter. Make a well in the flour mixture and slowly add the water. Knead for 10-15 minutes until soft and smooth (you can use an electric stand mixer with the dough hook attachment). Add more water if needed for tender dough.

Take 2 TB dough and roll out on floured board, very thin, about 5 1/2 inches in

Abuela Cata proudly shows me her knitting

diameter (it doesn't have to be perfectly round). Don't roll with a lot of force and don't use too much flour—both will make the dough tougher. Add 2 TB of either filling, fold over and crimp edges well to create a pocket. Brush both sides with egg wash and poke with a fork. Place on a greased baking sheet. For the raisin filling, sprinkle on about 1 tsp. sugar per empanada. Bake at 475° for about 15-20 minutes, until golden brown.

Prep. time: 1 hour
Cooking time: 15-20 minutes
Serves: 8-10

Abuela Cata's dog, Timmy, was being so obnoxious he was shut out of the kitchen but he would rather die via crushed skull than miss out on the action.

Grandma Moog,

my kids' Great Grandma Moog, became known long ago as the "cookie gamma." None of us have any memory of Grandma Moog appearing at the door empty handed, and she always seemed to know just the right thing to bring. Whether it was a platter of sandwiches during a move or a lipstick for a young new Mom, she got it right every time. Most of all, she loved baking, and she sure knew the way to a small child's heart – cookies, and lots of them.

Grandma Moog becomes a Great Grandma, proudly holding the first girls born to her family in three generations...

Grandma Moog - the queen of 60s chic...

The 60s were about more than tie-dye and jeans, the costume jewelry was really quite stunning, and Grandma Moog wore it to great effect. What a great day it was when she handed it to us like it was nothing. The girls will enjoy it all someday, I'm sure, but in the meantime, Mom's having a ball. My very favorites? Other than the earrings that are as painful as they are Mod? Black Cat - the brooch, & Silver Pear Necklace, the outfit maker.

Vintage earrings - the drill.

- Find special outfit earrings are perfect with.
- Wear earrings 3 hours.
- Fling into car ashtray.
- Cry while rubbing earlobes.
- Dig out 6 months later.
- Repeat.

Grandma Moog kept her collection of turtles when she downsized into her apartment, and there wasn't quite as much space for an active little boy there. So, while we chatted, the turtles were arranged and rearranged with every visit. Sometimes in a long marching line, largest to tiniest, sometimes stacked up improbably high. Like Grandma Moog's son, her Great grandson loves rocks, so these are his favorites, now that the turtles line his shelves...

Sometimes cinnamon rolls just aren't that easy to make. But this Grandma Moog recipe is as simple as it is delicious, and they don't take hours, either. So you can easily bake and serve them on a Sunday morning, and the whole family will be happy you did.

Thanks for all the treats! Great Grandma Moog

Carly Eva Lucas

Grandma Moog's Quick and Easy Cinnamon Rolls

Rolls:

3	Cups flour
¼	tsp. salt
4	tsp. baking powder
½	Cup sugar
2	eggs
⅔	Cup milk
½	tsp. pure vanilla extract
½	Cup butter or shortening–melted

Filling:

½	Cup white sugar
¼	Cup melted butter
1½	tsp. cinnamon - the stronger the better

Topping:

½	Cup brown sugar
½	Cup broken walnuts or pecans
3	TB melted butter

Icing:

1	Cup powdered sugar
2	TB warm milk
1	TB melted butter
¼	tsp. pure vanilla extract

Sift flour with salt, baking powder and sugar into a large mixing bowl, and make a well in the center of the dry ingredients. In another bowl, beat eggs until well mixed, pour into the center of the dry ingredients, along with milk, pure vanilla extract, and butter, which should be melted and cooled slightly, so it is warm, not hot. Mix by hand with a wooden spoon, or on the lowest speed with a mixer. Once the dough is holding together, turn out onto a floured board, knead for 1 minute. This dough is easy to work with–if it seems sticky, sprinkle a bit more flour onto it as you work. Turn the dough over once or twice as you are kneading, then roll the dough out into a rectangular shape about ¼ inch thick. Shoot for about a 9" by 13" rectangle, just like a baking pan, but don't worry if it is a bit bigger or smaller. Combine the filling ingredients, mixing well in a small bowl, then spread onto the dough using a flexible spatula, the back of a spoon or a pastry brush, smoothing out from the middle to ½ inch from the edge. Roll the dough up into a jellyroll from the long side, and, using a sharp knife, cut the dough as evenly as possible into 18 pieces. Mix the topping together in a small bowl. Use spray oil to grease a muffin pan, then divide the topping between 18 muffin tins. After dividing up the topping, place one piece of dough, cut side down, in each muffin tin, on top of the walnut mix. Bake in a preheated 350° oven for 20-25 minutes, until golden brown. Remove the cinnamon rolls right away to cool, if some of the topping stays in the tin, just pull it out with a spoon and replace it on top of the muffin while it's still hot. Prepare the icing by whisking all the ingredients together while the rolls cool for at least 10 minutes. Cinnamon Rolls look great served upside down or rightside up. Pick which you prefer, drizzle with icing and serve.

Yield: 18 Cinnamon Rolls
Prep. time: 15 minutes
Baking time: 20-25 minutes

Grandma Moog has collections. China shoes and turtles, costume jewelry she wore through the years - nice stuff that means something to her - stuff that has stories. The kids couldn't have been more than 5 or 6 when they came home from Grandma Moog's for the first time clutching precious treasures. Eyes shining, walking so carefully...delicate china shoes, a 1912 glass pitcher. It was hard to believe - what was she doing, giving such breakable and irreplaceable stuff to little children?

Look what Grandma Moog gave me!
It's Mr. Shoe and Mrs. Shoe - Kiss kiss kiss!
Clink clink clink!

Well, for one, she had a feeling they wouldn't break anything, but more importantly, she wanted to be the one to have the joy of giving. Sure the same things would have gone to the kids when they were adults, after she was gone, but to her, that wouldn't have been the same at all. And as for them, they have now owned these treasures for most of their lives, carefully seeing them through a move and safely placing them where curious cats won't get killed for knocking them down. Every shoe, every turtle, every piece of jewelry has strong connections and memories already, which somehow, in a way, means Grandma Moog is always going to be there for them...

Grandma Moog's husband Richard was quite the violinist and was given this violin somewhere around World War I. Neither of their sons played and neither of their grandsons played. She was adamant, however, that the violin stay in the family, even after she was gone if need be, because someday, somehow, someone in the family would play that violin - she just knew it. As luck would have it, she got to pass it on herself and hear it played again because her Great Granddaughter picked up a half-size violin in the second grade and hasn't put it down since. Once she graduated to full-size, Grandma Moog was ready. A little spiffing up and that old violin sounds as beautiful as she remembers, though these days it seems to show a marked fondness for Appalachian fiddle tunes.

Grandma Moog's Mom went to the state fair as a young girl and brought home this gift to give her own mother.

We fill it with flowers, though only on very special occasions, because it is the perfect height - short enough to see across on the kitchen table when filled with daffodils.

Once upon a time it was filled with flowers by the kids' great-great-great grandmother...

Butterhorns

A perfect bit of bakery to take along on a visit–greatly appreciated, and since the recipe makes oodles, you can still keep some at home for yourself.

Pins are in - again.
A tip from a master pin wearer?
Secure pin to undergarment in hollow below shoulder. It won't hamper arm movement (great for hand talkers) and no matter how heavy it is, it won't tip or drag down delicate fabrics.

Dough:

1	package yeast
$1\frac{3}{4}$	Cups milk, divided
$\frac{1}{2}$	Cup plus 1 tsp. sugar, divided
2	eggs
1	Cup butter
$5-5\frac{1}{2}$	Cups flour
1	TB cinnamon sugar

Filling:

$\frac{1}{2}$	Cup sugar
$\frac{1}{4}$	Cup butter
1-2	tsp. cinnamon

Icing:

1	Cup powdered sugar
2	TB softened butter
2	TB milk
$\frac{1}{4}$	tsp. pure vanilla extract

Heat $\frac{1}{2}$ Cup milk to lukewarm, (warm to the touch). Pour into a small bowl with yeast and 1 tsp. sugar. Let stand for 5 minutes. If your yeast is working, the mix will be brown, frothy and smell yeasty, if not–get some fresh yeast and start over.

In a very large mixer bowl, beat 2 eggs with $\frac{1}{2}$ Cup sugar until well blended. Melt 1 Cup (2 sticks) butter. Mix with $1\frac{1}{4}$ Cup warm milk–remember, warm, not hot. Yeast likes warmth to do its thing, but it doesn't respond well to serious heat. Pour milk, butter, yeast mixture and $2\frac{1}{2}$ Cups flour into mixing bowl. Blend by hand or use low mixer speed until just mixed. Over blending will toughen the dough, as will adding too much flour. The dough will be very moist at this point. Cover the bowl with plastic wrap or a towel and let rise in a warm place until doubled in size. Good warm places are 1) on top of a stove that is cooking something else, or 2) inside a stove that was heated to the lowest temperature setting, then turned off and left with its door ajar. The dough will rise in 45 minutes to $1\frac{1}{2}$ hours, depending on whether you have quick yeast or regular.

Once the dough has risen, mix by hand with $2\frac{1}{2}$ Cups flour. If the dough is sticky, mix in another $\frac{1}{4}-\frac{1}{2}$ Cup of flour 1 TB at a time. The dough won't be really stiff like bread dough, but it shouldn't stick to your fingers.

Preheat oven to 350°. Grab a hunk of dough the size of a small tennis ball and roll it in a circular shape on a lightly floured table. Turn the dough over while rolling, so it doesn't stick. Use as little flour as possible, so the dough doesn't toughen up. Combine the filling ingredients and spread on the dough circle lightly. Don't spread on too much filling (use about 1 tsp.) or the butterhorns will unroll during cooking. Cut the circle into 8 triangles–just like a pizza, and roll the butterhorns up, starting at the outside edge. Sprinkle with cinnamon sugar and place on a greased baking sheet. Bake on the center rack (if baking two pans at once, switch them halfway through) for 20 minutes, until golden. Remove from sheet, let cool, drizzle with icing and serve. For icing, beat together butter, milk, sugar and pure vanilla extract at high speed until creamy.

Yield: 74 or so butterhorns.

Prep. time: $1\frac{1}{2}$ hours.

Great Grandma Moog's Gingersnap Cookies

In an airtight container, gingersnaps are crispy– left out, they're chewy. Try some both ways. Gingersnaps are also the best dunking cookies. Kids love to help make them–rolling the dense, fragrant dough into balls, coating them in sugar, and then watching the cookies magically flatten out during baking. It's almost as much fun as eating them. A very traditional (and easy) recipe from the twins and Lucas's "cookie grandma."

Cocoa Snowflakes

Delicious, bite-sized chewy brownie cookies with a lacy powdered sugar topping. Fun for kids to make, even more fun to eat. We haven't found anyone yet who doesn't love these cookies.

Gingersnaps

- 2 Cups flour
- 2 tsp. baking soda
- 1/4 tsp. salt
- 3/4 Cup vegetable shortening (it needs to be shortening for this recipe - butter causes the cookies to be very flat)
- 1 Cup sugar
- 1 large egg
- 1/4 Cup molasses
- 1 tsp. ginger
- 1 tsp. cinnamon
- 1/2 tsp. cloves
- 1/3 Cup granulated sugar (to roll dough in)

Sift flour, baking soda and salt together, set aside. In a large mixing bowl, beat shortening and sugar until well blended. Beat in egg, molasses, ginger, cinnamon, and cloves. Add the flour mixture in two parts, blending well. Shape the dough into a ball, cover and refrigerate overnight or at least 2 hours. Preheat oven to 350°. Shape dough into 1 1/2" balls. Roll the balls thoroughly in sugar, place on ungreased cookie sheets. The cookies spread out during baking, so don't crowd them. Bake 15 minutes. Cool for a minute, then remove from cookie sheets. Store in an airtight container for crispy cookies, or in a regular cookie jar for chewy cookies.

Yield: 50-60 cookies

Prep. time: 10 minutes plus chilling (at least 2 hours)

Baking time: 30 minutes total (2 sheets at a time for 15 minutes each)

Cocoa Snowflakes

- 1 Cup all purpose flour
- 1 tsp. baking powder
- 1/4 tsp. salt
- 5 TB butter
- 6 TB natural cocoa powder
- 1 Cup sugar
- 1 tsp. pure vanilla extract
- 2 extra large eggs
- 1 Cup finely chopped nuts (optional—skip for kids)
- 1/2 Cup powdered sugar (for rolling cookies in)

In a medium bowl, sift flour, baking powder and salt, set aside. In a small heavy saucepan, melt butter over low heat, add cocoa powder, blend well with a fork or a small whisk until smooth. Remove pan from heat, stir in sugar until combined (it will be dark brown at this point). Transfer to a large mixing bowl, add pure vanilla extract, then eggs one at a time, stirring well with a wooden spoon or hand mixer after each addition. Add flour mixture and nuts if desired, mix well. Cover the dough with plastic wrap, refrigerate until chilled. The dough really should chill overnight, or the finished cookies won't be quite as puffy, but 2 hours will do in a pinch. The dough never gets really stiff, but it rolls and bakes best when thoroughly chilled. Preheat oven to 400°. Grab a handful of dough, enough for a cookie sheet, leaving the rest in the fridge. Roll each hunk of dough into a 3/4" ball, then roll in powdered sugar. It is easier to roll the dough into balls if you coat your hands with powdered sugar (kids love doing this). Place the sugar coated balls onto a greased cookie sheet, 2" apart. Bake cookies for 8 minutes at 400°, let cool a minute, then remove from pan. Store in an airtight container to maintain the soft and chewy texture of these cookies. If you'd like a crisper cookie, cook a minute longer (be careful not to burn the bottoms). Yield: 40-60 cookies. Prep. time: 15 minutes plus 2 hours chilling time. Baking time: 8 minutes per pan

Great cooks create more great cooks by sharing

Gingersnaps was the first recipe I requested from Grandma Moog, before she even became a Great Grandma. They were the Moog family favorite, and I wanted to learn how to make them myself. She was more than gracious about sharing, and when I asked if she would be kind enough to allow us to print the recipe for all our Penzeys customers (they are the best gingersnaps ever), she just laughed and told me to go ahead. Grandma Moog has always been so happy to talk about cooking, so kind and sharing of her wealth of knowledge and lifetime of skills, she has been an inspiration both to me and my children, and I can only hope to do half as well...

GINGER SNAPS

1 c WHITE SUGAR	2 t
3/4 c SPRY	1/2 t
1 EGG	1 t
1/4 c MOLASSES	
2 c FLOUR	1/4 t

MIX INGREDIENTS AS LISTED. LET AT LEAST 1 HR. OR OVERNIGHT. ROLL BALLS + ROLL IN SUGAR

When we understand that everyone has good reasons to be proud of both who they are, and where they are from, the world becomes a far less mystifying place.

one world Turkey

One World, One Wonderful World

The world is not something that only happens someplace else. We believe the world begins in your kitchen, yet we've had to travel to the far corners of the Earth, following the same routes our fellow spice merchants have traveled through the millenniums. In the process we have learned firsthand the world outside our borders is a very worthwhile place. It is filled with so many good and decent people, so many tasty dishes, that with so many pages in this magazine we should be able to spare some room for a few recipes from outside of the United States. For careful readers of the catalog the Turkey travel story will be familiar. It was featured in the summer of 2003, but it sums up our thoughts and experiences so well and has such a universal theme that it seemed right to use it here. We weren't doing recipes or photos of this quality back then; these are all new for this magazine. The writing and the thoughts hold up well. The plan for future One World sections is to focus on the stories and recipes of people who are willing to give up a little of their own comfort to build bridges between peoples and cultures. Those blessed peacemakers whose efforts keep this world in one piece.

We know our inclusiveness won't always be great for subscription sales. The thing is, we feel we owe our success to two groups of people. First, the people overseas, whose hard work, intelligence and integrity produce the spices we sell to make our living. And second, the truly diverse group of people here at home, bound together only by the act of caring that is cooking, who buy the spices we sell to make our living. Together these two groups are responsible for us getting to the point where we can make this magazine. They are the ones who brought us to this dance and however it works out for us we are very happy to be dancing with them.

Bill

This writing comes from a trip I took a month after 9/11. Like so many who travel the globe for a living, I felt the desperate need to do what I could in my small way to try and hold the world together. It seemed to be coming apart not because of its nature, but because of a chain of events intentionally set into play by a very small group of people. Now, years later we are only beginning to understand the enormous power of this chain of events. To overcome the act of hate committed by a handful over a few minutes will take billions of acts of kindness over many years. This is the story of one of those acts of kindness. Whenever I find the amount of work that still needs to be done overwhelming, I take heart in the knowledge that acts of kindness, like this one, are what being human is all about. It is this desire to do for others that I am convinced drives us to cook for the people around us. Yes it will take time, and there will be setbacks along the way, but slowly and surely acts of kindness are bringing this world together. I believe intentional acts of kindness are making us One.

Every trip has its moments; sometimes they are big, like when you reach your destination and you are standing in a field of spices and you are overwhelmed because the experience is more than you could ever have imagined. But those big moments are rare, very rare. Most travel moments are little – those times when a place or an idea or a taste suddenly seems to make sense.

This moment occurred in Turkey. In part because of its people and in part because of its history, Turkey is a magical place that never fails to delight. There is not another country that is both so important to America's relationship with Europe and our relationship with the Middle East.

You can't be a good spice business without having really good bay leaves and really good oregano. We have found Turkey to be the best location for both of these, as well as aleppo pepper. But this moment did not happen in the pepper fields or on the mountainous slopes outside of Izmir where the oregano and bay leaves grow. This moment happened in a taxi between Istanbul and Ataturk International Airport about a month after 9/11.

Everyone who travels overseas regularly knows one of the more annoying parts of travel is the foreign taxi ride. Every country has its share of unsavory characters, and there are few better opportunities for this crowd to make an unfair dollar than taking foreigners from the hotel to the airport. Meters (if they even

exist) always seem to break on airport taxis. Surcharges and tolls randomly appear, and there is always construction or traffic up ahead that justifies a ten-mile detour known as a "shortcut." Try and complain about what you are being charged and the driver, who has just explained to you that he has spent eight years living in Florida, will suddenly no longer understand English. Even the sharpest traveler at their most alert still gets taken for a ride now and again.

This ride started like so many–in silence. Istanbul (Constantinople) is a very old, very large city, and the airport builders had to go a long way from the center of town to find an open area big enough to land a 747. Along the drive we started to talk. The driver's English was not great, and my Turkish was non-existent, so communication was tough. He had studied to be an engineer in Germany and with my Wisconsin upbringing we were able to use a combination of a little English and a little German to get a conversation started. After a few minutes of small talk, he paused a moment and asked me where I was from. I was surprised to find myself nervous about answering that question. I must admit that even I was wondering in the weeks after 9/11 if my experience and belief that the world is a good place was correct. Before I left for my trip, there were warnings about not making it obvious to strangers that you are American. Here I was halfway around the world and miles from anyone I knew. No one back home knew where I was other than that I had checked out of the hotel and had a flight later that day. Bad thoughts go through your head a month after 9/11 when someone who

(Continued on page 111)

104

Phyllo Cheese Straws

Crispy melt-in-your-mouth golden phyllo stuffed with salty feta cheese. Perfect for appetizers with cocktails, or lunch with a simple salad.

1	lb. feta cheese (see tip)
½	Cup flat leaf parsley, finely chopped
14	sheets fresh phyllo dough
1	stick butter, melted

Preheat oven to 400°. Crumble the feta cheese and mix in the parsley, stirring to combine and break feta into smaller pieces. Start with good fresh or fresh frozen phyllo. The key is to purchase it at a place which sells a lot, so you know it's fresh. Take a sheet of phyllo dough and brush with melted butter. Place 2 TB of the cheese mixture along the bottom of one of the short sides. Don't put the filling too close to the edges or it will squish out the sides. Fold the long edges of the phyllo in, about 2 inches on each side. Flatten and fold the short end of the phyllo over the top of the filling. Roll up to give a tube effect (see photo), then brush with melted butter and place on a greased baking sheet. Continue using each sheet of dough and 2 TB of filling. Bake for 10 minutes at 400°. Serve warm from the oven. Makes 14 sticks.

Feta Tip:
Feta is a salty hard cheese sold in many packages. We tried vacuum packed squares, plastic wrapped in a little brine, and chunks in tubs of brine, which were the hands down favorite. If you only see the other types, soak the cheese in a small covered bowl of water in the fridge overnight to remove a bit of the extra salty flavor.

Yield: 14
Prep. time: 30 minutes
Cooking time: 10 minutes

Shredded Chicken and Walnut Sauce

This can be served as an appetizer on bread rounds, as a hearty dip with pita crisps, or on rolls as a delightful chicken salad lunch.

4	boneless, skinless chicken breasts or a 3 lb. chicken, cut in 8 pieces
3	Cups water
1½	tsp. salt, divided
1½	Cups walnuts
½	Cup finely chopped onions
3	slices white bread or 2 pita breads
1	tsp. paprika, divided
¼	tsp. black pepper sliced black olives to garnish

In a large pan simmer the chicken with water and tsp. salt until cooked, 20-40 minutes, depending on whether it is bone-in or not. Strain through cheesecloth or a fine strainer, set chicken aside to cool, and boil the water stock down until you have 1½ cups. Remove the cooled chicken from the bones while the stock is reducing and chop into 1 inch pieces. In a food processor or blender, blend the walnuts, onions and cooled, reduced stock. Break the bread into chunks and add to the blender, along with ½ tsp. paprika, 1 tsp. salt, and pepper. Blend to a smooth paste. Put the chicken pieces in a bowl, pour the walnut paste over, and toss gently to combine. Garnish with the remaining paprika and sliced black olives. Particularly nice served with fresh fruit.

Serves: 10-12
Prep. time: 45 minutes
Cooking time: 30 minutes

Phyllo Cheese Straws

Shredded Chicken and
Walnut Sauce

Eggplant Dip with Pita Crisps – Baba Ganoush

Spicy, zesty eggplant dip. We toyed with the traditional recipe a bit to make it easier, and were tempted to rename it Baba O'Penzeys, but we figured it is still close enough to the original Turkish recipe to call it baba ganoush. At any rate, it's a dip that by any other name would still taste as sweet...

Eggplant Dip:

2	medium eggplants
2	TB olive oil
1	small onion, minced (¼ Cup)
2	cloves garlic, peeled and minced
3	TB tahini (sesame paste)
2	lemons, juice of (roughly ¼ Cup)
1-2	tsp. salt
1	TB. chopped flat leaf parsley or cilantro for garnish

Pita Crisps:

6	pita bread rounds
1-2	TB olive oil
2	tsp. zatar

Preheat oven to 375°. Pour the olive oil onto a baking sheet. Cut the eggplants in half, place cut-side down on the baking sheet, rubbing the cut side in the olive oil on the pan. Roast until the eggplant is soft, about 30 minutes. While the eggplant is roasting, mince the onion and garlic and whisk the tahini and lemon juice together, which will make it easier to blend with the eggplant. Remove eggplant from oven and pan, let cool. Peel off skin, hand mash or puree with garlic, onion, tahini-lemon mix and salt to taste. Garnish with chopped parsley or cilantro, serve with pita crisps.

To make the pita crisps, cut each pita into 8 pizza-style wedges. Brush with olive oil (this can be done before cutting), sprinkle with zatar, and bake in a preheated 375° oven for 8-10 minutes, until crispy and golden brown.

Yield: about 2 cups dip and 64 crisps.
Prep. time: 10 minutes

Eggplant Dip with Pita Crisps – Baba Ganoush

Stuffed Eggplant – Imam Bayaldi

Turkish stuffed eggplant in olive oil is a classic dish with a classic story: The name roughly translates as "The Priest Fainted," though no one knows quite why. Some hold the imam was so overcome by the deliciousness of this dish that he fell into a swoon. Others say he was overcome with shock by the amount of precious (and expensive) olive oil in the dish. Those of us who know how much oil (or butter) the sponge-like eggplant can consume and how delicious it tastes can believe both stories.

3	medium eggplants
6	TB salt, divided
6	medium onions, finely sliced into rings
15	oz. can of diced tomatoes
½	Cup olive oil, divided
6	large cloves garlic
1	Cup water
2	TB flat leaf parsley, chopped
1	small red onion, chopped

Prepare the eggplant by chopping off the ends and cut in half lengthwise. Make slashes in the flesh along the length and sprinkle with 2 TB salt. Soak in cold water with a weighted plate on top. Toss the onion slices in 2 TB of salt and place in a strainer or colander over the sink. Leave both at room temperature–this removes excess moisture and any bitter flavor. After 30 minutes, rinse and dry the eggplant and onions. Mix together the onion, tomatoes and remaining 2 TB. salt. In a lidded pan that can go on the stove top put 2 TB olive oil and arrange the eggplant cut side up in a single layer. Stuff the tomato onion mixture into the slashes and then top with the remaining mixture. Place a garlic clove on top of each eggplant and drizzle with remaining olive oil. Pour 1 cup water around the vegetables and bring to a boil, reduce heat, cover and simmer for 1 hour until cooked.

Remove from heat and leave to cool before transferring to a serving dish and sprinkle with parsley and red onion to serve at room temperature. Serve with crusty bread and green salad for a meal that you can swoon over as well.

Serves: 4.
Prep. time: 1 hour (includes soaking and salting)
Cooking time: 1 hour

Stuffed Eggplant – Imam Bayaldi

Turkish Mixed Grill with Kofta Sausages

Kofta

This mix can be shaped into patties to go inside pita pockets, into meatballs to serve as an appetizer, or in small hot dog shapes on skewers for grilling.

1	lb. ground lamb
1	onion, grated
3	garlic cloves, crushed
1	tsp. medium crushed red pepper flakes
1	tsp. salt
1	tsp. pepper
1/2	tsp. ground cumin
1	tsp. ground coriander
2	TB bread crumbs
1/2	Cup flat leaf parsley, chopped

Mix all the ingredients together by hand or use a potato masher. The key is nice, fresh ground lamb, so use it the same day you purchase it or freeze it right away to use when you're ready. The seasoned mix can be covered and refrigerated overnight to allow the flavors to develop or used right away. Shape into little sausages and place on skewers. Grill or broil for 5 minutes each side and serve hot as part of a mixed grill, alone with yogurt/cucumber sauce for appetizers, or stuffed into pita bread with sauce and tomato for fabulous sandwiches.

Tip: If you are using wooden skewers, soak in water for 30 minutes before threading on the meat. It will make the kofta slide off the skewers and the wood should not go up in flames.

Yield: 20-30 meatballs
Prep. time: 15 minutes
Cooking time: 5 minutes per side

Sauteed Rice with Leeks

A nice side dish for our mixed grill, also a nice change of pace with simple baked chicken. The leeks add sweet and satisfying flavor to this simple dish.

2	leeks
1/4	Cup olive oil
1	Cup minced onion
1	TB flour
1	TB salt
1/2	tsp. sugar
4	Cups water
1	Cup rice, uncooked

Clean the leeks by cutting off and discarding the white bulb end and the upper green leaves. Slice into thin rounds then run under water to remove any sandy bits, leave to drain. In a lidded frying pan, heat the oil over medium heat and fry the minced onions until soft and translucent but not brown, about 5 minutes. Add the flour, salt, and sugar and fry for 1 minute, stirring constantly, then add the water. Bring to a boil and it will thicken slightly. Add the rice and leek rings. Turn to coat, cover, reduce heat to low and simmer until the leeks and rice are cooked and have absorbed the liquid. This should take about 20-25 minutes.

Serves: 4.
Prep. time: 5 minutes.
Cooking time: 30-35 minutes.

Turkish Mixed Grill

Turkish seasonings are a wonderful combination, bursting with flavor. Here we've rubbed them on lamb chops and chicken. Seafood also works seasoned and cooked this way, and though we kept the eggplant simple to complement the spicier meats, it also takes well to the same seasonings when grilled and served with bread and salad.

Grill:

4	lamb chops, 1/2 - 3/4 inches thick
2	chicken breast pieces (we used bone-in with drummettes, boneless works fine too)
1	TB olive oil
1	tsp. ground cumin
1	tsp. granulated garlic
1	tsp. Turkish oregano
1/2 -1	tsp. aleppo pepper
1/2 -1	tsp. salt
1/2	tsp. cilantro
1/2	tsp. black pepper
1	lemon

Eggplant:

1	medium eggplant, slim profile (chubby ones are hard to fit on a plate full of food)
1-2	TB olive oil
1/4	tsp. granulated garlic
1/4	tsp. salt

Cut the chops into individual pieces, remove excess fat. Don't remove all the fat though, it keeps the chops juicy during cooking. Cut away the outer wing section of the chicken if using a bone-in piece. Wash the meat and poultry, pat dry. Brush with olive oil, rub in cumin, garlic, oregano, aleppo, salt, cilantro and pepper. Set aside for at least a few minutes to let the flavors come to life. If possible, cover and refrigerate an hour or two for extra great flavor. Bone-in chicken takes about 45 minutes to cook, lamb chops about 15, boneless/skinless breasts about 12, so judge accordingly. We cooked our chops and chicken on a stove top grill, and popped the chicken into a 350° oven to finish, which isn't necessary for boneless/skinless. So, the bone-in chicken goes on first. Give it 10 minutes per side, then add the lamb chops. Give them 5 minutes per side. Remove the chicken to a preheated oven for 10-15 minutes to finish. While the meat is cooking, wash the eggplant and pat dry. Leaving the lush purple skin on is traditional, but it can be peeled off and discarded if desired. Slice the eggplant into rounds. Brush the eggplant slices with olive oil, season with garlic and salt. Add to the grill top as soon as the chicken has been put in the oven. Cook about 10 minutes, flipping carefully once or twice. Check the lamb chops after another 5 minutes, at which point they'll have been cooking for 15 minutes, and should be medium rare for a 3/4" chop–give them another 5 minutes if you aren't sure or like them a little bit more cooked. So the chicken has had 45 minutes cooking time, the lamb chops 15-20 and the eggplant 10, and everything is nicely done. Cut half the lemon into nice slices and divide between two plates. Squeeze the other half of the lemon lightly over the chops, chicken and eggplant slices just as you put them on the plate. Serve with rice, or for a special meal the sauteed rice with leeks, and for a feast add a few kofta.

Serves: 2.
Prep. time: 10 minutes.
Cooking time: 45 minutes total.

Hazim's Chicken and Pasta

Hazim's Chicken & Pasta is named after Todd Lowe's Turkish friend, Hazim. After he made it one evening for the Lowes and friends, they insisted that he do it again and provide a cooking lesson. Although Hazim lives in Istanbul and shops at the spice market, he commented that Todd Lowe's spices (from Penzeys) were stronger. The chicken should marinate for a day prior to cooking. The seasoned chicken also freezes well and is ready to cook when you are.

Hazim's Chicken:

2	lbs. boneless chicken thighs
3	oz. tomato paste (you need 3 oz. for the pasta as well, so a 6 oz. can is perfect)
6	oz. plain yogurt
2	TB olive oil
1	TB granulated garlic
1	TB salt
2	tsp. Turkish oregano
1-2	tsp. hot red pepper
1-2	tsp. crushed red pepper
5	tsp. ground cumin

Clean the chicken and remove excess fat. Lightly score the chicken. Mix the tomato paste, yogurt, and olive oil, then thoroughly mix in the spices. If you use the larger amount of hot pepper, the chicken will be pretty darn spicy. Remove 1/3 of the mixture and refrigerate it in a covered container separate from the raw chicken. Pour the rest into a quart storage bag with the chicken and refrigerate overnight. Remove the chicken from the bag and place in an oiled grilling basket, discarding the bag. Place the basket on a hot charcoal grill, turning frequently. After several turns, pour the extra refrigerated sauce over the chicken. Let it cook a few more minutes. Ideally the chicken should be lightly charred on the outside, but moist on the inside. If you don't own a grill basket or it's winter in Wisconsin, an electric grill pan works well too.

Serves: 4-6.
Prep. time: 30 minutes plus marinating time.
Cooking time: 25-30 minutes.

Hazim's Pasta:

16	oz. flat, wide egg noodles or dumpling noodles
1	TB butter
2	TB olive oil
3	oz. tomato paste
1	tsp. granulated garlic
1	tsp. salt
1	tsp. Turkish oregano
1/2-1	tsp. hot red pepper
1/2-1	tsp. crushed red pepper

Bring a pot of water to a boil and cook the noodles according to package directions. While the pasta is cooking, place butter, olive oil, and tomato paste in a small sauce pan over low heat and stir. Mix in the spices and stir well. Again, using the full amount of hot peppers will make the pasta quite spicy. Drain pasta, return to pan, and mix in the sauce. The pasta sauce can also be made in larger batches and frozen for later use.

Serves: 4-6.
Prep. time: 5 minutes.
Cooking time: 10 minutes.

looks like he could be one of the terrorist's roommates from Frankfurt asks you where you are from. Still, I was not going to let my thoughts get the best of me, so I told him I was an American.

I was watching his eyes in the rearview mirror and I saw a sadness come over him. It seems I was not the only one in this taxi that was having a hard time coming to grips with what the post 9/11 world would be. Like so many people I met on this trip across the Islamic world, from Turkey to Malaysia, my driver was having a tough time coming to grips with the emotions he felt. Through broken bits of English and German he got those feelings across to me. For him there was a deep sadness for the victims of the terrorists. So often we here in the States brush aside thoughts we don't want to deal with. But for my driver and many others I was surprised that they spoke of these deaths as though they were the deaths of their own family members. Their grief was immense, but coupled with their grief was anger. An anger that someone could have done this monstrous deed and then tried to say they did it for their religion. Over and over the driver said to me in English so I would not miss the point, that this was not Islam, not Islam, not Islam.

Though this alone is a good story, it is not the moment that this tale is about. That moment happened without me noticing about three miles from the airport. I pride myself on being a savvy traveler. In a taxi I sit where I can watch the road, see the meter and keep an eye on the speedometer. But what happened to me on that ride was something that has never happened to me before or since. I have never read of it in any

travel books or heard of it in talks with people who make their living abroad. As far as I know this may have been the only time it has ever happened.

Somewhere about three miles from the airport I must have been distracted by the taxi driver's words, thinking about what he had to say. Somewhere about three miles from the airport, while I was looking the other way, the driver reached over and turned off his meter and quickly restarted it. We got to the airport, I looked at the meter and for what should have been a $16 fare, the meter read the Turkish equivalent of $1.85. At first I thought I had dropped a zero when I did the conversion, but no, he wanted $1.85. I was stunned. I had taken the same trip three times in the last four days. I knew it should be roughly $16 plus a little extra for luggage and a tip. It is one thing to say you feel bad about what has happened; it is another thing to undercharge a random American by $15 to do something about it. Fifteen dollars is a lot of money in Turkey. We were standing there looking at each other and I was trying to figure out what to do. In the back of my mind was that old Harry Chapin song "Taxi." So I handed him the Turkish equivalent of $20 for a $1.85 fare and told him to keep the change. He tried to give me change; I would not take it. He shook my hand with more feeling than I had felt in a handshake in a long time. We walked away. Nothing in the world had really changed, but for the two of us it felt like it had. Turkey, it is a magical place.

❶

One from the Universal One

The Creative Cook
The Super Humanizing
Food Super Hero
(Haiku)

Because the very best in food is not
about competing with the world

it is all about connecting to it.

The Creative Cook

He remembers most of that night on the mountain in the most vivid of detail. He remembers the chill of the cold dry air; he remembers the rainbow colored lightning coming from the cloudless starry night. How the thunder had the sound of a woman's voice that was so familiar, but to this day he just can't quite place. He also remembers saying calmly, clearly, "I am here to become the Creative Cook" and how the thunder replied that if he wanted to be just a little bit creative she could give him some tips, but to hold the mantle of Creative Cook would require bearing the burden of total awareness. To be truly creative he must become truly open. It would require that he tear down the defenses that he had spent so many years building up around him. He would have to give up his anger at his parents, his teachers, all of mankind. And hardest of all he would have to give up his cherished sarcasm. He gave it a long moment's thought and uttered his now famous reply, "I could use a change." With that the thunder spoke "Your wish has been granted." There was a quiet thud and a flicker of blue light and the final words "good luck." Then all went black.

Welcome to the world of the Creative Cook who wanders the back alleys of consciousness with his four footed companion Brutus. Exploring the places of the mind that most happily avoid to bring ideas both new and tasty to the world of food.

Deviled Eggs à la Sam

115

Deviled Eggs à la Sam

10	large eggs (see tip)
2	slices double thick prosciutto (or 4 regular). If you don't have faith in ham, use pastrami.

Guacamole:

2	ripe avocados (see tip)
½	small red onion, minced
4	cherry tomatoes, minced
1	TB water
½	tsp. ground cumin
¼	tsp. granulated garlic
1	large lime (juice of)
1	tsp. salt
dash	hot red pepper to taste
2	tsp. fresh cilantro leaves, minced

Prepare the guacamole while the eggs are cooking. Mix water and spices together in a medium bowl. Halve avocados, remove pits. Remove skin, cut in thirds (discard brown spots) add to the bowl. Add onion and tomato, lime juice and salt. Mash with a hand potato masher, stir to blend. Add hot pepper as desired. Cover with plastic wrap patted onto the surface. Carefully peel the eggs and cut in half. Remove the yolks and save for salad. Cut a small slice off the bottoms if they don't sit nicely on the plate you've chosen. Cube the prosciutto, stir into the guacamole and fill the eggs. Sprinkle fresh cilantro over the tops and serve.

Yield: 20 Deviled Eggs à la Sam.
Prep. time: 15 minutes.
Cooking time: roughly 30 minutes for the eggs.

Tip: Hard-boiling Eggs:
Buy your eggs at least a few days ahead of time, as they'll be easier to peel once boiled. With a needle or a clean thumbtack, pierce the large end of each egg to a depth of 3/8 inch. This helps center the yolk. Place eggs carefully in a large kettle with at least 2 quarts cold water. Bring to a rolling boil over medium high heat. Remove the kettle from the heat, cover and let stand 18 minutes.

WHERE DOES CREATIVITY LIVE?

For the Creative Cook there is no one route to inspiration. There are those moments where an idea strikes the middle of the forehead like a diamond bullet. Or an idea can roll around at the back of the mind for days before emerging into the light of consciousness. At other times creativity can be a slow evolution in the kitchen as a familiar dish gradually becomes something more. Creativity really is that enigma wrapped in a riddle shrouded by a mystery. And though others will claim to be able to judge your creativity, it is only you that can stand in judgment of the processes of your mind. Creativity exists only in the eye of the beholder. Only you know if you have pushed your boundaries, slid through the looking glass, or hopped down the rabbit's hole.

This being the first issue of ONE the Creative Cook has found his inspiration in symbolism. In this case the egg, the symbol of birth, of life, of the fragile hope of new beginnings. This time the inspiration is not the taste or the texture of the egg, but rather its simple, elegant, even magical shape. Though in retrospect it seems the color of the egg has had an impact on his thinking as well.

Tip: Picking a good avocado
We like the smaller, bumpy-skinned avocados, because they have great flavor. When ripe, an avocado will give slightly when gently pressed. Unripe avocados are lighter green and hard, like an apple. Overripe ones are very dark, and under the hard skin, quite squishy. It is unusual to find perfectly ripe avocados just when you need them. Your best bet is to shop a few days ahead of time and let the avocados finish ripening at home. If the avocados are totally hard it will take about a week for them to be perfectly ripe. If they are firm but seem to give a little, then it will only be a day or two. Just don't squeeze the avocados too vigorously, this will bruise them, and then no one will want them.

IN ADDITION TO DOING MOST OF THE PHOTOGRAPHY FOR THE FIRST ISSUE OF ONE, JACK WEISSMANN ALSO PAINTED THE ORIGINAL ARTWORK FOR THE CREATIVE COOK.

WHAT ROLE THE ALMIGHTY DOLLAR PLAYS WHEN IT COMES TO COOKING?

It all comes down to where you feel comfortable. If you have that grin 'cause your ship's come in and you want to drop a C-note to put something fun on your friends' plates, the Creative Cook says go ahead, knock yourself out. If your ship is still far out to sea and you need to squeeze your quarters tight, the Creative Cook respects that all the more, for then creativity makes all the difference. What the Creative Cook has no respect for is the core message of so much of today's advertising that the more money you spend the better person you are. And it is not just about ingredients you drop into your meals. All the super luxury companies want to lay their racket down on the feelings you create when you cook and share food. You won't be seeing any diamond ads next to the

> *WHAT THE CREATIVE COOK HAS NO RESPECT FOR IS THE CORE MESSAGE OF SO MUCH OF TODAY'S ADVERTISING THAT THE MORE MONEY YOU SPEND THE BETTER THE PERSON YOU ARE.*

Creative Cook's recipes as long as the toe of his ground grippers still comes to a point. The thing is, nothing you can buy can make you a better person. The only way to become a better person is to work to make the ripples in the pond that is life, caused by the pebble that is you, lift everyone else up higher.

That being said the Creative Cook really does have a fondness for true Roquefort cheese (the runnier the better), for smoked duck breast, for quality beef (you should not eat that much so why not have the good stuff when you do eat it?), and for St. Emilion Grand Cru, some of the most reasonably priced grand cru wines you will find.

Yet if the Creative Cook was stranded on a desert isle and could only have one food, it would not be cheese or duck or even Kobe beef. It would be the potato, and not some fancy limited production variety but good Idaho #1 russets. The ways to cook and serve them are virtually endless, which the Creative Cook needs. Though if there could also be a dairy cow on the island the Creative Cook would promise not to eat the cow but only use it for condiments. Sour cream, yogurt, butter and even clarified butter (ghee) for frying pomme frittes, a

little evaporated seawater for salt. Most Copasetic. No need to float the rescue boat with any haste whatsoever.

119

Sushi Egg Filling

Delicious, lightly seasoned, sushi-grade tuna filling, topped with the smallest touch of caviar to add that special touch.

4	oz. sushi grade tuna
½	tsp. wasabi powder
1	tsp. water
4	tsp. soy sauce
1	TB seasoned rice wine vinegar
3-4	TB caviar

Rinse tuna, pat dry. Cut into small cubes. In a small bowl, cover wasabi with water. Let stand a minute, then add soy sauce and rice wine vinegar. Add tuna, toss gently to coat. Prepare the sushi rice eggs while the tuna marinates. Divide the tuna between the 12 sushi rice eggs (approximately 1 TB per rice egg). Top each with roughly ¼ teaspoon of your favorite caviar.

Yield: 1 dozen egg toppers. Prep. time: 5 minutes. Cooking time: none.

Sushi Rice Eggs

Make sure to use sushi rice for this recipe so the eggs hold together. As this is an absorption method, accurately measure the rice and water.

1	Cup sushi rice
1¼	Cups cold water
1½	TB seasoned rice wine vinegar

Rinse rice thoroughly with cool water, about 2-3 minutes. Drain and place in a heavy 2 quart saucepan. Cover with cold water. Heat on high until boiling. Reduce to low, cover and simmer 20 minutes. Remove from heat and let stand 10 minutes. Place rice in a non-metallic bowl and gently stir in rice vinegar. Fan or gently stir the rice occasionally during the 10 minute cooling time. Gently shape roughly 2 TB of rice into small egg shapes with a divot in the center. It is easiest if your hands are a little wet and you use your palm to form the bottom of the egg.

Yield: a dozen or so eggs. Prep. and cooking time: 30 minutes.

Lobster Chicken on a Nest

4	pieces boneless/skinless chicken breast
1	tsp. salt
¼	tsp. ginger
¼	tsp. garlic
1	TB. oil
1	medium (8-12 oz) lobster tail
1	lb. asparagus spears
½	cup hollandaise sauce

Prepare the hollandaise sauce (see recipe at right) just before you start the chicken, and leave it resting, covered, on the counter while everything else cooks. Simmer the lobster tail in water for 10-15 minutes, rinse to cool and set aside. Wash chicken, pat dry. Cut the tail bit off each breast to make a nice egg shape; don't worry if it doesn't look perfect, the chicken will get more egg-shaped as it cooks. Season lightly with salt, garlic and ginger. Heat the oil over medium low heat, cook chicken breasts, about 6 minutes per side, turning twice during cooking. The chicken should get no more than lightly golden, if at all,

since it is playing the white egg in this drama. While the chicken is cooking, remove the lobster from its shell and cut into bite-sized cubes. Bring water to a boil for the asparagus. Remove any tough lower stem bits from the asparagus. When the chicken is done, remove from the pan. This is the point to start the asparagus which needs 3 minutes to cook. Cut a yolk-shaped and slightly larger than yolk-sized piece of chicken out of each breast (and remove any little bits off the sides keeping it from being egg shaped). Cutting halfway into the breast is about right. Toss the lobster cubes in ½ cup hollandaise sauce. Drain the asparagus and rinse briefly to cool. Divide among 4 plates, arranging the asparagus to look like a nest. Place a spoonful of hollandaise on top of the asparagus. Place a chicken breast on top, then divide the lobster filling among the four breasts to fill the yolk position. Serve immediately, with extra hollandaise on the side if desired.

Serves: 4. Prep. and cooking time: 45 minutes total.

Easy Hollandaise Sauce

1½	sticks butter (cut the whole stick in half so you have 3 half sticks)
1½	TB lemon juice
3	egg yolks

Cut each half stick of butter into ½ inch cubes. Place the first ⅓ of the butter, the lemon juice and egg yolks in a glass bowl over gently simmering water. Whisk until the butter is melted, about 3-5 minutes. Add the next ⅓ of the butter, cube by cube, letting each cube melt as you go. Whisk all the time so the egg yolks do not scramble. Add the last ⅓ of the butter and whisk until you have a creamy, thick consistency.

Serve as soon as possible for the best temperature and consistency. If you must use later, cover directly with a layer of plastic wrap and refrigerate. To reheat, place over a bowl of simmering water and gently whisk/stir.

Prep. time: 5 minutes
Cooking time: 10-12 minutes
Yield: about 1 cup

Vanillawonderful Ice Cream

2 whole vanilla beans
2 Cups cream
1 Cup half & half
⅔ Cup sugar
1 dash salt

Remove the seeds from the vanilla beans by splitting the bean open down the middle, rolling the skin back and scraping the seeds out with the flat edge of a knife. Place the vanilla bean seeds in a chilled mixer bowl with all of the rest of the ingredients, which should be very cold. Beat well at high speed, then pour the cold whipped mix into the ice cream maker. That's it, a very easy recipe. Follow the instructions on the ice cream maker for the amount of time to freeze the ice cream. Spoon it into a plastic container and store in the freezer for an hour or two before serving, as even the best home ice cream makers usually don't make the ice cream quite hard enough.
Yield: 1 quart–eight ½ cup servings
Prep. time: 10 minutes
"Cooking" time: 20-30 minutes

Crème Anglaise

Rich and creamy traditional vanilla dessert sauce.

2 eggs + 2 extra yolks
2 Cups milk, 2% or whole
½ tsp. pure vanilla extract
⅓ Cup flour
5 tsp. cornstarch
½ Cup sugar

Blend the milk, vanilla, flour, cornstarch and sugar in a heavy-bottomed saucepan and heat gently over medium-low heat, stirring all the time until it boils, about 5 minutes. Crack the eggs and two extra yolks into a bowl, whisk lightly. Take the sauce off the heat and slowly pour in the eggs and egg yolks. Mix until it is glossy and a nice yellow color. Cool and keep in the fridge. Crème anglaise is also excellent warm, but for this recipe it should be chilled so it doesn't melt the ice cream.
Yield: 2 Cups sauce. Prep. and Cooking time: about 10 minutes.

Ice Cream Egg of Delight

½ Cup Vanillawonderful ice cream
2 tsp. (or so) your favorite orange sherbert
⅓ Cup Raspberry Enlightenment, or use fresh raspberry or strawberry sauce prepared   according to your favorite recipe
⅓ Cup crème anglaise

Pick two nice small to medium plates with rims. Print off a picture of a yin and yang if you have trouble remembering how it goes. Find your melon ball utensil. Practice making a quick little scoop of sherbert that looks like the top of a deviled egg—even the smallest container of sherbert has plenty. Make the ice cream eggs

first and return them to the freezer while making the design on the plate. Wash your hands with cold water, and drop a medium scoop of ice cream into your hands. Quickly shape it into an egg shape and pop on a plate into the freezer. It doesn't have to be perfect, you can smooth out imperfections once it returns to a fully frozen shape. The crème anglaise is thicker than the Raspberry Enlightenment, so use that first, and it will hold the Raspberry Enlightenment in place.

Using a spoon, smooth the chilled crème anglaise carefully into the shape of the yang. Next, using a light hand and a fresh spoon, lightly pour the Raspberry Enlightenment or fruit sauce into the middle of the plate and smooth out to the edges. Don't place the dots until just before serving. Take the ice cream eggs from the freezer and smooth any rough edges with your fingers. Use the small end of the melon baller to quickly make a half sphere of orange sherbert and place that in the middle of the egg. Place in the middle of the plate. Quickly drop a small dot of raspberry yin on the crème anglaise yang and vice versa, and serve.
Yield: 2 Eggs of Delight.

DOES THE CREATIVE COOK REALLY EXIST?

Well yes, but not in the way everybody else exists. It is more like the Creative Cook exists in the heart of every cook who sees a dish not as it is, but as it could be; in the cry of the baby that longs for something that is beyond puréed, something with taste and texture and sometimes even added coloring; and in the breeze that brings an aroma unknown yet delicious to you when your spirit needs it most. And when people sit down to eat, excited to know that someone cares about them enough to send something special their way, the Creative Cook will be there too.

Yet the Creative Cook is not just a single person. His reality is one of leaping from cook to cook. Fostering creativity, witnessing inspiration and then leaping on to the next kitchen that could use a change. His is the expression of many different individuals' styles, ideas and ultimately recipes. In many ways the Creative Cook is like the lines of perfect O's in your third grade penmanship book. Sure they tried to make you believe that they were produced one after another by a fellow third grader, when in reality they were the twenty best most perfect O's created by the most gifted calligraphers in the history of mankind. It would not be entirely wrong to call the penmanship book a lie, but at the same time it was nice for someone to come up with a place where all the perfect O's could hang out together and leave the real O's alone, unhampered by the burdens of imaginary perfection. The Creative Cook is kind of like that, an imaginary role model. Not real, so not a threat, but at the same time something more than real can ever hope to be.

slant swing

123

Cast a big net.
Net an abundant variety.
Variety is the spice of life.

Nate and Lori Christianson

Ms. Pam Penzey
Penzeys Spices
19300 West Janacek Ct.
Brookfield, WI 53045

"go pack!"

Pam Penzey
Penzeys Spices
19300 West Janacek Ct.
Brookfield, WI 53045

Dear Ms. Penzey:

My mom, Lori, and I are sending you a recipe for her homemade potato soup. She got the recipe from her mom, who is my grandma, but then my mom went on a diet and she changed things a little bit so it wasn't so fattening.

Here are some comments on this GREAT soup. This soup is so great that you'd really like it. I think you'd like this soup because it's GREAT, GREAT, GREAT and because it has things that kids and adults like. It has ham and tastes just like mashed potatoes. I'd rather have this soup than anything that comes out of a can. I feel pretty much like I'm in heaven when I eat this soup.

I think if kids like it, that's got to mean it's pretty good. Even my five-year-old brother likes it, and he usually hates soup. But he'll eat this. I hope you try it because When you try it, it will taste better than anything you have ever tasted in your life.

As you can see from our address, we are in Phoenix but we moved from Germantown out here just a few months ago. One of our favorite things to do when we lived near Milwaukee was to visit the Penzey's store in Brookfield and open all the jars and sniff all the great spices and herbs. We liked coloring pictures for you all, too. We miss Wisconsin a lot.

I hope you like the soup.

Sincerely,

Nate Christianson

Nate Christianson
Age 9

---

a note from

Penzeys Spices

Toll Free: 800.741.7787
Phone: 262.785.7676
Fax: 262.785.7678
www.penzeys.com

Dear Nate,

Thanks for sending us your Mom's recipe. It is great. So great we're going to use it in our magazine!

Your words really painted a delicious picture about the soup and your family, and showed that everybody will love this great soup! You are a very good writer already so keep on writing — you'll just get better and better.

I hope you like Phoenix, it is icy cold here today.

Thanks,

Pam Penzey

P.S. → Thanks for getting my name right too — it is Ms. :)

Sometimes

a letter jumps right out of the stack and into your hand. Maybe it was the handwritten envelope, maybe it was the "go pack!," maybe it was the fact that my name was actually correct, but it was obvious we had a good one before the letter was even opened. Sure enough, nine-year-old Nate had written a glowing tribute to his mom and her potato soup. He pretty much feels like he's in heaven when he eats that soup, and after giving it a try, we agree. It's Great! The Vegetable Soup is Great too! Thank you Nate, and thank you Nate's Mom, also known as Lori Christianson. And we appreciate the "go pack."

Nate's Mom's Vegetable Soup

Also known as "Everything but the Kitchen Sink Soup." Use whatever veggies are in the fridge and the freezer to make this fresh and flavorful soup the whole family will love.

6	14 oz. cans vegetable broth (chicken broth is good too if you aren't looking for vegetarian soup)
1	Cup diced onion (1 large onion)
1	red bell pepper, diced
2	cloves garlic, minced
1	TB vegetable oil
1	8 oz. package mushrooms, cleaned and sliced
2	stalks celery, diced
2	cups chopped cabbage or 1 small bag coleslaw
1	small bag frozen pea/carrot blend
1	Cup broccoli florets, chopped
1	Cup green beans, chopped
2	cups cauliflower, chopped (this was in our veggie drawer, so we added it)
3/4	tsp. thyme
1/2	tsp. basil
1/2	tsp. rosemary
1/4	tsp. cayenne pepper or
1/2	tsp. aleppo pepper
3	TB salsa (use your favorite) salt and pepper to taste

Ten cups total vegetables is about what you're looking for. Mixing and matching is fine, but the onion/red bell pepper/garlic mix should always start things out for the best flavor. Saute onions, red pepper and garlic in vegetable oil in a large stock pot until soft. Add the mushrooms and saute for a few more minutes. Add the broth, the rest of the vegetables, the seasonings and the salsa, cover and simmer on low for 30 minutes. Add more water if there isn't enough stock to cover everything. Taste before serving and add salt and pepper as desired.

Serves: 6-8
Prep. time: 10 minutes
Cooking time: 45 minutes

Nate's Mom's Potato Soup

As Nate himself said, this soup is so great that you'd really like it. It's GREAT, GREAT, GREAT. We also think it's easy, easy, easy.

4	large potatoes, peeled and diced
1	medium white onion, diced
2	stalks celery, finely chopped
2	large carrots, finely diced
1	16 oz. can chicken stock (or 2 cups water mixed with 2 tsp. chicken soup base)
1	Cup water
2	Cups milk
1	Cup diced ham
1	tsp. dill weed

Place the vegetables into a deep saucepan and add the stock and water. Simmer until the potatoes are soft—about 30 minutes. Puree the vegetables in a blender or food processor, then add the milk, ham and dill weed. Reheat gently on low but do not boil. Add more milk if the soup is a little thick. Serves: 6-8. Prep. time: 10 minutes. Cooking time: 45 minutes.

Note: Nate's Mom used a combo of skim milk and fat free half and half. We used all 2% milk and were very happy with the results.

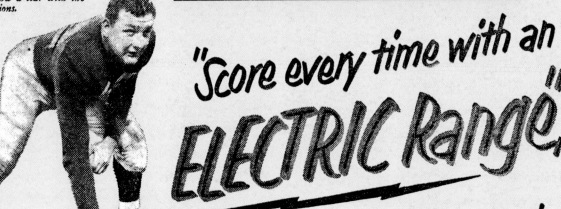
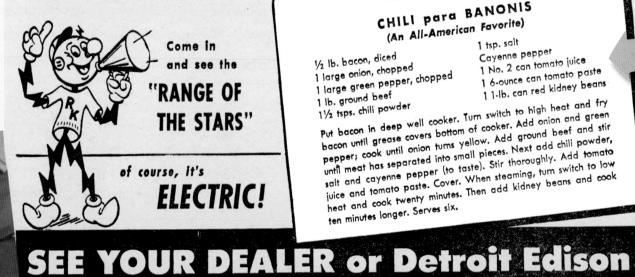

VINCE BANONIS

Cream of Broccoli Soup

Vince and Marilyn Banonis

The advertisement on the opposite page ran in Detroit area newspapers in 1952. Vince Banonis had been recently traded to his hometown Detroit Lions from the Chicago Cardinals where he helped them win the NFL Championship in 1947. With the Lions, he would go on to win two more championships in 1953 and 1954. But something more important than championships happened in 1947. He met Marilyn Schodowski. When they were introduced, a friend told Marilyn that Vince was "loaded." "I thought she meant with money. Boy was I wrong." They married a year later.

Vince was already a well known hometown football hero, having played at the University of Detroit. So the couple was asked to promote the new-fangled electric stoves that were gaining popularity. But this stove was special. It had a deep well, which was perfect for preparing soups such as Chili para Banonis. Recently, when asked if she

liked the deep-well feature on the stove, Marilyn laughed, "I never used it because I already had an electric stove. They gave me an electric dryer instead. It only lasted 26 years."

The chili recipe is a variation on the old Cardinals team recipe. The team cook would make a big pot full for the guys after cold, late season games. "It was good chili but it had pasta in it," said Vince. " I didn't care for the pasta but I still ate it after the games. I had to. When Marilyn made it she left out the pasta and it became Chili para Banonis."

After nearly 60 years of marriage Marilyn is still making soup for Vince, though chili is not on the menu too often. Today it's Cream of Broccoli. "I just make a white sauce, add a little white pepper, some garlic and broccoli. Vince loves it." Vince agreed and added that one thing has not changed since 1952, "Her cooking is still terrific."

Cream of Broccoli Soup

Vince loves this soup and often has it for lunch, and as Marilyn says, it's such a snap you can make it fresh every day with ease...

6	TB. butter
4	TB flour
$\frac{1}{2}$	tsp. granulated garlic
$\frac{1}{4}$-$\frac{1}{2}$	tsp. white pepper
$\frac{1}{2}$	tsp. salt
2	Cups milk
2	Cups chicken stock
2	Cups blanched broccoli (plunge

florets in boiling water for 2 minutes then into ice cold water)

Melt the butter in a heavy bottom sauce pan. Stir in the flour and seasonings and cook for 2-3 minutes to cook the flour. Add the milk and stock slowly, stirring until the soup is nice and thick. Add the blanched broccoli and gently heat through on low.

Prep. time: 5 minutes
Cooking time: 15 minutes
Serves: 2-3

No. 2 can is equal to 2 ½ Cups tomato juice

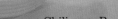

Chili para Banonis

Krzysztof & Deborah Mathews

Plip. Gleek.Clopp.Urd.Gurf.Yarp. That's not someone's stomach gleefully rumbling in anticipation of tasting these outstanding soups. Deborah Mathews of Warwick, Rhode Island loves to cook for family and friends. Her culinary creations, many made from ingredients fresh from her garden, provide the fuel for ideas and characters designed by husband and artist Krzysztof. People who live in the Providence area have seen his artwork on their local buses. If you want to learn more about Urd and his friends, go to: www. firstgearterritories. com. If you want to learn more about great soup, try Deborah's recipes. Flurp.

Carrot and Orange Soup

Tasty, pretty soup. Maple syrup adds wonderful flavor.

1	large onion, thinly sliced
¼	Cup olive oil + 1 TB
3	large carrots peeled and thinly sliced (2½ Cups)
2	TB fresh ginger (about 1 chunky inch), divided
2	Cups chicken stock, unsalted
½	Cup orange juice
2	TB crystallized ginger
½	tsp. salt
1	TB maple syrup
1	tsp. lemon juice

In a large soup kettle, saute the onions in the ¼ Cup olive oil over medium heat until caramelized—about 8-10 minutes. Add the carrots and 1 TB of the fresh ginger. Continue sauteing for a few minutes to coat the carrots with oil. Add the stock and the other TB of fresh ginger. Bring to a boil and then reduce heat and simmer for 30 minutes until the carrots are soft. Puree the soup in batches and return to the pan with the remaining tablespoon of olive oil, the orange juice, crystallized ginger, salt, maple syrup and lemon juice. Heat on low (don't boil), serve when ready.

Prep. time: 20 minutes
Cooking time: 45 minutes
Serves: 4

Simple Split Pea Soup

Hearty soup that's a meal in itself—perfect on a rainy day.

1 ½	Cups yellow split peas
4 ½	Cups water
½	tsp. turmeric
1 ½	tsp. salt
¼	Cup olive oil
1	TB cumin seeds
¼	tsp. crushed medium red hot pepper flakes

Wash the split peas in a sieve until the water runs clear. Place in a pot with the water and turmeric. Bring to a boil and simmer on the lowest heat for 1 hour. Mash with a potato masher to give a smooth consistency. Add the salt (to taste) and keep warm. In a small saucepan or frying pan, heat the olive oil on medium and add the cumin and crushed peppers. Do not have the oil too hot—3 minutes or so of cooking will flavor the oil, then stir the oil and spice mix into the soup. Serve with salad.

Prep. time: 5 minutes
Cooking time: 1 hour
Serves: 4

Eva Burns – Bill & Pam's Gram

Gram & Uncle Jimmy

Growing up, Gram

meant everything to us. She was always there, always strong, always cooking another great meal. With Dad working long hours and Mom working nights at the Post Office, as well as taking care of us, Gram helped hold it together on the home front, and boy were we lucky to have her. We wouldn't be the people we are today if we hadn't had her for all those yesterdays. She was a great cook across the board, but Gram's soups were out of this world good. Here are two of her (and our) very favorites.

Gram with a friend

Gram with Uncle Lamar, Mom and Aunty Patsy

Gram's Goulash Soup

Our favorite soup from childhood. These days, we can afford to put a lot more meat in, but it's awesome as potato soup too. Gramps (Joe Burns) said the more potatoes the better...

2	lbs. beef stew meat (chuck, Swiss, round)
3	medium yellow onions
3	TB vegetable oil, divided
2-3	TB Hungarian sweet paprika
1/8-1/4	tsp. cayenne pepper (1/4 tsp. will give the soup a bit of a bite, so use less to start if you're not sure)
8-10	Cups water
2	bay leaves
7	average sized white potatoes
2	TB flake salt (start with 1 TB if using regular salt) freshly ground black pepper to taste

Cube beef in small pieces. Peel and slice onions into thin rounds. Heat a large pan over high heat, add 1 TB vegetable oil, swirl to coat. When the oil is good and hot, add onions, cook until lightly browned, about 5 minutes, stirring often. Remove onions to a soup pot. Add another TB of oil. When hot, add one-third of the beef. It is important not to crowd the pieces, so the browning is best done in two-three batches. Brown beef for about 5 minutes (brown on both sides), add to the soup pot, then add more beef and continue to brown. Add a little more oil if necessary to keep things from sticking. When the final batch of beef is mostly brown, add the Hungarian paprika and the cayenne pepper, fry an extra minute, remove to soup pot. Add 8-10 cups of water. Make sure to pour 1/2 cup into the used fry pan, scrape up the browned bits, and pour into the pot. Feel free to use beef stock instead of water, but it really isn't necessary. Add the bay leaves at this point, bring the soup to a simmer, and simmer for one hour. Peel and cut potatoes, add to soup along with salt, which this soup, frankly, needs a lot of. Start with 1 TB but taste before serving and adjust if necessary.

Raise the heat to medium (soup should not quite boil) and cook for another 45 minutes. Serve with a simple salad, and, this is *very important*, fresh crusty white bread or rolls, which, eaten Gram and Gramps style, should be dunked or broken up into the soup in bite-sized pieces, though you could serve it on the side with butter. Make sure there is pepper on the table so each person can add their own.

Yield: 12 good-sized bowls
Prep. time: 20 minutes
Cooking time: 1 1/2 hours

Gram's Bean Soup

Our other favorite soup from childhood.

Stock:

3	quarts water
1	onion, halved
1	stalk celery, halved
1	meaty ham bone or a large ham shank
2	bay leaves
2	cloves

Soup:

1	lb. bag dry beans (navy, pea or northern) soaked in a large bowl of water overnight
1	lb. ham, diced (3-4 Cups)
2	carrots, peeled, ends removed, diced
4	medium potatoes, diced (about 4 Cups)
1/2	tsp. thyme leaves
1/2	tsp. savory leaves
1	tsp. salt (optional–some hams are salty)
1/2 - 1	tsp. black pepper

Don't forget to start soaking the beans the night before you start the soup. Place all the stock ingredients in a soup pot. Over fairly high heat, bring quickly to a simmer, then reduce heat and simmer at least 2 hours, skimming occasionally. Strain and return to the cleaned pot. Add beans, cook 1 hour, add ham, carrots, potatoes, thyme, savory, half the salt and pepper. Simmer another hour, until beans and potatoes are tender. Taste and add more salt and pepper as desired.

Yield: 3-4 quarts soup
Prep. time: 10 minutes
Cooking time: 4 hours

Two we left out

If I somehow was granted the ability to magically change one and only one thing about cooking it would be to change the way cooks see what they do. Virtually every recipe in our magazine, every recipe in this book had to be pried out of the cook that created it. For most every story we end up having to call back two-three times sometimes more to get people to finally open up about their cooking. At the heart of the hesitancy is always the same feeling: "You don't want me in your magazine because what I do is nothing special."

Nothing Special?!!! Arrgh!!! What cooks do is incredibly special, but for some reason it is invisible. Whether it is the quality of our recipes or the impact our cooking has on the people around us, as cooks we just don't see it. For people who do so much to hold this world together to feel anything other than amazing is just plain wrong. When we started this magazine I strongly believed the cause for this "we're nothing special" feeling was rooted in the way food writers and editors portrayed people who cook for a living. That by making a handful of chefs into Oz-like characters, food writers might have done wonders for boosting their television show's rating, or their magazine's news-stand sales, but it was doing long-term damage to cooking itself.

You never get a call from your doctor's office needing to reschedule your appointment because your doctor watched *Marcus Welby* / *Doogie Howser* / that *House* guy last night and is too down to show up for work. "That Doogie, he's such a better doctor than me, and he's only 16!"

Police response rates don't fall the Monday after a cable station runs a weekend *Starsky & Hutch* marathon because officers are too blue to show up for work. "I have been on the force twenty years and have never even hung from the landing skids of a helicopter while making a bust, not once!"

Yet somehow as cooks we believe the way people are portrayed in our favorite food stories is totally true to life, and judge our own actual successes against their created ones. We don't seem to be able to see the hundreds of names that roll in the credits after our favorite shows as incredibly talented people who work very hard to craft the images on the screen. Somehow we imagine that they must merely be people who get to stand in the back of the studio and enjoy the show as much as we do.

In my frustration with the way people who are wonderful enough to cook see themselves I intentionally decided to exclude food writers and people who cook for a living from the first issue of *Penzeys One*. It is the one thing I truly regret about an issue that otherwise fills me with great pride to this day. The truth is that among both food writers and chefs there really are a whole lot of very decent people struggling to find a way to make a career out of their love of food, while still not missing out on spending dinner time with those they care about. These are people who very much belong in the pages of our magazine. I was wrong to exclude them.

In the years since we started I have come to an understanding that the notion of celebrity chefs has followed its own storyline, a storyline that was beyond anyone's control, and had little to do with chefs or writers. When we started we were going to be about the rest of the pie not covered by the magazines of the day, but since then I have come to understand that to do what we want to do, to live up to our name of ONE, we really must be the magazine that covers the whole pie and includes everyone. To change the way cooks see what they do, to get them to appreciate the impact they are having, we don't need to do any excluding or putting down, all we need to do is lift up.

I have faith that by showing in issue after issue the wonderfulness that comes to life with cooking that we will reach our goal. Cooks will always be the modest sorts, but one day I'm pretty sure if we just keep doing what we are doing, I will see a slight pause and maybe even a twinkle in the eye and possibly just a little smile before the standard reply of "what I do is nothing special." With that pause, with that twinkle, with that smile I'll know that they know, and I'll know that we have succeeded.

With best wishes,

Edward Harris Heth

Move beyond yourself.
Give up on writing about what divides,
give in to what we share as cooks.
Your words will make the world a richer place.

Ed Heth:
WISCONSIN'S BEST

Greetings
from
The House
on the Hill

Even as a young man, Edward Heth showed promise as an author. His first novel was published when he was 26. In his lifetime, he authored eight books and wrote many articles.

"It was a long time ago but

I know that Virginia and Hazel saw quite a little of them," says 96-year-old Ruth Roberts of author Edward Harris Heth and his long-time partner, ceramicist William Chancey, "because of Hazel being the postmistress and Virginia was her good friend. They would go up to the house now and again."

The house is what townsfolk in Wales, Wisconsin used to call "The House on the Hill." Built and designed mostly by Heth with much input from Chancey, it was completed in the late 1940s and was where Heth wrote one of the best cookbooks of all-time.

Edward Harris Heth was born in Milwaukee in 1909, the son of a big-time gambler. It was the story of his father that led to his most successful novel, <u>Any Number Can Play</u>, which was made into a movie starring Clark Gable. Being the only son of a Clark Gable-like father was not easy for Ed especially since he had a love for writing and the arts, not gambling.

After college he made his way to New York City to make it big as a writer but like so many he needed a job to survive. He kicked around at different jobs and had some success writing short stories but he eventu-

(continued on page 140)

Roast Duck with Sauerkraut Stuffing

Whole ducks are usually sold frozen, so make sure you purchase your duck at least a day ahead of time and thaw it overnight in the fridge.

2	whole 4-5 lb. ducks
2	tsp. salt
1	tsp. black pepper
2	Cups red wine (we used Merlot)

Preheat oven to 375°. Wash ducks, remove and discard the giblets, and pat dry. Cut off any extra fat around the cavity. Season heavily inside and out with salt and pepper. Place on a rack in a roasting pan, cook at 375° for 15 minutes, while making the stuffing. When ducks have cooked for 15 minutes, remove from oven and lower heat to 325°. Spoon stuffing lightly into the duck cavities, tie legs shut with a string, if desired. Excess stuffing can be placed in a small casserole dish and baked, covered, for the last hour the ducks are in the oven. Roast the ducks for 2 hours at 325°. Pour the wine over the ducks after the first 30 minutes. Baste every 30 minutes. When the 2 hours are up, remove ducks from oven, and let rest for 10 minutes. Remove stuffing from the ducks to serving plates, cut the ducks in half. Do this with a sharp, heavyweight knife or cleaver. Cut carefully through the breast along one side of the bone, then spread the two halves out and finish the job by cutting along both sides of the backbone, which is then discarded.
Serves: 4. Prep. time: 15 minutes
Cooking time: 2 hours, 15 minutes

Sauerkraut Stuffing

3/4	Cup salt pork, diced
1	large onion, chopped
1	garlic clove, chopped
1/2	tsp. salt
1/4	tsp. pepper
1/8	tsp. thyme
1	TB brown sugar
1	TB raisins
1	jigger brandy (3 TB)
2	Cups sauerkraut, drained and coarsely chopped
1	tart apple, peeled, cored and chopped

In a heavy skillet, lightly brown the salt pork. Remove salt pork with a slotted spoon and set aside. Brown the onion and garlic in the salt pork drippings, about 10 minutes. Add the salt, pepper, thyme, brown sugar and raisins to the pan and heat for about 1 minute. Add the brandy to the skillet, mix well, being sure to scrape the bottom of the pan. Remove from the heat, add the sauerkraut, apple and browned salt pork and mix well.

SAUERKRAUT STUFFING FOR DUCK

Drain and chop coarsely 2 cups of sauerkraut. Season with salt, pepper, a pinch of thyme, 1 T brown sugar, 1 chopped clove garlic, and add a large chopped onion, a tart apple (peeled, cored and chopped) and ¾ cup diced and partly fried salt pork. A few raisins or currants and chopped water chestnuts are good too. Moisten with a jigger of brandy, stuff the duck lightly and baste the bird with red wine while roasting as usual.

139

What a moment—your book a Clark Gable movie. Ed admires a movie marquee on Wisconsin Avenue in Milwaukee.

scription was a stay in the country.

"Six months out of the city, some place quiet in the country, and you'll be yourself again," he promised. *"And I'd advise you to get out of town for at least half of each year afterward. It's a good policy for people in your line of work. Say you're in advertising?"*

He headed back to his hometown of Milwaukee and at the urging of his mother bought land about 30 miles west of the city, in the Welsh Hills where his parents and grandparents were raised.

Friends had urged me to build my house in Connecticut where it is fashionable for writers, actors and agents to build their homes. They murmured about the countryside, the great hills, the old lovely towns. But I defy them to show me hills more beautiful than my own Welsh Hills, rolling and pastoral in the summer, always reminding me of the biblical Canaan, or sleeping like a ring of grey and blue camels on the dunes of snow in the winter.

Too, I would enjoy having my mother nearby in Milwaukee, where she still lived; and she could know these hills again.

Still, as his house was being built, he could not wait to return to his beloved New York.

I wanted to move into the house, spend a week or two there, then lock up, leave, return to New York where everything was waiting. I was ready to grapple again.

He contacted his employer in New York, Ernie Pollock and told him he was ready to get back to work. He received this telegram in response:

```
SORRY COULDN'T HOLD POSITION OPEN
ANY LONGER STOP AFTER MEETING TODAY
HAVE TURNED ALL YOUR ACCOUNTS OVER TO
STANLEY MERRIAM HOW'S YOUR HEALTH KEEP
PLUGGING GOOD LUCK ERNIE
```

As autumn came to an end so did Heth's dreams of returning to New York. His partner Bill had joined him in the country and through the building of the house they began to meet some of the people

(continued on page 144)

ally ended up being very successful in the advertising business. Yet the fast New York way of life began to take a toll on his health as he tells in his loosely veiled and partially fictionalized autobiography <u>My Life on Earth</u>.

But earning big money had grown pleasant, living in New York was pleasant, success was pleasant. Wasn't all else folly? So one learns diabolically almost to woo the sleepless nights that finally come, they'll pass, come on, come on... until the nerves sever, the body collapses, the sprit breaks. And the heart with it.

In the 1940s doctors did not have myriads of pills to prescribe to cure "nerves." Back then the pre-

Yum-Yum—Old-Fashioned Hamburger Casserole

1	lb. ground beef
1	tsp. butter
1	TB butter or oil
1	Cup coarsely chopped onion
1	Cup chopped celery
½	green bell pepper, chopped
1	can cream of mushroom soup
½	soup can of water
3	oz. can chow mein noodles

Heat the butter over medium heat. Add the ground beef and cook until nicely browned. In a separate pan, heat the 3 tsp. oil or butter and brown the onions, celery and bell pepper until the onions are pale gold. Mix the meat and vegetables together in a covered casserole dish. Deglaze the frying pans with the water and pour into the casserole dish. Add the mushroom soup and mix well. Cover the dish and bake at 350° for 45 minutes. Remove the cover, sprinkle the noodles on top and heat through.

Prep. time: 20 minutes
Cooking time: 45 minutes
Serves: 6

"I like to remember my mother's respect for her kitchen: it was a kind of holy place from which she ministered lavishly to her family

via stove and sink and cupboards and flour bin. There were rag rugs on the floor; usually wild white daisies or goldenrod stuck in a milk bottle, or garden flowers (her favorite bunch was snow on the mountain and small deep red dahlias); and almost always a rolling pin or flour sifter or earthenware mixing bowl was in sight."

"Good cooking was a way of life and enjoyment. You did not save time but you spent it recklessly, proudly, and with full reward inside those four spotless walls."

Onion Pie with Bacon

Pie crust:

¼	lb. butter
1	Cup flour
	pinch salt
	pinch sugar
2	TB milk

Filling:

4	strips bacon, finely diced
2	large onions, very finely diced
1	egg, beaten
1	egg yolk, beaten
½	Cup sour cream
½	tsp. salt
¼	tsp. pepper
2	tsp. chopped chives
½	tsp. caraway seeds

To prepare the crust, cut the butter into small pieces; it doesn't have to be cold, but it should not be warm to the point of melting. Add the flour, salt, and sugar to the butter and beat or mix by hand to combine. Add the milk in a thin stream, mixing until thoroughly blended. Form into a ball and chill until it can be easily handled. Preheat oven to 350°. Sprinkle a wooden board or counter top with flour, place the dough on the board, and sprinkle the top of the dough with flour. Using short strokes, roll it from the center to the edges until it is 1/8 to 1/4 inch thick. You will want to turn the dough over and re-dust with flour halfway through. Roll until the crust is about an inch larger than your 9-inch pie pan when inverted. Fold the crust in half and in half again so that it looks like a triangle. Place it in the ungreased pie pan with the point in the center. Unfold the crust and ease it into the pan. Roll the edges of the overhanging crust under so that you have a nice rim around the pie plate. Prick the crust all over with a fork and bake for 10-15 minutes or until lightly browned.

*Ed **loved** Onion Pie.*

For the filling, fry the bacon until done. Remove the bacon from the pan, reserving some of the drippings. Cook the onions in the bacon drippings until nicely browned. Drain off the drippings. In a roomy bowl, combine the bacon, onions, egg, egg yolk, sour cream, salt, pepper, chives and caraway seed. Mix well and pour into the crust. Bake at 350° until the filling is firm, about 30-35 minutes. This should be eaten warm.

Prep. time: 45 minutes
Cooking time: 45-50 minutes
Serves: 12 as an appetizer, 6 as a meal

ONION PIE

Mix together a dough of 1 cup flour, ¼ lb. butter, 2 T milk, and a pinch each of salt and sugar. Form into a ball and chill until it is easily handled. Roll out to fit an 8″ pie tin. Bake 10 minutes in a moderate oven, but be sure you have pricked the crust all over with a fork, or you are likely to end up with a tent.

For the filling, fry 4 strips of finely diced bacon until done. Drain, and in the bacon fat cook, until they are transparent, 2 large onions that have been diced *very* fine. Drain off fat, and mix bacon and onions with 1 egg and 1 egg yolk, previously beaten, a scant ½ cup sour cream, salt and pepper, some chopped chives and a sprinkling of caraway seeds. Pour into crust and bake at 350° until the filling is firm, about 20 or 25 minutes. This should be eaten warm, cut into narrow wedges that can be taken up with the hand.

around town.

Joyce Evans, now 81, said that her husband Clayton did the electrical work on The House on the Hill. "We had a commercial store that sold electrical supplies. Ed and Bill would come in occasionally," she tells. "Bill would come in more often. Our chit-chat was nonsensical and he had a nice sense of humor and I enjoyed him but I really didn't know anything about his personal life." Asked if she knew if Bill and Ed had a relationship she said, "Oh yeah." Did she think they were brothers? "It was a little bit beyond that," she laughed. "It didn't seem to be a problem at all around town. They minded their own business and they were always pleasant. Maybe some of the older folks had their tongues clicking but nobody ever objected. It was probably fun for Wales because it was our first experience with anything like that and we could all gossip about it. It was good-natured. Nobody formed a protest march or anything like that."

In fact the town seemed to embrace them according to Ruth Roberts's daughter Shirley, "They used to go down to the corner tavern. They used to have a good time down there. I remember people saying they were very interesting people and Wales always felt very honored to have them in the community. They called him 'The Author.'"

Frustrated about losing his job in New York, Ed seemed determined to live a hermit-like existence in the country. He admits as much, "Because I had come to want no friends inside these very four walls I had raised to harbor friends." According to Joyce Evans, Bill was "the more outgoing of the two" and the one who helped draw Ed out. But there were also the neighbors, who would invite him to church suppers or over to their houses for coffee and dessert. After his first visit with the Litten sisters he came away with a basket full of goodies that included pears, peaches, garlic dill pickles and even a duck.

I felt strangely laden driving away from their house – I had not expected such a bounty. Something was being thrust on me without my wanting it; a sense of community perhaps. When I looked back, the startling thought struck me. I had neighbors.

Ed began to embrace family as well. Richard Luper was in junior high school when his family began visiting The House on the Hill. Richard's brother and Ed's niece Marilyn Engle were high school sweethearts. The Engles and the Lupers made regular Sunday trips to Wales. "You had to go up this big steep hill and it wasn't paved and it wasn't plowed half the time," says Richard, now 78 and living in Atlanta. "Sometimes it was kind of hard getting up that hill with a car." Getting down wasn't easy either. When it was time to leave on snowy nights, everyone left at once to make sure the steep drive was negotiated successfully.

According to Richard, the trip up the hill was worth it. "He made the best leg of lamb I have ever had. It was just delicious." What was Richard's favorite? "I'd have to say the Yum-Yum. Everybody loved it."

It was those Sundays and many others like them that led Edward Harris Heth to write <u>The Wonderful World of Cooking</u> first published in 1956. It is a cookbook lyrically written by a writer with a love of cooking. The recipes are not just lists of ingredients but narratives interwoven with short stories as the author guides you through the seasons starting with spring. Naturalist Euell Gibbons wrote the introduction for the second edition published in 1968, "Here is a book that titillates the appetite and captures the soul." He goes on, "The author is a modest man and doesn't demand that you slavishly follow his directions, but encourages you to flout his recipes or adapt them to your needs and opportunities."

Lamb and Cabbage Stew

3	lbs. lamb shoulder, cut into small pieces
1	TB butter
4	Cups water
2	tsp. salt
1	medium onion, sliced
1	tsp. caraway seeds
1	tsp. whole allspice
1	tsp. whole black peppercorns
3	bay leaves
1	cabbage
3-4	large potatoes, peeled and cubed
20	pearl onions, peeled
3-4	carrots, cut into coins
	white vinegar

Heat half of the butter in a large stock pot or Dutch oven. Add half of the lamb and brown on all sides. Remove the lamb and set aside. Brown the rest of the lamb. Place all of the lamb in the pot and add the water, salt, sliced onion, caraway seeds, allspice, peppercorns and bay leaves. Simmer, covered, for about 1 hour, until the meat is nearly tender. While the stew is simmering, quarter the cabbage and soak in cold water for 30 minutes. Slice the cabbage coarsely and add it to the stew along with the potatoes, pearl onions and carrots and cook for another 30 minutes. Have a cruet of white vinegar on the table for sprinkling over the stew, if desired.

Prep. time: 30 minutes
Cooking time: 1½ hours
Serves: 8-10

LAMB AND CABBAGE STEW

Brown in butter 3 lbs. of stewing lamb cut into small pieces and just barely cover with water. Add salt, a sliced onion, 1 t caraway seed and the trinity of whole allspice, peppercorns, and bay leaf. Simmer covered for several hours until the meat is nearly tender. Quarter a cabbage, soak it in cold water, and slice it coarsely. Add this to the stew, along with 3 or 4 large cubed potatoes and a few whole small onions, and continue cooking for another half-hour until all is done. Have a cruet of white vinegar on the table when you serve this and let the guests sprinkle a little over each serving. And use deep plates because the stew should be quite soupy. You mash the cubed potatoes in the golden gravy as you eat.

Ed's way of writing recipes can even bring a chuckle as he says that a cabbage should not resemble an old wig or describes large zucchinis as "monsters." Cooking for his friends and loved ones was pure joy.

And in our kitchen the seasons are always present: in a basket of freshly gathered wild asparagus or dandelions or in the year's first peas; then in the glory of dill and later in the comfort of squashes; then in the butternuts and black walnuts and a partridge and winter soups and at last the pickled herring salad for New Year's Eve. You notice one evening that the days have grown longer, a new light hangs in the sky, the wiry willows have brightened their yellows. It is spring again.

Here in this kitchen you also sit around dreaming up perfect combinations of herb and vegetable and fowl and beast to make perfect food, as I have tried to do in this book.

Though he took such delight in cooking, Ed's writing was often melancholic such as his description of the motivation to write his Great American Novel, <u>Any Number Can Play</u>.

Too, as I remembered my grandfather, I remembered his son, my father, who had run away from these hills as a young man to become a big city gambler. I began to remember many things about my father and mother together, stories they told me, stories I had watched unfold, how they met, loved, fought for each other, bore a son, grew rich, grew poor again, stood faithful to each other, and how always mother and son were the staff of life to the father, but the whisper of dice, the hushed click-clack of the chips, were its blood. Perhaps unknowingly I began that novel as long ago as the previous autumn, when one of Ernie Pollock's wires had wisecracked cheerfully, as he was cutting me out of a job and livelihood: "Why don't you write a book?" I know I saw the wire often on the pages as I typed away. I wrote with fury for Ernie and love for my parents, with rage toward life and hope for tomorrow.

A month ago, that book had been quietly published. Its success was critical, not financial. So now there could be no more waiting to return to New York. There was a job to find, new clients and accounts, the work,

Broiled Chicken

1	whole chicken (about 4 lbs.), quartered
1	tsp. salt
1	tsp. black pepper
½	tsp. paprika
1	TB fresh minced parsley
	juice of ½ lemon
½	stick butter (4 TB)
¾	Cup heavy cream (2% milk works well)
2	tsp. cornstarch
½	Cup water

Preheat oven to low broil. Wash the chicken and pat dry. Mix together the salt, pepper, paprika and parsley. Place the chicken skin side up in a shallow pan. Sprinkle the chicken quarters with the spice mix and then with lemon juice. Dot with the butter and broil in the middle of the oven on low for 45 minutes, basting often. After 35 minutes, pour the cream or milk over the chicken for the last minutes of baking. When the chicken is done, remove to a platter and add the cornstarch mixed with the water to the pan and stir up the juices to make a nice gravy.

Prep. time: 35 minutes if you are cutting up the chicken yourself.
Cooking time: 45 minutes
Serves: 4

the rushing, the need to make noise and be heard and to find sudden success again.

That fear, grown swollen in the past year, was a large part of my not wanting to return. That I had, ironically, grown used to small places. That youth can start out in big cities with empty pockets, but for an older man...?

Around us the woods, hills, kettles, lay in such self-enclosed silence as if they were in another country, superiorly governing themselves, and glancing indifferently sometimes toward their neighboring nation of human beings. I was thinking of myself not walking through these woods but racing through a hot and airless subway. It doesn't matter to the woods and hills whether you or I or anyone else walks here or not. They have no need of us. They don't know grief. You might say a man has his own glory because he can think and feel and the trees cannot. But also a man knows he must die, but the tree doesn't, which does not make man the lucky one.

Ed continued to struggle with his yearnings to return to New York. Though he was a successful author his books had not earned him a lifetime supply of money. His biggest paycheck came from selling the movie rights and much of it was spent completing The House on the Hill. Shortly after the house was finished his mother passed away. It was assumed he was building such a large house in anticipation his mother would live there or at least visit regularly. Now she was gone and the lure of New

Toward the end of his life, Ed had a popular show on Wisconsin Public Radio, weaving tales of the Wisconsin countryside, plucked from his lifetime of writing.

York was strong. So too, was the lure of the land.

I gradually came to know that I was back in the land where my grandfather had been born. New York seemed farther and farther away, now that I had friends, was making a life. I still would return to New York, almost any day now. I was strong enough to grapple again, my humor was back. I got train schedules. I wrote letters of application to New York agencies. I received cordial answers and sent them cordial answers in return. I set a date to return; made an appointment with the most cordial of answerees. The date just slipped by. I wrote a note of apology, was urged to set another date. Soon I would...

Soon enough he would return finding "a job at another agency, at half the salary I had earned before, and with three men sharing my office, where once I had gloried in my own." He realized he was not the same man that had left a few years ago. Even his fellow New Yorkers were different to him.

Once I had loved cities but suddenly didn't. The Verdi Square women were still there, looking colder now, walking aimlessly along the street, shopping for a single pork chop or a half pint of whiskey, going back to their no less cold or barren rooms. That winter I walked the

Postmaster Hazel Mason at the counter of the Wales Post Office in 1960, where Bill and Ed used to get their mail. She struck up a friendship with them and had dinner at the House many times.

(continued on page 149)

147

As the leaves fell, as the earth prepared for sleep, I began to understand that I might have to spend the winter in the Welsh Hills - which, all at once, looked cold. They seemed to close around me in impatience. I could escape them, of course. I could go to New York, find other agencies, other clients and accounts...

Only, there was no money left to live on while I beat my way back to New York and got myself on my feet again. Nevertheless, I could still make it. Except that the loud, wracked nights had begun once more. The sound of night wind became thunderous - it blew all sleep away. I felt my nerves pulled tight again, then snap, like rubber bands. My heart raced without provocation. In panic I watched all that the summer months had done become undone. Quickly I packed my bags. A day or two more and Joe would have the house finished, ready to lock up for the winter. I could abandon it, flee from it.

As an afterthought, or pehaprs final precaution, I stopped at the village doctor's office. Dr. Beemiller is a chunky, friendly man, but his eyes kept blinking nervously.

"I doubt if you could take a New York winter right now - your nerves and blood pressure. Hypertension. Not too good, man. take it easy. And I don't like the way you've been loading yourself with sleeping pills. What kind of business you say you're in back there?"

"Advertising." I said it clearly.

"Pretty rough business? Hard work?"

I nodded.

He shook his head. "You'd never make it. I'll tell you, you spend six months or so right here in the country where it's quiet."

"But I've just spent six months here, quiet as a mummy' And I've got to earn a living."

Dr. Beemiller smiled. "Why?"

"Why earn a living?"

"Haven't you got a roof to sleep under. and a good-sized piece of land? What's the matter, man? You just stay here."

He looked at me soberly. "You'd really better."

As I drove home, I noticed the last leaves had fallen from the trees.

streets of my old neighborhood with the feeling I had never been there before, so little are you remembered and so quickly do new curtains hang in your window.

He thought about his friends and neighbors back at his country home and his mind was made up.

I was walking down Madison Avenue. I swerved over toward the New Weston bar. It was only when the men inside kept looking at me that I knew I had tears in my eyes. But this was a mist of happiness. I took the next train home.

And I knew I would never have to leave these Welsh Hills again, unless I wanted to. But it bothered me, with the remote passive affection one feels toward an old love, that I left New York with such relief. I was growing old, or disgruntled, or sour.

Upon his return to the country one of his neighbors suffered "that great rural tragedy," a barn fire.

While the fire itself was a tragedy, the response of the community heartened Ed.

But while the fire was burning, well over half a hundred men appeared from nowhere, three-quarters of whom the stricken farmer had never seen in the neighborhood before. These men fought the fire, singeing their own clothing and bodies to rescue the cattle, and when their effort to save the barn itself proved useless, as it always is, and the barn was gone, stayed on to spend the rest of the evening driving the farmer's frantic cattle a mile away to safety and shelter and warmth.

To Ed these men "had just enacted the best possible definition of the word 'neighbor.' I knew then without a doubt that this was the world I wanted to live in forever."

As he wrote of the farmer's misfortune, he did not know that he was telling of his own future to come just seven years later.

The barn and everything in it, harvest and machinery, along with the farmer's hope for a winter of rest and security burned to the ground in a great shock of light, and as swiftly as any human hope can die. Against the flaming light the farmer stood silhouetted, watching himself fall in ruins and ashes.

On July 27, 1960 Edward Harris Heth's beloved House on the Hill burned to the ground while he and Bill were out of town. The house had been struck by lighting in the night and by the time the fire was discovered at 4 am, it was too late. From the Waukesha Daily Freeman:

Heth's book collections, as well as his antiques, were completely destroyed in the blaze. Amid the debris cluttering the six rooms were charred and burned scrapbooks tracing the author's career. Under a pile of burned letters and photographs lay a charred autographed picture of Gable and Miss Totter.

Housed in the basement were Chancey's brick kilns which he used to supply gift and floral shops with his exclusive pottery. Shelves of finished pottery products had been pushed to the floor.

The couple's life began to unravel. They designed and began construction on a new House on the Hill that included a beautiful kitchen with a fireplace for Ed and a light-filled pottery studio for Bill. A year later, as the house neared completion, tragedy struck once again. In the garage of the house they rented while the new house was being built, Bill Chancey sat down behind the wheel of his car and started the motor with the garage door closed. As Ed's partner and companion of the last 20 years passed, so did Ed's desire to live in the country. The house was completed but he never moved in. Neighbor Joyce Evans adds, "He would have been very lonely up there without Bill." He must have felt the loneliness or isolation would be more than he could handle so he sold the house and the beautiful land on which it sits, and took an apartment in Milwaukee.

Now in his 50s, Ed wrote some short stories and began a novel called <u>Clear to the End of Summer</u>. That novel would never be finished. On April 26, 1963 he was found dead in his apartment with

(continued on page 154)

Ed probably didn't need to look at his own book to make a salad, but publicity shots work.

Shrimp in Dill Sauce

1   lb. large, raw, frozen shrimp,
    thawed, shells on
1   tsp. caraway seed
1/2 Cup Hollandaise Sauce
1/2 Cup Homemade Mayonnaise
1   TB chopped, fresh dill weed
    or 1 tsp. dried dill weed
1   tsp. capers
    dill weed for garnish

Bring a large pot of water to a boil.
Add the shrimp and caraway seeds.
Boil for 3 minutes. Drain the shrimp, let
cool, peel and chill. To prepare the Dill
Sauce, mix together the Hollandaise
Sauce and Mayonnaise. Add the fresh
dill weed and capers and mix well.
Chill well. An hour before serving, mix
the sauce gently with a fork. Spoon the
sauce over the shrimp and sprinkle with
the dill weed.
Prep. time: 10 min. not including chilling
time. Cooking time: 3 min. Serves: 4

Hollandaise Sauce

1/2 lb. butter
    juice of 1 lemon
pinch salt
6   egg yolks
2   TB light cream or water

Melt the butter in a saucepan.
Remove from the heat and add
the lemon juice, salt, egg yolks and
cream or water. Whisk well. Return
to the stove and cook over medium
heat, rapidly stirring constantly with
a whisk or wooden spoon until the
desired consistency, about 5 minutes. If
it is too thick, add a bit more cream or
water. If it is too thin, add another egg
yolk.
Prep. time: 5 min. Cooking time: 5 min.
Yield: 1 2/3 Cups

Homemade Mayonnaise

2   eggs
1   tsp. salt
1/2 tsp. mustard powder
2   Cups extra virgin olive oil
    juice of 1 lemon, strained

SHRIMPS AND DILL SAUCE

Here again the ever-accommodating fresh dill blends tauntingly with the shrimp. Boil as many shrimps as are needed until they are tender in water to which 1 t caraway seed has been added. Peel and chill. Then make whatever amount of sauce is required as follows, allowing 1 cup sauce for each pound of frozen shrimps:

Mix equal parts of homemade mayonnaise (see page 63) and hollandaise sauce, which has been allowed to cool. If desired, the hollandaise may be omitted, using instead all homemade mayonnaise with 1 heaping T sour cream whipped with a fork into each cup of mayonnaise. Add a dash of cayenne. For each cup of sauce, add 2 large heads of finely chopped fresh dill and 1 t capers. Chill, and an hour before serving whip the sauce gently with a fork. Heap lavishly over the shrimps on a deep platter and sprinkle generously with more chopped dill. Garnish with thin-sliced tomatoes from which the seeds and juice have been squeezed before slicing, parsley, and a good supply of tiny pickled onions.

Break the eggs into a bowl and add
the salt, mustard powder and about 1/4
cup of the olive oil. Beat the mixture for
a minute, add another 1/4 cup oil, beat
again, and when it begins to thicken
(about 2-3 minutes) add the oil in large
dollops until you've added about 2
cups total. Beat until thick (about 5 minutes) and then beat in the lemon juice
and mix well.
Prep. time: 10 min. Yield: 2 1/2 Cups

"One perfect evening a really bang-up snowstorm began just as we sat down to a partridge dinner. The hunter's wives had joined up to make it a celebration, Hank had worked with fervor, cocktails had been soothing, and dinner was being served family style on the long oak table before the kitchen fireplace. We listened only in comfort to the wind howling outside – and up here on the hill on stormy nights it blows a tempest. Let winter come, we all thought, let it come. The snow flew like hunted white birds against the windows.

The partridge was so juicy and crisp-skinned, the wild rice smoky and the Burgundy so clear and dry that none of us bothered to notice the drifts piling six feet high outside. None of the guests could leave that night; friends slept cheerfully on sofas and mattresses in front of the fire, and in the morning we shoveled and shoveled our way down the interminable hill. But even that had its own reward. The icy air filled our panting lungs. Inside the warm house the girls kept coffee hot and were cooking soup and baking fresh rolls. They opened preserves (this was the moment for the first jars of relishes and jelly, stored away in summer against just such a day) and brought up apples from the basement for a cobbler. Luncheon became as festive as last night's dinner had been."

Rare Roast Leg of Lamb

1	leg of lamb, about 8 ½ lbs.
3-4	garlic cloves
1	TB salt
2	tsp. ground black pepper
2	TB flour
½	Cup brewed, strong black coffee
½	Cup red wine

Preheat oven to 350°. Make slits in the leg of lamb with a sharp knife and insert the garlic cloves. Sprinkle the lamb with the salt and pepper and then the flour. Place in a roasting pan and put into the oven. After 20 minutes, pour the coffee and red wine over the lamb. Cook for another hour and 10 minutes, basting occasionally. A meat thermometer should read about 130° for lamb on the rare side of medium-rare.

Prep. time: 10 min. Cooking time: 90 min. Serves: 10-12

Fried Green Cabbage

1	head cabbage
pinch	caraway seeds
1	medium onion, minced or 4-5 scallions, chopped
4	TB butter
½	tsp. prepared mustard
2	tsp. salt
½	tsp. pepper
3	drops lemon juice
2	TB sour cream

Cut the cabbage in quarters and soak for 30 minutes in salted ice water. Drain well. Coarsely shred the cabbage and steam in a small amount of water with the caraway seeds, covered, for about 5 minutes. Drain again and make sure the cabbage is completely dry. In a large frying pan, heat the butter and sauté the onion or scallions for about a minute or until lightly golden. Stir in the mustard then add the cabbage, salt and pepper. Cook for about 5 minutes. Remove from heat and add the lemon juice and sour cream before serving. This dish is best served immediately.

Prep. time: 45 minutes, including soaking. Cooking time: 6 minutes. Serves: 8

ૐ RARE ROAST LEG OF LAMB

Insert 3 or 4 cloves of garlic into the leg of lamb, and don't use too large a leg. Salt and pepper it, dredge it lightly with flour. Put into a 350° preheated oven. After 20 minutes pour over ½ cup strong black coffee, or ¼ cup coffee and ¼ cup dry red wine, continue basting with this, and hold your breath while I tell you to cook the roast no longer than one hour in all. You won't want gravy to serve with this. Put the leg of lamb on a heated platter, let a few pats of butter melt over it. The butter will blend with the natural juices of the pink, succulent roast as you slice it *as thinly as possible*, and a little of this sauce should be served over each portion. It is amazing how cooking lamb as rare as you would steak or a beef rib roast makes it a wholly different meat than any you have tasted before—and delicious too.

ૐ FRIED GREEN CABBAGE

A cooked cabbage should bear no resemblance to a discarded wig. This, properly prepared, is one of the gentlest and most delicate vegetables. Choose a summer cabbage that is light in weight, pale green in color, not too large or sullied by time. Cut the cabbage in quarters and soak ½ hour in salted ice water. Drain, shred coarsely, and steam in a very small amount of water with a pinch of caraway for 5 minutes, covered. Drain again, this time absolutely dry. Fry 1 medium minced onion, or 4 or 5 scallions chopped with their tops, in 4 T butter for a minute or so, only until it is palest gold. Stir in ½ t prepared mustard, add the cabbage, salt and pepper. Fry for only 5 minutes more. Add a few drops lemon juice and 2 T sour cream before serving. It must be served at once and the cabbage should be crisp, green and tenderly delicious.

Above: Bill Chancey (on right) was a popular ceramicist, working in the mid-century modern style. His work was highly regarded and he exhibited at the U.S. Nationals in 1951. We would dearly love to see more examples of his work. Below: Salem Jerusalem Cemetery, Wales WI. The wildflowers are from the hill Ed and Bill loved.

the phone off the hook and a bottle of tranquilizers nearby. Was he not feeling well and trying to contact the doctor when he collapsed? Or had he simply chosen to take the same road as his partner? The results of the toxicology tests were never published.

Jan Singer, a licensed clinical social worker for 25 years, has worked with many people in same sex relationships that have lost a partner. She knows how hard it is to cope with that kind of loss today, much less 50 years ago, "You have two people who can't talk about their relationship and have been in that relationship long standing. Then the first person kills himself, so you can't even talk about that, which adds another layer of isolation and silence. You can't grieve about the death, you can't grieve

(continued on page 157)

Pork Chops with Green Onions and Sour Cream Sauce

6	bone-in pork chops
1½	tsp. salt
1	tsp. black pepper
1	TB Hungarian sweet paprika
1	Cup sour cream (light works well)
1	bunch green onions, ends removed
1	TB butter or olive oil

Preheat oven to 300°. Sprinkle the chops with salt and pepper. In an oven-proof skillet, brown the pork chops in the butter, 3-5 minutes per side. Liberally sprinkle the chops with the paprika. Spoon the sour cream between the chops. Top with the green onions and bake, covered, at 300° for 20-40 minutes, depending on the thickness of the pork chops. Remove chops to a platter and whisk the sauce over medium-high heat for 3-5 minutes, until reduced to desired thickness. If you want to keep the onions bright and green, steam them in a bit of water and top the chops before serving instead of including them in the sauce.

Prep. time: 5 minutes
Cooking: 30-50 minutes
Serves: 6

❧ PORK CHOPS AND GREEN ONIONS IN SOUR CREAM

Brown 6 pork chops in an iron skillet. Salt and pepper them and add 1 T paprika. Remove to a casserole (I leave them right in the skillet). Clean a handful of young garden onions but leave part of the green tops on them. Put over the chops and cover with 1 cup sour cream. Bake covered in 300° oven about 40 minutes, until chops are tender. The gravy is delicious over rice. If you prefer, the green onions may be stewed separately in as little water as possible, drained, buttered, and put over the chops before serving.

And I can't let those first tender scallions ripen in the garden without telling what they will do for a humble fried egg sandwich.

Hickory Nut Torte

½	Cup butter
1	Cup sugar
3	egg whites
½	Cup milk
1	Cup all-purpose flour
¾	Cup finely chopped pecans
1	TB milk
1	tsp. cream of tartar
1½	tsp. baking soda

Preheat oven to 350°. Cream the butter and sugar together until light and fluffy. In a separate bowl, beat the egg whites until stiff peaks form. Fold the egg whites into the butter mixture. While stirring constantly, alternate adding the milk and flour a bit at a time until well blended. Mix in the pecans. Dissolve the cream of tartar and baking soda in the TB of milk, add to the batter and mix well. Divide batter between two large, lightly greased and floured loaf pans and bake at 350° for 30-35 minutes.

Prep. time: 15 minutes. Baking time: 30-35 minutes.
Serves: 8-10

Coffee Icing

2	sticks butter
2	Cups powdered sugar
¼	Cup brewed strong coffee
1	tsp. vanilla extract

In a large bowl, cream the sugar and butter until light and fluffy. Add the coffee and vanilla and mix well. Once the loaves are cool, frost and sprinkle with more finely chopped pecans if desired.

HICKORY NUT TORTE

To conclude a game or wild poultry dinner, there is no better dessert than this torte, the tang of the woods still lingering in each slice. Cream together ½ cup butter and 1 cup sugar, add the whites of 3 eggs whipped stiff and beat until light and smooth. Alternately add ½ cup milk and 1½ cups flour, stirring all the while. Then stir in ¾ cup hickory nuts, chopped but not too fine, 1 t cream of tartar and 1½ t baking soda dissolved in 1 t milk. Beat well, pour into a buttered and lightly floured loaf pan and bake in a moderate oven. Serve plain or frost sparingly with a coffee or caramel frosting and sprinkle heavily with more nuts, this time chopped fine.

"And in our kitchen the seasons are always present: in a basket of freshly gathered wild asparagus or dandelions or in the year's first peas; then in the glory of dill and later in the comfort of squashes; then in the butternuts and black walnuts and a partridge and winter soups and at last the pickled herring salad for New Year's Eve. You notice one evening that the days have grown longer, a new light hangs in the sky, the wiry willows have brightened their yellows. It is spring again.

Here in this kitchen you also sit around dreaming up perfect combinations of herb and vegetable and fowl and beast to make perfect food, as I have tried to do in this book."

about the closeness, you can't grieve in public, and you can't get any support because you weren't supposed to have this relationship in the first place. Where do you go with that?"

It is a testament to the people of the tiny religious village of Wales that this couple was as accepted as they were–truly remarkable, especially for that time. But acceptance is not support. Today there are still people in all lines of work who must hide their sexuality. They live with the knowledge that this could be the day it all comes out and much of their life as they know it will be over. Many are in long term committed relationships just like anyone else. Yet at work they can't talk about something funny their partner said last night or what a great time they had last weekend because it could be detrimental to their jobs or make others uncomfortable. Jan Singer adds, "It's all the corners of society that don't want to deal with something they're uncomfortable with and therefore make the other person the enemy, instead of recognizing the enemy is within themselves in their preconceived notions."

The couple lives on through lives they touched and what they left behind. Bill through his pottery and Ed in his books, stories and especially in his recipes. Sit down to the rare roast leg of lamb, lightly basted with coffee and red wine, with a helping of buttery oven-roasted potatoes and all at once it's a Sunday in the country. A slice of onion pie during cocktail hour transports you to the terrace overlooking the meadow with the smell of fresh air no doubt mixing with the laughter of friends. The flavors are simple and delicious and take you to another place and time: A comfortable place, where Ed and Bill could just be happy being themselves.

With best wishes,
Edward Harris Heth

"Whether you like it or not, dogs are integral to the country landscape, like wheeling hawks or fencerows or haystacks and silos. Move to the country and you'll have dogs, as immutably as you'll have fresh air. You may fear, despise, disapprove of, regard them as unsanitary, be allergic to them or prefer a camel to a chihuahua in your antique-laden parlor - you'll have a dog anyway. If they don't just come by themselves, possibly waiting patiently outside your window some fine, peaceable morning, city friends will bring them to you. ... Buy an acre of land. You have a dog."

SOUR CREAM MUFFINS

Into a well-beaten egg, beat 2 T melted butter, 2 T sugar and 1 cup thick sour cream. Sift together 1¼ cups flour, 1 t baking powder, ½ t each of baking soda and salt, and stir into the cream. Pour into greased muffin tins and bake at 400° about ½ hour. Serve these piping hot.

Ed Heth's Sour Cream Muffins

These muffins are tender and delicious, almost like pancakes in muffin form.

2	TB butter, melted
1¼	Cups flour
1	tsp. baking powder
½	tsp. baking soda
½	tsp. salt
1	egg
2	TB sugar
1	Cup sour cream (reduced fat results in an equally delicious muffin)

Preheat oven to 400°. Melt butter; set aside to cool (it should be warm but not hot when it is eventually added). In a bowl mix together the flour, baking powder, baking soda, and salt. Set aside. In a large bowl, beat the egg well. Gradually add the butter, sugar, and sour cream while blending. Add the flour mixture and beat well. Pour into greased muffin tins and bake for 20-25 minutes, or until the tops are golden brown. When they are finished remove immediately onto a cooling rack. The easiest way to do this is to bang the muffin tin sideways on the table, holding the rack close so the muffins don't fall far. Serve these piping hot with butter.

Prep. time: 15 minutes
Baking time: 20-25 minutes
Yield: 9 muffins

CHOCOLATE NUT PIE

When you have beaten 2 egg whites foamy, add ⅛ t each of salt and cream of tartar. Continue beating and when soft peaks form add ½ cup sugar gradually and beat until stiff. Fold in ½ cup broken walnut meats and ½ t vanilla, spread in greased pie tin and bake in a slow oven for 45 minutes. For the filling of this light, crunchy pie, melt ¼ lb. German sweet chocolate in a double boiler, and add 3 T hot water and 1 t vanilla. When this has cooled, stir in 1 cup cream, whipped. Place into the crust and chill at least 2 hours.

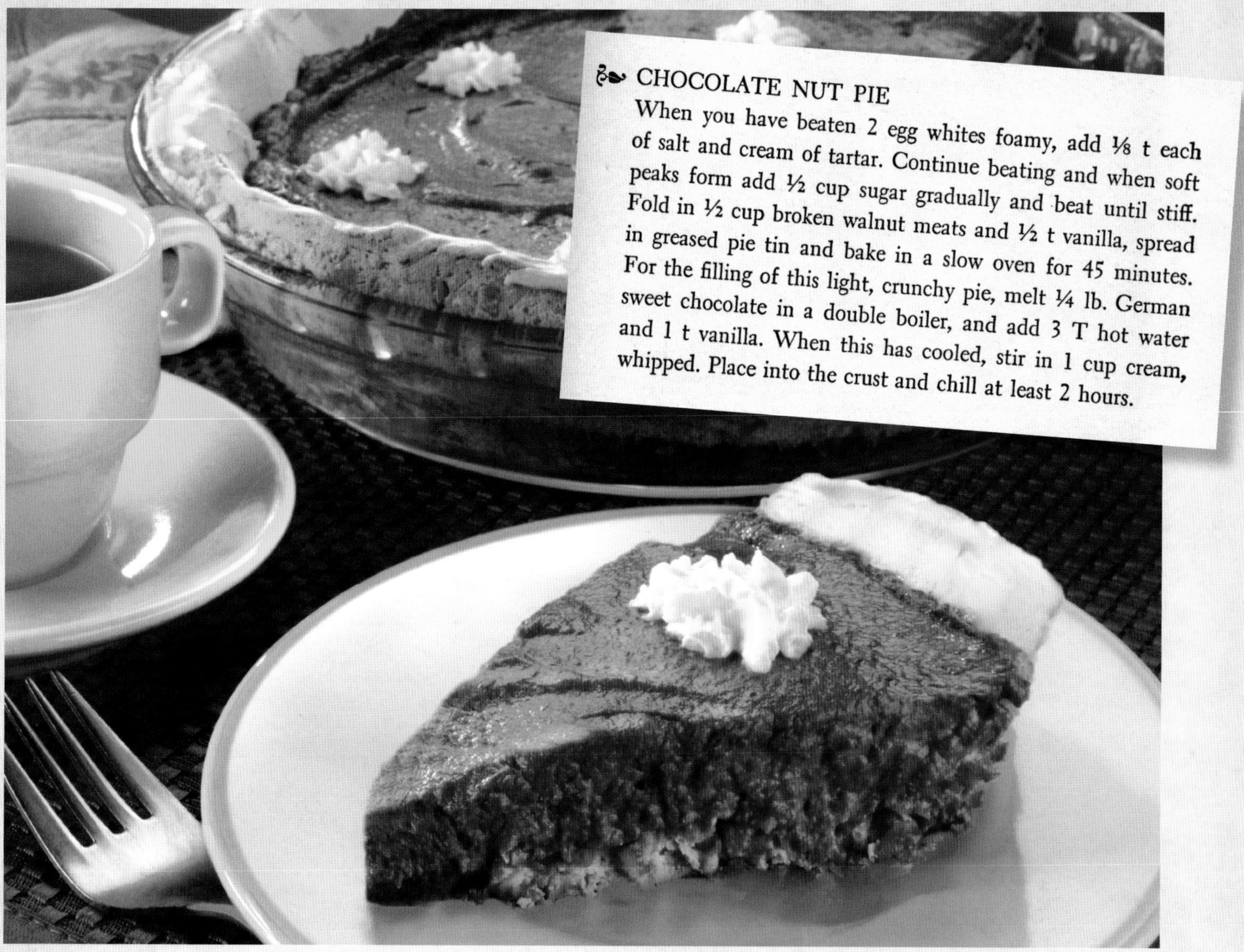

Ed Heth's Chocolate Nut Pie

An original, creative pie so delicious you'll want to share your love with the world! As Bill Penzey said, "It turns everything I knew about pie upside down!"

Pie:
- 2 egg whites
- ⅛ tsp. salt
- ⅛ tsp. cream of tartar
- ½ Cup sugar
- ½ Cup walnuts, finely chopped
- ½ tsp. vanilla

Preheat oven to 325°. Use a small mixing bowl (this is important, as using a large bowl will force you to beat the eggs for much, much longer). Beat the egg whites until foamy. Add the salt and cream of tartar. Beat until soft peaks form, and then gradually add the sugar. Beat until stiff. Gently fold in the walnuts and vanilla and spread into a greased glass pie plate. Bake at 325° for 45 minutes. Allow to completely cool before adding the filling.

Filling:
- ¼ lb. German sweet baking chocolate
- 3 TB hot water
- 1 tsp. vanilla
- 1 Cup cream, whipped

Melt the chocolate in a heavy saucepan over the lowest possible heat, or use a double boiler. Stir frequently even before the chocolate seems to be melting at all. Just before the last pieces have completely melted, add the water and vanilla, stir, and remove from heat as soon as possible to stop the mixture from "seizing." If this happens, and it gets gritty, you will have to start over. When the mixture has cooled, gently stir/fold in the whipped cream. Place the filling on top of the completely cooled pie and chill for at least 2 hours before serving.

Prep. time: 20 minutes
Baking time: 45 minutes
Serves: 8

Many start cooking professionally for the food, but the ones who make a life of it stay for the people.

SOUTH WATER MARKET, CHICAGO
View looking west along 15th St. from Morgan St., shows Chicago's principal produce market. Over 80,000 carloads of fruits and vegetables come into this market by rail and truck yearly. It is an important factor in contributing to Chicago's fame as the great central market.

POST CARD

POSTAGE ONE

SOUTH WATER MARKET, CHICAGO

268

Louie Danegelis has traveled a long road to come full circle. From growing up working in his family's Greek restaurant in Chicago to teaching his own children the business at Lee John's Catering, his long and interesting history has delivered him to the present.

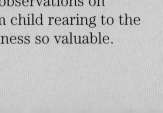

Louie Danegelis with his daughter Gina, working together at the family business, just as he worked with his dad.

We caught up with Louie on a classically busy working day. He was camped out in the front office after getting 40 gallons of stock on the simmer; setting up daughter Gina with basil to clean; letting mom-in-law Marlene in to start the baking and looking after him; plus answering the door and phones for various clients, old friends, and, of course, wife Lisa from home. He's had close to 50 years of experience, including 20 years of teaching – paying attention to everything from how to handle a knife to how to handle people. So many years of such great experiences are what have made his observations on everything from child rearing to the restaurant business so valuable.

rowing up in Chicago in the late '40s and early '50s, Louie learned the family business by working in his Dad's Greek restaurant at Chicago's South Water Market – feeding the workers of Commission Row where all the fruit came in. His Dad was a Greek immigrant and his Mom a transplant from Michigan, and together with the 3 boys they ran the place. By 3-4 in the morning, someone was always there with Dad, getting ready for the breakfast crowd. Mac and cheese with a fried egg on top would give way to a lunch of roast lamb shanks with orzo, as the busiest market in the world reached its peak. By early afternoon, it was a ghost town, and

"I was an energetic young man in Chicago."
Brothers George (left), Gus (second from right) and Louie (far right) enjoy a meal with a friend.

Louie's family gathers for a festive meal.

1958
Milwaukee Athletic Club

they'd close up shop until the next day.

Louie knew he wanted to go to school, had the idea of turning from a cook to a chef, and in 1956 got his chance, taking off for the Wisconsin Restaurant Institute in Madison.

As Louie said,

"I worked around after the Institute. I had a sort of career awareness, I guess, and I wanted to see it all and learn it all. So I'd always look for the oldest German French European trained chef looking for a gofer to train, and I'd run around trying to impress him, get all the information I could. I got a job at the country club, and I said, Chef, when should I come in? And he said 10. And I said, well, when do you come in? And he said 7-8, so I asked if it was okay could I come in then - not punch in or anything. So, after a week or two, he saw I was actually, you know, doing it, and he said - Louie, you punch in, I've been writing you in - you start punching in.

"So he knew he could train me and I'd work hard and do it his way and I wouldn't be gone in three months, and that's a good thing. So I worked around - Madison, Elkhart Lake, hotel, restaurant, country club, the Red Circle Inn, where we did tableside Caesars and Shrimp Denise and Bananas Foster and Sabayon - Lisa still does that.

Louie and Lisa in:
"Too Much Pepper!"

Louie and Lisa met in 1978. When Lisa was a student in the cooking program where Louie was the chef, he brought her to tears by pouring her big batch of onion soup down the drain saying, "Way too much pepper, start over." She got over that quickly when the next batch brought smiles.

Lisa began helping Louie cater a few weddings here and there, and before you know it, they were spending all their time together. After 4 years of various cooking jobs, they started catering full time in 1985. They married in 1986 (Lisa proposed to him!) and rented their own building the same year. In 1992 Louie retired from 20 years of teaching as the time had come to devote all their time to catering.

As Louie said, "Yeah, you know Lisa, she's a, well, what can I say? She's a great mom, caregiver, wife, administrator – sharp. God bless her, I woulda given the shop away a long time ago. I don't know what I'd do without her."

Lisa and Louie share a kiss in the kitchen in the 1980s.

"Then I wanted something bigger, so I moved to Milwaukee –The Athletic Club, and I worked with some great journeymen there. Started doing some catering with Schuster's - the old Gimbels, that was the place back then - but I wound up teaching and darned if that wasn't for 20 years. Had a great time doing it, met some great kids, gone on to great things. And, of course, met Lisa.

We had summer off, so I started catering - for the church, for friends, a little here and there. Once Lisa and I got married, well, the catering really took off from there."

165

CARROT CAKE
2 LOAF PAN
2 CUPS SUGAR
4 EGGS
1½ CUP OIL
2 CUPS GRATED CARROTS
3 CUPS FLOUR
2 TBR. SODA (TSP)
2 TBR. BAKING POWDER (TSP)
¼ TSP. SALT
2 TSP. CINNAMON
1 CUP NUTS - OPTIONAL
COMBINE: OIL-SUGAR-EGGS
CARROTS. ADD DRY INGREDIENTS

Bill Carrott
MAKES 6 CAKES

Louie's Mom (Yai Yai) and Dad

Carrot Loaf Cake

Yai Yai's favorite—she'd make 24 loaves at a crack.

2	Cups sugar
4	eggs
1½	Cups vegetable oil
2	Cups carrots, grated (about a pound)
3	Cups flour
2	tsp. baking soda
2	tsp. baking powder
¼	tsp. salt
2	tsp. cinnamon
1	Cup chopped nuts, optional

Preheat oven to 350°. Combine the sugar, eggs, oil and carrots. Stir in the dry ingredients and mix well. Pour into two greased loaf pans (we used 4-cup loaf pans). To remove the loaves from their pans, try this trick: double a sheet of aluminum foil, cut it to half the width of the pan and place it in the greased bread pan, up and over the edges, then pour in the batter. This will give you a handy way to lift the bread right out of the pan. Bake at 350° for 1 hour.

Prep. time: 5-10 minutes
Baking time: 1 hour
Yield: 24 slices

The womenfolk in Louie's family live a long long time. His Mom, long known simply as Yai Yai (Greek for Grandma), "just passed at 92, God bless her. Spanikopita, kappema, the horta salad with the grilled meats, she gave us all the recipes – Lisa uses them all – we still carry that over." Yai Yai would often come up from Chicago to visit and make giant batches of her carrot cake (an old fashioned loaf cake, which we'd call a bread). As you can see from her notation, 6 lbs. carrots = 6 batches, she made a lot. In fact, 6 loaves was her smallest batch, she'd often make 24 at a crack.

Kotta kappema, Greek tomato chicken with pasta, is still one of Louie's favorite meals. Do you need to whip the butter for 30 minutes to make kourabiedes, the legendary Greek powdered sugar covered cookie? Well, that's what Yai Yai did, and if you do it too you sure won't be disappointed...

Kourabiedes
(Greek Butter Cookies)

Wow—one of the world's great cookies.

- 1   lb. sweet butter, unsalted (4 sticks)
- ½   Cup powdered sugar
- 1   egg yolk
- 3   Cups cake flour (fine flour that produces more tender, finer-textured baked goods)
- 2   Cups all-purpose flour
- 1   tsp. baking powder
- 2   Cups powdered sugar for dusting the cookies, divided

Preheat oven to 350°. Soften butter at room temperature. Beat butter with an electric mixer for ½ hour at medium high speed (don't skimp, the long beating time is crucial). Add the ½ cup of powdered sugar, followed by the egg yolk and continue beating so the sugar and egg yolk mix in well. Add cake flour a little at a time, then the regular flour and baking powder. The dough should be soft but not sticky to the hand. Make sure you mix the dough well. Roll the dough into ¾ inch balls and make a small indentation on top to hold the powdered sugar. Bake at 350° for about 20 minutes. Sprinkle with 1 cup of powdered sugar. Remove from pan and place cookies on a board or rack to cool and sprinkle with remaining powdered sugar. Let them cool overnight.

Prep. time: 40 minutes
Baking time: 20 minutes
Yield: about 60 cookies

Yai Yai's Chicken

This was Louie's favorite meal growing up.

- 1   whole chicken, cut in 8 pieces, or 8 boneless/skinless chicken breast halves
- 3   TB oil
- 4   oz. tomato paste
- 2   cloves fresh chopped garlic
- 3   Cups chicken stock/broth or water
- 2-3 3-inch cinnamon sticks
- ¼   Cup Romano cheese for sprinkling

In a large, deep sauté pan, brown the chicken on all sides in the oil. Remove chicken from pan and pour off all but 1 TB of the fat. Put the tomato paste, garlic and chicken stock/ broth or water in the pan. Add the chicken and cinnamon sticks. The liquid should almost cover the chicken; add more if needed. Bring to a simmer, cover, and braise until tender, about 40 minutes for chicken pieces, 30 minutes for chicken breasts. Serve over Greek Spaghetti with the Romano cheese.

Prep. time: 10 minutes
Cooking time: 30-40 minutes
Serves: 6-8

Greek Spaghetti

- 1   lb. spaghetti noodles
- 1½   Cups Romano cheese, freshly grated
- ½   Cup butter (1 stick)

Cook spaghetti according to package directions and rinse with cold water. Place on a large platter and toss well with cheese. Melt the butter in a skillet until it begins to brown, stirring constantly. When butter foams and is a light brown, remove from heat and pour over spaghetti. Rewarm in oven or microwave.

Prep. time: 3-5 minutes
Cooking time: 10 minutes
Serves: 6-8

Lisa's Mom, Marlene, helps out in many ways. In her own words, she's a "Grandma, mother-in-law, caregiver, part-time baker, cleaning lady, cook and bottle washer." She also makes one of the kids' favorite meals – a big pan of chicken and rice. She lives close to the shop, so she can pop in and do a bit of clean up or get some bread dough started, giving Lisa an invaluable extra hour at home with the kids before school.

When you have 5 kids and a business to run, having a dedicated grandma around is truly a blessing.

From left: Lisa's father and mother, Richard and Marlene Landers, and Lisa's grandmother, Josephine Landers, along with the rest of Lisa's family.

Marlene with David in the kitchen baking.

Grandma Landers's Chicken 'n' Rice

Lisa grew up with this family favorite and sent it along to us. Even though it has cans of cream soup in the recipe (which we hardly ever use), her kids love it so much that we had to give it a try. We're happy we did. Lisa suggests doubling the rice and liquid and using an 11x17" pan to satisfy everyone—there was never enough rice when she was a kid.

1	Cup dry white rice
1	onion, diced
1	whole chicken, cut into 8 pieces
	salt and pepper, to taste
1	can Cream of Chicken soup
1	can Cream of Mushroom soup
2½	Cups chicken stock/broth (or 2½ Cups water mixed with 1-2 TB chicken soup base)
1	tsp. fresh garlic, chopped
1	pkg. dry onion soup mix (or 3 TB minced toasted onions and 2 tsp. salt)

Preheat oven to 350°. Pour uncooked rice on the bottom of a 9x13" pan. Top with diced onion. Season the chicken with salt and pepper and lay over the rice. Combine the soups, stock/broth and garlic and pour over the chicken. Sprinkle with soup mix. Cover with foil and bake at 350° for 1-1½ hours, until chicken is tender and the rice is cooked.
Prep. time: 10 minutes
Cooking time: 60-90 minutes
Serves: 4

Citrus Martini

Two puddings that are very good on their own. Put them together and WOW—looks as good as it tastes.

White Chocolate Mousse:

2 Cups whipping cream
3/4 lb. white chocolate, finely chopped
1 1/2 tsp. vanilla extract

In a small heavy saucepan, heat whipping cream to boiling over medium heat. Remove from heat and pour cream over chocolate in mixing bowl with vanilla. Stir to dissolve all the lumps. Chill overnight. Whip mousse with flat beater attachment of electric mixer (not the whisk attachment) until thick and creamy, about 5-8 minutes (do not over-mix as it will curdle). See photo.

Lemon Curd:

12 egg yolks
2 Cups sugar
1 Cup fresh lemon juice (roughly 6 lemons)
1 Cup cold unsalted butter, cut into chunks (2 sticks)

Whisk together egg yolks, sugar and lemon juice in a heavy-bottomed saucepan. Heat over low heat, stirring constantly with a flat-bottomed wooden spoon. Stir until mixture thickens and coats the spoon. Do not boil. Strain into a large bowl. Whisk in butter chunks gradually until incorporated. Chill.

Layer mousse and curd in martini glasses with fresh berries and/or crushed cookies of your choice. Garnish with a mint leaf.

Prep. time: 20 minutes
Cooking time: 20 minutes plus overnight chilling
Serves: 12

Lee Johns Catering

When the food must be perfect, and the service beyond compare, it is time to call Lee John's Catering. With Louie and Lisa you know the sea bass or rack of lamb will be coming out of the oven just as the salads are served, arriving at the table freshly cooked and piping hot whether you are serving 12 for an intimate dinner, 500 at a very special wedding, or 1000 for the opening of the Calatrava addition to the Milwaukee Art Museum.

The foccaccia with carmelized onions will have been baked fresh that day, and the cheesecake lollipops dressed up just before they head to the party.

As Louie likes to say, being kind to us as he has for 20 years, "It's the Spices, man!" After watching him in action for 20 years, we can say "It's Louie, man, and Lisa too!"

Lamb Chop Persillade

As served at Bill and Jeri's wedding.

1	rack of lamb (about 8 chops)
1	TB. olive oil, divided
½	tsp. salt (we use kosher flake salt)
½	tsp. pepper
½	tsp. granulated garlic
½	Cup fresh bread crumbs
1	tsp. dried rosemary, cracked
½	tsp. dried oregano
½	tsp. dried basil
½	tsp. dried parsley
2	tsp. regular or country Dijon-style prepared mustard

Preheat oven to 400°. Wash the lamb, pat dry. The rack of lamb should have the chine bone (a thin, flat bone on the bottom side of the rack) removed and the rib bones cleaned (which is called Frenched). If you are getting the lamb from a butcher, ask that those two things be done–if the lamb is wrapped at the grocer, it probably has been done already. If there seems to be lots of fat, carefully trim a bit away. Rub the lamb with 2 tsp. olive oil, then sprinkle with salt, pepper and garlic. Combine the fresh bread crumbs (2 slices of bread ripped up and whirled in a blender or food processor should do it) with the herbs and 1 tsp. olive oil; toss to combine. Spread the top side of the rack of lamb with prepared Dijon-style mustard, place the lamb in the baking dish, then carefully pack on the bread crumbs over the mustard. Don't worry if you don't use it all. Place the lamb in the preheated 400° oven. It should take 25-30 minutes to reach rare in the center, medium rare for the outer chops. Use a meat thermometer if you are unsure, and remember it will rise a few degrees once it is out of the oven resting. Overcooked lamb is just plain sad, so keep a close eye on it. After 15 minutes cooking time, if the breading is already brown, place a piece of aluminum foil loosely on top of it. Once out of the oven, let the lamb rest 10 minutes before cutting. Cut the lamb between the ribs using a large, sharp chef's knife.

Prep. time: 10 minutes
Cooking time: 40 minutes or so
Serves: 4

Risotto with Chicken, Lemon Grass and Coconut Milk

1	lb. boneless, skinless chicken breast, sliced
3	TB oil, divided
2	TB fresh ginger root, peeled, chopped, sliced or grated (about a 2 inch piece of ginger)
2	whole garlic cloves, finely chopped
4	scallions, sliced
1	stalk lemon grass, peeled, chopped 3 inches from the bottom, kept whole
	salt, to taste
1	Cup onion, diced
2	Cups Arborio rice (risotto)
⅛	tsp. red pepper flakes
6	Cups chicken broth
1	Cup unsweetened coconut milk
2	TB Thai fish sauce
2	TB fresh cilantro
2	TB scallions, chopped
⅓	Cup unsalted roasted peanuts (optional)

Heat 1 TB of oil in a heavy-duty pan. Add the ginger, garlic, scallions and lemon grass stalk and sauté for 3-5 minutes. Add the chicken and sauté for 5 minutes. Season with salt to taste and set aside. For the risotto, heat the remaining oil in a heavy saucepan. Add the onion and sauté for about 2 minutes. Add the rice and red pepper flakes and stir. Add the chicken broth, ½ Cup at a time, stirring well after each ½ Cup, until the liquid is absorbed. When rice is tender but firm (about 20 minutes), turn off the heat. Add the coconut milk, fish sauce and cilantro and stir. Add the chicken mixture. Remove the lemon grass stalk. For garnish, sprinkle with scallions and peanuts, if desired.

Prep. time: 10 minutes
Cooking time: 30 minutes
Serves: 6-8

Chinese Duck Pizza

One of our favorite Lee John's appetizers—we were very happy to get this recipe. It seems long, but it's really pretty easy, and if you are lacking one of the more unusual marinade ingredients, it'll still taste great!

Crust:

2	TB yeast
2	tsp. sugar
1	Cup warm water
3	TB olive oil
2	tsp. salt
2 3/4 - 3	Cups all-purpose flour

Marinade:

2	TB brown bean sauce
2	cloves garlic
6	TB soy sauce
2	TB hoisin sauce
1/4	Cup dry sherry or white wine
2	TB sugar
2	TB oil
1	tsp. Chinese five spice powder

Topping:

2	duck breasts (approximately 6 oz. each)
1/2	Cup shiitake mushroom caps (6-8 mushrooms), diced
1/3	Cup white sesame seeds
3/4	Cup hoisin sauce
2	TB fresh ginger root, minced
1	tsp. Chinese chili paste or 1/2 tsp. crushed red peppers
1	bunch green onions, minced (about 1/2 Cup)
2	Cups mozzarella cheese, grated (reserve 1/2 Cup for garnish)
1/2	Cup fresh cilantro, chopped

Mix all of the marinade ingredients together and put in a zip-top bag or a covered container. Add the duck breasts, put in the refrigerator and marinate overnight.

Crust: Place yeast and sugar in a mixing bowl. Add warm water (not too hot, you just want to wake up the yeast, so the water should feel very warm to the touch, but not so hot you jerk your hand out). Mix with a spoon to blend–the yeast won't all dissolve, don't worry about that. Let stand for 5 minutes. This is called proofing the yeast. Since the bread won't work if the yeast isn't active, it pays to take a look. Active yeast mixed with sugar and water will be a rich, foamy brown. Add 3 TB olive oil and 2 tsp. salt, mix well. Add flour 1/2 Cup at a time, blending in with a spoon. Stop once you have added 2 1/2 Cups of flour. If necessary, use the rest of the flour on the table while you are kneading. The dough will be a bit sticky; dust the dough and your hands with flour and work it into the dough. As you knead it, the dough will go from wet and sticky to smooth and elastic–don't add too much flour, as then it will be dry and hard once baked. Adding just the right amount of flour is the trickiest bit. Even though this is a very easy recipe that will give good results the first time, it usually takes until the third try to truly understand how the dough acts, and to really feel just when the dough turns elastic and exactly how much flour is needed to reach that point. Once the kneading is over, roll out to fit a 13x17" baking sheet. Let the dough rest another 20 minutes while the oven is preheating to 400°. Bake for about 15 minutes, until golden brown.

While the crust is baking, heat a pan on medium-high heat. Place the duck breasts in the pan, skin side down, for 5 minutes. Flip the breasts and cook for 5 more minutes. Remove from the pan, remove the skin, and dice the meat. In the same pan, sauté the mushrooms and sesame seeds. Combine the hoisin sauce, ginger, chili paste, green onion and cilantro. Stir in the duck, mushrooms, and 1 1/2 Cups of the cheese. Spread over the pizza crust. Sprinkle with the remaining cheese. Bake at 350° for about 5 minutes to melt the cheese.

Prep. time: 1 hour plus overnight marinating
Cooking: 20 minutes
Serves: 4-6 as a meal, or makes 100-120 little triangles for appetizers

"Oh yeah, man, they are great kids, just super, super kids. I am really, really happy to have them – and Lisa, what can I say? God bless her, I don't know what I'd do without her."

Family Life

When Louie and Lisa got married, they knew they wanted to start a family. They looked into adopting, and while it took some time to complete the paperwork for their first son Casey, suddenly over the course of just a few years they had five kids, all from Louie's hometown of Chicago.

Casey is in high school now with Jordan close behind. Gina is in sixth grade, and even the little ones aren't so little anymore. David is in first grade now, and Lily Rose has officially broken her mother's heart by leaving home to start kindergarten.

As Louie said, "There's an old Greek saying – little children, little problems, big children, big problems. It's a maintenance program, trying to help them stay centered. I grew up in Chicago, that says it all. Some of my friends went one way, some the other. I just thank God I got to where I am."

Family time is important to Louie and Lisa and is worked right into the catering business. The realities of life in food service are a lot different from the

image. There is that glamorous moment of the customer smiling while enjoying the perfect food, but that moment comes at the end of a whole lot of hard work. As Louie calls it, "bull work." Catering is even harder than a regular restaurant, as the kitchen needs to be packed up and taken on the road for every event.

Family mealtime revolves around how busy the catering weekend will be. As Lisa says, "The three older children help out quite a bit and work parties with Dad. The little ones are good for an hour or so, sneaking chocolate whenever possible. Sundays are a family day with church and a nice sitdown Greek meal. Greek salads and homemade pita are favorites,

as is anything Mexican. Lamb is a staple, and the Greeks always have crusty bread with dinner.

"Sometimes we have 'Take-home' night, where we all go down the line and each family member gets to choose. For Louie, his favorite is a Chicago all beef hot dog, properly prepared."

You can take the boy out of Chicago...

Casey in the shop, hard at work. The days Louie would come in for a single cup of lavender are far in the past. We didn't even sell it that way, but he was so very, very charming...

What is it to raise good kids – to work side by side with them? To teach them skills – how to hold a knife, how to work smart, get the basil cleaned quick, keep cool. These are life skills, and Louie has spent a lot of years learning them. His incredible way with people, along with his ability to hold the family together and keep the business going, have given him an enormous amount of knowledge to pass on, and in a family business, you really do come full circle, repaying your debt to your parents by working with your own children.

"All the kids have a recipe book started – whenever they help prepare something it is written down."

Left to Right: Jordan, Lily Rose, Casey, Gina and David

173

Spaghetti Pie

Here's another great recipe from Louie and Lisa—baked spaghetti in a creamy sauce; a tasty crowd pleaser!

1	lb. spaghetti
4-6	Italian sausage links
¼	Cup vegetable oil
1	Cup chopped onion
1-2	cloves garlic, chopped
¼	Cup ground almonds
4	eggs
1½	Cups cream
½	tsp. salt
¼	tsp. pepper
1	tsp. dried oregano
4	Cups marinara sauce, divided
½	Cup grated Parmesan or Romano cheese

Preheat oven to 350°. Bring a large pot of water to a boil for the spaghetti. Cook the sausages by browning them in a skillet with a little bit of water or grilling them. Leftovers work well. Set them aside to cool. Heat the oil in a skillet over medium-high heat. Add the onion and garlic and cook until softened, about 5 minutes. Cook the spaghetti according to the package directions and drain well. Slice the sausages. Combine the ground almonds, eggs, cream, salt, pepper and oregano with 3½ cups of the marinara sauce. Mix everything together in a 9x13 pan. Top with the remaining sauce and sprinkle with cheese if desired. Bake, covered, at 350° until set, about 45 minutes.

Prep. time: 30 minutes
Cooking time: 45 minutes
Serves: 8

Hoisin Chicken

This combination of white meat chicken and sweet and spicy hoisin sauce will please both the kids and their parents.

1	boneless/skinless chicken breast, cut into bite-sized pieces
1	TB olive oil
1	Cup sliced onion
3	TB hoisin sauce
4	TB rice wine
5	TB soy sauce
1½	TB sugar
1	TB sesame oil
2	TB minced garlic
¼	lb. green beans, trimmed
1	tsp. arrowroot starch mixed with 1-2 TB water (optional)

Heat the olive oil in a skillet over medium-high heat. Add the onion and cook until softened. Remove from the skillet and set aside. Add the chicken to the skillet and cook until lightly browned on all sides. While the chicken is cooking, whisk together the hoisin sauce, rice wine, soy sauce, sugar, sesame oil and garlic. Add to the skillet along with the onions. Stir well. Add the green beans. Cover the skillet and reduce the heat to a simmer. Cook about 10-15 minutes or until the green beans are cooked to the desired consistency. If necessary, thicken the sauce by adding the arrowroot/water mix. Serve over rice or noodles.

Prep. time: 10 minutes
Cooking time: 25 minutes
Serves: 4

celebrate
100 YEARS
of Hope

LIVE THE 40'S USO THEME CLUB

THIS WILL BE A VERY FUN TIME

SEE THE CLASSIC MOVIES, HEAR AMERICA'S #1 RADIO PROGRAM.

BOB HOPE INSPIRED FOOD AND BEVERAGES

PLAY THE 5 HOLE TILLISON DESIGNED MINI DESERT CLASSIC GOLF TOURNAMENT FOR PRIZES GALORE.

EXPERIENCE THE REMARKABLE CAREER OF A REMARKABLE MAN: BOB HOPE. FROM VAUDEVILLE TO TELEVISION, BOB'S LONG STRANGE TRIP WILL COME TO LIFE AT THIS CAN'T-MISS EVENT.

THE MORNING OF THE 31ST THERE WILL ONLY BE THOSE WHO CAN TELL THE STORY OF THIS EPIC EVENT AND THOSE WHO WILL BE FORCED TO LISTEN. REARRANGE YOUR CALENDAR. YOU WON'T REGRET IT.

7:30, MAY 30TH AT THE PENZEY HOME

To Otto—
I hope I look
this good.
Bob
Hope

It really was Bob Hope and the party we threw for his 100th birthday that got this whole magazine rolling. It was a great party. I could not imagine a better starting point, or a better outcome. Here's to hoping the party goes on for years and years.

one *for the road* TO UTOPIA

Thanks for the magazine.

Our original goal was to write a book. For a long time people had wanted us to put out a compilation of our recipes. It was actually eight years ago that Bantam/Doubleday/Dell approached me about a cookbook. At the time I thought we weren't ready. We were still trying to get our footing back then and I feared all the attention would have swamped us. Two years ago I thought we were almost ready. We still needed to improve our writing skills and add a few more people to make a really good book, but the time had come. Then a funny thing happened along the way to that book -- Bob Hope's 100th birthday.

As part of building up to the book we added some more pages to the catalog. There were extended travel pieces, the Creative Cook saw the light of day and we began to do some longer entertaining pieces. We always push our catalog deadlines, so it was not until a week before going to press in April of 2003 that we came to the conclusion that we just had to do an entertaining piece on Bob Hope's 100th. I am a real fan of Bob Hope. It began with an obscure line from the movie Caddy Shack, but what started as kitsch grew into a sincere admiration. The work he did to perfect his craft. Vaudeville, Broadway, Movies, Radio, TV -- he was a star in all. What he did for so many decades with the USO, bringing a piece of America to so many troops so far from home. But it was not

just the troops - he went out into the world to put a human face on what America is all about. At the very height of the cold war he traveled to Moscow to use his unique humor to break the ice. He was America's Ambassador of Comedy, a position that has been vacant for far too long.

So it was a week from our deadline and we contacted Bob Hope's people about a catalog piece on throwing a Bob Hope 100th birthday party. There were concerns. They sensed my admiration, but there were questions about whether this would show an implied endorsement of our spices by Mr. Hope. They apologized and said if they had six months notice they thought it would most likely go through, but with only a week until our deadline they would have to say no. Then they added the magic words that have you reading this now, "If you were a magazine it would be no problem."

Even though we could not feature it in the catalog, we threw our Bob Hope party and a great time was had by all. Months passed and sadly even Bob passed, but still I kept thinking about "If you were a magazine it would be no problem." In November I brought up the idea of a magazine with my wife Jeri and she was positive. In December we told my sister, and now managing editor, Pam while waiting around the delivery room for our daughter Teddi. Since then it has been well over a year of us thrashing out the details. I hope you liked it and if you did please do us a huge favor and tell each and every person you know. We've spent decades supplying good spices and seasonings to people who cook to make the lives around them better. In that time I really have come to believe people who cook are the glue that holds this whole world together. Your support in spreading this message is greatly appreciated.

And to the spirit of Mr. Bob Hope, thanks for the magazine. Without your love of life, and strength to hold on, who knows if it would have ever come to be. A very sincere thanks,

Bill

BOB HOPE'S LEMON MERINGUE PIE

Lemon Meringue Pie

This is a 1950s lemon pie recipe; it's everything a pie should be. Feel free to use your favorite pie crust recipe or our very easy No Roll Pie Crust recipe below.

Filling for a 9" pie shell:

1½	Cups sugar
6	TB cornstarch
¾	Cup water
3	TB butter
5	egg yolks (save the whites for the meringue)
6	TB fresh lemon juice (about 1½ lemons)
	pinch of salt
	grated rind of 1 lemon (or 1 tsp. minced lemon peel rehydrated in 1 TB water)

Meringue:

5	egg whites
1/4	tsp. salt
1/4	tsp. cream of tartar
1	TB sugar
½	tsp. vanilla extract (optional)

Preheat oven to 350°.
Lemon filling:
Mix sugar and cornstarch together. In a heavy saucepan bring water to a boil. Slowly add sugar mix, whisking until smooth. Reduce heat to low, cook, stirring constantly, until you have a thick consistency (3-4 minutes). Stir in the butter until melted. Remove from stove and whisk in the egg yolks one at a time, then lemon juice, salt and lemon peel. Return to stovetop on low, stirring for 2-3 minutes until thick, golden and glossy—do not boil or you will scramble the eggs. Pour into the pre-baked pie shell, let cool, then top with meringue and bake.

Meringue:
Start with a very clean, dry glass bowl, and make sure there isn't even one speck of yolk. Beat the egg whites, salt, and cream of tartar until stiff peaks form, which is close to 5 minutes on high speed, then fold in the sugar and vanilla by hand, being careful not to smash all the air out of the whites. Spread the meringue over the cooled pie all the way to the edge of the pie crust, which keeps the filling from shrinking. Bake for 15 minutes in a preheated 350° oven until meringue is lightly browned. Cool to room temperature, then refrigerate until ready to serve. The pie is easiest to slice when cold.

No Roll Pie Crust
We used a no roll pie crust, which was probably unheard of in the 1950s, but it is so simple and tasty that we're sure you won't mind bending from tradition.

9" pie shell:

1½	Cups all-purpose flour
1	TB sugar
½	tsp. salt
½	Cup oil (we used canola)
3	TB milk

Preheat oven to 375°. Put all of the ingredients into a 9 inch pie pan. Mix with a fork until well blended and pat into the pan. Push the pastry up the sides and form a nice edge with your thumb and finger. Generously prick the crust with a fork to prevent bubbling of the pastry during baking. Bake at 375° for 15-17 minutes until nicely browned. Let cool before filling.

Prep. time: 25 minutes
Baking time: 30 minutes
Serves: 8

volume one, issue four, 2006

Penzeys
one

The food magazine by & for everyone

Johnny
Cash
&
Curry

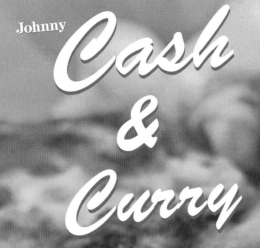

penzeysone.com
$4.95 U.S.

1 87732 00004 8

PLUS: **one** NAME: Smith, INSIDE SCOOP, WEEKNIGHT PIRATES, 4 X 2 and so much more.

Part II

So we had a magazine, what then? Looking back, I think the fourth issue went a long way in answering that very question. I realize now how much of my desire to start a food magazine really came from my experiences of thirty-plus years in the spice business. Spices have taken me around the world more times than I can remember. I have met many, many people in my travels and I can honestly say that human kindness does not stop at the border, any border. Here at home it is much the same story. Each of our stores has 10 to 20,000 regular customers, people who share in their desire to make the lives around them better by cooking. To spend years with these customers is to understand that the goodness of cooking does not live in just one segment, or one group of this country. The goodness of cooking really is universal, and to meet these cooks opens your eyes not only to the richness of their recipes, but the richness in the diversity that so often goes unseen.

I think that in people who have experiences like mine, experiences that have brought them face to face, time and again with so many people from so many different places and backgrounds, there is a desire to find the one thing to say or show that will magically open everyone's eyes to this idea that kindness knows no borders, that goodness is not the possession of any one group. All too often the desire for that quick fix starts with cleverness and humor, but over time slips into sarcasm and bitterness. It is all too easy for what starts out as an earnest effort to make a difference instead to end up creating even greater division. At times I have been guilty of this myself.

I have come to the belief that there is no silver bullet, no magic fix. The only way anyone ever comes to see the goodness in the world is to meet that goodness one person at a time. At times it can seem too slow or too gradual, but the progress is real. Ultimately there may be nothing wrong with how we see the world we live in that can't be cured by a 30-year-long parade of people who care enough to cook. If that is what we need to be then that is what I hope our magazine can become. Thirty more years, think of the recipes...

This was fun. It had energy and great recipes, but it was not right for us. Cooking is all about building up those around us. Though sarcasm and cleverness are very popular, they are not a foundation that you can build on. For us, cooking without humanity really is not cooking.

It does remind me of what a talented group of people we have here. We have the ability to photograph more than just food close-ups and we should find a way to use that ability in a way that is more us. I still love the whole *Creative Cook / Matrix / School House Rock* ending—good stuff.

WHAT'S WITH ALL THIS "CURRYING FLAVOR"?

Haven't had much time for the news lately, though we did see this on-line at the Washington Post the other day;

"When politicians align themselves with charities, it allows special interests to donate unlimited sums of money and curry favor while acting as if they are doing it out of the goodness of their souls... charitable foundations allow politicians to play both sides of the favor-currying street, taking money from corporate interests looking to curry favor then turning around and using that money to curry favor with groups and organizations that might prove helpful down the line."

We were shocked. First off at the dismal state of spelling in the media. It's "f l a v o r" not "f a v o r." And second, at the idea that big business would be giving huge sums to politicians for curry flavor when they could make it themselves at home for not much money. We figure it must be that big business lacks good curry recipes and thought if we printed some of our best, the Capitol could get back to that "by the people thing."

ROGAN JOSH CURRY

Rogan Josh is the popular red lamb dish from Northern India and Pakistan. This version comes from Rajasthan. Rogan Josh can be made with beef, but it is a perfect example of how crafty seasoning can change the stronger flavor of lamb into something far more delicious. Rogan Josh is traditionally served with roti, (round flat bread), instead of rice. Roti is torn into rectangular pieces, and then used to grab a piece of meat and scoop up some sauce. It takes some practice to do this gracefully, but like using chopsticks, everyone should know how.

Mix all of the spices (except the cayenne) with water, let stand while browning the lamb. Preheat a large, heavy, deep pot over medium high flame. Add 2 TB oil, heat, then brown lamb in 3 batches. To reduce sticking, add another TB of oil before the second and third batches, allowing the oil to get hot before adding the meat each time. Remove browned meat to plate. Add 1 TB oil to pot and brown the onions. When brown, add spice mix, 1 tsp. cayenne and salt, stirring constantly for 45 seconds. Add the browned meat with any juices that have accumulated. Continue to stir, adding yogurt ¼ at a time. Add water, bring to a boil, reduce heat to low for a slow simmer and cover. Cook for 1-1½ hours, stirring

occasionally. When meat is tender and most of the onions have disintegrated, remove cover, increase flame to medium, and reduce liquid until sauce is thick. At this point the extra oil can be drained off the top by blotting with a paper towel (although it tastes better if some of the oil is left and mixed back in). Taste the Rogan Josh and add extra cayenne at this point if desired. Serve with roti (Indian flat bread—pita bread is a reasonable substitute), white or saffron rice and a simple salad with lemon juice and oil dressing.

Preparation time: 20 minutes
Cooking time: 1½ hours (approximately)
Serves 6-8

3	lbs. lamb shoulder blade chops, bones and fat removed, cut into 3/4" cubes
5	TB vegetable oil
2	medium onions, finely minced
1	TB paprika
1	TB garlic powder
1½	tsp. ground cumin
1½	tsp. powdered ginger
1	tsp. ground coriander
1	tsp. black pepper
½ - 1½	tsp. ground cardamom
½	tsp. cinnamon
¼	tsp. ground cloves
1	pinch saffron
2-4	TB water
1-2	tsp. cayenne pepper (optional)—without any cayenne, the dish will be spicy but not hot, with 2 tsp. cayenne it will be about as hot as it is when prepared in India
1	tsp. salt
1	Cup plain yogurt
1	Cup water

Rogan Josh

ALOO GOBI CURRY

Aloo Gobi (curried potatoes with cauliflower)

Aloo Gobi -- Curried Potatoes with Cauliflower

6		medium red potatoes
2		Cups or so cauliflower florets (½ a medium head)
1		small onion
2		TB butter, olive oil, or ghee (clarified butter)
1–2		TB curry powder
1		tsp. ground coriander seed
1		TB water
1		tsp. whole brown mustard seed
½		tsp. whole cumin seeds
2–3		TB lemon juice (juice of 1 lemon)
3		TB fresh cilantro leaf, chopped
1		jalapeño pepper-thinly sliced and seeds removed (optional)
½		Cup water
		salt to taste

Bring 2 quarts of water to a boil, then add red potatoes. Cook as you would for potato salad, reducing heat to a high simmer and cooking until fork tender but not mushy—usually about 20 minutes. Drain the pot and rinse the potatoes until cool to the touch.

While the potatoes are cooking, bring a second smaller pot of water to a boil for the cauliflower. Cut the cauliflower into florets, and mince the onion. Combine the curry powder (start with 1 TB if you don't eat curry often) and coriander with 1 TB water, let stand a few minutes. At this point the potatoes should be done, and the cauliflower water should be boiling. Cook the cauliflower 3 minutes, rinse and drain. Peel the skin off the potatoes (a paring knife works best) and cube. Heat the butter/oil over medium-high heat. Add the minced onion, brown mustard seed and cumin seeds. When the seeds start to sizzle and pop, add the curry/water mix, stirring well to evenly coat the onions. Cook 3 minutes, then add the lemon juice, along with cubed potatoes and cauliflower, stirring well to coat. Add the cilantro and jalapeño, along with ½ cup water, turn the heat down a bit, and simmer till the vegetables are heated through and the sauce is thick—10 minutes or so. Taste and add salt as desired. Traditionally served with saffron rice.

Serves: 4 Prep. Time: 15 minutes. Total Cooking time: 30 minutes.

SIMPLE CHICKEN CURRY

This is a nice starter curry, great flavor but not too spicy. Serve with rice and bread and maybe a steamed vegetable such as broccoli. Fresh ginger and garlic are preferred for this recipe because they help thicken the sauce.

1	lb. chicken–we used breast meat, which we boned and chopped
2	TB vegetable oil or butter
1	medium onion, peeled and minced
4	inch section fresh ginger, peeled and grated–or 1 tsp. powdered ginger
2	cloves garlic, minced, or 1/2 tsp. garlic powder
2	tsp. curry powder
1	tsp. garam masala (see tip, or if you don't feel like making garam masala, use an extra tsp. curry powder)
1/2	Cup plus 2 TB water, divided
2	ripe tomatoes, good-sized, washed, cored and chopped into large pieces
1	Cup plain yogurt (we definitely prefer low fat yogurt over nonfat yogurt)

Place ginger and garlic (if using powdered), curry powder and garam masala in a small bowl, cover with 2 TB water. Let stand while de-boning and chopping the chicken into bite-sized pieces, mincing the onion, grating the fresh ginger and finely mincing the garlic. Heat oil or butter over medium heat. When hot, add onion, plus ginger and garlic if using fresh. Sauté, stirring, for about 3 minutes, until onions start to brown and everything smells really good. Spoon in the curry/water mixture, stirring quickly. The mix will become quite dry, keep stirring until everything is a smooth paste, about 2 minutes. Add the chicken pieces, saute quickly for a few minutes until well coated, then add water and chopped tomatoes, stirring well. Reduce heat to a simmer and cook 20 minutes, stirring every 5 minutes or so. Add yogurt, stir well, raise heat to medium and simmer until the sauce is thick and golden. This usually takes about 10 minutes. Taste and add salt if desired; most Americans would like 1/2 a teaspoon or so.

Serves: 4
Prep. time: 10 minutes
Cooking time: 35 minutes

Chicken Curry

Tip: How to Make Garam Masala

Garam Masala is a traditional Indian spice blend called for in many recipes. It has a cool deep flavor that is a really essential component to many fine Indian dishes. It is available in Indian grocery stores and often in supermarkets. However, it is even better when you make it fresh.

$3\frac{1}{2}$	tsp. ground coriander
2	tsp. black pepper
$1\frac{1}{2}$	tsp. ground cardamom
$1\frac{1}{4}$	tsp. ground cinnamon
1	tsp. ground caraway seed
1	tsp. ground cumin seed
$\frac{1}{2}$	tsp. powdered ginger
$\frac{1}{2}$	tsp. ground cloves
$\frac{1}{4}$	tsp. ground nutmeg

VINDALOO CURRIES

Duck Vindaloo

Vindaloo is a wonderfully flavorful pork and potato stew from Goa, the beautiful region on the southwest coast of India. Pork dishes are unusual in Indian cooking, but Goa was under Portuguese influence for hundreds of years and developed its own tradition of fragrant, tender, spicy dishes. Vindaloo is a dish best served hot. The larger amounts of seasoning listed will yield authentic (spicy) flavor. If this is your first Vindaloo experience, you may want to start with the smaller amount listed. Vindaloo takes a bit of prep work, but then it can be ignored while it slowly simmers to tender perfection.

Lamb Vindaloo

Pork Vindaloo Curry

1½	tsp.	ground coriander
2	tsp.	garlic powder
1½	tsp.	ground cumin
1	tsp.	ground cinnamon
1	tsp.	powdered ginger
1	tsp.	crushed brown mustard seed
¼ - ½	tsp.	powdered jalapeno pepper
½	tsp.	ground cardamom
½	tsp.	powdered turmeric
¼	tsp.	black pepper
⅛	tsp.	ground cloves
4	TB	water
4	TB	vegetable oil or ghee, divided
1½	lbs.	boneless pork cut into 3/4" cubes (pork chop suey cubes, already cut at the grocers, work fine and save time, or cut up a roast or shoulder chops; tougher cuts are perfect, as they will become tender in the cooking)
2		medium onions, finely chopped
4		medium red potatoes, peeled, cut into 3/4" cubes
½	tsp.	salt
2	Cups	water
¾	Cup	vinegar
1-5	tsp.	cayenne pepper

In a small bowl, mix all of the spices (except the cayenne) with water, set aside. Have pork, onions, and potatoes cut and ready to go. Keep the potatoes in a bowl of water to prevent browning. Preheat a large, deep, heavy pot over a medium-high flame. Add 1 TB vegetable oil, heat, then brown pork in two batches, adding and heating another TB of oil before the second batch of pork. If you have a non-stick pan, you may not need any oil to brown the pork. Remove pork when brown, add the last 2 TB of oil, heat, then add onions. Stir over medium-high heat until onions are deep brown, about 5 minutes. When onions are a very deep brown, add spice paste. Stir constantly for about 30 seconds until paste begins to burn on the bottom of the pot. Add pork, potatoes, salt, water, and vinegar. When water comes to a boil, reduce heat to a slow simmer, cover and cook for 30 minutes. After 30 minutes, taste the Vindaloo. Adjust heat to the maximum tolerable level with cayenne or other hot peppers (fresh jalapeños work well). Simmer uncovered over low heat until potatoes and pork are very tender and the liquid has reduced to a thick, glossy sauce, about 1 hour and 30 minutes. Serve with white or saffron rice, a plain vegetable, like steamed broccoli or cauliflower, and plenty of ice water. Serves: 4. Preparation time: 30 minutes. Cooking time: 2 hours.

Duck Vindaloo Curry

Spice mix:

1½	tsp.	ground coriander
2	tsp.	garlic powder
1½	tsp.	ground cumin
1	tsp.	ground cinnamon
1	tsp.	powdered ginger
1	tsp.	crushed brown mustard seed
¼ - ½	tsp.	powdered jalapeño pepper
½	tsp.	ground cardamom
½	tsp.	powdered turmeric
¼	tsp.	black pepper
⅛	tsp.	ground cloves
1		whole duck, breast removed
2		medium onions, finely chopped
4		medium potatoes, peeled, cut into 3/4" cubes
1	tsp.	salt
2	Cups	water mixed with
¾	Cup	white vinegar (or 3 cups red wine)
½	tsp.	cayenne pepper (or a fresh hot pepper)

Preheat oven to 375°. Mix together all of the Spice Mix ingredients and set aside. Wash duck, pat dry. Remove giblets and neck, discard or save for other dishes. Carefully remove the duck breast with a sharp knife, and reserve for another recipe. Rub the duck all over with 1 TB of the Spice Mix. Roast for one hour. After roasting, disjoint the duck--basically cut it into a few pieces so it'll fit into a soup pot, and cover with water/vinegar mix or red wine. Place the pot on low to simmer. Using 1-2 TB duck fat from the roasting pan, sauté the chopped onions. After about 5 minutes cooking time, add another 1-2 TB Spice Mix (depending on how hot you like it) to the pan with the onions. Stir and cook a minute or two, then add the seasoned onions to the pot. Simmer away for a few hours, then pull out the duck pieces. Let them cool a bit, then remove all the meat from the skin and bones. Discard the skin and bones and put the meat back in the pot. Refrigerate overnight. In the morning or a few hours before serving time, remove the layer of fat from the top of the pot and discard. Put the pot on to simmer. Add potatoes and salt to the pot for the final hour of cooking time. Adjust heat with cayenne pepper or other hot peppers (fresh jalapeños work well). Simmer uncovered over low heat until potatoes are very tender and the liquid has reduced to a thick, glossy sauce. Serve with white or saffron rice.
Serves: 4. Preparation time: 30 minutes. Cooking time: 4 hours divided, with an overnight in between.

CHICKEN BIRYANI CURRY

Biryani are fragrant rice and meat dishes from the North of India. The key is to know the rice you are using, so it will cook properly. Biryani should have nicely cooked rice that is not mushy or dry, which is then mixed with the seasoned meat and onions, and baked for a bit to marry the flavors. Lamb is traditional, chicken also works well.

1	lb. chicken meat, cubed
½	Cup plain yogurt (regular, not fat free)
1 ½	Cups white rice (we used basmati)
2	tsp. salt, divided
3	Cups water
¼	Cup butter (1/2 stick), divided
1	large onion, peeled and thinly sliced
½	Cup golden raisins (optional)
2	tsp. garam masala (see tip)
1	tsp. powdered ginger
½	tsp. garlic powder
¼	tsp. cayenne pepper
2	TB water (to soak the spices in for 5 minutes)
¼	tsp. (1 large pinch) saffron threads, soaked in 3 TB warm milk for 5 minutes
¼	Cup chicken stock

Mix the chicken cubes with yogurt, let stand 30 minutes. While the chicken is marinating, start the rice. For basmati rice, measure the rice, rinse it several times, place in a small, heavy-bottomed saucepan with a tight-fitting lid, add water and 1 tsp. salt. Cover, bring to a boil, then reduce heat and simmer for 20 minutes. Turn the heat off and let the rice stand, undisturbed, for another 10 minutes. In a large skillet, melt 2 TB butter over medium high heat. Sauté onions until brown—about 5 minutes, stirring regularly. For the final minute, add the raisins, and stir continually. Make sure the heat is not so high that the onions are blackening, a nice golden brown is what you are looking for. Remove the onions/raisins from the pan and set aside. Add 1 TB butter. When hot, add the chicken and yogurt mixture, 1 tsp. salt and the spices, which

should soak in water for about 5 minutes before using. Sauté over medium-high heat, stirring regularly, about 7 minutes, until the mixture starts turning brown. Preheat oven to 350˚. Melt the remaining tablespoon of butter and pour it into a large casserole dish (the standard 8" by 12" oval works well), swirling to coat the bottom. Sprinkle in a bit of the onions and raisins, then add half of the cooked rice. Sprinkle half of the saffron and milk mix over the rice, then add half of the chicken, spreading it out over the rice. Sprinkle on more onions and raisins, add the other half of the rice, sprinkle with the remaining saffron and milk, top with the rest of the chicken, onion and raisins. Slowly add the quarter cup of chicken stock, pouring it down the sides of the dish so it doesn't disturb the layers. Tightly seal the casserole with foil over the dish, then a lid on top of that. Bake at 350˚ for 20 minutes, until the liquid is mostly absorbed. To serve, turn the entire dish out onto a serving platter , mound it up in a large bowl, or serve straight from the baking dish. For a festive occasion, cashews, pistachios, or slivered almonds can be sautéed and sprinkled on top.

Serves: 6
Prep. time: 15 minutes
Cooking Time: 55 minutes

Chicken Biryani

Tandoori Chicken Kabobs

TANDOORI CHICKEN KABOBS

Tandoori Chicken Kabobs (Murgh Tikka)

Tender, richly seasoned chicken chunks. In India, Murgh Tikka is served on a bed of lettuce with lemon wedges, as a main dish with roti or other flat breads. It also works well as a flavorful appetizer.

2	whole (4 half) chicken breasts
3/4	tsp. ground coriander
3/4	tsp. ground cumin
3/4	tsp. paprika
1/2 - 3/4	tsp. garlic powder
1/8	tsp. powdered ginger
1	pinch ground cardamom
1	pinch saffron
1	TB water
1	Cup plain yogurt
2	TB lemon juice
1/2	tsp. salt
1/2	tsp. red food coloring (optional)
4	TB (1/2 stick) butter
24	thin metal or wooden skewers (if using wood, be sure to soak overnight in water to prevent them from bursting into flames)

In a medium-sized bowl, mix spices with water, let stand while boning and skinning the chicken. Cut the chicken into 1/2" cubes. Add the yogurt, lemon juice, salt and food coloring to the spices in the bowl, mix well, then add the chicken pieces and stir to coat. Cover tightly with plastic wrap. Refrigerate for at least 2 hours. Overnight is even better, but even an hour or two in the yogurt marinade will tenderize the chicken. Preheat oven to 475˚. Put the chicken on the skewers, leaving 1/2" between the pieces– usually 5-6 to a skewer. Balance the skewers across a glass baking dish, which will catch any drips. Melt the butter in a small pan or a bowl in the microwave. Brush or drizzle the kabobs liberally with melted butter. Place in the oven to cook for 12 minutes. Be careful not to overcook, or the chicken won't be as tender. Depending on the size of the baking pan, the chicken may have to be cooked in 2 batches. Serve warm out of the oven, or let come to room temperature.

Serves: 4 for lunch, 6-8 for appetizers
Prep. time: 20 minutes
Cooking time: 12 minutes

And the Creative Cook Tosses in a Recipe for Change:

TUNA WITH CURRY SAUCE

Tuna with curry Sauce

Curry Sauce:

1	TB butter
1	TB curry powder
1	TB wasabi powder
1/2	tsp. powdered ginger
1/2	tsp. garlic powder
2	TB water
1 1/2	tsp. soy sauce
1/2	Cup mayonnaise
1/2	Cup sour cream
1	Cup plain yogurt
1/2	tsp. salt
2	tsp. honey
2	tsp. rice vinegar
1	lb. dry pasta— vermicelli or angel hair, cooked and drained
2	TB olive oil
3	TB rice vinegar
1	TB finely minced, fresh cilantro (optional)
6	8 oz. tuna steaks canola or olive oil
1/2	tsp. powdered ginger
1/2	tsp. garlic powder
1/2	tsp. ground white pepper
1/2	tsp. white sesame seeds

In a heavy-bottomed sauce pan, melt the butter over medium heat, then add the curry powder. Cook for 1 minute, stirring occasionally, then remove from heat. In a small bowl, combine the wasabi powder, ginger, garlic, water and soy sauce and set aside. To the curry/butter pan, add the mayo, sour cream, yogurt, salt, honey and rice vinegar. Return to very low heat, stirring now and again. Just before tossing with the pasta, stir in the wasabi/soy mix.

For the tuna, lightly coat both sides of the tuna with oil. Sprinkle with the ginger, garlic, white pepper and sesame seeds. Grill over high if using an electric stove or griddle, or medium high if using a gas or charcoal grill. Grill to desired doneness (about 3-5 minutes per side), turning once. Toss the pasta with 6 TB of the curry sauce, olive oil, rice vinegar and fresh cilantro. Serve the tuna with the pasta and Tomato salad. Drizzle 1 TB sauce over each serving of pasta and put the rest of the sauce in a gravy boat on the table for those who can't resist.

Prep. time: 15 minutes
Cooking time: 15 minutes
Serves: 6

Tomato Salad

1	pt. grape tomatoes
2	TB olive oil
1	TB balsamic vinegar
	pinch garlic powder
	pinch dried oregano
	pinch dried basil
	pinch whole fennel seed
1/2	tsp. sugar
1/4	tsp. salt

Halve the tomatoes lengthwise. Mix together the oil, vinegar and seasonings. Pour over the tomatoes and let sit for 10 minutes before serving.

In many ways we settled into our path with the Johnny Cash party story. With our first issue we already had an idea what we wanted to be, it was just a matter of getting to a place where we had a strong enough belief in our idea. Johnny Cash was a part of us finding our way to that place.

one PARTY

JOHNNY CASH— THE PARTY

The time is right to celebrate the life of The Man In Black. His music alone is enough to make for a great time, but with Johnny Cash there is so much more. His life was not an easy one. He was a private man, yet his struggles were public because he refused to be merely an image. Though he rose from rural poverty to international super stardom he carried with him the knowledge of what it meant to be a sharecropper's son. From North to South, Presidents to prisoners, he sang his songs for all of us. And in doing so used his stardom and his voice to speak for those whose voices had been forgotten. Plus, he loved good food.

THE 50TH ANNIVERSARY OF
THE MAN IN BLACK

MUSIC, MOMENTS MAYBE EVEN

Parties start with a spark, the spark gets fed, the flames burst forth, and the whole thing takes on a life of its own. Like socks, no two parties are exactly the same, but they all start with the energy of the hosts and hostesses, and the caring attention that makes a guest feel "to home" as Gram used to say. So give some thought to the menu, get yourself energized, and greet those guests!

MUSIC

Plan the music - can't say it enough - theming the party relies so much on music, but there's more. High energy music that your guests recognize at least some of provides both a comforting ambient noise level to help them settle in and relax, and the energizing force to get the party going. Let's not forget those potential sing and/or dance along moments throughout the evening that may become some of your best party memories.

Think about the guests - high school kids? Your oldest friends? A Reunion crowd you don't know too well? - and do a little planning according to what you know about the group.

AND MENUS...
A SOUVENIR.

Energize yourself before the first guest even arrives - Whatever it takes for you - loud music works well to Pump it Up, as it were (that's an excellent choice, btw).

If you have a high energy level greeting the guests, they'll give it straight back to you and the party is off to a roaring start.

Having a great soundtrack is essential in pulling off a party theme. We created an individual sound track for each area of the party. Guests entered to the sound of "Walk the Line" playing in a continuous loop on the front porch. The living room ran Johnny Cash video clips on the television while the patio had a mix of classic country with an underscore of carnival midway sound effects. The kitchen Diner jukebox was loaded with Johnny Cash 45's and the basement prison area played "Johnny Cash Live at Folsom Prison" with an occasional siren thrown in for good measure. Even the restrooms had their own sound track, a continuous loop of "The Mercy Seat".

No need to worry about expensive sound systems. We just borrow boom boxes and small shelf stereos from friends to place in each area.

The Man in Black

Well, you wonder why I always dress in black,
Why you never see bright colors on my back,
And why does my appearance seem to have a somber tone.
Well, there's a reason for the things that I have on.

I wear the black for the poor and the beaten down,
Livin' in the hopeless, hungry side of town,
I wear it for the prisoner who has long paid for his crime,
But is there because he's a victim of the times.

I wear the black for those who never read,
Or listened to the words that Jesus said,
About the road to happiness through love and charity,
Why, you'd think He's talking straight to you and me.

Well, we're doin' mighty fine, I do suppose,
In our streak of lightnin' cars and fancy clothes,
But just so we're reminded of the ones who are held back,
Up front there ought 'a be a Man In Black.

MOMENTS

Plan the Moments - yes you can, at least some of them. We are about food, so many of our 'moments' revolve around the little theatrical bits inherent in the cooking and serving of food. For Johnny Cash, the Carnival fryer area with John manning the vats was a crowd pleaser - the golden bubbles, the spattering sounds, the lifting and draining of the awesome chicken and catfish, and then, of course, the eating. We've found you don't want everything out at once - a short wait for a food item makes people more excited about receiving it and more invested in watching it cooking.

Sno Cones and Cotton Candy - nothing more awesome than watching a kid's face as he's watching a friendly teen wind him up his very own cotton candy.

Sweet Summer Corn Bread

This is the nicest corn bread, as it stays moist and sweet, never dry and crumbly. Perfect served with anything Southern, from fried chicken to ribs.

3	Cups flour
1 ½	Cups yellow cornmeal
1 ⅓	Cups sugar
3	TB + 1 tsp. baking powder
1	tsp. salt
2	sticks butter
2	eggs
2	Cups milk
1	TB vanilla extract

Preheat oven to 350°. Grease a 9"x13" glass baking dish. In a large bowl, combine flour, cornmeal, sugar, baking powder and salt. In a separate bowl or small saucepan, melt the butter. Whisk the eggs lightly while the butter cools a bit, then add the eggs, milk and vanilla extract to the butter. Make a well in the center of the dry ingredients and pour in the mixed liquid, stirring lightly until just blended. Don't over-mix or the bread won't be as tender. Pour the batter into a greased 9"x13" glass baking dish. Bake in the preheated 350° oven for 45-50 minutes, until bread has risen a bit, is golden brown and springy to the touch. Let cool for at least 20 minutes before slicing.
Yield: 24 squares. Prep time: 10 min.
Baking time: 45-50 min.

Southern Style Baby Back Ribs

Spice Rub:

2	TB coarse flake salt
1	TB brown sugar
1	TB ground black pepper
2	tsp. Hungarian sweet paprika
1	tsp. rubbed sage
1	tsp. garlic powder
1	tsp. onion powder
½	tsp. ground nutmeg
¼	tsp. cayenne pepper
¼	tsp. medium hot crushed red pepper
2	racks baby back ribs (about 2 ½ lbs. each)
2	Cups Barbecue Sauce

Sift together all the spices except the crushed red pepper, which should be added after sifting. Peel the skin off of the bone side of ribs. Rub both sides of the ribs with the spice rub, heavier on the meaty side. Place the ribs in a shallow roasting pan and roast in a low oven (220°) for 3 hours. You may need to cut the racks in half to fit in the pan. The key is not to get the bones too hot, as that can cause the ribs to fall apart. You can roast the ribs a day ahead and refrigerate them until you are ready to finish them on the grill.

In a kettle-style grill, light about 70 coals, heat for about 20 minutes until they are hot and gray. Split the coals in half and spread to each side. Place a disposable aluminum pan in the middle to catch the drippings. Fill the pan with ½ inch of water to help keep the ribs moist.

If you would like the ribs to have a smoky flavor, make a foil packet with 1 cup of dry wood chips. We used a combination of hickory and apple. Be sure to punch some holes in the top of the packet.

When the coals are hot, place the wood chip packet directly over one pile of coals. Cover the grill leaving the top and bottom vents ¼ open. After 5 minutes, arrange the ribs bone-side down in the center of the grill so they are not directly over the coals. Cover and cook about 15 minutes. Give them an extra 5 minutes if they are coming out of the refrigerator. Turn the ribs over and lightly brush the bone-side with warmed BBQ sauce. Cover and cook for 5 minutes then turn the ribs over again and brush a heavier coating of BBQ sauce on the meaty side. Cover again and let them cook for another 10 minutes.

The ribs will hold nicely in a warm oven (170°) for up to 2 hours.

Tips: Cut the ribs into 2 or 3 rib portions prior to putting them on the grill. It's not as messy and everyone gets a crispy end piece. You can fit 2 or 3 racks of ribs on a 22" kettle grill. If you are making more than one batch, add 3 coals to each side and leave the grill uncovered for about 5 minutes to let the coals heat up. Remember to make a fresh wood chip packet.

Prep. time: 10 min.
Roasting time: 3 hrs.
Grilling time: 30 min.
Serves: 10-12 as an appetizer, 4-6 as a meal

Southern Style BBQ Sauce

2	TB vegetable oil
1½	Cups onions, chopped
2	cloves garlic, minced
1	6 oz. can tomato paste
2	tsp. beef soup base or bouillon (2 cubes)
½	Cup honey
3	TB lemon juice
1	tsp. Tabasco sauce or your favorite hot sauce
3	Cups water
1½	tsp. ground black pepper
1	tsp. kosher salt
1	tsp. onion powder
1	tsp. garlic powder
½	tsp. white pepper
½	tsp. cayenne pepper

In a large skillet, heat oil. Add chopped onions and sauté for 3-5 minutes. Add minced garlic and cook for a minute. Add tomato paste, beef base, honey, lemon juice and hot sauce. Stir to make a paste, then add water and mix well. Add remaining spices. Bring to a boil. Reduce heat and simmer uncovered for 30-45 minutes, stirring occasionally. Cook to desired thickness.

Prep. time: 10 minutes. Cooking time: 30-45 minutes. Yield: about 5 cups.

 Christmas lights strung outside add a wonderful ambience to any party – they make you feel as though you're stepping back in time. We used them to add to the feeling of a carnival midway.

If you're lucky you've got a handyman in the family to help you make a Ring of Fire. We used a metal tube, welded in a circle, with holes drilled in the top. Blue tubing goes from the propane tank (hidden in a festive box beside the pool) to the ring which is floating on styrofoam blocks in the pool. It's a lot of work, but the lighting ceremony alone was worth the effort.

Blueberry Pie

Fruit pies are wonderful, but many cooks don't attempt them for fear they won't turn out. This crust is the most forgiving thing in the world, and the arrowroot coating for the berries makes for thick, juicy filling every time.

Crust: Makes 2–9" pie crusts
2	Cups all-purpose flour
1	Cup butter or shortening
1	tsp. cream of tartar
1	tsp. salt
½	Cup milk

Crust topping:
1	large egg–white only
1	TB. water
2	TB. sugar (for sprinkling on top - we like to use vanilla sugar)

Filling:
4½	Cups fresh blueberries
3	TB. arrowroot starch
¼	Cup cool water
⅔	Cup granulated white sugar
½	tsp. pure vanilla extract
1	TB. butter (optional)

Wash the blueberries, drain thoroughly, discard any mushy berries and place remaining berries in a large bowl. In a small bowl, combine arrowroot starch and water, whisk thoroughly to blend. Add sugar, mix again. Pour the mix over the blueberries, making sure to scrape it all out. Add vanilla extract, then mix gently with a wooden spoon to thoroughly coat the berries. The berries need to sit in the sugar mix for at least 15 minutes, which is about as long as the crust will take. Stir the berries gently every so often as you are making the crust.

Start preheating the oven to 450° right when you start the crust. To prepare crust, cut the butter into small bits–it doesn't have to be cold for this easy crust, but it shouldn't be warm to the point of melting. Add the dry ingredients, beat or mix by hand to combine (or use a food processor to make it even easier), then add the milk in a thin stream, mixing until thoroughly blended. Divide the dough in half. Sprinkle a wooden board with flour, place half of the dough on the board, sprinkle the top of the

dough with flour too. Starting from the center of the dough ball, roll out gently to form a larger and larger circle. Flip the dough once when you are about halfway there, sprinkle again with flour. This will help keep the dough from sticking when you move it from the board to the pie dish. Place the pie dish (we use glass), next to the crust. The crust should be rolled a few inches larger than the dish, to allow for the sides. Gently pick up the edge of the crust, and drape it over the side of the rolling pin. Roll the dough loosely over the rolling pin, then unroll over the pie plate. Make sure to eyeball the crust and set it down over the plate with room to spare on all sides. You can move it if you must, but it's easier just to set it down right the first time.

Gently pat the crust into place, then trim the edge so only about half an inch of crust is overhanging. Don't add the blueberry filling until the top crust has been rolled out. Repeat the rolling process for the top crust. Whisk the egg white and water together, then brush the bottom crust with about half the mixture. Gently stir the blueberries one last time, pour gently into the pie shell. Dot with bits of butter if desired, then place the top crust on. Cut the edges off, then fold both crust edges under and press gently into the rim with your fingers–or use a pastry tool if you are into designs. Vent the crust with a few pokes with a fork, then brush the top with the remaining egg white. Sprinkle generously with sugar and place on the center rack in the preheated oven. Bake at 450° for 10 minutes, then reduce heat to 350° and bake 40 minutes, at which point the pie should be golden brown. Place a cookie sheet on the bottom rack of the oven while it is preheating, as this will catch any drips from the pie. Sometimes the edge of the pie has a tendency to get dark brown. To prevent this, you can lightly press a ring of tinfoil over the outer edge of the pie crust for the first 10 minutes of baking, then remove it when you turn the oven down to 350°. After 50 minutes of total baking time, remove the pie from the oven and cool on a rack. Pies really must cool for 6-8 hours before cutting; any less and the filling won't be set, (though it will still taste wonderful if you just can't wait).

Yield: 1 pie: 8-12 pieces. Prep. time: 30-40 minutes. Baking time: 50 minutes.

MOMENTS

Pie - Pie Pie Pie. Everyone loves pie, and the great thing about pie is you can make it a day ahead, freeing up party day for other things. Now you might think having the pies all sliced up and ready to go on individual plates is what the people want, but it isn't so. People just love to watch pie in the act of being cut and served, it is one of the greatest of the small food theatre moments, even if it means they have to wait a minute to have their very own serving delivered by the friendly waitress helper.

Other moments can be the making of a special drink, a short speech by the host (or in our case the lighting of the Ring of Fire), and the opening of different areas. The booking procedure for the prison bar was one such great moment - though the lines got a little longer than we'd like, and the booking agents worked up a sweat, the Folsom prison bar was oh so worth it. Not to mention the Lanyard and Tin Cup, which brings us to the Souvenirs (see page 215 for really cool souvenir ideas).

Give a little thought to crowd flow. If people will be arriving over an extended period and the space is big, it helps the party develop if the guests are clustered in one area. We started with the Carnival Space outdoors - great for the kids, perfect while the sun was up, lots of chances for the guests to interact, just an awesome way to get things rolling. That way the excitement built for the opening of the Diner or the Prison Bar later in the evening when there were enough guests to fill multiple areas.

Pecan Pie

Crust: makes crust for one 9-inch pie
1	Cup plus 2 TB. flour
½	Cup butter or shortening
½	tsp. cream of tartar
¼	Cup milk

If you are using butter instead of shortening, cut it up into small pieces into a bowl. It does not have to be cold for this recipe, but it should not be very soft. If using shortening, just put it in the bowl in a lump. Add the dry ingredients, mix well with a fork. While mixing, add the milk in a thin stream and continue mixing until well blended. The pastry may still be very wet and sticky; if this is the case, add more flour by the tsp. until you are able to form it into a ball. Sprinkle your rolling surface with flour. Place the dough in the center, sprinkle it with flour and begin to roll out the pastry. Use short strokes from the center out, forming a circle. Turn your pastry occasionally to prevent sticking. Roll the pastry out until it is about 1 inch larger than your pie plate inverted over the pastry. Fold the pastry in half and then in half again. Lift it into your pie pan and gently unfold it. Ease the pastry into the pan, gently patting it into place. Trim the overhanging edge to extend about half an inch. Roll this under and make a nice decorative edge to your pie.

Preheat the oven to 375°. Mix the flour and sugar in a small bowl and set aside. In a medium bowl, beat the eggs with an electric mixer. Add the butter, salt, flour/sugar mixture, corn syrup, and vanilla. Beat until well mixed. The butter may not be fully mixed in, but that's ok. You will probably have small pieces of butter floating on the top. Stir in the pecans. If you would prefer the pecans to be broken up, you can beat them in with the rest of the ingredients. We gave you a range of pecans, 1-2 Cups, depending on your preference. Pour the mixture into the unbaked pie shell. You may want to put a strip of aluminum foil around the edge for the beginning of baking to prevent over browning of the crust. Remove this after the first 10 minutes. Bake at 375° for 10 minutes then lower the oven temperature to 350° and bake for an additional 50 minutes. The pie will set as it cools.

Filling:
2	TB. flour
½	Cup sugar
3	eggs
½	Cup butter, very soft
	dash of salt
1	Cup light corn syrup
1	tsp. vanilla extract
1-2	Cups pecans

Prep. time: 20 minutes
Baking time: 1 hour
Yield: one 9 inch pie

Most cities have a variety of party rental companies. We worked with one of our local companies to rent the popcorn wagon, cotton candy and sno-cone machines. These rental companies also carry all of the supplies from popcorn, oil and popcorn bags, to sno-cone syrup and cotton candy floss (sugar), making the entire process painless.

Get local kids to help out. You can use the help – they can use the money. Plus, they're fun to have at parties!

Buy paper diner baskets at your local warehouse club store for a real diner feeling.

COTTON **CANDY**

FREE! FRESH ROASTED CORN-ON-THE-COBB

FREE! CAT FISH NUGGETS

Whatever you serve, make sure it's easy to carry so people can walk around and enjoy the party.

Rental tents and tables decorated with party store pennants and bright paper are an easy way to make festive carnival booths. Add a couple of computer generated signs to the booth and you've got the beginnings of a midway.

As kids, we would always get the neighborhood together and produce an MDA Carnival. These were promoted through a local television station and the Muscular Dystrophy Association and were always tons of fun. As adults, we used that childhood experience and expanded on it to create our County Fair Midway for the party.

Jambalaya

Simply delicious, great for a party.

1	TB flour
2	TB oil
1	large onion, diced
2	cloves garlic, finely chopped
1	green pepper, diced
4	chicken thighs
1	Cup diced ham
2	Andouille sausages, sliced
2 ½	Cups chopped fresh tomatoes
1	can diced tomatoes
2 ½	Cups chicken stock
1 ½	Cups uncooked rice
½	tsp. salt
½ -1	tsp. Tabasco sauce (depends on the heat level you like)
1	TB sugar
1	Cup shrimp (we used medium-sized, cooked, frozen shrimp and defrosted them before adding to the jambalaya), peeled and de-veined

In a large skillet, heat the flour and oil until brown, stirring constantly. Add the onion, garlic and green peppers, and continue to sauté. Toss in the chicken, ham and sausage, cook about 5 minutes to brown a little. Then add all the remaining ingredients except the shrimp. Cover and let the pan simmer for 20 minutes to cook the rice. Stir from time to time to prevent the rice from sticking. Then add the shrimp and continue to cook for 5 more minutes (if you are using fresh shrimp, cook for 10 minutes). Serve hot from the pot with extra Tabasco or hot sauce for those who like extra heat!!
Serves: 8-10. Prep. time: 10 minutes. Cooking time: 45 minutes.

MOMENTS

People love to have their picture taken with the guests of honor, so make sure they're at the party! A copy store can reproduce pictures in extra-big sizes, which you then spray-mount on to foam core (found at most art, craft or office product stores) and cut out with a box cutter or exacto knife. Be careful though, they sometimes get into the food!

Some parties just cry out with a need for costumes and Johnny Cash was one of those parties. The southern diner wouldn't be complete without waitresses in classic waitress uniforms. We also wanted the prison booking experience to be one of the most memorable of the evening. After a little internet searching we found actual California Department of Corrections Officer jumpsuits that made the mugshot experience a reality. All of our costumes were purchased for less than $60.00 each.

MENUS

People love to eat, and food is an important part of any party. The most important thing is to not run out of absolutely everything.

Any one item, well, it can go fast, and if you missed out on meatloaf because you were still trying to hit those balloons with darts at the carnival, oh well. But there should always be something that there is more than plenty of - something that makes good leftovers, you personally like it (ribs), or it's great to send home with guests as an added bonus nibbler (fried chicken pieces, pie, sub sandwich hunks).

Think about the theme of your party, the time of year and the guests involved. Children need simple food choices, and they love sweets; teens tend toward the polar opposites of incredible heavy meat eaters who can down 4000 calories without a second thought and total vegetarians who actually don't much care for vegetables. So for the most part, allowing them to assemble their own meal from multitudes of choices works best. Adults are easier, just make sure to offer something pork free and something meat free, and you're golden. We don't much figure people are really dieting on a party night, but still, it makes good sense to offer some tasty veggie trays and keep the dips low fat - they taste great that way anyway. Also, leave the mayo dressings on the side, and keep the portions of any one item reasonably on the small side.

The key is just making sure everyone has a beverage and a nibbler they enjoy, because it helps them have fun and relax, and it shows you care about them as a guest.

Keeping serving sizes small serves two purposes, it allows guests to sample their way through the evening without getting overstuffed, and it may encourage them to try something they wouldn't necessarily order a full portion of, and find they like it!

Also, it is important to consider the table space or lack thereof. If there aren't tables or places to set a plate, knives are out - you can't hold a plate and use your knife. So keep the food "fork friendly", like a pasta salad, serve finger food like burgers or catfish nuggets or better yet, for an outdoor party, food with a handle like grilled meat on a stick or chicken drumsticks. We kept our plated food in the diner area, where there were plenty of tables.

At the end of the night, and that can be late, it's great to bring out a platter of sandwiches that has been waiting in the fridge - turkey on a nice roll, salami on rye, whatever - it's a nice way for the last guests to wind up the evening and get ready for the ride home.

And it's great to have some leftover for the next day.

Iron Pot Chili

A Johnny Cash Special. He would add more hot peppers, but said this is great for a party when the ladies are present.

2	lbs. sirloin steak
3	TB oil
1	onion, diced
2-3	TB medium-hot chili powder
½	tsp. ground cumin
1	TB sugar
½	tsp. thyme
¼	tsp. sage
2	tsp. garlic powder
2	tsp. onion powder
2	28 oz. cans whole tomatoes
1	TB tomato paste
2	cans dark kidney beans, drained
2	cans light kidney beans, drained

Heat the oil in a stock pot. Dice the steak into small pieces then fry until brown. Add the onions and continue to cook until the onions are golden. Toss in the seasonings and cook for 2 minutes. Swirl a knife around in the can of whole tomatoes to break them up a bit. Add the canned tomatoes, tomato paste and the beans to the pot. Cover and continue to simmer until the meat is tender (1-1½ hours). You may need to add more water if it is too thick. Taste and add salt if necessary.

Prep. time: 30 minutes.
Cooking time: 1-1½ hours. Serves: 8-10

SOUVENIRS

A party souvenir is really sweet. It doesn't have to be big - use your imagination. A cup, a lanyard, maybe a photo with a cardboard frame or a CD of the party theme songs - the possibilities are endless, but just like a kid at a birthday party, it's so nice to go home with a treat bag.

Meatloaf

The perfect winter comfort food, especially when served with mashed potatoes and peas. Just like Mom used to make.

1½	lbs. ground chuck
1	medium onion, minced
2	eggs
1	15 oz. can stewed tomatoes
2	slices of bread, torn into small pieces
¼	tsp. ground black pepper
2	tsp. salt
1½	tsp. chili powder
1½	tsp. mustard powder
½	tsp. garlic powder

Preheat oven to 350°. Put the ground chuck in a roomy bowl. Add the onion, eggs, and tomatoes and mix well. It is easiest to mix meatloaf with your hands. Add the bread bits, pepper, salt, chili powder, mustard powder, and garlic powder and mix thoroughly. Put the meat mixture in a loaf pan and pat it to fill the pan evenly. Place the loaf pan on a cookie sheet and bake at 350° for 1½ hours. Every 30 minutes, check the meatloaf and remove any excess fat with a turkey baster.

Serves: 6. Prep. time: 10 minutes.
Cooking time: 1½ hours.

Mushroom Gravy

This vegetarian delight is great when paired with our Johnny Cash meatloaf. Start to roast the veggies, then put the meatloaf in the oven after 30 minutes so they finish cooking together.

8	oz. button mushrooms, sliced
6	oz. portobella mushrooms, sliced
1	medium onion, diced
2	tomatoes, diced
¼	Cup olive oil
1	TB seasoned salt
6	Cups water
4	TB flour
4	TB butter

Preheat the oven 350°. Slice the mushrooms and place with the onions and tomatoes in a big bowl. Drizzle with the olive oil and toss with the seasoned salt to coat. Place in a deep roasting pan and bake for 1½ hours, turning the veggies over every 30 minutes. While the veggies are roasting, mix the flour and butter together. When all the veggies are cooked, add the water and cook for another 30 minutes. Strain the gravy and thicken with the flour/butter mixture.

Prep. time: 20 minutes
Cooking time: 2 hours
Yield: 3 cups gravy

The basement bar area was fully decked out with prison bars in our re-creation of Folsom Prison. Our guests were the prisoners, complete with mugshots and tin cups. The bartenders were on the other side of the bars and dressed as correctional officers. The bars were made with plastic conduit and simple lumber. We had a small stage on one end of the room with a single microphone just in case Johnny decided to stop by and perform.

FOLSOM PRISON
BOOKING
OFFICE

Menomonee River Prisonway
061105077
June 11, 2005

PENZEYS
JOHNNY CASH PARTY
FOLSOM PRISONER NO.
061105 077

INMATE

The magic of Johnny Cash, beyond his music, was in his openness. In his refusal to hide his own struggles in life, he found a way to connect with a much wider circle. It wasn't his thing to use his microphone and spotlight to tell right from wrong, or how to live our lives. Instead he used his celebrity to shine a light on, and give a voice to, those who otherwise would have been beyond the view of the popular culture of the day. From the experience of his own early life in rural America, far beyond the footlights, he understood just how much of the richness and strength of this country goes unseen.

As a food magazine committed to the idea of variety, and willing to go down roads less traveled to find it, we found a kindred spirit in Johnny Cash. It is great to share a culture and have things in common, but many times the best songs or even the best recipes come from looking beyond our own experiences and connecting with those who have different tales to tell. In that connection we just might find that we have far more in common with far more people than we had thought possible. Plus with so many different peoples, ideas and experiences out there, we never have to worry about there being a shortage of new and tasty recipes.

Restorative Justice

What Would Johnny Cash Do?

After our Johnny Cash party we sent a check off to the American Diabetes Association. Cash in his later years suffered from the disease and it seemed a good tribute, but somehow it did not seem to be enough. We found ourselves asking what would Johnny Cash do if he was us? It did not take long to figure if Cash had a food magazine he would use it to promote prison reform. Not something we had spent a lot of time thinking about before we started working on this piece, but it did not take us long to find some good people out there with some good and proven ideas on how to make prisons work better. And wherever you find people working to make things better, you know good recipes will be close at hand.

Sautéed Chicken

"This recipe was adapted from a recipe of Sylvia Sebastiani's, who owned Sebastiani Vineyards with her husband, August. Their son, Don, is a dear friend and was a colleague of mine in the California State Assembly for many years."

—Pat Nolan

6	boneless, skinless chicken breasts
2	TB butter
2	TB olive oil
	salt and pepper to taste
2	cloves garlic, pressed
1/2	Cup chopped onion
1	Cup white wine

Season the chicken with salt and pepper. Heat butter and olive oil in frying pan, add chicken and cook until golden brown, about 5-6 minutes per side. Remove chicken pieces and keep warm. Add garlic and onion to juices in the pan and fry for about 1 minute. Add the wine to deglaze the pan. Cook for 2 minutes then return chicken to pan and cook 8 or 9 minutes longer, uncovered. Serve immediately.

Prep. time: 5 minutes. Cooking time: 20 minutes. Serves: 6

Note: For bone-in, skin-on chicken breasts, fry chicken for about 25 minutes, turning often. Follow the remaining instructions.

Pat Nolan

T he FBI raid on California Assemblyman Pat Nolan's office came in 1988. It took the US Attorney's office 5 years to figure out an indictment. He was reelected twice during this period yet when the indictment came, he was facing a maximum of 21 years and a minimum of 8 for taking a campaign contribution from an FBI sting operation. His son Jamie was just 10 months old and his daughters Courtney and Katie were 5 and 4. "With my children so young, I had to choose. I would miss most of their childhood at a minimum or all of their childhood if it was the maximum. Or say I did something I didn't do and instead do the sentence of 33 months. So to me the calculus was easy. My family is too important to me." He took a plea deal and admitted to racketeering. He ended up serving 29 months. "I sucked it up and went to prison and I was able to come home to my family while I was still young."

Family has always been important to Pat Nolan. A fifth generation Californian, he grew up with eight brothers and sisters in Los Angeles and even attended the same parish grade school as his grandparents. At the age of 4 he started to learn Irish dancing. "My parents were looking for a healthy activity for my sisters when they became teenagers. They saw an ad for the Irish Rovers and my sisters joined. When the rest of us came along we were taught by my sisters and we joined the group." Once all of the Nolan children were old enough to dance they formed their own group. "We were The Nine Dancing Nolans." The pay wasn't great but the venues they danced had some perks. "Disneyland, before they had the electrical parade, used to have groups come march in the parade and then perform in the park in return for free services. We did that probably thirty or forty times." They went on to be regulars at the Los Angeles International Folk Dance Festival. The family kept the group together for many years but alas, children get older and they stopped performing in the early 1960s. Pat was elected to the California State Assembly in 1978 at the age of 28 and The Nine Dancing Nolans, well, most of them, danced again. "When I got in the Assembly we started up again. I used to throw a St. Patrick's party every year and my brothers and sisters and I would dance."

Maybe the negotiations involved in being the sixth of nine dancing children caused Pat to become active in politics. He worked on all four of Ronald Reagan's campaigns for President. "Few people remember he ran in 1968 against Richard Nixon." He even had the honor of being a delegate for Reagan at the 1980 Republican National Convention. He was elected to his assembly seat eight times over the course of 16 years and was known for being tough on crime. "I was a very strong law and order guy. I carried several tough-on-crime bills and supported the dramatic expansion of prisons in California." Part of this toughness came because his old neighborhood in L.A., where three generations of his family grew up, was changing. "The neighborhood had deteriorated and crime was just awful. So I supported all those policies because I thought it would make people safer. Then I went to prison and saw that those policies

In the Oval Office, behind President Bush, as he signs the Prison Rape Elimination Act.

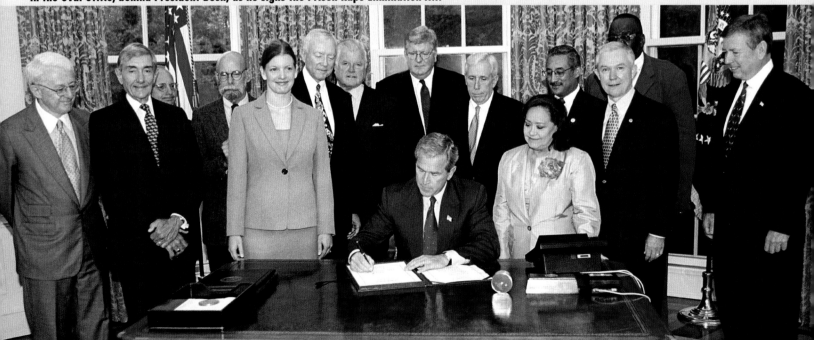

Eight of the Nine Dancing Nolans. My brother Jack was missing. We are wearing costumes that my mom and sisters designed and sewed.

Left to right: Maureen, Tom, Michele, Pat, Mike, Bijou, Denise, and Bill

I had been so ardently advocating really weren't turning the folks' lives around. People weren't coming out of prison better than they went in."

After finishing his sentence he began a career with and eventually became president of Justice Fellowship, which is the criminal justice reform arm of Prison Fellowship Ministries, founded by former Nixon aide Chuck Colson of Watergate fame. "Now I'm in a position to help talk to conservatives, because I am a conservative Republican, about these policies we've all supported that aren't really working. Aren't making us safer."

> "I supported all those policies because I thought it would make people safer. Then I went to prison and saw that those policies I had been so ardently advocating really weren't turning the folks' lives around. People weren't coming out of prison better than they went in."

Pat says that he did not change his philosophy, "But I changed how I apply that philosophy. As I sat in prison I wondered, as a conservative who was suspicious of the bureaucracy and how ill served the public often is, why would I turn a blind eye to the corrections department? And why wasn't I holding them accountable for public safety? We entrust them with tens of thousands of inmates each year yet two out of three end up committing a crime and are rearrested within three years. Well, in any other business that would be called a failure."

Irish Soda Bread

"My dad was all Irish, and my mom had no Irish blood. Yet, they both encouraged us to celebrate our Irish heritage. We did Irish dancing together as the "Nine Dancing Nolans" at such venues as the Los Angeles Philharmonic Auditorium and Bovard Auditorium. We performed on numerous occasions at Disneyland, including many St. Patrick's Day celebrations. Irish Soda Bread is a special treat we always enjoyed."

2	Cups flour
1/2	Cup sugar
2 1/2	tsp. baking powder
1/4	tsp. salt
1/4	Cup butter
1	Cup raisins
2	TB caraway seeds (or to taste)
1/2	Cup buttermilk pinch of baking soda
1	egg

Preheat oven to 350°. Sift together the flour, sugar, baking powder, and salt. Cut the butter into slices and work into the dry ingredients with your fingers. Place the raisins in warm water for a few minutes, then drain and dry them and add them to mixture. Add the caraway seeds.

In a separate bowl mix together the buttermilk and baking soda. Add the egg and mix again.

Gradually mix wet ingredients into dry. Add more buttermilk if too dry, more flour if too wet. Mix with a spoon. Then, with floured hands, shape into a small round ball. Place on a greased and floured pan and do not flatten, leave as a round ball. Draw a cross on top with a dull knife and bake at 350° for 40-50 minutes. When golden brown, remove from oven and wipe top with a little butter and sprinkle with a little bit of sugar as well.

Prep. time: 15 minutes
Baking time: 40-50 minutes
Yield: 1 large loaf (about 8 servings)

"The purpose of the corrections department is not stronger prisons. It's a safer community. Prisons exist so we're protected. Now part of that function is quarantine, we keep people locked up so we're safer. But the sad thing is a lot of the folks we lock up aren't dangerous. We're just mad at them. They haven't followed our rules." Today he is promoting the Second Chance Act in Congress. It is designed to assist states in retooling how their departments of correction function. "The preparation for release should begin when they enter prison not just at the back end. It should all be aimed at equipping them to make good decisions when they get out. Part of the bill is funds to help establish mentoring programs in communities so there's a loving member of the community that has met with them in prison and helped them develop a life plan. The mentor helps hold them accountable when they get out and helps them think through the challenges they face when they get out."

Getting out is surprisingly difficult. An example comes from Pat's testimony in front of Congress in 2005.

Shortly after my release from prison to the halfway house, some friends took me to lunch at a local deli. The waiter came over to take our orders. Everyone else told him what they wanted, but I kept poring over the menu. My eyes raced over the columns of choices. I knew that I was supposed to order, but the number of options overwhelmed me. My friends sat in embarrassed silence. I was paralyzed. The waiter looked at me impatiently. I began to panic. How ridiculous that I wasn't able to do such a simple thing as order lunch. Finally, in desperation I ordered the next item my eyes landed on, a turkey sandwich. I didn't even want it, but at least it put an end to this embarrassing incident.

For two years I hadn't been allowed to make any choices about what I ate. Now I was having a hard time making a simple choice that most people face every day. If I had this much difficulty after only a couple of years in prison, think how hard it is for those inmates who haven't made any choices for five, ten, or fifteen years. And what about those who didn't have the wonderful home, the loving family, the strong faith and the good education that I had? They face a baffling array of options and little preparation. Is it any surprise that so many newly released prisoners make some bad choices and end up back in prison?

Pat's wife Gail was instrumental in holding their family together. Pat spent ten months in a Dublin, California correctional facility, about 70 miles from his home in Sacramento. Later he was moved to Spokane, Washington, 1700 miles away. She was able to bring the kids to visit every two months thanks to friends contributing their frequent flyer miles. Pat says, "My wife was just terrific at keeping me a vibrant part of their lives." She regularly sent their homework for him to look at. She would even send the books the kids were reading so he could read them at the same time and discuss them during phone calls. However, they could not share meals together and the food in prison was as Pat describes it,

"Awful... I never had a tomato slice. It was always the butt ends. I don't know where the center pieces went but they sure didn't come to us." Because of those years apart, the Nolan family rarely misses a meal together. "Virtually every night we gather around the table. It's very important to them and to me."

And he still occasionally kicks it up with some of the Nine Dancing Nolans. "Yeah but I'm a lot heavier (laughing). It takes its toll on my knees. It doesn't leave you. It's like riding a bicycle." His experiences in prison haven't left him either as evidenced by his life's work and his memories. "Dropping my daughter Courtney off at kindergarten before I went to prison... I literally drove from there to the prison... I mean it's still painful to think about."

❶

With wife Gail and children Courtney, Katie, and Jamie at Disney's California Adventure in 2002. They were 14, 13, and 9. They are 17, 16, and 12 now.

With brother Tom, on the right, when they were altar boys at St. Paul's Parish in Los Angeles.

A proud moment riding as USC's mascot, Tommy Trojan, in the 1974 Rose Parade

The Agoure family on their ranch. My great-grandparents, Kate and Pierre Agoure, are in the center and my grandmother, Bijou, is on the right holding the reins of the burro.

Enchiladas

"My great-grandparents Pierre and Kate Agoure, pictured below, were pioneers in southern California, and owned a large ranch in what is now the city of Agoura. Each New Year's Day they held a grand fiesta for the family and all of the ranch hands. The menu consisted of pots of chili con carne, tamales, enchiladas, beans, rice and salsa."

Sauce:

1	TB chili powder
2	tsp. salt
3	Cups water
1	large can (29 oz.) tomato sauce
3	cloves garlic, pressed
1	medium onion, chopped
1	tsp. Mexican oregano
1	tsp. sugar

Mix ingredients and simmer for 20 minutes.

36	6-inch corn tortillas

1	Cup canola oil
1½-2	lbs. cheddar cheese, grated
2	5.75 oz. cans black olives, sliced
3	medium onions, chopped (about 1¼ Cups)
6	green onions, sliced

Preheat oven to 350°. Heat the oil in a small frying pan. Dip tortillas, one at a time, into hot oil and then briefly into sauce to coat. Place coated tortillas on a baking sheet, and sprinkle cheese, olives and onions into center of each. Spoon sauce over this mixture and fold sides of tortillas into center. Arrange in baking dishes. Spoon more sauce over outside of enchiladas, and sprinkle with remaining cheese and green onion. Bake at 350° for 10 minutes or until warmed through.

Prep. time: 45 minutes
Cooking time: 10 minutes
Yield: 36 enchiladas

Janice Little

"I firmly believe that every person coming out of prison needs someone, who is not their family member, to help hold them accountable, to be there to encourage, and to walk them through things. "

Janice's mom, Andrew and Eric Little at Andrew's 8th grade graduation.

Janice and Andrew at Disneyland, Christmas 2005

Family Portrait. Taken in 2002 the day after Eric came home.

"I'm proud of my husband... I am. He's made some poor choices but he readily accepts the responsibility for them. He doesn't put it off on anybody else. He takes full responsibility," says Janice Little about her husband Eric. They have been married for 17 years yet he has spent most of that time behind bars. "He was convicted of armed robbery although he did not have a gun. He had a Black and Decker drill." Janice has kidded Eric about that and it has been her sense of humor, and even Eric's, which has helped this couple stay together and raise their son Andrew.

Eric and Janice had known each other for a long time. Janice is the daughter of a Baptist minister and began teaching Sunday school at the age of 15. She first met Eric when teaching Sunday school near Fresno, California. Years later when they met again, Eric had custody of his six month-old baby boy Andrew. Janice had been engaged before but never married and at that time was medically not able to have children. "I had made peace with that. It was God's will. Then here came Andrew. I looked at it from this perspective, God knew I always wanted kids and I couldn't. And God knew Andrew would need a mother. So He met both of our needs. Andrew is the joy of my life."

Soon she would be needed more than she imagined. Two years after they married Eric fell off the wagon and began doing drugs, which led to his power-tool armed robbery. He was convicted and sent to prison for 11 years. His incarceration eventually led Janice to a new career path. "When Eric went in the first time I found myself helping people out around the prison." She was well dressed, spoke English and was able to get her questions answered. But others were having a hard time. "I stood there and thought – there is such a need here. I'm able to ask and get my questions answered but many of these people are not. They are really in need of a support group for women going through the system." She started a support group for women with incarcerated family members. Soon she had over 40 people in her group so she started a second group. "I would not let the women talk about the crime. The crime was not the important issue. The issue was we were all in the same boat dealing with the system and dealing with emotional issues."

She hosted these groups while raising Andrew and working her full-time job when Prison Fellowship Ministries opened an office in the Fresno area. Part of their mission was to create support groups similar to Janice's. Eventually they were brought under the Prison Fellowship umbrella and Janice was working full-time for them as a field director. Janice says Eric jokes with her about it: "I'm so glad my incarceration can enhance your ministry."

Yet her most important job is raising Andrew. She knew that Eric's childhood was not good. His father was killed in San Quentin during the riots that eventually led to the San Quentin Six trials. His stepfather was physically and emotionally abusive. It was important for her to break this chain. Though much of the

me out today, I would go straight to an inpatient drug program. Even though it had been 11 years, what did they really do to help me in here?" Janice goes on, "Drugs and alcohol are really at the root of why most people are in prison. To me it would make far more sense economically and socially if we spent the money putting these men and women into intense programs rather than spending all of it incarcerating them forever." And Andrew, speaking of his dad, summed up the plight of many who are released from prison, "I loved having Dad home but it was almost like he was an alien. As hard as he tried, he just didn't quite fit in." **Continued on page 227**

With Eric's family, Christmas 2005

time she is raising him alone, Eric still helps, "My son and husband have a wonderful relationship. He is one of the best long distance dads. I remind him that he is a better dad sometimes in there than many of the dads that live at home." And she has support from her family. Her parents always treat Andrew like their own flesh and blood.

Janice says her mom and dad are both good cooks but "Dad's mom was phenomenal. There was nothing she could not make." Her grandmother taught her to make cornbread dressing which she served to Eric's family one holiday. She took the leftovers to her grandmother to try and Grandma told her, "I really think it's not too good!" Janice's aunt was there and told Grandma not to hurt her feelings. "Well she needs to know the truth," she said. "She's got to improve. It's not too good." She proceeded to explain to Janice how to fix it. Janice adds, "We are a big loving family, very forgiving, but we pretty much tell it like it is. I think that's part of why it's been easy for Andrew and all of us to deal with Eric's situation, because we are so up front."

Andrew is enrolling in college this fall and plans on following his father Eric's footsteps only so far. Eric fought in the "little war" in Grenada, which isn't considered "little" if you fought in it. Andrew will join the Air Force ROTC at Fresno State. His mother couldn't be happier. "I'm very proud of Andrew and the young man he is turning out to be... against some pretty tough odds."

Tough odds indeed. Eric was released in 2002 but 10 months later got mixed up in drugs again and pulled another robbery. He was sent away for another 20 years. Janice says they have learned a lot about aftercare. As Eric says, "If they were to let

Janice and Eric

Janice, Andrew, Pops and Grandmom with Aunts in Branson, MO.

Chicken and Grape Salad with Cashews

2	TB fresh lime juice
1	TB Major Grey's Chutney, minced if necessary
1	small garlic clove, minced and mashed to a paste with 1/4 tsp. salt
2	TB sour cream
3	TB vegetable oil
1-2	drops Tabasco sauce
1 1/2	Cups shredded, cooked chicken
1	Cup seedless green or red grapes, sliced
1/2	Cup roasted, salted cashew nuts
2	Cups watercress sprigs, coarse stems discarded, rinsed well and dried

In a small bowl, whisk together the lime juice, chutney, garlic paste and sour cream. Add the oil in a stream, whisking until the dressing is emulsified. Whisk in the Tabasco. In a separate bowl, toss the chicken and grapes with the dressing and let marinate for 15 minutes. In a salad bowl, toss together the chicken mixture, cashews and watercress. Add salt and pepper to taste.

Prep. time: 15 minutes
Cooking time: 15 minutes to marinate
Serves: 4

"Drugs and alcohol are really at the root of why most people are in prison. To me it would make far more sense economically and socially if we spent the money putting these men and women into intense programs rather than spending all of it incarcerating them forever."

Mom's Meat Loaf
Eric's Favorite

1 1/2	lbs. lean ground beef
1	Cup quick-cooking oatmeal
1	8 oz. can tomato sauce
1	Cup chopped onion
2	eggs, beaten
1/2	tsp. salt
1/2	tsp. pepper
1	tsp. garlic powder

Mix all of the ingredients together and press into a glass loaf pan. Top with ketchup and let set overnight in the refrigerator. Bake at 350° for 1 hour and let cool 10 minutes before slicing.

Prep. time: 15 minutes plus overnight chilling
Cooking time: 1 hour
Serves: 4-6

Scalloped Potatoes

"They all love my scalloped potatoes," says Janice. After trying them we have to agree.

2	Cups milk
8	medium potatoes, peeled and thinly sliced
1	medium onion, chopped
2	TB flour
1	tsp. salt
1	tsp. pepper
1	stick butter, melted
2	Cups shredded cheese
16	saltine crackers, crushed

Preheat oven to 325°. Layer, in a 9x13 casserole dish, all of the flour, 1/3 of the salt and pepper, 1/3 of the potatoes, 1/3 of the butter, 1/3 of the onion, and 1/3 of the cheese. Continue layering to fill the casserole dish. Pour the milk into the dish and cover the top with the cracker crumbs. Bake, uncovered, for 1 hour at 325°. Cover with foil and bake for another 15 minutes.

Prep. time: 30 minutes
Cooking time: 1 hour 15 minutes
Serves: 8-10

Carrot Cake

This cake was served at the baby shower when Janice got custody of Andrew. The frosting may soak in which only makes it more delicious.

2	Cups flour
2	Cups sugar
2	tsp. baking soda
2	tsp. cinnamon
1	tsp. salt
1½	Cups vegetable oil
3	eggs
1	small (8 oz.) can crushed pineapple
2	tsp. vanilla extract
2	Cups grated carrots (about 4 medium carrots)
2	Cups unsweetened, shredded coconut
1	Cup nuts

Preheat oven to 375°. Sift together the flour, sugar, baking soda, cinnamon and salt. In a separate bowl, beat together the oil, eggs, pineapple, vanilla and coconut until well mixed. Combine the dry and wet ingredients and mix well. Fold in the nuts. Pour into a 9x13 greased pan or a 9-inch tube pan. Bake at 375° for about 45 minutes. If using a tube pan, bake for 20 extra minutes. Remove from oven and let cool.

Frosting

1	Cup sugar
½	stick butter
1	TB white corn syrup
½	Cup buttermilk
½	tsp. baking soda
½	tsp. vanilla extract

Combine all of the ingredients in a heavy-bottomed saucepan. Bring to a boil and cook for 5 minutes, stirring constantly. Pour over the cake while frosting is still hot.

Prep. time: 30 minutes
Cooking time: 45-65 minutes
Serves: about 16

Janice Little

Helping those men and women fit in will be Janice's life work. "I firmly believe that every person coming out of prison needs someone, who is not their family member, to help hold them accountable, to be there to encourage, and to walk them through things. It's hard for a man or woman to have been gone for so long and come out and say 'I don't know how to do this, I don't know how to do that.' They need someone to bounce things off of. We are finding how helpful it is if a mentor can be assigned to an inmate a year before they get ready to get out so the mentor can develop that relationship with the individual and be there when they get out. Then continue that relationship at least for a year after release."

Janice has much to be proud of - her family, her son, sticking with her marriage. She makes a difference in people's lives. "What a shame it would be to go through something like this and not use it," says Janice. "I believe God allows us to go through things and then He expects us to use it to help somebody else. Part of my healing is being able to help somebody else because of what I've gone through."

The Rolen Family Disneyland Trip (Janice's Family)

Scott Koser

On Christmas Day 1996, 26-year-old Scott Koser went snow tubing with some friends. As he zoomed down the icy hill he hit a homemade jump that some kids had made weeks before. "I was airborne and I was kind of laughing to tell you the truth," says Scott, "because I thought, 'Oh… this is going to hurt,' and when I hit, immediately it was nothing from the waist down. Maybe a slight tingly feeling for a split second and then everything was gone."

Scott had landed at the bottom of the hill, backwards, against a U-shaped dried up riverbed. He shattered three vertebrae in his back and the impact was so great that bone fragments cut into his spinal cord. "I knew immediately that I was paralyzed. As much as I knew that, in my mind, I was trying to thrash around and get up right away. Your initial reaction is to get up and start walking. I just couldn't do it, not to mention that the back pain was extremely severe at that point. I was just seeing stars all over." He knew his life had just changed forever. "I mean it didn't take anyone in the medical field to tell me that, well, I'm in a lot of trouble. I knew it was going to be a permanent thing just by the way I felt when I hit."

A three-month stay in the hospital included surgeries to install 13-inch titanium rods on both sides of his spine and to reconnect nerves that are 1/1000th of the size of a human hair. In the hospital he was encouraged to work out and develop his upper body so he could deal with his life to come. After two years of complete paralysis from the waist down, something bordering on miraculous happened. "I noticed one day I started getting some very light movement in my legs." Scott began to work even harder. Though he has no balance at all and no movement in his ankles or feet, he has enough strength in his quadriceps that he can pull himself up and get something off a shelf in the kitchen. "If I hang on to something, I can stand up and can hold myself up for probably a good 15 or 20 minutes before my legs start shaking."

He feels very lucky. "It was a godsend. I do counseling and it's something that you just don't see too often. It's an improvement I thank my lucky stars for. It has allowed me to become much more mobile than what we would term a typical paraplegic. I am in a very, very select category of what the doctors call a walking paraplegic. It was a one in a million thing."

Though his employer prior to the accident was supportive and willing to make accommodations for him, he decided not to return to his old job. "My doctor and I had determined years ago that I likely would not be able to return to work full-time ever again, as much as I would like to. I was raised with a very strong work ethic and I was a very hard worker but the pain issue is such that I'm usually spending my days off recuperating from the back pain. And that's something that unfortunately is always going to happen." Scott is now working part-time as an aid to the activities director at a senior center. His other part-time job

Scott and his dog Shep two years after his accident. Scott wanted to get more active and, "Nothing will get you active like a puppy," he laughs.

Scalloped Corn

1	16 oz. can creamed corn	¼	Cup sugar	
1	8 oz. can corn niblets, undrained	½	Cup flour	
2	eggs, beaten	¼	Cup cornmeal	
1	Cup sour cream	2	TB sugar	
½	Cup melted butter	1	tsp. baking powder	

Preheat oven to 375°. Combine all of the ingredients together. Pour into a greased 9-inch square casserole dish. Bake at 375° for 40 minutes or until the center no longer jiggles when the dish is shaken.

Prep. time: 12 minutes
Cooking time: 40 minutes
Serves: 9

is volunteer counseling in the spinal cord unit of the hospital where he recuperated. "It's a very fulfilling thing. I certainly would never give that up no matter what."

The counseling gives him perspective on his own situation. "If this had to happen to me, thank God it happened at the time it did. I've had 26 years of my life to know what it was like to be an active normal human being, and I can't imagine going through puberty and my teenaged years dealing with something like this." What is hard for Scott is seeing the 8 or 9-year-old children who have been in a car or diving accident. "You know, their whole lives have been changed at that age and they're not going to be able to experience their teenage years like they should. So at least I felt like I had plenty of years to live my life fully."

Scott rented an apartment for a short time after the accident but decided to stop throwing money away and he bought a small house. "My first home was a great starter home but I could sit in the middle of the kitchen and practically touch all four walls with my arms spread. So you can imagine, being in a wheelchair, it was no fun to cook or bake at all." When the time was right, Scott sold his starter home and built a place that would work better for him, especially in the kitchen. "Once I decided to build I wanted to make a kitchen that would work for me. I would never claim that this is an accessible kitchen to someone else in a wheelchair just because I can hold on to the counters and stand up to get product out of the cupboards. So really, it's basically a normal kitchen. One of the things I insisted on was I wanted a design that did not have an island. In a wheelchair, it really is very difficult to work around an island. The second thing I insisted on was a stove that did not have controls in the back." There is only one thing he wishes he could change: "I still wish someone would design a range-oven with a side opening door. It's difficult to reach past the door especially if

something is in the back."

The larger kitchen has opened up a new world for him. "I just wanted a kitchen that was big enough for me to get around in. Now I'm having a blast. I call my mom on just about a daily basis and say 'Ma, how do I bake this or that,' because I'm still learning. But I can say without reservation that baking is becoming my favorite hobby. I absolutely love it."

His love of baking comes honestly. "For 30 years, my father was a commercial food photographer. He was working for Ideals Publishing and they moved to Tennessee and he decided not to go. So he started his own studio and started freelancing. The cool thing was, growing up, my father would do the food shots and my mother did the cooking and baking." This was a benefit for his friends as well. "Mom was always, always cooking. And she was always cooking or baking for an army. I was one of these guys in high school and early college, I'd bring home 12 or 15 friends at a time, unannounced, because I knew she always had food and I knew she always had a ton of it. The best thing too was to eat the food after the photo shoot because, well, ya gotta eat it. If you liked eating, it was the best household to grow up in. There was always the smell of baking or cooking."

The world outside of Scott's kitchen poses many challenges. If you are going to cook, you need groceries. "I can push a regular cart as long as it doesn't get too heavy. I can maneuver a regular cart with one hand while pushing my wheelchair with the other. Or I'll set my feet on the bottom rack of the cart and push myself along that way. If there's something up on a top shelf that I don't feel comfortable with standing up and reaching, I have never been somewhere where someone has not offered to help me."

"...I consider my life normal now. It's a different kind of normal. A lot of times I kind of forget I'm in the wheelchair because it's become a part of me; it's part of my body. This is my personal space."

Beef and Cornbread Bake
(See recipe on next page)

Beef and Cornbread Bake

Cornbread:

½	Cup flour
¼	Cup cornmeal
1	TB sugar
1	tsp. baking powder
½	Cup milk
2	TB vegetable oil
1	egg, slightly beaten

Beef Filling:

1	lb. ground beef
1	tsp. dried oregano, crushed
¾	Cup picante sauce
1	can (8 oz.) tomato sauce
1	can (about 16 oz.) whole kernel corn, drained
½	Cup shredded cheddar cheese

For Beef Filling: Preheat oven to 375°. Cook beef and oregano in a skillet until browned. Drain off the fat. Add the picante sauce, tomato sauce, and corn. Heat through. Stir in the cheese. Place in a shallow, 2 quart baking dish.

For Cornbread: Mix dry ingredients together in a large bowl. In a separate bowl, beat the egg and add milk and vegetable oil; blend together. Add egg mixture to dry mixture and mix until just moistened. Spread over the beef filling. Bake uncovered for 25-30 minutes until the crust is golden brown. Let stand for 10 minutes before serving.

Prep. time: 25 minutes
Cooking time: 30 minutes
Serves: 6

Scott at his 8th grade confirmation with his Godfather Terry Mitton and Terry's wife Mary Ann.

For Scott, the fun part is getting to the store. "I love to drive," he says. His car has a motorcycle-like throttle mounted to the steering column. It twists to accelerate and it is attached to a lever that you push forward to apply the brakes. "It's connected to a bar that attaches right to the brake pedal," says Scott. "So when you push that bar you are actually pushing on the brake pedal. Anyone can get in the car and drive it regularly. It does not affect the gas pedal or brake pedal at all." Getting in and out is something of a process. "My outdoor wheelchair is slimmer and quite a bit lighter. It disassembles in a matter of 10 or 15 seconds. I can recline my front driver's seat once I get in and reach down to the wheelchair, which is outside of the car, pull the wheels, put all the parts in the passenger side front seat and lift the body of the wheelchair over me as I'm reclined. Then just bring my seat back up and go." It is well worth the effort. "Anyone who's in a wheelchair will tell you, when they are in a vehicle driving, they consider themselves completely normal. It's the coolest feeling to have, especially if you are feeling down. As much as I try to put the best construction on everything, you're going to have days where you're just not feeling good. Get in the car and start driving and everyone around you who sees you in the car never knows you're in a wheelchair. You just blend right in with everyone else."

Blending right in is not easy in a wheelchair, especially out in public. "In the ten short years I've been in a wheelchair I've seen a vast improvement in public facilities. Every new construction public building has to be wheelchair accessible, which means flush entry and wide doorways." He adds, "Still, there is a huge difference between wheelchair accessible and

Scott and his parents, Jerry and Diane, at a wedding reception in 2000.

wheelchair friendly." Going to a restaurant for example. "Sure, a restaurant can be wheelchair accessible with a flush entry you may be able to get in. Once you enter, they have the tables so jammed packed in that the staff has to either move a table or ask someone who's dining to please get up and move for a minute so they can get me through. Or they may have to bring me in through the back door or the kitchen. That tends to draw attention and I do not like attention being drawn to me in that kind of way."

He loves to travel and a recent trip out east opened his eyes. "The state of Massachusetts really takes their senior citizens and people with disabilities very, very seriously. I would have to say that in my experience with traveling, which since I've been in a wheelchair I think I've been to nearly every state, I would say Massachusetts is the number one state. They are making even their historical buildings very accessible. They are doing it in such a way that they maintain the integrity of the original buildings but in the back they have a nice wheelchair ramp or a flush entry."

He was able to adapt his home and his vehicle to his situation. Society is slowly making things better but there is one thing that can't be adapted. "Of all the things I do miss, it's going deep into the woods, forests or fields, hunting or fishing. I was always really into that. Now I have to enjoy things sort of from afar, sort of from the outside looking at the whole big picture instead of getting deep down and into the woods. Other than that, I have to say I have so much more now than back before the accident that I really don't miss anything else.

"Now looking back on it, ten years have gone by and I consider my life normal now." He adds, "It's a different kind of normal. A lot of times I kind of forget I'm in the wheelchair because it's become a part of me; it's part of my body. This is my personal space."

Above: Scott and his best friend Chris enjoying time at the lakefront last summer. Chris was an EMT and was with Scott when his accident happened. **Left:** Scott is a true animal lover.

Blueberry Muffins

¼	Cup butter, softened
2	eggs
½	tsp. salt
1	Cup sugar
2	Cups Flour
2	tsp. baking powder
1	tsp. vanilla
½	Cup milk
2	Cups fresh or frozen blueberries

Preheat oven to 350°. Cream together the butter, eggs, salt, and sugar. In a separate bowl, mix flour with baking powder and sift into the first mixture, alternating with adding the milk. Blend in the vanilla and gently fold in the blueberries. Pour into greased muffin pans and bake for 25 minutes.

Prep. time: 15 minutes
Baking time: 25 minutes
Yield: 12 muffins

Jennifer Longdon

Jennifer prepares a fruit and cheese platter in her new accessible kitchen.

There are plenty of challenges in the kitchen. "That's the biggest problem for me as I only have this little bit of body left that works," says Jennifer Longdon. "And it works very well but for example, if I lean forward, I have to brace myself so I can't lean forward and use both hands to pick up something heavy." She uses a rolling cart that is the same height as her modified countertops for moving things around the kitchen and for chopping or other prep work. "That was my thing. How will I take a roast out of the oven? How will I move a pot of spaghetti or pot of soup? How will I get dirty dishes from the kitchen table back to the sink to wash? How will I cook a Thanksgiving dinner? This rolling cart we came up with has really saved me. I can move it around and it just works for everything. I love it."

On the evening of November 15, 2004, the lives of Jennifer and her fiancé David Rueckert changed forever. "I woke up the next morning in inten-

sive care and my son and ex-husband were there," Jennifer recalls. "My son was holding my hand and the doctor came in and told me I was paralyzed." But there was a bit of good news. "I also found out David was still alive."

The police are still investigating what happened to Jennifer and David but this much is certain. On the way home from teaching Tae Kwon Do, David was shot three times leaving him permanently blind. Jennifer was shot once in the back, damaging her lungs and shattering ribs and vertebrae.

Of that night Jennifer recalls, "There was a man who was an off-duty paramedic and I remember talking to him and I told him David was dead, I was dying and please tell my son I love him."

Jennifer and David are two of the tens of thousands of Americans who survive gunshot wounds every year. Sent to different hospitals, they were separated from each other until a brief visit at Christmas. Released from the hospital two months later, Jennifer and David's lives were very different. "He went to his son's home. I went to live with friends. In the interim there were no paychecks, we lost the house, lost the car. The dogs went into foster care." Despite help from friends, it was frustrating for Jennifer to not be able to control her life. "I had no idea where the furniture went, had no idea what I had. Some friends went over and packed up my house based on what I told them to keep or not to keep. It was just a few months ago that I finished unpacking boxes and found out what I had."

It was eight months after the incident before they were finally living together again and it wasn't until a year post injury that they were alone and could start to rebuild their lives as

Rosemary Roasted Sweet Potatoes

3	large sweet potatoes
2	TB olive oil
	salt and pepper, to taste
3-4	cloves garlic
3-4	sprigs fresh rosemary (or 1 tsp. dried cracked rosemary)

Preheat oven to 350°. Cut the sweet potatoes into large spears. Brush with olive oil and season with salt and pepper. Strip the rosemary from the stems and sprinkle over sweet potatoes. Bruise the stems (partially crush to release flavor) and lay them over the potatoes. Smash the garlic cloves with the back of a knife and lay them, unpeeled, on the potatoes. Bake 45-60 minutes or until tender. Remove garlic and rosemary stems before serving.

Prep. time: 5 minutes
Cooking time: 15-60 minutes
Serves: 4-6

Pork Chops with Apples and Onions

4	6 oz. pork chops
	salt and pepper, to taste
2	TB olive oil
1	large Granny Smith apple, peeled and chopped
1	large onion, peeled and chopped
3	cloves garlic, peeled and chopped
1	Cup apple juice

Season the pork chops with salt and pepper. Heat the olive oil in a large pan, add the pork chops and brown on both sides. Remove chops from the pan and add the apple juice and stir to lift any browned bits from the pan. Add the chops, apple, onions and garlic to the pan, cover, and simmer until cooked, about 20-30 minutes.

Prep. time: 5 minutes
Cooking time: 20-30 minutes
Serves: 4

"Preparing food together, playing in the kitchen together and cutting and chopping and nibbling and talking and that sort of thing. It's such a bonding to prepare a meal like that. I love doing it."

"I love food and I refuse to compromise. I'm not going to eat light…My philosophy is I'll just hike another mile."

a couple. "Our martial arts training came in there because you start off as a white belt and slowly, bit by bit, you gain skills and there are a lot of setbacks along the way," says Jennifer who had earned three black belts. "So I remember telling people that I'm a white belt again. It took me years to get to black belt and it will take me years again. That was the approach we took."

Getting back into the kitchen was high on Jennifer's list of priorities. "I love to cook and David and I, that was our ritual, preparing food together, playing in the kitchen together and cutting and chopping and nibbling and talking and that sort of thing. It's such a bonding to prepare a meal like that. I love doing it. And I honestly thought that was gone. Seriously, I would cry in the hospital thinking I

used to have such beautiful dinner parties and it's all gone now."

It wasn't all gone thanks to their perseverance and indomitable spirits. "I now cook every night. David helps when he's feeling well. He has actually made his signature meatloaf twice. It's a meatloaf that people say, 'When you make it, can I come over?' He definitely does some cutting and chopping. He lifts things for me that I can't lift and provides a lot of muscle in the kitchen when I need it."

The height of things in a regular kitchen presents problems. "Go into your kitchen, sit in a chair and imagine that you can't get out of that chair," says Jennifer. "Now realize what it is that you can't reach. You can't reach the top two shelves of the refrigerator, most of the upper cabinets are now useless for you, and on top of it things that are very low are difficult."

The solution for Jennifer was obvious. "In our kitchen, everything is lower. The cook-top sits in the middle of a peninsula. There is a seating area on one side and on the other side I cook. The controls are along the side so I don't have to reach over hot pans. My oven is built in and it opens like a microwave." One problem with everything being lower is that David is 6'5" tall. The solution was simple. When he cooks with Jennifer, he uses a rolling office chair.

"We eat very healthy," Jennifer adds. "We have very athletic minds. My cooking is simpler. I don't cook things with as many steps as I used to. I used to love really complex recipes just to do it. That's harder for me to do. It's harder for me to move around the kitchen, I have to think things through more carefully."

Keeping things clean for example. "I have to move by touching the wheels of my chair. When I have raw chicken on my hands and then touch the

Savory Oranges

3	large oranges
2	TB extra virgin olive oil
½	tsp. kosher salt
½	tsp. ground pepper

Wash the outsides of the oranges. Score the skin along one side so when the orange is sliced, there will be a handy slit in each slice, making it easier to eat. Slice the oranges into ¼-inch slices. Brush the olive oil on both sides of each orange slice. Sprinkle salt and pepper on one side of each slice. Lay flat on a large baking sheet or platter, salt and pepper side up, and refrigerate until icy cold, about 20 minutes. To eat, open at score, nibble the orange from the rind and enjoy.

Prep. time: 10 minutes
Cooking time: none
Serves: 3-4

Ceviche-Style Shrimp

Cooked shrimp in a tangy, salsa-style marinade. Perfect for parties.

1	lb. raw shrimp, peeled and deveined
6-8	lemons (juice of)
1	lb. tomatoes, diced in ¼-inch pieces
¼	Cup celery, finely diced
1-2	jalapeños, finely diced
½	Cup red onion, finely diced
2	TB minced garlic
2	TB chopped fresh cilantro
¼	tsp. black pepper
1	TB salt

Thaw shrimp under cool running water. Drop the shrimp into boiling water for 3-4 minutes, until cooked. Place in ice water to cool. Remove from water and mince. Mix the minced shrimp with the remaining ingredients and chill for 3-4 hours before serving. Serve with lots of avocado slices and lime wedges. Goes great with fresh corn chips or on a tostada shell topped with sliced avocado.

Prep. time: 15 minutes
Cooking time: 4 minutes
Yield: 1 medium bowl of shrimp salad which will make 8-12 good-sized servings for tostadas

Jennifer uses her "grabber" to reach the high shelves. "The grabber is great until you drop it and can't grab the grabber."

TENETS OF TAE KWON DO

여의 **COURTESY:** To be thoughtful and considerate of others. Tae Kwon Do students and instructors should be polite, and show consideration for others.

염치 **INTEGRITY:** To be honest and good. Tae Kwon Do practitioners should live by a code of moral values and principles

인내 **PERSEVERANCE:** To never give up in the pursuit of one's goals. Students should welcome challenges, because challenges cause us to grow and improve.

극기 **SELF-CONTROL:** To have control of your body and mind. A Tae Kwon Do student should practice controlling his actions and reactions.

INDOMITABLE SPIRIT: To have courage in the face of adversity. A Tae Kwon Do student should never be dominated by, or have his spirit broken by another.

백절불굴

wheels... you really have to think things through so you don't make a stupid mistake and end up making a huge mess or doing something that would make someone sick later on. I wash my hands so much while I'm in the kitchen and I keep little wipes so I can constantly wipe my rims while I'm cooking."

There is another reason to think things through. "Now remember, I can't feel either. So I have to be very careful not to accidentally touch my belly with a hot pot. It will sit there and I'll never know it happened. A friend of mine had an interesting story. After a while everything below your level of injury kind of disappears. It's almost not there most of the time. He was cooking and didn't think things through and put a hot pot of spaghetti right on his lap and wheeled it over to the sink. You can't feel it and you don't know you've done it."

"I love food and that's part of why I have to work out so hard," Jennifer adds. "I love food and I refuse to compromise. I'm not going to eat light. I'm going to enjoy the food that I enjoy and I'm not going to make any apologies for it. My philosophy is I'll just hike another mile."

David is still suffering chronic head pain but that does not stop the fifth-degree black belt and four-time Tae Kwon Do world champion from resuming his work in martial arts. "He has competed and he does train students on a very limited basis," Jennifer says. "It's hard but it's amazing what he can do. He can hear when they are not doing the technique properly. He'll say things like 'you're not breathing properly, you're not looking in the right place' because he can hear them stumble. It's amazing how right on he is when he is critiquing someone's form. He can't hear if their hand is open or closed but he can hear a lot of the rest of it."

In addition to teaching Tae Kwon Do, Jennifer was a well-known massage therapist and renowned spa consultant. She is now focusing on mak-

ing people's minds feel better instead of their bodies. "I've trained as a life coach and I'm looking forward to doing more disability advocacy. When I woke up in the hospital and started rehab, there were a lot of people who taught me how to get my body from here to there. But there was really no one there to tell me how to get my spirit from here to there.

"I understood from the start that my injuries were complete and they were permanent. I still also refuse to accept that. So I'm one of those. I'm working with research projects and I'm very involved and hoping one day to find some way to make some sort of accommodation to get us up and moving. I'm not going to say I will get up and walk or feel again. I might be able to stand which would make me very happy."

That would only be the beginning because Jennifer has bigger plans. Before their injuries Jennifer and David loved to hike to the top of a nearby mountain. "Piestewa Peak is the mountain I used to climb every day. It's a good 45-minute hike up. I still plan to climb that trail one more time. It will be with a neuron-stimulator or some sort of something but I am getting up that mountain one more time."

Jennifer washes up after another meal well prepared.

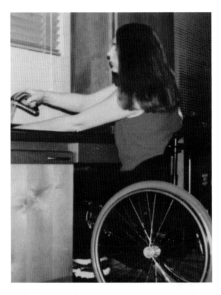

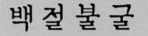

Stuffed Steak

2   1 lb. pieces sirloin, sliced in half length-wise
3   garlic cloves, coarsely chopped
6   Roma tomatoes, chopped into large pieces
2   Cups fresh spinach, coarsely chopped
     salt and pepper, to taste
2   TB olive oil
8   oz. tomato sauce
¼   Cup red wine
1   TB Worcestershire sauce

Preheat oven to 350°. We pounded the steak a bit to make it thinner and easier to roll, but that is optional. Sauté the garlic, tomatoes and spinach in a bit of olive oil and then let cool. Salt and pepper the steak. Spoon a line of the spinach mix down the center of each slice of steak (reserve the juice from the pan) and roll. Hold the rolls together with toothpicks or bamboo skewers. Heat an oven-proof skillet on the stove top with 2 TB olive oil, and quickly brown the rolled steak. Season the vegetable juices with salt and pepper, add tomato sauce, wine and Worcestershire sauce and mix, and pour over browned steak. Cover with foil and bake until cooked to your liking, about 30-45 minutes. Baste with juice often. Remove the steak to a platter and keep warm. Put the skillet on the stove over high heat and reduce the juice to the desired consistency. Spoon the sauce over the steak and serve.

Prep. time: 20 minutes
Cooking time: 30-45 minutes
Yield: 4 rolls
Serves: 4-6

Lynn Reed

Lynn & Don in Puerto Vallarta April 2006

a *TV Guide* but certainly not a legal document. That's 45% of the popula- tion." She goes on, "And yes, part of it is due to immigration. But only 11 million of that 93 million don't speak English. The rest were able to be tested in English. So we can't blame this on the immi- gration problem." Lynn doesn't want to play the blame game because as she puts it, "It's a national crisis."

Lynn got into her current position almost by accident. She was voluntarily serving on the board of directors for the Literacy Volunteers while running her account- ing business. She was asked to fill in for about six months until they found a new director. Her uncom- mon combination of college degrees, sociology and accounting, were a perfect fit and this year is now her tenth on the job. "The poster I'm staring at, that the staff made me, says 'The Longest Six Months in History.'"

Lynn has been married for 31 years to her husband Don who is a retired rancher. "Traveling is my thing," says Lynn. "I love to travel." They've visited far away places in Europe, Asia and especially Lynn's favorite place, Africa. Another "thing" is cooking but the long hours at the office interfere. "I love to cook but I don't have a lot of time to do it." She says Don enjoys cooking partly, "...because I'm here so much he has to do it to survive." She and Don do find time to cook and entertain friends on the weekends.

A native of Northern California, her father's job with Kaiser Aluminum caused her to spend much of her youth in Louisiana. "I grew up partly in New Orleans and Baton Rouge so cooking was bred into me at that point. To me that's the most wonderful food." She adds, "I'm not good on super hot but I like spicy. It was well spiced and that was the secret to it. I like good flavors."

Her real "thing" however, is literacy and adult educa- tion. The agency has almost tripled in size since Lynn took over. "We've gone from having one little center and a

"We need to assimilate the people that we have," says Lynn Reed, Executive Director of the Literacy Volun- teers of Maricopa County in Phoenix, Arizona. "We need to improve their educations so we don't have whole neighborhoods of poverty. We need to get them [undocumented workers] to a point where they are legally here to work, "says Lynn. "Whether we want to make it five years, ten years, whatever. It's so they're not looking over their shoulder, they're not in fear all the time, and they're paying taxes." She is not con- vinced that everyone wants to be a US citizen. "I don't know if we need to provide a pathway to citizenship. If it takes a compromise I could give in on that."

Lynn and her staff are "literally" on the front lines of this issue. Recent government statistics on literacy rates in the US are staggering. In the United States, 93 million adults read at a "basic" level or "below basic" level. Basic is defined as able to perform simple and everyday literacy activities. Lynn says that these folks "...could read maybe

Carrot Cake

2	Cups raisins
1³⁄4	Cups sugar
5	eggs
1½	Cups corn oil, cold
2½	Cups flour
2	tsp. baking soda
1	tsp. salt
1	tsp. cinnamon
1½	Cups pecans, chopped
1⅓	Cups apples, chopped
3	Cups carrots, grated

Soak the raisins in 2 Cups warm water and let stand for 5 minutes. Drain well in a colander and blot dry with a paper towel. In a roomy bowl, beat together the sugar and eggs. Slowly add the corn oil which has been cooled in the refrigerator. In a separate bowl, sift together the flour, salt, baking soda and cinnamon. Gradually add to the sugar/egg mixture and mix well. In another bowl, combine the pecans, apple, carrots and raisins. Add to the batter and mix well on low speed until just combined. Pour into a greased and floured 9x13 inch pan. Bake at 350° for 45 minutes. Ice with Cream Cheese Icing.

Cream Cheese Icing

1	8 oz. pkg. cream cheese, softened
2½	Cups powdered sugar
¼	Cup butter, softened

Place the cream cheese, powdered sugar and butter in a mixing bowl and beat until smooth. Spread over the top of the cooled cake.

Prep. time: 30 minutes
Baking time: 45 minutes
Yield: 18-24 pieces

lot of volunteer tutors to having three centers and being tied to one of the largest family literacy programs in the state." They take on the problem from two angles. "We do adult education which encompasses lots of things but essentially is for anyone age 16 or older who is out of school. We help people learn to read, we help them prepare for the G.E.D. exam and we teach people to speak English." The other program is called Family Literacy, which has an interesting approach. "We go on-site in the elementary schools and we recruit the parents of kindergarten age children." By assuring that the parents know how to read, they hope to create a

Puerto Vallarta 1986

July 2005
Blenheim Palace Woodstock, England, with friends Les and Barbara.

Botswana, Africa, October 2002 with our guide Chobe.

Lynn and her brother Kevin, 1952.

better environment for the child to learn at home. "A lot of families, you go into their home for the first time and believe it or not the written word isn't anywhere. There's not a newspaper, not a magazine, nothing." Lynn says just getting books and newspapers in the home can help. "The kids need that environment, they need to see it, be around it and the most important thing is they need their parents to participate in their education."

Which is exactly what Family Literacy tries to do. Targeting schools in poorer areas, they ask the administration if they would like a program in their school. "We pick the schools with the highest free and reduced lunch ratios. If 95% of the kids qualify for a free lunch because of their family's income level, then we know we are in the right school." The school needs to provide cooperation and a classroom. "Other than that we bring in a full-time teacher, a coordinator and a family liaison who works with all the families. The most important part is that the teacher becomes a part of the team that works with the children. Most of the schools are very excited to get a pro-

"We need to get them (undocumented workers) to a point where they are legally here to work, whether we want to make it 5 years, 10 years, whatever. It's so they're not looking over their shoulder, they're not in fear all the time, and they're paying taxes."

gram like this. But the challenge is the space, whether they have an extra classroom. You pick your spots where you think you can help people and hope that school has space." It can be difficult for working parents to participate but hopefully one of them is able. "They have to be really devoted to spending that 22 hours a week in school, same as their children. It's quite a commitment."

Of course reality always rears its ugly head and for Lynn that reality is money. Her accounting background helps them to cope with budget pressures. "Unfortunately family literacy is more expensive but it is a life changing event for the families that participate in it. It really serves to bring people out of poverty and out of the cycle. As an old social worker we always talked about the cycle of poverty but I have learned that there is a cycle of illiteracy too." Lynn thinks involving the family is not just important, it's necessary. "I love when they throw out statistics of the number of children living in poverty. The children aren't just living in poverty,

December 2004 8:00 am
Gourmet brunch after balloon ride over the plains of Masai Mara in Kenya, Africa.

Lynn taking pictures in Africa, October 1999.

the whole family is living in poverty." Whether they are immigrants or from the US, Lynn says parental involvement in education is key. "If their parents don't speak English there are already some challenges trying to live in the United States. So we teach the family literacy activities and we teach the parents how to help their kids in school because that's the part that is so necessary. A lot of parents don't understand how children learn. It doesn't matter if they were born in the US or in some other country."

Nationwide, the need for literacy services is great and the resources are stretched. "Every single program in Arizona and across the nation has a waiting list," says Lynn. "There are hundreds of thousands of people that we are not able to serve that have finally gotten the guts... because a lot of times it takes guts. If you're an adult and you don't know how to read, the

"Unfortunately family literacy is more expensive but it is a life changing event for the families that participate in it. It really serves to bring people out of poverty and out of the cycle."

hardest thing you can ever do is walk through our door. You do that and we have to turn you away because we don't have space." She adds, "We are nowhere near serving the adults in this nation that have figured out the only way to truly have a meaningful life is to be able to read well and have a high school diploma so that they can get a better job, so that they can support their families."

Lynn and others like her just try to win those little battles. Like the 50-year-old dyslexic man who was regularly tutored across the hall from her office. "I watched him start and he was not able to read at all. A year later I would walk by the door and hear him read from a book. It let me know that I was in the right place." To Lynn, reading isn't just fundamental. "It's such a precious thing. It opens up the world for you and it opens up opportunities."

Botswana Africa, learning about the elephants. October 2002

Sweet and Sour Basting Sauce

This recipe was given to me by my dear friends Al and Audrey of Baton Rouge, Louisiana. I have made this at least 100 times over the last 15 years. It is a family favorite.

2	TB salad oil
1	tsp. salt
2	TB diced green bell pepper
1	6 oz. can pineapple juice concentrate
1/3	Cup brown sugar
1/2	of a 2 oz. jar pimento
1/2	clove garlic
1/2	Cup wine vinegar
1	tsp. soy sauce

July 2004 Italy with friends Meredith and Tom.

Place all of the ingredients in a blender and process on high until thoroughly blended.

We used the sauce on pan-fried pork chops. We melted 1 tsp. of butter in a pan over medium-high heat, browned 3-4 pork chops on both sides, added 1/2 Cup of the sauce and cooked for 10 minutes, turning once. Heat the rest of the sauce and spoon over mixed vegetables or rice.

Prep. time: 10 minutes
Cooking time: 15 minutes for pork chops
Serves: 3-4

Chicken with White Wine Sauce

I developed this recipe soon after I was married, 30 years ago. It has been a great recipe for entertaining.

1	3 lb. chicken or 3 whole chicken breasts (bone-in, skin-on)
1½	Cups dry white wine
1	TB lemon juice
¼	tsp. black pepper
¼	tsp. paprika
¼	Cup melted butter
¼	Cup chopped green onions
¼	Cup minced fresh parsley
1½	tsp. salt

Divide chicken breasts or quarter chicken. Place chicken, skin side down, in a large casserole dish. Blend the remaining ingredients together and pour over the chicken. Remember—good wine makes even better chicken. Cover the casserole dish with foil and cook the chicken for 1 hour at 325°. After 1 hour, remove the foil and turn the chicken so that the skin side is up. Increase the temperature to 375° and bake for 30 minutes, basting often. After 30 minutes, increase the temperature to 425° and cook for an additional 30 minutes.

Prep. time: 20 minutes
Cooking time: 2 hours
Serves: 3-4

Sara Ocampo

For Sara Ocampo, leaving Mexico was not an easy decision. "In Mexico, it's beautiful," said Sara. "I love the city where I came from because of the weather, the flowers and everything." Her son Christian was already in America and encouraging her to come stay with him. Sara's teenaged daughter Sandra was with her in Mexico but Sara's elderly mother had recently passed away, so maybe the time was right. Finally, there was one overriding factor in her final decision to leave home. "Unfortunately for handicapped people, there are no places like in the USA," says Sara. "In Mexico I have to stay home. Here I can go places and do things and that's what I love about the United States."

Sara contracted polio when she was just a year old. "I was just learning to walk. I have always either used a walker, crutches or a wheelchair." People immigrate to the US for many reasons. Besides reuniting her family, for Sara, it was the freedom that America offers people with disabilities.

Christian and Sandra

Mother's Day 2004

Once in the States, Sara began doing clothing alterations for folks around the neighborhood. A skilled seamstress, she quickly found plenty of work and has developed it into her own business. She can do just about anything from simple alterations all the way to wedding dresses. "It takes me about a week to make a wedding dress," says Sara.

Sara and a friend at a wheelchair competition in Peru

Sara's mother and father with her niece Jessica on a hill overlooking her hometown

Pollo en Pipian (Chicken in Peanut Salsa)

2	lbs. chicken or pork (we used bone-in, skin-on, legs, thighs and breasts)
1/2	onion, quartered
2	garlic cloves, coarsely chopped
1/2	tsp. salt
12	dried guajillo chili peppers
2	TB corn oil
1/2	medium onion, chopped
4	garlic cloves, chopped
3	oz. peanuts
1	bay leaf
4	whole cloves

Place chicken in a stock pot and add enough water to cover the chicken. Add the onion, garlic and salt and simmer for 30 minutes.

While the chicken is simmering, open and remove stems and seeds from chiles. In a pan add the oil and fry the chiles, two at a time. They don't take long at all, so watch them carefully. Put the chiles in a blender. Add the peanuts to the frying pan and sauté, stirring frequently to prevent burning. When lightly toasted, add the peanuts to the blender. Add the onion, garlic and bay leaf

to the pan and sauté until nicely browned. Add more oil to the pan if needed. Put onion, garlic, bay leaf and cloves in blender with the chiles and peanuts. Blend with 6 ounces of liquid from the chicken pot until very smooth. Add pepper to taste. Place sauce in frying pan and cook to reduce to about 1 1/2 cups. To serve, coat chicken with sauce and serve with corn tortillas and extra sauce.

Prep. time: 1 hour
Cooking time: 30 minutes
Serves: 4-6

People around the barrio love Sara's cooking. Especially her pazolé says daughter Sandra. "My mom's friends always ask her to make pozolé for their birthdays." Son Chris says his mom's skills were passed down. "She loves to cook," says Chris. "She learned cooking by looking... from my grandmother." She moves around the kitchen with surprising ease despite her disability. "I tried one time to do what she does in the wheelchair," Chris says. "I couldn't."

Chris likes American pop culture because of the modern conveniences. "Like when you have a party, usually people say let's go to a restaurant or you buy things," says Chris. "But my mom likes to do everything. I say no, we can do it the American way. You can do a little bit of cooking and we can buy the rest. She says, 'No, no, no, I want to make it myself.'"

"My mom is my inspiration," says Chris. "She showed me that there are no limits."

Pechugas Verde (Green Chicken Breast)

1	8 oz. container sour cream
2	chicken breasts, skin-on and bone-in
4	poblano peppers
5	garlic cloves, chopped
2	large onions, quartered
2	TB butter
¼	Cup Chihuahua cheese
	chopped cilantro (optional)

Bring enough water to cover the chicken breasts to a boil and add chicken, garlic and onion. Simmer chicken breasts for 30 minutes; discard skin, garlic and onion when done. Blacken peppers over an open flame, such as a gas stove top, portable gas burner, or grill. Put peppers in a plastic bag or plastic wrap for a few minutes; uncover and remove skin and seeds.

Blend peppers and sour cream in blender. Melt butter in skillet and brown chicken breasts on high heat. Lower heat to low/medium. Pour sour cream/pepper mixture over chicken, and top with cheese. Cover with lid and simmer on low, until cheese is melted. Top with chopped cilantro.

Serves: 2
Prep. time: 10 minutes
Cooking time: 40 minutes

"I was in Europe for a couple of weeks visiting. I decided to come and see my aunt," says Christian Ocampo. "It was very exciting because everyone talks about the USA. I came and I decided to work so I could bring some money back with me." He found work in a local restaurant. "Then I decided to stay and my mom and my sister were in Mexico. You shouldn't have two women by themselves and that's why I wanted to bring them here."

Though Chris started out working in a restaurant, he has recently moved into healthcare. "I work for a health and wellness company. I focus a lot on the Hispanic community. Right now we are taking people to different places to learn how to exercise and make a better life." Many who come to the United States to work find isolation in their new surroundings, something Chris experienced firsthand. " I was depressed before my mom came. I think a lot of people get depressed because they are away from their families. They come for the American dream and end up

with something much less." A program, such as the one Chris works in, helps with those feelings and also puts people into positive social situations.

Sandra Ocampo was in high school when she and her mom came to the States. She is now hoping to win a scholarship to technical school to learn medical translation. When Sandra first arrived in the US she was in the hospital and at that time did not speak English. "I did not know what was going on," says Sandra. After learning the language she had a much better experience. "I was at the hospital with my friend and she did not speak English. So I translated for her and thought I like this. I like to help people."

Both Sandra and Christian speak nearly perfect English. "I had to learn English," says Chris. "I know it's not easy. It's a challenge. But I think that's what my mom taught me. Life is a challenge, that's what life is about. You deal with it and that's what makes it so fun and exciting."

"My mom is my inspiration," says Chris. "She showed me that there are no limits."

Making Pozolé

Pozolé is a traditional Mexican dish made for special occasions. It is commonly served with tostadas.

Arbol Chili Salsa

1   oz. dried arbol chili peppers, stems removed
    juice of 4 limes (½-1 Cup)
    dash of salt
1   TB corn oil

Sauté peppers in the corn oil for about 3-5 minutes, stirring occasionally, until crisp. Add whole peppers, lime juice, and salt to blender and process until smooth. Serve with pozolé.

CAUTION: This sauce is very hot.

Pozolé

Stock:

2	lbs. pork shoulder butt roast
1	gallon water
4	garlic cloves
½	onion
½	tsp. dried Mexican oregano
2	bay leaves

1	6 lb. 12 oz. can white hominy
9	dried guajillo chili peppers
	salt and pepper to taste
1	clove garlic, minced
¼	onion, diced

Rinse the pork. In a large pot, add water, pork, garlic, onion, oregano and bay leaves. Bring to a boil, and simmer for 2-3 hours to make stock. Once the meat is cooked through from simmering, strain stock and discard any onion, bay leaf, and garlic pieces. Bring the stock back to a simmer. Open the can of hominy, do not drain, and add to stock. While the hominy is simmering, remove the seeds from the guajillos, put in a separate pot with 2 cups of water, the minced garlic, and onion. Simmer to soften the guajillo peppers (approximately 5 minutes). Remove from heat and transfer to blender. Blend until smooth. Add this mixture to the pot of stock. Simmer for 30 more minutes. Do not over cook. Shred the meat for the soup. Top each serving bowl of soup with a bit of the pork. Serve pozolé with sour cream, arbol chili salsa, lettuce, avocado, Mexican oregano, lime wedges, and onion on the side.

Serves: 6-10
Prep. time: 30 minutes
Cooking time: 2-3 hours depending on initial simmer time

Al Parajecki

Al proudly shows off the fish he and his dad caught in Little Muskego Lake in the 1940s.

Here in Milwaukee, we're not much on Mardi Gras, but we're pretty big on Lent.

The Friday fish fry, a tradition in every corner tap, dates way back to the pre-Vatican II days of not eating meat on Friday – any Friday. Fish fries are big year 'round, but on those Lenten Fridays, where the old No Meat rule prevails, every parking lot is crammed and in every church basement, neighborhood tavern and family restaurant the fish is frying and the potato pancakes are flipping. All-you-can-eat fried lake perch with homemade potato pancakes, tangy slaw and marble rye is one of the best meals out there, which might not be what Lent is quite about, but you aren't eating meat, and that's the rule.

When we talk fish fry, we think of Al in the woodshop. Not only has he been to every fish fry in 2 counties, he's serious enough about Lent to make sure he's having the vegetarian offering on our Friday Soup day. Once we got talking to him, with the thought of getting a fish fry recipe, it reminded us that Al's a great cook with a great story. No fish fry recipe though; why would you do that at home?

Born in 1939 to Lithuanian parents, Al grew up on Milwaukee's south side in a working class neighborhood with a mix of homes and factories, churches, family-run butchers and bakeries. In a city built on beer, there truly was a tavern on just about every corner. Living close to Lake Michigan in the 1940s and '50s, there was plenty of fishing to be had and no shortage of lake perch to catch.

Following tradition, on Friday nights Al would walk to the nearest tavern to buy the full fish fry dinner - perch, potato pancakes, coleslaw, applesauce and rye bread - to take home to his parents and brother and sister.

Al's parents worked hard to put good food on the table for their children. They always bought day-old bakery and Al's mother Laura would make "gourmet" meals using whatever was at hand – macaroni, rice, soup, chicken, herring and liver. A favorite meal was homemade beef stew with lots of gravy. A least favorite was "Creamed corn with milk," he said, with a wrinkle of his nose.

Al started working at the age of 12 as a pinsetter at the local bowling lanes. He moved on to picking radishes, which paid better but was backbreaking work. Radishes grow so very close to the ground. Every morning he would be picked up at 6 a.m. to go to work in Muskego, which was a pretty long drive in those days, on the outskirts of Milwaukee.

He worked hard, weeding and picking row after row in the hot summer sun. He was paid 12 cents a crate and at the end of the day, he'd have about $7, all of which went to his mother to help pay the household expenses, except for $1 that he was allowed to keep – "for a hamburger and an ice cream."

Most days, though, Al's lunch was a radish sandwich, spread with bacon grease.

"I still remember the coffee can that sat on top of the stove my Mom filled with bacon grease. She made those piecrusts with the bacon grease; she was the best baker. We were poor, I make no bones about it, but when she baked the whole neighborhood knew it."

In the winter, Al and his father, Michael, would go fishing

Kathleen and Al

"My Mom was the best baker, and then I got lucky, because my wife is the same way."

on Little Muskego Lake for bluegills or on the Milwaukee River for perch.

"He would call me and say, 'Bring the boards and the poles and I'll meet you there.'" The thing about ice fishing is it takes awhile, and sitting right on the ice isn't so pleasant.

After high school, Al joined the Marines and was stationed at Camp Pendleton Marine Corp Base in California. He saw tours of duty in Lebanon, Southeast Asia and Cuba, and he'd join up all over again without hesitation.

After the service, Al became a firefighter for the City of Milwaukee, a job that spanned almost three decades. His easy way with people kept them calmer during a fire, car accident or in the not as rare as you would think delivery of a baby. Al

Al moves up in rank.

tried to remember how many babies he's delivered, but gave up with a shrug. "More than I can count."

Being a firefighter wasn't all about fires, though there does come a time when the hair on your hands just doesn't grow back. It wasn't long before Al was recruited by the boss to be the firehouse cook.

"One year to the day I was on the job, he said 'You're the cook,' and I was like, 'It's Sunday, what do I even get?' He said go to the butcher, and get five pounds of beef and five pounds of onions and don't even worry about anything else. That was goulash and I was a hero." Al's mentor was Hungarian and had cooked at Milwaukee's famed Serb Hall, and told Al everything he needed to know.

Eventually, Al was making all the hearty meals firefighters love, and became famous for his firehouse lasagna.

Today, Al and his wife Kathleen have three grown sons and live in a home they built on the outskirts of Milwaukee, not too far from the farm in Muskego where he picked all those radishes. On wintry days, when he isn't hammering away in Penzeys' woodshop, Al still loves ice fishing, and is happy as a clam sitting on a bucket in his snowmobile suit waiting for that lunker.

Every month or so, Al and his wife Kathleen meet up with their friends for a fish fry. They have their favorite hotspots, but once in awhile, they like to try a new place; they'll drive a half hour for a good fish fry, Al said.

"Fish fries are a part of my life," he said. "They're tradition."

Al as a young Marine

Al (front) and his cousin Ronald stand beside one of the boats that Al's father built in the 1940s.

Al's Firehouse Lasagna

As Al says, "If the corners are good, the whole thing will be good." So don't skimp on the edges.

³/₄ lb. lasagna noodles
1 lb. ground chuck
1 lb. Italian sausage
1 medium onion, diced
2 cloves garlic, diced
8 oz. mushrooms, sliced
1 3 oz. can tomato paste
1 28 oz. can whole tomatoes
1 15 oz. can tomato sauce
2 tsp. dried basil
¹/₄ tsp. fennel seed
1 tsp. dried oregano
1 tsp. Italian herb blend
1 tsp. salt
15 oz. ricotta cheese, divided
4 oz. Parmesan cheese
1 lb. mozzarella cheese
10 slices provolone

Bring a large pot of water to a boil. Soften the pasta in the water for 5 minutes then plunge into cold water and set aside. Brown the ground chuck in half pound sized batches in a large frying pan over medium-high heat. When first half pound is brown set aside in a bowl and brown the second half. Do the same for the Italian sausages, brown in half pound batches and add to the bowl. Using the same pan, add the onions with 2 tsp. oil, cook until clear, about 5 minutes. Add the garlic and mushrooms and continue to cook until lightly browned, about 5 minutes. Add the meat back into the pan and mix. Pour in the tomatoes and seasonings and let simmer for 20 minutes. Preheat oven to 350 degrees at this time. Add 1 TB ricotta to the meat sauce. Slice the provolone into strips. Begin to assemble the lasagna in an ungreased 9x13 inch pan. It is also nice to do one 8x8" pan and two bread pans to freeze for later use if your family isn't large enough to eat a whole 9x13 pan at once. Add a bit of the meat sauce to the bottom of the pan, then add a layer of pasta, and then some meat sauce. Sprinkle with Parmesan. Add some strips of provolone and dot with ricotta cheese (see photo) in between. Top with mozzarella. Continue with two more layers of pasta, sauce and cheese. Finish with meat and the remaining cheese. Bake at 350° for 30 minutes to heat through and brown the top.

Serves: 9-12
Prep. time: 1 hour
Baking time: 30 minutes

"When my mother baked the whole neighborhood knew it."

Walnut Coffee Cake

3/4 Cup butter
1 1/4 Cups sugar, divided
1 tsp. vanilla extract
2 eggs
2 Cups flour, sifted
1 tsp. baking powder
1 tsp. baking soda
1/2 tsp. salt
1 Cup sour cream

Topping:
1/4 Cup light brown sugar, firmly packed
1/2 tsp. cinnamon
1/2 Cup chopped walnuts

Preheat oven to 350°. Cream together the butter and 1 cup of sugar until light and fluffy; add vanilla. Add the eggs, one at a time, beating well after each addition. In a separate bowl, sift together the flour, baking powder, baking soda and salt. Add to butter mixture, alternating with sour cream, beginning and ending with dry ingredients. Spread evenly in a greased 9x5x3 inch loaf pan or a 9-inch square pan. Mix together the brown sugar, remaining cup of sugar, cinnamon and walnuts. Sprinkle over the top of the batter. Bake at 350° for 45-55 minutes.

Serves: 10-12
Prep. time: 10 minutes
Baking time: 45-55 minutes

Cinnamon Sour Cream Coffee Cake

1/2 Cup butter, softened
1 Cup sugar
2 large eggs
1 Cup sour cream
2 Cups flour, sifted
1 tsp. baking powder
1/2 tsp. baking soda
1 tsp. almond extract
3/4 Cup chopped almonds
1 tsp. cinnamon
2 TB dark brown sugar, packed

Preheat oven to 350°. Cream the butter and sugar together until light and fluffy. Add eggs, one at a time, beating well after each addition. Stir in the sour cream. In a separate bowl, sift together the flour, baking powder and baking soda and add to the butter mixture. Stir in the almond extract. In another bowl, combine the almonds, cinnamon and brown sugar. Spoon half of the batter into a greased and lightly floured 9x5x3 inch loaf pan or an 8 inch tube pan. Sprinkle half of the almond mixture on top. Cover with the remaining batter and top with the remaining almond mixture. Bake at 350° for 1 hour, or until a toothpick inserted in the center comes out clean. Serve warm or cold.

Serves: 10-12
Prep. time: 10 minutes
Baking time: 45-55 minutes

"I enjoy my job and the people are great to work with," Al said. "This is my life."

Al in woodshop:

Al figures he's made around 40,000 – yes, that's right, 40,000 – gift boxes and crates for spices in the 10 years he's worked at Penzeys.

Spice waits for Al to sit down and relax.

LLOYD RAHLF

Advisory teams usually consisted of a Major, a Captain, two Sergeants (one was a medic) and a radio operator. Their primary job was to train foreign soldiers but sometimes the training was first hand.

In September 2005 Lloyd J. Rahlf, SGM (Ret) and his wife Dee celebrated their 40th wedding anniversary. They were married in England but his first tour of Vietnam started a month later. "We had a short honeymoon and then I'm in the jungle." Whether he is talking about a major battle or dinner with his family, Lloyd's nonchalance makes the stories of his life sound ordinary even though many of these events were anything but.

The oldest of 11 children, Lloyd started to help in the kitchen when he was 7 or 8. "Everybody did a little cooking." When asked what it was like with 11 kids in the house, he joked, "I'm not sure, I was out of the house when some of them came along." Then he added, "Mother always cooked a big meal and the children had to help her get it ready. Everyone had to be at the dinner table when Dad said to sit down and eat. There was no tardiness." The family ate together every night except during the war years. Though Dad didn't serve during WWII, he contributed to the effort, working 12 hours, 7 days a week at A.O. Smith Co., making propellers, landing gears and jeep chassis.

After serving in the National Guard for two years Lloyd entered active duty in 1952 with the 101st Airborne Division and fought in the Korean War. After Korea his involvement with infantry operations and intelligence took him to Iran, Iraq, West Germany, France, and two tours in Vietnam. He participated in seven Vietnam campaigns during 1965-66 and 1969-70. He has received many medals including the Bronze Star. He trained soldiers, fought battles, fed many men and women, and had some very interesting experiences. "I was in Baghdad on St. Nicholas Day 1959. You know the big Mullah of the Kurds, Massoud Barzani, who is the bigwig now? Well I had a cup of hot tea with his daddy (Mustafa)."

During his first tour of Vietnam he was the senior non-commissioned officer of an operations and intelligence advisory team, "And I was also the cook... and I was an infantry man all rolled into one." Active duty units had mess halls and cooks. Not the advisory teams. "When you were on an advisory team, out there just the five of you, you had no cooks."

Just the five of you, out in the jungle, far from home. From a distance war can look like the total abandonment of civilization, but up close it is all about holding on to all the little moments of civility you can. When you are so far from home and the ideals you were raised on, little things take on a much greater meaning. In Vietnam, where everywhere was behind enemy lines, simple things like a letter from home, a picture of loved ones, or a good home cooked meal could mean the world. Lloyd knew this and did his best to make sure those around him had good food whenever it was possible.

After that tour Lloyd was stationed in Germany where in 1968, his daughter Karen was born. "We lived in government quarters so we usually had an evening meal together. Breakfast was kind of difficult because I was out the door at 4 a.m. But lunch was usually at home because you were so close. You ran home for a quick bite to eat. My wife is an excellent cook and being from England she cooked some of the British stuff and me being from the old Yankee country, I cooked the normal stuff, ham, beef roasts, and a lot of barbecue while I was in Europe. The foreign nationals I had as friends and guests loved the barbecue. They would come from far away places, my buddies and German friends, just to have a barbecue on the weekend."

After his second tour of Vietnam, Lloyd and his family landed in Sparks, NV where he taught ROTC until his retirement from the U.S. Army after 27 years of active service. Lloyd worked in outside sales until he retired for good 2 years ago. Now he is able to devote time to another love— gardening. Growing conditions are difficult in Sparks so he concentrates on what he calls the six basic root crops: onions, rutabagas, parsnips, turnips, celery root, and carrots. "I have a row of each and I make a stew or a soup out of it. Sometimes it's chicken, or beef, or lamb. It depends on what's available."

That's the magic of Lloyd Rahlf's cooking and his life. Bringing people together by taking what's available and turning it into something special. Whether he is making Christmas dinner in the jungle, barbecuing in Germany, or growing vegetables in the desert of Nevada, Lloyd makes the best of a tough situation.

Christmas Dinner 1965: Five advisory teams gathered. They had two turkeys, canned sweet potatoes, canned cranberries, "... everything was in cans except the turkeys. I had to cook them in a kerosene oven. We had a kerosene range that was hooked up to an oxygen tank. It would force a mixture of kerosene and oxygen and produce a blue flame just like gas."

Marmalade Glazed Turkey with Stuffing

Folks on this side of the ocean aren't as familiar with the tart taste of marmalade as Lloyd and his British wife Dee are. You may want to start with a smaller amount in the basting sauce and see how you like it. Lloyd always roasts a whole bird, but we tried it with just the turkey breast and liked the results.

6-7   lb. turkey breast, thawed according to instructions

Bread Stuffing:
2/3   Cup butter or margarine
3   medium onions, minced
1 1/2 tsp. poultry seasoning or use thyme or sage or other herbs to taste
2   tsp. salt
1   tsp. pepper
1   Cup celery leaves, chopped
2   tsp. ground sage
3 1/2 qts. soft (a few days old) white bread cubes, crust removed

Sauté all ingredients except bread cubes in skillet over medium heat for 5 minutes. Toss with bread cubes. Let cool.

1   Cup pineapple juice
1/2   Cup orange marmalade
2   TB steak sauce
1   TB brandy or bourbon

Mix all ingredients together in a small saucepan. Warm over medium heat,

stirring frequently, just until it starts to bubble, then turn off the heat.

Preheat oven to 325°. Place the turkey breast in a roasting pan and fill with stuffing. We used bamboo skewers to hold the cavity together. Place the excess in the pan around the turkey. Roast at 325° until the internal temperature is at least 165°, about 3 1/2–4 1/2 hours. Baste several times with drippings from the pan. When breast starts turning brown, cover with a foil tent. After 2 hours, begin basting with the basting sauce until the turkey is done.
Prep. time: 30 minutes
Cooking time: 4 hours
Serves: 10-12

Courtesy of the 1st Infantry Officer's Mess. (Unbeknownst to them) – Lloyd used bricks, oven racks and Vietnamese charcoal to cook the ribs. "We mixed honey, ketchup, and mustard together. We put some salt and pepper in there and I think we even had some Scotch whiskey or bourbon lying around so I threw that in. I just slapped it on those ribs with a paintbrush."

Vegetable Beef Soup

This is a hearty soup for the colder months. Lloyd has made this for many years and makes a few variations depending on what is in the garden or at the market. The roots add a delightfully sweet flavor and hold up well during cooking. This soup is even better the second day.

1	lb. chuck steak, cubed into ½ inch pieces
1	TB vegetable oil
1	medium onion, chopped
2	carrots, sliced
2	celery stalks, sliced
1	rutabaga, cut into bite-sized chunks
1	parsnip, cut into bite-sized chunks
1	celery root (also known as celeriac), cubed
2	purple-top turnips, cubed ½ inch
8	Cups beef broth/stock (canned or homemade)
½	tsp. kosher salt
½	tsp. pepper
1	TB oregano
¼	tsp. cayenne pepper
1	tsp. ground cumin
2	zucchini, sliced (small)
4	Roma tomatoes, chopped
⅓	Cup fresh cilantro or 1 tsp. dried cilantro

In a skillet over medium high heat, brown beef. Remove from skillet, drain, and set aside. In the same skillet over medium heat, warm the oil and sauté the onions, carrots, and celery stalks for 5 minutes until onion is translucent. Put into soup pot. Then add rutabaga, parsnip, celery root, and turnips to the pot along with beef, beef broth/stock, salt, pepper and oregano. Bring to a boil, turn down heat to medium-low and simmer for 2-3 hours, or until vegetables are tender. About 20 minutes before serving, add the cayenne, cumin (see note), zucchini, tomatoes, and fresh cilantro. Serve with garlic bread or fresh baked biscuits.

Note: Caution, add cayenne pepper and cumin at the end before you add the last vegetables. Also, add them a little at a time, so that the soup is not too spicy. Taste as you add them—once they are added it's too late to lessen the spicy flavor. To get the soup to the proper consistency, add or reduce beef broth.

Prep. time: 45 minutes
Cooking time: 3 hours
Serves: 6-8

This 28 lb. ham was served at Lloyd's 70th birthday party and fed about 100 people. You guessed it; he baked it himself.

Baked Ham with Spicy Sauce

Recipes that take all day scare many of us off, but this ham is easy and well worth the time you invest. Not to mention, the sauce is wonderful.

2	Cups orange or pineapple juice
1½	Cups light brown sugar, packed
4	tsp. powdered mustard
½	tsp. ground cloves
¼	tsp. nutmeg
1	tsp. ginger
6	tsp. rum extract or 3 teaspoons dark rum, divided
8-12	lbs. bone-in ham
15-30	whole cloves
1	Cup raisins, plumped in boiling water and drained
2	TB fresh lemon juice
2	TB arrowroot or cornstarch
2	TB water

Mix first six ingredients and bring to a boil. Simmer, stirring, until sugar is dissolved. Add 4 tsp. of rum extract or 2 tsp. of dark rum. Let cool. Score the ham fat with a knife. Stud the ham with cloves, using a skewer to poke holes. Cover with marinade when cool. Let stand in the refrigerator for 4 hours, basting occasionally with marinade. Preheat oven to 325°. Remove ham from marinade and place on a rack in a roasting pan. Bake at 325° for 5½ hours covered with aluminum foil. Baste every half hour or so. With 30 minutes to go, remove foil, baste one more time, and place back in the oven. Increase heat to 425°. After 30 minutes, remove ham from roasting pan, re-cover with foil and let rest. Deglaze roasting pan with lemon juice and drained raisins. Transfer to sauce pan. Blend arrowroot with 2 TB water and stir into lemon juice mixture. Cook and stir sauce until thickened. Add remaining 2 tsp. of rum extract or 1 tsp. of dark rum. Serve sauce with ham.

Prep. time: 1 hour
Marinate time: 4 hours
Cooking time: 6 hours
Serves: 12-18

Shrimp Kabobs

This is a great recipe Lloyd sent to us after he had appeared in our magazine. We held onto it because it was too good not to share.

- 1 lb. medium shrimp, peeled and deveined
- 1 tsp. vegetable oil
- 1-2 tsp. Singapore Seasoning (or 1 1/2 tsp. lemon pepper mixed with 1/2 tsp. sweet curry powder)
  wooden or metal skewers

Toss the shrimp with the vegetable oil and Singapore Seasoning or lemon pepper mixed with sweet curry. Cover and refrigerate for at least 30 minutes. If you are using wooden skewers, soak them in water while the shrimp are marinating in the refrigerator. Heat your grill to medium heat. Remove the shrimp from the refrigerator and thread on the skewers. Grill the kabobs over medium heat for 4-5 minutes per side.

Prep. time: 45 minutes
Cooking time: 8-10 minutes
Serves: 4-6

Vegetable Kabobs

Lloyd loves to garden, and this recipe is a great way for him to enjoy his beautiful bounty.

- 1 green bell pepper, cut into chunks
- 1 red bell pepper, cut into chunks
- 15-20 small onions (pearl or cipollini or scallions), peeled
- 1 8 oz. package button mushrooms
- 2 tsp. vegetable oil
- 2 tsp. lemon pepper
- 1/2 tsp. salt
- 1/4 tsp. pepper
  wooden or metal skewers

Toss the vegetables with the oil, lemon pepper, salt and pepper. Cover and refrigerate for at least 30 minutes. If you are using wooden skewers, soak them in water while the veggies are marinating in the refrigerator. Heat your grill to medium heat. Remove the vegetables from the refrigerator and thread on the skewers. Grill the kabobs over medium heat for 5-6 minutes per side or until the vegetables are tender.

Prep. time: 45 minutes
Cooking time: 10-12 minutes
Serves: 4-6

Chris Swann

"I am undaunted in the kitchen, I will try anything," says Chris Swann, an economist and writer for the Bureau of Economic Analysis (BEA) in Washington, DC. "I follow recipes that I don't know but once you do it a couple times, then you add a little of this. That's what I like about cooking; I'm free to do whatever I want."

After a long career in the private sector, Chris decided to ply his trade for the Bureau of Economic Analysis, an analytical arm of the U.S. Department of Commerce. When in the kitchen he is free to do what he wants; it can be a different story at the office. His monthly article, called "GDP (Gross Domestic Product) and the Economy," must be delivered in a non-biased, non-partisan way. "And it really is remarkable how we can do that," says Chris. "You have to be very careful about the words you pick."

Any concern he had transitioning from the private to the public sector was short lived. "Over the last several years, BEA has made strides toward innovation in how we communicate with the public and how we present our products." Noting that he had used the word "products," a private sector term, Chris laughs, "I still carry my private sector mentality with me and no one has thrown me out.

"What I do principally revolves around writing an article for our monthly journal, *The Survey of Current Business.* To me, content management is just what we did in the private sector. We were in the information business and that's exactly the business we are in at BEA." There is a long tradition in this journal that goes back decades. "It encompasses all of the important analyses that BEA has done over the course of some time but mainly presented in the course of a month," says Chris. "My article is a broad summary of what the current economic data shows." His article, and much of the survey itself, has been subject to much modification because the readership has changed. "Not many have time to read long paragraphs and decipher arcane terminology. So BEA has tried to respond to that market change. Sure, there are traditional economists who read it. I bet Alan Greenspan reads it still. But the new sort of reader is not the economist. They are probably involved in making decisions or providing information to decision makers. We've tried to make the article an easier read with a short overview to results and reduced table reading."

Chris's monthly article, "GDP and the Economy," is the result of many people working hard. "I have a great job and I'll tell you what, I work with a lot of smart people. They work on these numbers, comb through these articles and get the numbers and language right. I'm honored to have my name on the article but there are a lot of people who look at this thing."

The only problem with his great job is

Chris with Aunt Mary (The Stromboli Aunt).

Chris and Aunt Mary's Stromboli

This is something that Deb's Aunt Mary (she's about 90 now) and I decided to do over several glasses of wine about ten years ago for our Christmas Eve party. I used to make the pizza dough from scratch (mixed and kneaded by machine), but now I buy the dough from our favorite pizza restaurant. Stromboli is a baked pizza dough filled with meats and cheese of your choice. Some favorites are the Italian (recipe which follows); meatball and cheese; sausage and cheese; and the American—ham and American cheese. Serve it with your favorite pizza sauce on the side for dipping.

Pizza dough:

1	tsp. yeast
2	Cups high gluten pizza flour (we used bread flour)
1	tsp. olive oil
½	tsp. salt
½	tsp. sugar
1	Cup lukewarm water

Add the yeast and flour to a bread machine or mixing bowl. Add the olive oil, salt, sugar and water. Knead for about 5-10 minutes. Sprinkle the dough ball with flour or polenta (Italian corn meal) and put it in a container to rise a bit, about 1 hour. If you're not going to use the dough for a day, put it in the refrigerator to retard the rising.

Dressing:

¼	Cup olive oil
1	clove garlic, minced
1	TB dried oregano
1	tsp. sugar

Filling:

¼	lb. Italian (Genoa) salami
¼	lb. sliced pepperoni
¼	lb. cappacola (sweet or hot, your choice)
¼	lb. sharp, sliced provolone cheese
1	Cup shredded mozzarella cheese
¼	Cup grated Romano or Parmesan cheese

Preheat the oven to 450°. Roll the pizza dough out in a rectangle, about ¼-inch thick (too thick and you have bread; too thin and it won't be sturdy enough for the filling). Layer the meats in the center of the dough followed by the sliced cheese and the mozzarella. Top with the grated cheese. Fold the sides in and pinch them together. Whisk the dressing ingredients together. Brush the dough with dressing to help seal it together. Fold up the ends and pinch to seal. Bake at 450° for about 15 minutes. The dough will be nicely browned and the cheeses will have melted together. Slice it and serve it with pizza sauce on the side for dipping.

Prep. time: 1 hour, 30 minutes, **Cooking time:** 15 minutes, **Serves:** 8

that it's far from home. Chris and his wife Debra live in Paoli, Pennsylvania, a suburb of Philadelphia, along with their daughters Stephanie (19) and Casey (16). Which means a long commute on Amtrak. "It's about a 3-hour commute, all things considered, each way. People are shocked by that but interestingly enough there are a lot of people who do that. Many more are going to New York than Washington. The other thing is that a lot of people in the Washington, DC area, particularly on the Virginia side, they have a 2 to 2 ½-hour commute and they're not more than fifty miles away." The advantage is with the taxpayers who pay his salary. "The train is a great place to work. I once told my division chief: If I were you, I would never want me to move down here because you get more work out of me this way," Chris laughs.

The long commute makes family time precious. "I don't think this would have been possible even a couple of years ago. Now our oldest daughter is in college. The younger one is within months of having her license. The biggest thing is that it would not have been possible if Deb had

"MY ITALIAN GRANDPARENTS CAME FROM SICILY AND MY GREEK GRANDPARENTS EMIGRATED FROM GREECE—BETWEEN THE GREEK AND THE SICILIAN, THERE'S AN AWFUL LOT OF OLIVE OIL AND GARLIC THAT RUNS THROUGH THESE VEINS."

been working." Up until two years ago, Debra was an executive vice-president for a communications company where she and Chris met before they married in 1985. "She has had a good time frankly, taking a pause. It has refreshed her," says Chris adding, "But she's back in the saddle again, just accepting a VP position at a professional organization."

Cooking during the week is difficult because of his schedule. "When I first got the job I was eating late and I'd get home and… oh God, it was horrible. But I made some adjustments and I'm back down in the suits I was wearing when I first started. It can kill you, the long days and the commute because if you end up eating late you're dead. I try to manage what I'm eating during the course of the day a little better."

The weekends are when Chris can start cooking and drawing on his heritage. "My Italian grandparents came from Sicily and my Greek grandparents emigrated from Greece," says Chris then adds with a laugh, "Between the Greek and the Sicilian, there's an awful lot of olive oil and garlic that runs through these veins. If I don't

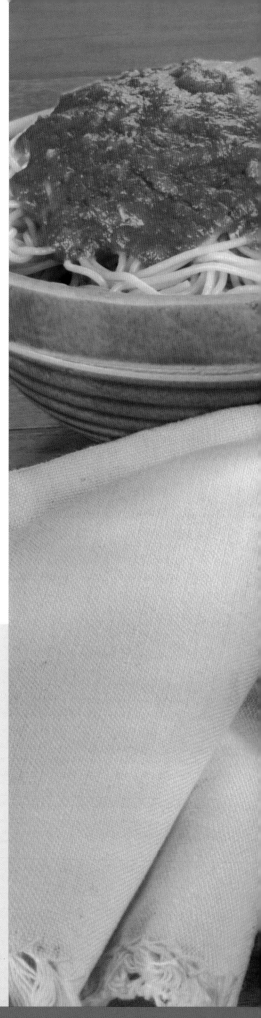

Aunt Pat's Pizza Meat

This is a braised meat dish, so you can use a cheaper cut of meat, like round steak, but you should pound it a bit. The braising will help tenderize it also.

1	lb. veal or round steak (we used round steak)
¾	Cup Italian bread crumbs (if you make them yourself, make sure there's plenty of garlic, grated cheese and parsley)
4	TB olive oil, divided
1	16 oz. can tomatoes (crushed are good)
1	8 oz. can tomato sauce
2	tsp. salt
2	tsp. pepper
1	tsp. dried basil
3	TB dried oregano (it has to taste like pizza!)
1	tsp. sugar
1-2	large onions, diced (about 1½ Cups)
4	oz. Italian cheese slices (sharp provolone or Romano are good) Grated Romano cheese and oregano

Preheat the oven to 350°. Pour 2 TB of the olive oil into a wide, shallow bowl. Coat the meat in the olive oil and then coat in bread crumbs. Heat the remaining oil over medium-high heat and brown the meat, about 2-3 minutes per side. Place in a baking pan. In a medium saucepan, mix together the tomatoes, tomato sauce, salt, pepper, basil, oregano and sugar. Cook over medium heat, stirring and mixing well, about 5 minutes. Spoon the sauce over the meat. Place slices of cheese liberally over the sauce. Spread the onions over the cheese. Shake a little grated Romano cheese and oregano over the top. Cover with aluminum foil and bake at 350° for about 45-60 minutes (the sauce should be bubbling).

Prep. time: 20 minutes, **Cooking time:** 45-60 minutes, **Serves:** 4-6

Cracchiola Family Sauce

This is for a big pot. I've never made a small pot. I learned the measures by the handful and the pinch, but the amounts here were measured.

Ingredients:

- 4   12 oz. cans tomato paste
- 6   TB olive oil
- 6   cloves garlic, minced
- 1   TB salt
- 2   TB pepper (adjust to taste—if my aunts were caught up in a soap opera while cooking, more seemed to get added)
- 3   TB dried basil
- 1   TB dried oregano (too much and you'll have pizza sauce!)
- 1   TB dried parsley
- 1   TB sugar (Aunt Eleanor added some sugar, Aunt Pat added none. Add as you need to cut the acidity of the tomatoes.)
- 4½   qts. water
- 1   lb. ground beef, pork, veal, or a mix of all three (the beef will make a heavier sauce; the pork and veal make for a lighter, sweeter sauce), we used ground beef
   Other meat: meatballs, sausage, pork butt, etc. to your own taste

If you're making meat sauce, brown the meat and set aside in a colander to drain the fat. Cover the bottom of a large stock pot with the olive oil and sweat the garlic (cook over low heat to prevent browning) until soft. Add the tomato paste and water (you may want to do this off the heat so the paste doesn't stick to the bottom of the pan). Then, stir as the paste melts and mixes with the water over medium heat. Add all of the other ingredients except the ground meat. Stir, turn up the heat and bring to a boil. Lower the heat to a simmer and add the ground meat, if you're making meat sauce. Simmer and stir often over the next 2 hours. The water will evaporate and the sauce will thicken. Taste along the way to see if it needs more salt and pepper. Feel free to dunk some bread in and taste too. It's part of the fun and ritual. Add any meatballs, sausage, pork, etc. to the sauce to heat in the last 30-60 minutes. I always brown these separately and let them finish cooking in the sauce.

Prep. time: 15 minutes, **Cooking time:** 2 hours, **Yield:** 6 qts.

Chris's wife Deb presents the 30 pound Thanksgiving turkey.

get a dose now and then, I start to have withdrawals." Being born in St. Louis influenced him as well. "Barbeques have always been big from when I was a kid from the St. Louis connection. You know, barbeque, baseball and beer."

Being in the Midwest exposed him to things other than the three B's. "My grandfather on my stepfather's side had a farm in Illinois. So my grandmother, who I knew very well, brought in the farm element. That's where I got clued into those great green beans with the bacon. There are just some things… the cobblers. That

woman would make blackberry cobblers that would knock your socks off."

His main cooking influence comes from his aunt. "Predominantly I learned how to cook from my aunt, who took care of me while my parents worked. I learned to cook from her and do domestic things, which served me well when I got on my own as a bachelor. I always tell guys, listen, if you want to score high with the ladies, a little Fettuccine Alfredo and a bottle of wine will score you big points."

He still needed to get over the notion that real men don't cook. "What got me

Chris's Baked Ziti

Once you've made the Cracchiola Family Sauce, you're home free.
This is a layered, baked pasta dish like lasagna.

- 4½   Cups Cracchiola Family Sauce
- 1   lb. pasta—ziti or rigatoni (we used ziti)
- 8   oz. sliced, sharp provolone
- ½   Cup grated Romano or Parmesan cheese
   optional: 16 oz. ricotta cheese mixed with 1 egg and 1 TB fresh chopped parsley

Preheat the oven to 350°. Cook the pasta al dente (slightly undercooked); the pasta will finish cooking in the oven. Using a 9x13 pan, spoon 1½ cups of sauce over the bottom of the pan. Layer the pan as follows: half of the drained pasta, half of the

cheese slices, half of the grated cheese, and 1½ Cups of sauce. Repeat the layers. Finish with a sprinkle of grated cheese, about 2 TB. If you are using the ricotta mixture, layer it between the cheese slices and the grated cheese. Bake at 350° for 30-45 minutes or until the sauce is just bubbling. That's a good sign that the cheeses are thoroughly melted and mixed.

Prep. time: 30 minutes
Cooking time: 30-45 minutes
Serves: 12

Aunt Eleanor's Spedini

These are little rolled-up meats ("veal birds") that are best on the grill. They are basted with a lemon-garlic-oil mixture that keeps them moist and adds flavor.

1	lb. veal, thinly sliced (chicken or a tender cut of beef can also be used, just make sure it's thinly sliced)
2	TB olive oil
1½	Cups Italian bread crumbs (there should be grated cheese, garlic and parsley in the mix)
1	medium tomato, thinly sliced
1	medium onion, very thinly sliced
4	oz. small, thin slices or chunks of sharp Italian or Sicilian cheese (sharp provolone is good)

Basting sauce:

¼	Cup lemon juice
¼	Cup olive oil
4	cloves garlic, minced

Pound and cut the meat into thin slices, about 4-6 inches long, about 4 inches wide, and about ¼-inch thick. Pour the olive oil in a wide, shallow bowl. Dip the meat into the olive oil and then into the bread crumbs, coating both sides. Shake off any excess bread crumbs to prevent sogginess. Place some bread crumbs, tomato, onion and cheese on top of the meat and roll. Hold the meat together with toothpicks. Mix the lemon juice, olive oil and minced garlic together for the basting sauce. Put the spedini on the grill over medium-high heat, baste with the basting sauce and grill for 5-8 minutes, turning frequently to brown all sides. If you are using chicken, bake in a 325° oven for 10 minutes after grilling as chicken takes a bit longer to cook through.

Prep. time: 20 minutes, **Cooking time:** 5-8 minutes, **Yield:** 8-10 spedini

Chris's youngest daughter Casey helping out her dad in the kitchen.

by the image of the guy cooking was two things. First of all as an enquiring young man I would come across an occasional *Playboy* magazine lying around. I'm gonna tell you—I didn't just read the articles. But beside the pictures, I'd see these guys dressed up in tuxedos and they'd have the chafing dish and be serving these good-looking women. I thought these guys know what they're doing." The other influence came from a friend he stayed with one summer in college. "His dad was this big guy who was an all-American mention at Illinois in the 50s as an offensive guard. And he did all the cooking. So it was like, okay, I got this. You can be a macho guy and do all this cooking too. From that time on I really took an interest in food and cooking."

Being raised in an Italian family means that he doesn't mind cooking for a crowd. "My wife's aunt is first generation Italian and she's like ninety now," says Chris. "Well a few years back, over several glasses of wine, we got this idea that we would make homemade stromboli for part of the big Christmas Eve gathering. I think we're up to about fifty people for this thing. So last year we made about eight stromboli in addition to the seafood tray and the ham and all the rest of it."

The other crowd he cooks for is work-mates at the Bureau of Economic Analysis. Every summer they have a picnic and

Chris volunteers to help out. "It turns out I love to do these parties," laughs Chris. "There was one guy who pretty much co-ordinated it but I think he was at the end of his rope with it and needed a rest. So they asked me if I would like to coordinate it. I said yes and I decided that my contribution would be to barbeque some chicken. I brought down about one hundred pieces of barbequed chicken from Philadelphia in the back of my Explorer. So that pretty much sealed my fate." With help from his coworkers the picnic was a big success. "This past Christmas the finger of fate pointed in my direction. I de-

cided it was just cheaper and better to get two 30-pound turkeys and roast them. Then I de-boned them and vacuum sealed them at home. Then I brought them down with some sides that I bought. I pretty much catered the event. It was a lot of work but it was a lot of fun."

Chris is also on the board of directors for the National Association of Business Economists (NABE). "I love the organization and I love my profession," says Chris. NABE is a great source of information for business economists whether seasoned or just starting out. They also lobby for adequate funding for data for agencies like the Bureau of Economic Analysis, the Census Bureau or the Bureau of Labor and Statistics. "Those are the three big organizations that provide government data and survey work," says Chris. "They rely on the private sector to provide data. If you don't have the surveys, you don't get the data." As important as that data is to all of us, it's not always an easy case to make on Capitol Hill. "It would be nice to have a bake sale to get that funding but that would be hard to pull off," Chris says with a laugh.

To see Chris's writings visit the BEA website, http://bea.gov/, and click on *Survey of Current Business.* If only getting some of his barbeque chicken was that easy.

Chris's daughter Stephanie (right) celebrates her birthday with younger sister Casey.

Belle Sawhill

sabel Sawhill is a senior fellow with the Brookings Institution and regular panelist on Concord Coalition's Fiscal Wake-Up Tour. Her mother's name was also Isabel so as she grew up in the Washington, DC area family and friends called her Belle. Belle's years of experience in and around government make her well qualified to comment on the nation's fiscal crisis.

Belle was the executive director of a commission on employment policy under President Carter. "I later joined the Clinton administration as an associate director of the Office of Management and Budget (OMB)." She held that job from 1993 to 1995. "It was fascinating. It was exhausting," recalls Belle, "It really gave me a bird's eye view of how government works. When you have the job that I had at OMB you oversee a very large part of the government. The way it's structured at OMB,

you have the director but then the associate directors, of whom there are four or five, oversee a quarter or third or whatever of the government. My chunk was all of the social programs, Social Security, all of the Department of Education, all of the

Department of Labor, all of the social programs in Health and Human Services. I had the Veterans Administration under my wing and a lot of smaller agencies. So it's a huge job and very interesting." Difficult as well. In her position she had to say no to many wonderful sounding programs because the money just wasn't there. "It is indeed a thankless job. In fact I always tell anyone who takes a job with OMB, you better buy a dog before you take the job because the only friend you'll have in Washington when you get out of government is that dog," she says laughing.

While two years at the OMB doesn't seem like much, there is a burnout factor to overseeing those budgets. "I had a third of the Federal budget under my jurisdiction," says Belle adding, "You never stop working. I used to carry two briefcases home on the weekend because I had so much reading to catch up on."

Belle was born and raised in the Washington, DC area and is the granddaughter of former U.S. Supreme Court Justice Willis Van Devanter, who served from 1909 to 1937. "He was conservative and when Roosevelt tried to pack the Supreme Court, you know increase the number of

Belle with members of Congress at the launch of the National Campaign to Prevent Teen Pregnancy.

Roasted Sweet Potatoes

"People just seem to love these."

6	sweet potatoes (yams), about 4 lbs.
6	TB oil (we used canola)
1-2	TB ground nutmeg
1½	tsp. salt
1	tsp. black pepper

Preheat oven to 375°. Wash the sweet potatoes and remove the rough ends but leave the skins on. Cut into ½-1-inch cubes. Toss in olive oil, salt, black pepper, and ground nutmeg. Bake at 375° for 30 minutes or until tender.

Prep. time: 15 minutes, **Cooking time:** 30 minutes, **Serves:** 12 (1 cup servings)

members in 1937, my grandfather was one of his targets. The conservative justices at that time were not supporting the President's New Deal legislation. So Roosevelt wanted to do something about that and he proposed an expansion of the size of the Supreme Court, which failed. My grandfather retired anyway around that time which gave Roosevelt the majority he wanted."

But Belle's father wanted nothing to do with politics. "My father was in the investment advising business and did that most of his life," says Belle. "He was quiet, had good values and was an outdoorsman. We used to go to Canada, to the Georgian Bay, which is part of Lake Huron. There are 30,000 islands in that area and my father had a small cottage on one of those islands. We would spend a lot of time there in the summer. He was very much into fishing, as am I."

Not so for her mom however. "She was very smart, very funny, though she did not like all that outdoorsy type of thing," recalls Belle. "She used to call the place my father had in Canada 'Little Alcatraz.' There was no phone and in the begin-

1 OUT OF EVERY 5 INCOME TAX DOLLARS IS GOING JUST TO PAY INTEREST ON THE DEBT.

ning, no electricity. It was fairly primitive. She liked her creature comforts and she also liked her friends and it was pretty isolated."

She learned to cook from her mom, though these days, finding time to cook can be difficult. "I am involved in a huge number of things. Anyone will tell you that. Up until September I was a vice-president and director of Economic Studies at Brookings. In addition to that I'm a senior fellow and one of the hats I wear is a co-director of the Center for Children and Families at Brookings." About ten years ago she also helped start a non-profit organization in Washington called The National Campaign to Prevent Teen Pregnancy, of which she is still president of the board. "So I'm constantly running around doing this stuff and I don't have time to cook."

Like her father, she likes to get away from Washington and enjoy the great outdoors. Rather than an island in Canada, Belle chose a mountain in Colorado. "We're a big skiing family. We have a ski place in Steamboat Springs." Her late hus-

No Bowl Cake

"This is a recipe I've always gotten a huge kick out of because it's unusual and quite good. This came from my grandmother on my mother's side. I remember my mother making it and I've certainly made it."

1½	Cups flour
1	Cup sugar
3	TB cocoa powder (we used natural)
½	tsp. salt
1	tsp. baking soda
5	TB melted butter
1	Cup cold water
1	tsp. vanilla extract
1	TB white vinegar

Preheat oven to 350°. Combine all of the dry ingredients in an un-greased 8x8-inch square cake pan. Then make three holes or depressions in the dry material. Into one hole you pour the butter, into the second hole you pour the water and vanilla, and in the third hole you put the vinegar. Stir everything to blend it well. Bake at 350° for about 30 minutes or until the cake shrinks a little from the sides. Let the cake cool, and then frost.

Frosting

1	square semisweet chocolate (½ oz.)
3	TB butter
3	TB heavy cream
1	tsp. vanilla extract
1¾	Cups 4x confectioner's sugar (slightly finer than regular confectioner's sugar, although regular will work just fine)

Melt the chocolate and butter in a double boiler or microwave. Remove from heat. Stir in the heavy cream and vanilla extract. With an electric beater, mix in the sugar and beat until smooth.

Prep. time: 15 minutes, **Baking time:** 30 minutes, **Serves:** 9-16

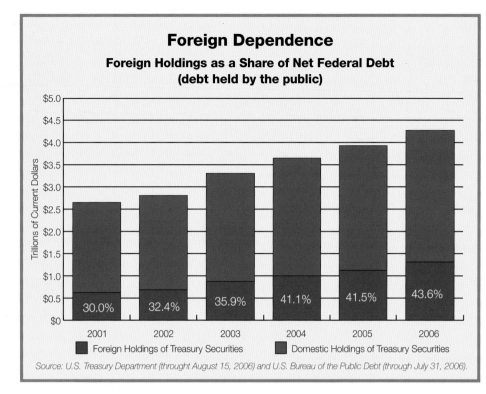

Foreign Dependence

Foreign Holdings as a Share of Net Federal Debt
(debt held by the public)

2001	30.0%
2002	32.4%
2003	35.9%
2004	41.1%
2005	41.5%
2006	43.6%

Trillions of Current Dollars

■ Foreign Holdings of Treasury Securities   ■ Domestic Holdings of Treasury Securities

Source: U.S. Treasury Department (throught August 15, 2006) and U.S. Bureau of the Public Debt (through July 31, 2006).

band, John Sawhill, passed away about six years ago and was also a lover of the outdoors. "He was president of The Nature Conservancy, a very large environmental organization. Before that he had several other interesting jobs including being president of New York University (where Belle earned her PhD) and Deputy Secretary of Energy in the Carter Administration." In addition to skiing, Belle gets to try her hand at angling, just like the old days on "Little Alcatraz" in Canada. "We're right on a lake and a river and the fishing there is fabulous."

Steamboat is also where Belle gets to do most of her cooking. "I like good food and I like having friends over and I will cook on vacation or when I'm having guests. As an economist I have to be efficient with my time." Belle laughs, "I have a lot of friends and relatives who are better cooks than I am. I like to have them over and I like to, particularly out in Steamboat, when people are staying with me, get into doing a group thing in the kitchen. Either we will cook a meal together or one person will take charge one evening and produce some fabulous feast and we'll all enjoy it."

On the Fiscal Wake-Up Tour Belle's segment is titled "Why Deficits Matter and What Elected Officials Need to Do." In Columbus, Ohio she was lucky enough to have her teenaged grandson, John Sawhill (named after her husband) in the audience. As she introduced him she showed a picture of him on the golf course and he received a nice round of applause. "So

Left: Belle and her late husband John Sawhill. "We're a big skiing family," says Belle. **Below:** At the Fiscal Wake-Up Tour stop in Columbus, Ohio, Belle's grandson, John Sawhill (named after her late husband) was in attendance. She could not resist poking a little fun at him during her talk.

Belle received an award from V.P. Al Gore for chairing a task force to make government more effective and less costly.

Belle's good friends Ed and Pietro taking a bow for a fabulous meal."I have a lot of friends and relatives who are better cooks than I am," says Belle. Try her salmon mousse and you may disagree (see page 281).

they're clapping for you now," said Belle, "but what you don't know is that you're not going to be able to afford all those golf balls and nice golf games in the future because you're going to be paying off the debt that people in my generation and your parents' generation created for you. So… good luck."

Her comment was met with laughter but the truth of the matter is not very funny. Belle says there are four reasons why the Federal deficit matters. First is dependence on foreigners. "About half of our publicly held national debt is owned by foreigners. Most of the new borrowing that we are doing is from foreigners often from central banks. That is putting us in a very vulnerable position.

"The second problem with deficits is they bring with them a larger and larger national debt," Belle continues. "Each year's deficit adds to the debt and we have to pay interest on that debt. Those interest costs are a very large part of the budget now. When you send your tax dollars to Washington, you probably think you're paying for the war in Iraq, education, highways and a whole variety of other things. How many people know that one

out of every five of their income tax dollars is going just to pay interest on the debt? That number is going to go up much higher in the future."

The third reason is the burden that deficits and the ever growing national debt puts on future generations, which is where she used her grandson and his golf balls as an example. Lastly we need to worry about deficits because it constrains our ability to invest in our future or to deal

with unforeseen contingencies. "Suppose there is a flu epidemic and we need to spend money on that. Suppose there is a new international crisis. Suppose you think we should be investing more in education or reducing global warming or in being the first in the world in science and technology. We do not have the resources to do those things now. And most importantly, it is a certainty that because of the retirement of the baby boomers we are going to have massive costs in the future for Social Security, Medicare, and that's going to require that we get started now in putting our fiscal house in order. So we will be better prepared to address the retirement of that group when the time comes."

Preparing for the future is what Belle Sawhill and economists like her are all about. Don't be afraid of the future, look into the future and plan for the future. "For too many people deficits are a very abstract concept," says Belle. "If we are going to be successful, we are going to have to convince a lot more people that this does matter to our future as a country and to the strength of our economy."

ON JAN 7, 2007, THE FISCAL WAKE-UP TOUR STOPPED AT THE JOHN GLENN SCHOOL OF PUBLIC AFFAIRS AT THE OHIO STATE UNIVERSITY.

JOHN GLENN: "I have been more concerned for the past few years about my country than I ever have in my whole life. And I mean that. It's not Iraq. It's the very basic foundation of our economy that I have been concerned about and the direction that we are going. It has been building up for a long time. It will determine all of the other things we can do in our society, in this democracy of ours."

one for the road

If the goal is to make wisdom a bigger part of our culture, there is something to be said for trying to make it fun and exciting, something to be said for attempting to make it the "in" thing. There is also something to be said for simply using it. The Fiscal Wake-up Tour seems to be just that. People from all ends of the political spectrum seeing the dangers of the deficit and putting politics aside is a big step. The idea of moving the discussion out of Washington, taking it on the road and delivering it directly to the people is huge, maybe even revolutionary.

For years now we have been caught in political gridlock. In our politics, as in the sports world, where there can't be a winner without a loser, the success rate is only fifty percent. Yet in the real world Dr. Seuss had it pretty close to right in the notion that if you really, really try, you will succeed 98¾% guaranteed. No sense in blaming our elected officials, they are just being who we want them to be. But maybe the economists are right and the time has come to stop trying to build consensus in the halls of power and try building it on Main Street instead.

It is all like this Salmon Mousse recipe. For years we've been giving our leaders in Washington the money to buy the ingredients for Salmon Mousse and demanding they make it for us, but they just have not been able to agree on a shopping list. Maybe if we want Salmon Mousse it is time for us to get our own ingredients, mix them all together and while we are letting it chill for a full 4 hours, work to build support for Salmon Mousse across the country. If we can serve the Mousse to our elected officials already prepared, and tell them the Mousse has an 80% approval rating, all that will be left for them to do is take a big forkful and smile.

Can the economists succeed? Hard to say; they are up against a lot. Still they are very sharp people and they have some time to figure out what is working and make adjustments. The important thing is that right now in this country there are people from opposite sides of the political spectrum working together to solve problems for the common good. That alone is reason enough to hope, and with hope anything is possible.

Bill

It's the Salmon Mousse!

Belle Sawhill (far right, being hugged by the Grim Reaper) and friends at a dinner party re-enacting a scene from the Monty Python movie The Meaning of Life.

Salmon Mousse

This recipe came from Belle's mom. She sometimes used canned salmon back in the old days but Belle says that freshly cooked or leftover salmon works best. Sometimes she will use smoked salmon or a combination of smoked and fresh. "Make it look pretty," says Belle. "It's very rich and people eat small portions. Serve with fresh parboiled vegetables such as asparagus or beans in a marinade. There are a lot of things you can do. I serve it as a main course in the summer or spring with a nice loaf of crusty bread and a good wine."

1	envelope gelatin
2	TB lemon juice
1	slice onion, ½-inch thick
½	Cup boiling water
½	Cup mayonnaise
¼	tsp. sweet paprika
1	tsp. salt (if using already cooked, seasoned salmon, you may want to omit the salt)
2½	tsp. fresh dill weed (1 tsp. dried)
1	lb. fresh cooked salmon
1	Cup heavy cream (we also made it using 2% milk and it was still good but not as rich)

Add the gelatin to a blender or food processor (we tried it with both and found the food processor easier, as it could hold more). Then add the lemon juice, onion and water. Blend on high for about 40 seconds. Turn off and add the mayonnaise, paprika, salt, dill weed and salmon. Blend briefly, about 20 seconds. Add the cream ⅓ at a time blending briefly between, then blend for about 40 seconds longer. Pour into a 4-cup mold and chill for 4 hours. Then un-mold it on a platter (dip in hot water to loosen it) and decorate with parsley, dill, cucumbers, cherry tomatoes or anything else that appeals to you.

Prep. time: 35 minutes if cooking the salmon first. Serves: 12

We owe a special debt to the cooks we met in the days following Hurricane Katrina. Their stories shined a light on how the values of hope and optimism found so often in those who cook can mean everything in times of trouble. That optimism is not merely an emotion, a pleasant breeze floating along on a sunny summer's day, that it is very real and very concrete and possessing it can mean all the difference. When times get hard, those who not only possess optimism, but have the ability to spread it, are valuable beyond calculation.

I really am not a Pollyanna who thinks everything happens for a good reason. Still, I can't help but feel that in 2005 we needed what it is that the people of New Orleans and the Gulf Coast have in abundance, and that we still need it today. The winds of Katrina spread the people of the Gulf through every state in this country. With them came their spirit of life, their joyous celebration of friends and family and what we are all about: their food.

When we started we could have gone a lot of directions with our magazine. We could have been one more publication selling the notion that great food and great wealth go hand in hand, but that is so not us. It is great food and great people that make up our world, and the cooks we found in the aftermath of Katrina really left me feeling that we chose the right direction.

Katrina also reminded us that opportunity in this country is not evenly distributed, and that the burden brought by an event like Katrina does not get evenly shared. Equality is a very long march and we have not reached the finish line. But who would want to stand still anyway when there are so many interesting people to meet, and great meals to eat, along our way?

one for the road

Think of how many really good moments you have had since August 29th. How many relaxing evenings sitting around the dinner table, how many holidays, good times, and even good night's sleep you've enjoyed since last summer. For those whose lives were in the path of Katrina, the months since have been rough. This is not like the fall you had your kitchen remodeled, and had to put up with the workmen's dusty footprints through your house for a month. This is so much more.

The burden of Katrina is not just being borne by those in its path. The communities around the gulf, the places that have reached out to those in need are paying a heavy price. This is a national problem and it should be solved with Federal funds. Tragedies like this are the reason we hang together, to share the burden and help each other get on with our lives. Yet it seems all of our tax dollars are too busy elsewhere to help. If you know people who live in Texas, Atlanta or even Slidell please thank them for what they are doing. Their caring, the love that they are sharing, means so very much.

And that's kind of our whole approach to food, why we think that cooking is so very important. Life gets hard at times. There are moments when it seems no one cares what happens to you. It is then that being able to fall back to the memory of it being your birthday and your grandmother, who loves you very much, has made you your favorite cake because you are someone special. It is those birthday treats and all the meals in between that give us strength for the future, and heal moments from the past. It does not matter if you are on the giving or receiving end, the magic of cooking flows both directions. Cooking is not a surface thing, it is the mortar of love that gets layered on day after day, year after year. Katrina has shown the limit of our control. Our stuff can be washed away, but people who cook know deep down that love is real and that is something that can never be washed away.

284

Gram's Banana Birthday Cake

Gram's Banana Cake

Every year when those April birthdays rolled around, Gram would make our special request–banana cake with chocolate frosting. This cake is just the best, and it is pretty darn easy, too. Make sure those bananas are really ripe, and follow our tips to make frosting the cake a snap.

2½ Cups sugar
 1 Cup shortening or butter
 4 eggs
 1 Cup sour cream
 3 Cups all-purpose flour
 2 tsp. baking soda
 6 very ripe bananas, mashed (2½ Cups)
 1 TB vanilla extract

Preheat the oven to 350°. Grease and flour three 9-inch cake pans and set aside. Cream together the sugar and shortening or butter.

It will be dry and crumbly. Add the eggs and beat well. Mix in the sour cream. In a separate bowl, sift together the flour and baking soda. Add to the creamed mixture and beat well. Add the mashed bananas and vanilla extract and mix well. Divide evenly between the prepared cake pans. Bake for 30-35 minutes or until a toothpick inserted in the center comes out clean. Check the cakes partway through baking and swap the pans around in the oven, top to bottom, bottom to top. Cool a few minutes and remove from pans. Finish cooling on a wire rack. This cake freezes very well if you'd like to bake it ahead of time to frost later. Wrap each layer in waxed paper and plastic wrap. There is no need to thaw before frosting the cake; it actually frosts quite nicely while the layers are still a bit frozen.

Frosting:

 6 Cups powdered sugar
½ Cup natural cocoa powder
½ Cup butter, softened
½ Cup, brewed, strong black coffee

Sift the powdered sugar and cocoa together into a large bowl. Add the softened butter and mix on very low speed until they are incorporated. Add the coffee and mix until smooth. **Serves:** 8-10. Prep. time: 15 minutes + 10 to frost. Baking time: 30-35 minutes.

Tip: Icing Layer Cakes

Choose the smoothest layer for the top layer of the cake. To keep your plate clean while icing the cake, place four strips of waxed paper ½" under the cake, extending over the sides of the plate. Just pull them out when you're finished. Put about ¼" of frosting between each layer of cake. Frost the sides next, and the top of the cake last.

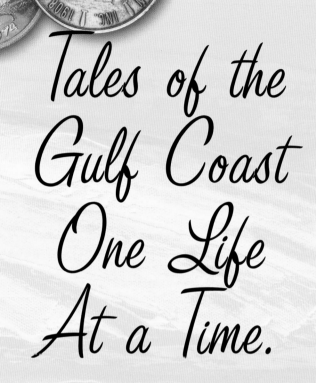

Tales of the Gulf Coast One Life At a Time.

Hundreds of thousands of homes destroyed is a statistic, one home destroyed is something very different. We salute those with the strength to leave. We salute those with the strength to stay. So many good recipes, so many good people. Here are just a few.

Amy Cyrex Sins

Amy and George's home, just three years old.

George and Amy's home in New Orleans, along the 17th St. Canal, was destroyed by Hurricane Katrina. Like many others, they've begun the journey of rebuilding their homes and their lives.

Amy Cyrex Sins was in Chicago with a college friend when she got news from her husband George back home in Louisiana that the hurricane on the way looked to be a bad one and she shouldn't come home just yet.

Instead of flying home the Sunday before Katrina hit, she made her way to her sister's home in Houston. Once there, she fixed herself in front of the television to monitor the news of the storm. Pictures of Louisiana flashed on the screen, showing miles upon miles of devastation.

"We were watching the local news, because at that point there was nothing on the national news about the flooding. The anchors were crying and saying that they lost their homes. A few hours later we started watching CNN. There was a helicopter flying over New Orleans and pictures of the levee break. When the announcer started saying the break was in the 17th Street Canal, I was glued to the TV."

The home George and Amy built, a mere three years ago, backed right up to the 17th Street Canal in Orleans Parish. She knew George had boarded up and evacuated safely with Frank and Dean, their two cats, but what of family photos? With all that work,

Boarded up and ready to evacuate. Both cats, Dean and Frank, made it through the storm, though they probably found it all quite annoying.

287

The view down Amy and George's street, 5 weeks after Katrina.

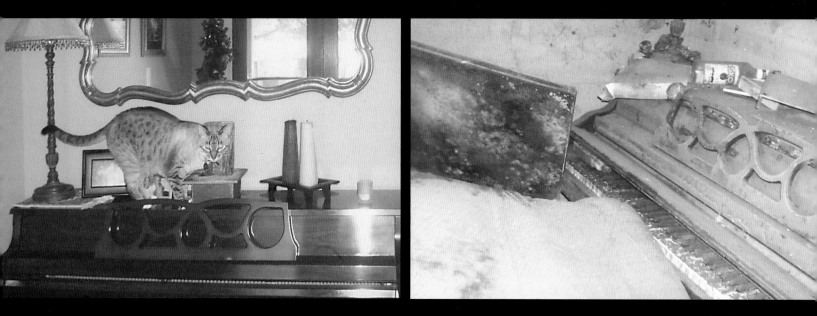

"The lake went through my living room," she said. "We had 7 or 8 feet of water in our house. You almost have to see it to believe it ... and the smell..."

would he have thought of the Wedding Pictures?

"Later in the day, I saw my house. I could tell because the video zoomed right up to it. You could see the roof of the shed in our back yard and the entire house. At the time all I was thinking was at least I know what we are dealing with, a lot of water."

And yes, George thought of the photos; picking up every one and moving them to a safe upstairs closet shelf.

"The lake went through my living room," she said. "We had 7 or 8 feet of water in our house. You almost have to see it to believe it ... and the smell. We had 6 inches of mud in the downstairs we had to shovel out. It looked like someone had bombed it. Everything was gray - not a green leaf in sight."

They were able to salvage their clothes and some pots and pans, but only the stainless steel ones.

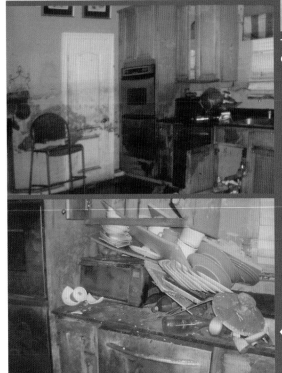

Their swimming pool became a home for garfish, crabs and turtles and who knows what else.

Everything on the first floor of the house was destroyed. If you figure salt water « might ever race through your kitchen, stick to stainless steel. Copper pots just couldn't handle the tough prerequisites of life in a New Orleans kitchen.

"If there's one thing I've learned, that's to invest in stainless steel," she said, trying to look on the bright side of things. "The saltwater ate holes in our copper pots; they were like sieves. Everything that survived was stainless steel."

A way Amy has been able to make herself feel better is through her cooking. "When I am stressed, I cook for everyone that will eat," she wrote to us. "If I won the Powerball, I'd be in the kitchen cooking."

Last fall, she prepared a meal of Sauce Piquant with Cheese Grits for 35 at her cousin's wedding rehearsal dinner in Baton Rouge. The majority of the guests were from New Orleans and

"When we were setting the table, my Mom went to the pantry to get something and said, 'What happened to my iris bulbs?' She was storing them in the pantry for the winter to plant in the spring. Needless to say, I confused iris bulbs with garlic and we stuffed them in the roast. After a call to poison control and them laughing at us thinking it was a prank call, they told us not to eat the roast. Iris plants can be toxic so they assumed the bulbs were too. So we all went out to dinner and laughed about the experience. I've been cooking ever since."

Despite their losses, Amy says she and her husband will pick up the pieces and together, with the support of her family, many of

A way Amy has been able to make herself feel better is through her cooking.

had lost their homes, too, Amy said.

She owes her love of cooking to both her mother and father. "My Dad loved to cook," Amy said. "Growing up I'd stand over Dad's shoulder and I'd get so excited to cook for others!

"At 9 years old both my Mom and Dad were cooking Sunday dinner — roast and rice and gravy. My Dad said that I could help stuff the roast but first I needed to chop the garlic. So I eagerly proceeded to peel and chop up garlic, stuffed in the roast and set the timer for the oven.

whom also lost their homes, will rebuild their lives.

"I do think five years from now, the city is going to come out of it," she said. "There's a lot of culture still intact. If people can do it right, it can be a nice, clean place to live but it will take a lot of time, energy and patience.

"It's hard to feel sorry for yourself and feel sad, because there are so many people that lost everything they had," she said. "You're all in the same boat."

Bananas Foster Bread Pudding

This is a party pudding, so cut the recipe in half if you aren't serving a crowd, or plan on eating way too much, since it is so delicious!

Bread pudding:

12	Cups stale bread (poorboy loaf is perfect dried out and broken up by hand—Amy saves and freezes bread throughout the end of the year and uses it all for a Christmas Pudding)
5	eggs, separated
2	egg whites (reserve yolks for sauce)
1¾	Cups sugar
5½	Cups whole milk or half and half
1	TB vanilla extract
1	tsp. almond extract
¼	Cup dark rum
¼	Cup crème de banana liqueur
1½	tsp. cinnamon
3	bananas, mashed
2	bananas, sliced on the bias
½	Cup raisins
2	TB butter

Custard Sauce:

2	egg yolks
¾	Cup of sugar
1	Cup evaporated milk
1	Cup whole milk
3	TB cornstarch
½	tsp. vanilla extract
¼	tsp. almond extract
¼	Cup dark rum
¼	Cup crème de banana liqueur

Bananas Foster Sauce:

4	TB (½ stick) butter (Amy uses unsalted)
1	Cup dark brown sugar, packed
¼	Cup dark rum
¼	Cup crème de banana liqueur cinnamon
⅓	Cup of the Custard Sauce
1	Cup chopped pecans

Preheat oven to 350°. For the bread pudding: Mix egg yolks with sugar and beat until light yellow. Add milk, extracts, liquors, cinnamon and the mashed bananas, mixing well. In a mixer, beat the seven egg whites until stiff peaks form, then fold into the egg yolk mixture. Add the sliced bananas and raisins, folding them in gently and being careful not to deflate the egg whites. Place the stale bread pieces into a large bowl, then pour half of the egg mixture over and mix well. Let soak for at least 10 minutes, then add the other half, and soak another 10 minutes. Melt 1 tablespoon of butter and use it to coat a 9" x 12" baking dish. Pour the bread mixture into the dish, then cover with foil and place into a bain-marie (water bath) or put the dish into a roasting pan and pour hot water into the roasting pan until it's about ⅔ the way up the side of the baking dish. Bake at 350° for one hour. Remove foil, then finish baking until the center is set, about 15 more minutes (or longer if necessary). Glaze the top of the pudding with 1 TB of butter while it's still hot.

For the custard sauce: Beat the 2 egg yolks and sugar together until light yellow, then add the milks and mix well. Make a slurry with the cornstarch and 3 tablespoons cold water, mix until dissolved, then add the cornstarch slurry, extracts and liquors. Cook in a double boiler until thickened, and the sauce coats the back of a spoon. If you don't have a double boiler, you can use a bowl placed over a pan of boiling water or simply cook in a saucepan and watch it like a hawk, as the eggs can scramble.

For the Bananas Foster sauce: Melt the butter, add the brown sugar and cook over medium heat for 4 to 5 minutes, stirring frequently, until the sugar has melted and dissolved. Add the liquors, stir well, and heat until warm. Very carefully ignite the sauce and gently swirl the pan to keep the sauce from sticking. If you're nervous, you don't have to light the sauce, but it's a crowd-pleaser and not as scary as you might think. Toss a few pinches of cinnamon into the flames (tell everyone to make a wish and watch it sparkle), then add ⅓ cup of the Custard Sauce and the pecans; cook for 1 minute.

Assembly: Slice the pudding into individual servings. Place a pool of Custard Sauce onto a dessert plate and place a slice of bread pudding in the middle. Drizzle liberally with the Bananas Foster Sauce.

Start a diet tomorrow!!!

Serves: 18-24. **Prep. time:** 30 minutes.
Baking time: 1 hr. 15 minutes.

Bananas Foster Bread Pudding
"Start a diet tomorrow!"

Amy labeled these photos "Bar- looks like a really rough party!" These days those World Famous Bloody Marys of George's probably taste even better than they did in the old days.

George's World Famous Bloody Mary

1	bottle (about 33 fl. oz.) Major Peter's Bloody Mary Mix, or your favorite mix
1	lemon, squeezed
1	lime, squeezed
3	TB Worcestershire sauce
1	TB celery salt
1	TB lemon pepper
1	TB LA Red Hot or Crystal Hot Sauce—add more if you like it really spicy! Use your favorite!
1½	Cups vodka

Garnish:

1	lemon and lime, sliced
	jalapeño olives
	celery stalks
	spicy pickled okra or beans

Combine all ingredients except vodka, stir well and chill. Add vodka immediately before serving. Serve over ice and garnish.

Prep. time: 5 minutes
Yield: 1 pitcher

Daddy's Sauce Piquant with Cheese Grits

Last fall, Amy prepared a meal of *Sauce Piquant with Cheese Grits* for 35 at her cousin's wedding rehearsal dinner in Baton Rouge. The majority of the guests were from New Orleans and had lost their homes, too.

Will Amy and George celebrate Mardi Gras this year? "Yes, Yes and Yes! Popeye's Chicken, red beans and rice, and for dessert – King cake from Randazzo's Bakery, and Bloody Marys to drink!"

Amy and her friends from New York celebrating Mardi Gras last year – they don't know who that guy is – he jumped into all the photos at the last second.

Daddy's Sauce Piquant

This recipe was originally "deer sauce" for venison, but it's really great with beef. Don't bother paying extra for a tender cut, the cooking tenderizes round steak perfectly.

2	lbs. of meat (we used round steak)
½	Cup flour
¼	tsp. cayenne
1	Cup olive oil, divided
3	onions, chopped (about 1½ Cups)
3	green onions, chopped
3	cloves of garlic, chopped
2	8 oz. packs of fresh, sliced mushrooms
2	red, yellow and/or orange bell peppers, chopped
1	Cup celery, chopped
1	Cup of red wine, more added as remaining after you have a glass or two while cooking
2	8 oz. cans of tomato sauce
2	10 oz. cans canned, chopped tomatoes & green chilies
3	Cups of beef broth, more added as needed
4	TB Worcestershire sauce
1	TB dried thyme
1	TB dried oregano
1	TB dried parsley
2	tsp. dried basil
3	bay leaves
	salt to taste
	black pepper to taste

garlic powder to taste
onion powder to taste
cayenne pepper to taste

Pound meat flat to tenderize, then cut into serving-size portions. Put flour and cayenne in re-sealable plastic bag. Add the meat and shake to coat. Pan-fry in ½ cup oil, browning both sides and set aside.

In same pot, make a roux with ½ cup oil and remaining flour from bag and cook until dark brown. Don't burn it—cook it slowly. Add all onions, garlic, mushrooms, peppers and celery and cook down until soft. Add ½ cup of red wine to deglaze pan.

Add meat, tomato sauce, chopped tomatoes & green chilies, beef broth and Worcestershire. Add thyme, oregano, parsley, basil, bay leaves, salt and pepper. Simmer for 2 hours, covered, or until meat is falling apart.

Add garlic powder, onion powder, cayenne and any leftover red wine. You may also need to add more beef stock if the sauce is too thick. If too thin, remove lid. Simmer a little longer and serve with garlic cheese grits.

Prep time: 45 minutes. **Cooking time:** up to 2 hours. **Serves:** 6-8

Garlic Cheese Grits

This is a really good side dish that most of us Northerners were unfamiliar with—easy and hearty as well as tasty. It can also easily be doubled to feed a hungry work crew.

1	Cup regular grits
4	Cups water
1	tsp. salt
2	tsp. garlic powder
8	oz. Kraft cheese log or grated cheddar (Velveeta cheese works well too)
1	stick of butter, sliced
2	eggs, well beaten
¼	Cup milk
	dash of cayenne

Preheat oven to 325°. Cook grits according to package directions in salted water. After the grits are cooked, add garlic, cheese and butter. Stir in eggs, milk and cayenne. Put in a greased, 8x8-inch glass dish and bake at 325° for 40 minutes.

Prep time: 10 minutes
Cooking time: 40 minutes
Serves: 6-8

Judith Wenger

Judith looking out onto the Gulf from the deck at her favorite Perdido Key rental spot. Now destroyed, it was the perfect nearby beach escape.

"During these past 100 days I have driven almost 8,000 miles and stayed in 14 different places. My longtime friends and neighbors who know exactly what I am going through are scattered all over the country, and all of us are just trying to get home."

Judith Wenger, longtime New Orleans resident, was forced to evacuate twice last year, first from Katrina in August, and then from Houston when Rita came ashore a month later. Even her vacation spot on Perdido Key was destroyed.

When Katrina loomed, she left her home in New Orleans and headed to Jackson, Mississippi, then made her way to family in Chicago. After returning to her studies in Houston, where she is finishing up her law degree, she had to evacuate for Rita and went to Pumpkin Center, Louisiana - across Lake Pontchartrain from New Orleans - and stayed with friends.

"I showed up with pancake mix, a ham, syrup and a bottle of bourbon, and slept on a recliner," she recalled.

In early December, Judith wrote to us from her temporary home in Houston about her day-to-day battles getting her life back up and running.

"I have had to make multiple trips back to New Orleans to meet with adjusters and contractors and roofers and to try to salvage some of my belongings. Dealing with the insurance companies has been a nightmare.

"People are certainly interested in hearing our storm stories, but only someone who has gone through this experience truly understands the loneliness of displacement and the frustration of having a monumental task ahead of you while your hands are tied by 350 miles of distance and insurance and contractor and government problems and the sheer enormity of the task of rebuilding New Orleans.

"Then there are the nightmares, the inability to concentrate, anxiety over the flood protection system, the need to be there with your people... everything has changed forever."

A friend helped Judith find a furnished garage

The Wenger family at Al and Ad's 60th anniversary party, October 3, 2004.

Cool Cuke and Tomato Salad

The yogurt adds a delicious, low fat creaminess to this recipe—give it a try!

1	large cucumber, peeled, halved, seeded and cut into bite-sized pieces (we like English seedless)
1	large tomato, coarsely chopped
1	medium avocado, diced
¼	Vidalia onion, finely diced
1-2	TB balsamic vinegar
1-2	TB plain yogurt
2	TB olive oil
	salt and pepper
1	TB. fresh basil or 1 tsp. dried basil

Combine fresh ingredients and mix gently. Add oil and vinegar, salt and pepper until it tastes right to you. This will taste best if it sits for about an hour before serving. Stir in yogurt and fresh basil just before serving.

Prep time: 10 minutes
Serves: 4-6
Cooking time: Let sit for 1 hour in dressing before serving

Simple Sautéed Greens

Don't forget the hot sauce! This makes a nice simple lunch with just some bread or rice on the side.

1	bunch of fresh greens, about 6 Cups (stems removed), washed thoroughly and chopped (kale, collard, mustard, beet, or even spinach if no other fresh greens are available)
2-3	cloves garlic, minced
½	medium onion, finely diced
2	TB olive oil
1-2	tsp. sesame oil
	salt and pepper
2-3	TB of rice vinegar

In a deep skillet, sauté garlic and onions in olive oil over medium heat. Add greens and mix well to coat with oil. Cover the pan and give it an occasional shake so the greens don't stick, but be sure to keep the pan covered. Check after 5 minutes. You want the greens to be wilted, but be careful to not overcook! When almost done, add sesame oil, salt and pepper. Remove from heat, and stir in vinegar just before serving.

Prep time: 10 minutes
Cooking time: 5-8 minutes
Serves: 3-4

apartment with low rent in the Heights neighborhood of Houston. The owner welcomed her with freshly baked banana bread on her arrival and she has made lasting friendships. So, on the surface, her life seemed fine, filled with her studies, grocery shopping, volunteering. It was all very surreal, she said.

One thing that remains a familiar comfort to her is her love of cooking. Judith loves pork roasts, beans and roasted vegetables, and she's a big fan of fish: red fish, flounder, speckled trout, crabs and crawfish.

> "I showed up with pancake mix, a ham, syrup and a bottle of bourbon, and slept on a recliner."

"I like to try new recipes, to mix French and traditional foods. I can cook fish six thousand ways," she said. "My specialty is to adapt the recipe to be healthier, lower in fat and to taste really good."

One of her favorite dishes is koo be-yawn, (court bouillon), poaching fish by simmering with vegetables, seasonings and wine or vinegar.

Judith loves to create new dishes, and worked out her Perdido Key Fish recipe while vacationing on the island, about a three-hour drive from New Orleans near the Alabama/Florida state line. Her vacation spot was also destroyed by Katrina.

Now back in New Orleans, Judith is living in a mobile home while her house is being rebuilt. Her heart belongs to the Uptown district where she lives and she believes that the city can and should be rebuilt.

"I was stunned about the destruction in New Orleans," she said. "It really did look like a war zone. But I love New Orleans. It's so laid-back, culturally diverse and racially mixed. That's so important to me. I think it'll be slow to come back, but it will come back."

Amidst all the upheaval Judith has continued working on her law degree from Loyola University at the University of Houston. She plans to graduate in May.

Judith started law school as a second career after considering ways to work in the field of social justice, and now that work is all the more important.

"I think my life in New Orleans will be determined by how the city begins to rebuild after I graduate," she said. "There are landlord-tenant issues, and family law issues, and insurance issues and immigrant issues. I want to do work that has meaning and I am committed to New Orleans."

> "I think my life in New Orleans will be determined by how the city begins to rebuild after I graduate...I want to do work that has meaning and I am committed to New Orleans."

Perdido Key Fish

Judith Wenger is one great cook, and we loved this light and lively but really satisfying dish. Here's to Perdido Key coming back better than ever!

1	lb. fish filets (we used tilapia)
3	cloves garlic, chopped
1	medium onion, chopped
1	red bell pepper, chopped
2	ribs celery, chopped
2-3	TB olive oil
1	15 oz. can diced tomatoes
1-2	TB balsamic vinegar
1½	tsp. fresh basil, chopped or ½ tsp. dried basil
¼-½	Cup oil-cured black olives, chopped
	salt and pepper
½	tsp. cumin
⅛	tsp. nutmeg*
¼	Cup red wine
1	lime
4-5	oz. goat cheese, room temperature

Buy the freshest full-bodied saltwater fish you can find: redfish, black drum, sheepshead, red snapper, tilapia.

Preheat oven to 400°. Sauté garlic, onion, bell pepper, celery, all coarsely chopped, in olive oil over medium heat until veggies are soft. Stir in tomatoes and their juice; add balsamic vinegar. Warm through.

Remove from heat, add basil and oil-cured black olives. Depending on your mood, add either ¼ tsp. ground cloves and a dash of cinnamon, or add cumin and a dash of nutmeg (see note). Splash in a shot of red wine if you have an open bottle and pour yourself a glass when you do.

Grease baking dish, rinse off fish and pat dry with paper towels. Spread a cup of sauce over bottom of baking dish. Salt and pepper filets lightly on both sides, place in baking dish and squeeze juice from half a lime on filets. Cover entirely with remaining sauce.

Bake, covered tightly, for 20 minutes in a 400° oven. Remove from oven, dot with teaspoon-sized dollops of room temperature goat cheese. Return to oven and bake for 5-8 minutes, uncovered, until cheese is melted.

Serve by candlelight with red wine, salad, more olives, lime wedges and plenty of warm, crusty French bread to mop up the sauce.

Note: We chose Cumin/Nutmeg to give a warm and spicy flavor, as opposed to Cloves/Cinnamon which would lend the recipe a sweeter flavor.

Serves: 4 to 6 people
Prep time: 10 minutes.
Cooking time: 30 minutes

Judith and her law school classmates celebrate a daughter's birthday in January 2005.

Judith wins the jackpot on Ad and Al's 1917 nickel slot machine.

Judith and a classmate at the Barrister's Ball, Loyola law school's annual dance, at the New Orleans Aquarium in May 2005

Louisiana Stuffed Eggplant from Judith Wenger

A traditional meal that has stood the test of time.
It's great!

1	medium eggplant
1	rib celery, diced
1	medium onion, diced
1	small red bell pepper, diced
1	Cup mushrooms, chopped
2	TB extra virgin olive oil
1	15 oz. can diced tomatoes, juice drained
1	Cup red wine
1	Cup cooked shrimp, chopped into bite-sized pieces
$1/4$	Cup seasoned bread crumbs
$1/4$	Cup grated Parmesan cheese
$1/4$	tsp. crushed red peppers or cayenne pepper
$1 1/2$	tsp. fresh basil or $1/2$ tsp. dried basil
$1/2$	tsp. salt
$1/4$	tsp. pepper

Slice eggplant in half lengthwise. Cut insides out, leaving $1/3$ inch of eggplant next to skin. Chop eggplant you scooped out. Grease baking dish, and rub olive oil on the outside of the eggplant skin.

Sauté celery, onion, bell pepper and mushrooms in 2 tablespoons of olive oil over medium heat. Add chopped eggplant, $1/2$ can tomatoes and cook 10 minutes. Pour in the red wine and give it a stir. Remove from heat. Stir in shrimp, bread crumbs, Parmesan, crushed red pepper, basil, salt and pepper. Blend thoroughly. Fill eggplant halves with mixture, cover with remaining tomatoes, and finish with more Parmesan cheese on top.

Bake uncovered at 425° for 25 to 30 minutes until top is nicely browned.

Serves: 2 for dinner, 4 for lunch
Prep time: 30 minutes
Cooking time: 25-30 minutes

Bob & Dorothy Olson

"We thought we could ride it out, so we chose not to evacuate," said Bob Olson. But ride it out he did along with his wife Dorothy, son Thor, mother-in-law Dorothy (a.k.a. "Mrs. B." for Beckerman) and brother-in-law George Beckerman. Retired from the Army after 32 years, Bob had weathered hurricanes before but this one was different. "Staying here was not a good move."

As the storm went through, the five of them passed the time in the dining room by playing cards and watching shingles, gutters and other chunks of houses fly by. When they heard a crash, Mrs. B would react. "Mom would say 'Oh my God!' or 'Jesus!'" said Bob's wife Dorothy, a retired nurse. "We were getting a little tense so I told Mom to stop. I told her it was like saying 'oops' in the operating room." The water began to rise and then started to seep into the house through the weep holes in the bricks. "We didn't know we were supposed to plug them before a hurricane. At one point George was holding Bob's belt as he hung out the window trying

Like so many high school sweethearts, Bob and Dorothy Olson went their separate ways. Unlike many, they managed to reconnect nearly thirty years later.

297

Dorothy's Jambalaya

Julianna loves her mother's jambalaya, and we do too.

1	whole chicken
1	TB chopped garlic
¼	Cup oil (bacon drippings are best)
4	Cups long grain rice (NOT instant)
1½	lbs. smoked sausage (spicy)
2	tsp. (or more to taste) Cajun seasoning
4	Cups chopped onions
2	Cups chopped green onions
2	Cups chopped celery
2	Cups chopped green peppers
1	heaping TB brown sugar

Skin and bone the chicken, throw the skin and bones into a pot with salt, pepper and sufficient water to make 5 cups of stock. Bring to a boil. While stock continues to boil, rough-chop the chicken meat, garlic, onions, celery and peppers. Slice the sausage into ¼ inch slices.

Heat the oil and brown the chopped chicken and sliced sausage. Remove the chicken and sausage. Add the brown sugar and caramelize. Add and sauté the garlic, onions, celery and green peppers. Return the chicken and sausage to the sautéed vegetables. Strain the chicken stock and add to the pan along with Cajun seasoning. Bring to a boil.

Add the rice and return to a boil. Cover and reduce heat to a simmer. Simmer for about 10 minutes. After 10 minutes remove cover and stir rice up from bottom. Continue cooking, uncovered, for an additional 15 minutes, or until rice is done. Add the chopped green onions.

Serves: 10-12. **Prep. time:** 15 minutes chopping. **Cooking time:** roughly an hour.
NOTE: To adjust the recipe to feed more people, use these rough rules of thumb: 1 cup of long grain rice will feed three people. Use 1 cup of rice to 2 cups of sautéed onions, celery and green peppers. Use 1¼ Cups stock to each cup of rice. Over-season to compensate for the rice.

Bar-B-Cue Shrimp

This is a very delicious recipe which makes a lot of sauce, suitable for French bread, rice or pasta.

1	lb. butter (seriously, this is NOT low fat)
¼	Cup fresh garlic, minced (6-8 cloves)
2	Cups Italian dressing (1 16 oz. bottle of your favorite, or 3-4 TB. Italian dressing seasoning mixed with 1⅓ Cups vegetable oil and ⅔ Cup regular or red wine vinegar)
1½-2	lbs. large shrimp (18-20 count or larger)—do not peel or remove head (the photo has the heads off because we couldn't get any with heads on here in Wisconsin)
	Cajun seasoning to taste

Melt the butter in a skillet on medium heat being careful not to let the butter burn. Add the garlic and sauté for about 30 seconds. Add the Italian dressing and Cajun seasoning. Stir to mix well. Add the shrimp, cook on each side until pink. Be careful not to overcook or the shrimp turns to rubber—just a few minutes will do it.

Serve with a green salad with French bread (the good crusty kind) to sop up the juice.

Serves: 8
Prep. time: 10 minutes
Cooking time: 8 minutes or so

to plug them." Finally a neighbor waded over with some duct tape and helped them. Fortunately their house was on a bit of a rise so they were able to keep the water out. It was not easy. "Everything is electric today, the scrubbers and so forth. With no electricity, all we had was one sponge mop and some towels."

With phone lines down it was frustrating. Other than looking out the window, they could not get any news of what was happening in Slidell. The only radio station they could get was WWL out of New Orleans. "That was heartbreaking," said Dorothy, "because some people still had cell phones working and they were calling into the radio station saying that water was up to their chest and to please get help." But no one was calling in from Slidell which had them worried. "We could not get out," said Bob. "We were in the middle of a moat for three days."

The gas stove was still working so Dorothy got creative in the kitchen. "She made some of the most amazing stuff," Bob said. "She'd take canned chicken, some tomato sauce, and put cinnamon in it to serve over noodles." Dorothy added, "It was so hot. You didn't want to eat. I tried to keep things interesting."

When the water receded, a neighbor helped them get in touch with their daughter Julianna, who was mobilizing to come and get them. They decided to make their way out and meet her somewhere. They discovered George's van had a flat tire and when

Dorothy's daughter, Julianna, followed in her footsteps and became a nurse.

George's Chicken Salad

A great recipe to use up leftover chicken. Throw it together after a nice roast chicken dinner, and by tomorrow's lunch, it'll be perfect. In a pinch, you can even start with a deli chicken and go from there.

2	Cups cooked chicken, chopped
1	rib celery, chopped
¼	Cup onion, minced
1	dill pickle spear, chopped
6	seedless red grapes, halved if large
6	seedless green grapes, halved if large
⅛	tsp. cayenne pepper
1	TB golden raisins
1	TB crystallized ginger
2	TB pine nuts
1	TB craisins (dried cranberries)
¼	red apple, chopped
¼	green apple, chopped
2	dashes Worcestershire sauce
2	TB mayonnaise

Combine all of the ingredients in a roomy bowl and mix well. Let sit in the refrigerator for at least an hour, but a day is even better. Serve with sourdough bread. For the photo, we split a whole, 8-inch loaf of sourdough and added some lettuce for garnish, which made 4 good-sized sandwiches.

Prep. time: 10 minutes
Chilling time: at least 1 hour
Serves: 4-6

Thor and his uncle, George Beckerman, formed a very special bond during Katrina. Thor, 36, is cognitively disabled and lives in a group home in New Orleans. Thinking he would be gone only a few days, he evacuated the home with only a book and an Elvis costume. But being the most able-bodied, he was very helpful at the house during the storm, mopping up and keeping the water out. George adds, "I just had surgery. Mom wasn't feeling so good. We were all kind of at the end of our ropes. But Thor, with the wisdom of a happy 5 year old, wakes up everyday to a brand new day, raring to go. He kept us going." Thor's home took 4 feet of water but fortunately his room is on the second floor. His beloved Elvis collection is still intact.

they tried to change it, the van fell off the jack. "We didn't know what we were going to do," said Dorothy. Then a group of guys from around the corner showed up and physically lifted the van up and on to the jack. The guys changed the tire for them and the family was on its way.

> # The gas stove was still working so Dorothy got creative in the kitchen. "She made some of the most amazing stuff," Bob said.

Once they got a ways from home their cell phone began working and they contacted Julianna. They agreed to meet at the Cracker Barrel in Jackson, Mississippi. Dorothy said it was a strange experience. "When we walked into the Cracker Barrel it was such a shock. There was electricity on. People smelled nice, food was there. It was as if nothing had happened." Everyone got cleaned up, fed and re-hydrated for the trip north.

In Mississippi, lines for gasoline were up to three miles long. When a station ran out of gas, people would just sleep in their cars so they didn't lose their place in line. "My daughter was driving a Molotov cocktail, she had so much gas." said Dorothy. "If she hadn't we would not have made it to Chicago."

George and Thor stayed in the basement of a house near Chicago. The house was occupied by 5 midwives and Thor would regularly entertain them with his Elvis impersonations. Mrs. B and her cat Tawny stayed with her grandson's family, much to the chagrin of the family dog. Bob and Dorothy and their two cats stayed with Julianna and her two cats. Things were tense at first ... between the cats, but they smoothed out. Bob and Dorothy enjoyed the time with their daughter.

They have all returned home. Thor's job was literally swept away but he has found another one. Dorothy says the neighborhood is changing because many people don't want to face another hurricane. "Folks from other towns that were wiped out are buying up houses in Slidell. So many of our neighbors have left." The family feels fortunate to be back home intact. "Basically we came through it pretty good," George said. "You can always look down the street and see someone who had it worse." Bob sums it up with some well earned advice: "The first rule to surviving a hurricane is to leave. Get out. Go! Never again will we sit through something like that."

Mrs. B's Royal Cajun-Swedish Pot Roast

This old-fashioned recipe is a gem, especially on a cold grey day—it warms the soul.

3½ -4	lbs. beef rump roast or eye of round	1	onion, cut in half
2 or 3	cloves garlic, thinly sliced	8	whole allspice berries
1	tsp. salt	6	white peppercorns
½	tsp. pepper	1	TB dark corn syrup
2	TB butter	2	TB vinegar
1½	Cups beef stock	6	anchovy filets
2	bay leaves	2	TB flour
		½	Cup cream

Cut slits around the beef. Insert pieces of sliced garlic. Rub the roast with salt and pepper. In a heavy saucepan heat the butter and brown the roast well on all sides. Add stock, bay leaf, onion, allspice, peppercorns, syrup and vinegar. Place the anchovies on top of the meat. Cover and simmer for about 2 hours or until the meat is tender. When the meat is ready, remove from the pot to a platter, keep warm. Take the anchovies off and add them to the juice in the pan and stir to blend. Simmer briefly, then strain juice and pour back into the pan. Stir in 2 TB flour and ½ cup cream to make gravy. Simmer gently until thickened. Serve gravy with sliced beef.

Prep. time: 10 minutes
Cooking time: 2 hours
Serves: 6-8

Mary celebrates Mardi Gras with her daughter, Sydney, in 2004.

Her son Matthew (left, with Sydney and dad, Jason) was thrilled to be there. Looking at New Orleans he said, "I can't believe I'm here. I never thought I would see the city like this." When Mary visited New Orleans after the flood she recalled his words and thought the exact same thing.

Sydney with her "baby" Molly.

Mary English

A simple pot of spaghetti was the first meal Mary and Jason English of Slidell, Louisiana cooked in their home nearly a month after Katrina came and went.

Mary and Jason moved to Slidell about 3 years ago with their 1-year-old daughter Sydney and teenage son Matthew. Jason had begun law school at Loyola University in New Orleans and the couple planned to move back to their hometown of Pensacola, Florida after Jason graduated from law school and Matthew from high school. Then Katrina appeared on the radar screen. Mary had experience with hurricanes over the years in Pensacola. "We had been hit multiple times so we knew what to do, we knew what to expect, somewhat. It was worse than what we were used to." Mary tried to talk friends and neighbors out of staying through the storm. She knew from experience they would not have water, sewage, or power for quite a while and it would not be a good situation especially for the older neighbors. "They said they would be okay and see me when I got back. I said, 'I sure hope so.'"

They packed up and headed for Pensacola. Watching the destruction on TV they grew more concerned. Leaving was definitely a good decision. "We had friends that stayed and they were swimming for hours with their children. Their house just split in half. I talked to so many people who stayed because their parents stayed through Camille... this wasn't Camille."

Two days after the storm, Jason could not wait anymore and

had to go check on things. He and his father loaded a pick-up truck with gas, ice, water, food, chainsaws and even an ATV. On the drive, there were live cattle wandering the interstate that had apparently floated away from their farms. Cars and trucks were overturned everywhere. Even massive gasoline storage tanks had floated up from Gulfport. "It was like driving through a maze." Fortunately Jason found the damage to their house was relatively minimal. With a little work it could be made livable once services were restored. The same could not be said for many neighbors. "The amount of people that were affected ... it's phenomenal because it's just gone. You can't describe it. In Pensacola the storm surge comes and then it leaves. It doesn't stay for a month."

Since all communication was cut off, Jason and Mary acted as information couriers for friends and neighbors. Jason would haul ice and food in and messages out. Mary would take care of making the phone calls.

It was two weeks before Mary and Jason decided to return to their house and stay. When they arrived, there was still no water. The garbage was not being picked up but at least the sewer system was working. Even when the water was restored it still needed to be boiled before use, which was just right to make a pot of spaghetti, sit at a table and eat as a family. Well, almost. Oldest son Matthew was not there. He enrolled in a high school near Pensacola because his school was too damaged to open. But that spaghetti was a step in the right direction.

Jason was able to continue his studies via on-line classes and frequent trips to Lafayette for live classes. Though he will have to take a heavy load, he vows to graduate this year. Mary was pleased that 4 year-old Sydney's preschool resumed in December. "When Sydney started back to preschool it felt really good, like we were moving ahead. When my son Matthew comes home it will be another big hurdle cleared. When my husband returns to school then ..." she paused, "... it's just baby steps."

They still plan on moving back to Pensacola this summer to be near their parents. Mary has mixed feelings about leaving all the friends they have made. "It's a guilt. I feel really guilty. I thank goodness I'm getting out of here but then I feel so bad leaving because it is going to be years and years and years of recovery. I have too many friends spending Christmas in a camper. But at least they are together and alive."

UPDATE
Matthew's high school reopened just as this issue was going to print. He's back home now and enjoying his favorite meal, mom's red rice and beans.

"Monday is Red Beans and Rice Day. Anywhere you go out and get the special on a Monday it's red beans and rice. That's wash day, that's why. It's an old tradition that Monday is wash day so you just put the beans on and wash all day. My daughter calls it 'red rice and beans'."

Red Rice and Beans

According to Mary's daughter—otherwise known as Red Beans and Rice.

1	lb. dry red beans
1	large onion, minced
1	whole ham hock
1	clove garlic
1	whole bay leaf
1	tsp. salt
1	lb. fully cooked smoked sausage, sliced (Mary prefers Green Onion brand sausage)

Soak beans in water overnight. Discard the water. Combine all ingredients except sausage. Cover with water and simmer, covered, for 2 hours, or until beans are tender. Add sausage, heat through and serve over freshly cooked rice.

Prep. time: 5 minutes plus overnight soaking
Cooking time: 2 hours
Serves: 6

Shrimp Creole

Quick and wonderful, a great taste of the Gulf Coast.

12	oz. fresh shelled shrimp, smallish or cut if bigger
1½	Cups Trinity, diced (½ Cup each of onion, green bell pepper and celery)
2	cloves garlic
2	TB butter
16	oz. can diced tomatoes
½	tsp. salt
½	tsp. sweet paprika
1	whole bay leaf
2	TB water
4	tsp. cornstarch
2	TB fresh parsley

Sauté Trinity and garlic in the butter. Add the tomatoes, salt, paprika, and bay leaf. Simmer, covered, for 15 minutes. Mix water with cornstarch. Stir into the pan along with the shrimp. Cook about 5 minutes. Stir in the parsley and serve over rice with hot sauce on the side.

Prep. time: 15 minutes
Cooking time: 30 minutes
Serves: 4

Crawfish Étouffée

Étouffée is a nice, quick, simple stew that is great served over rice or pasta. We found crawfish meat readily available in the frozen seafood section.

1	medium onion, diced, about 1 Cup
1	green bell pepper, diced, about 1 Cup
4	stalks celery, diced, about 1 Cup (first 3 ingredients are collectively known as "the Trinity")
1	stick butter
1	clove garlic
1½	TB flour
1	lb. frozen crawfish meat, thawed
1	whole bay leaf
½	Cup chicken broth or seafood stock
¼	Cup half & half
2	TB fresh parsley
	salt and pepper to taste

Melt the butter over medium heat and sauté "the Trinity" along with the garlic for about 5 minutes until softened. Add the flour and stir until dissolved. Add the crawfish, bay leaf, stock and half & half. Simmer uncovered for about 10 minutes. Add the parsley for the last 5 minutes of cooking. Salt and pepper to taste. Serve over rice.

Prep. time: 15 minutes
Cooking time: 15 minutes
Serves: 6

Étoufée starts with what Mary calls "the trinity" which is onion, green bell pepper and celery. It is the base for many meals along the Gulf coast.

Above, Kelly holds her dog Sasha. Below is her photo of the rosebush her husband planted many years ago, the same rosebush that managed to survive the hurricane. She even wrote a special note on the back.

Our message from Jim that we'd survive 09/20/05

Kelly Leachman

It was that last little tick to the right that Katrina made just before landfall. It spared New Orleans even worse devastation, but caused the eastern eye-wall to pretty much smash into Gulfport head-on. Three hours after landfall, the winds were still being clocked at over 90 mph. The casino barges washed ashore all the way across highway 90 and the 20-30 foot storm surge left people swimming for the roof-tops of any building that still had a roof.

The picture that emerged once help arrived was a far cry from the streets of stately old homes dotted with ancient oaks and pines, bustling beachfront restaurants, thriving oil industry and quiet harbors dotted with fishing boats that had made Gulfport, Mississippi such a wonderful place to live for Kelly Leachman and her late husband Jim.

"Cooking was our hobby," she said. "Jim was very creative. He could take unusual ingredients and turn them into masterpieces, like paella with local blue crabs and Oysters Rockefeller. He was a master at making cornbread.

"Until you walk in your house and see the refrigerator bent around a corner... I've never had a feeling like that in my life."

Kelly has been a teacher all of her life. She taught junior high and high school students, as well as gifted students in New Orleans. She has been a substitute teacher and was a principal too. In recent years, she has been working as the director of a child care center in Gulfport.

"I've taught everything, from 6 weeks old through freshmen in college. I've retired, like, three times. They just won't let me retire!"

As a longtime Gulf Coast resident, she'd weathered many a hurricane, and had no intention of leaving for Katrina either, but the night before Katrina hit, in the calm before the storm, Kelly Leachman had a change of heart. She packed up her little dog Sasha,

"Cooking was our hobby," she said. "Jim was very creative. He could take unusual ingredients and turn them into masterpieces, like paella and Oysters Rockefeller. He was a master at making cornbread"

collected a belonging or two and evacuated to a friend's house in nearby but inland Macon, Mississippi. The next morning the towering wall of water rushed down her street, submerging everything in its wake. Her neighbor, who decided to ride out the storm, was left to swim out of his house.

From her friend's house in Mississippi, Kelly was able to make contact with her nephew, Robert Leachman, a sheriff's deputy from Houston. When Kelly asked him to come for her and Sasha, he was pretty much on his way before he hung up the phone, loading supplies of bottled water and food, and driving first to Macon, then into Gulfport to see what could be salvaged.

When the two returned to her condominium she had to stand outside for a bit before she could venture inside. Robert helped her make her way up to the second floor of her home, which had not been flooded, where the enormity of the situation finally sunk in.

"I've never had a feeling like that in my life. I had just about collapsed from shock and fatigue," she said. "I just sat down and Rob put Sasha in my lap and that's what got me back."

Rob, Kelly and Sasha then made the 14-hour drive back to Houston, where she stayed with Robert and his family until Rita struck. Kelly was forced to evacuate again, this time to a relative's

The first floor of Kelly's condominium was flooded by the storm surge and had to be totally gutted.

Her new kitchen, which was rebuilt after the hurricane, is a blessing, Kelly said.

Kelly prepares Christmas dinner in her new kitchen with her godchildren in December 2005.

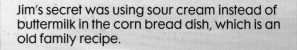

Jim's secret was using sour cream instead of buttermilk in the corn bread dish, which is an old family recipe.

Jim's Skillet Cornbread
(also known as Rich Corn Cake)

Yum! Great for breakfast by itself, or as a side to almost anything. We're really grateful Kelly shared this with us.

1	Cup yellow cornmeal
1	Cup flour (We use "Better for Bread" brand of flour)
2	tsp. cream of tartar
1	tsp. baking soda
¾	tsp. kosher salt
2	eggs, slightly beaten
3	TB vegetable oil
⅓	Cup milk
1	Cup sour cream

Preheat oven to 425°. In a large bowl, mix the cornmeal, flour, cream of tartar, baking soda and salt. In a small bowl, mix the eggs, vegetable oil, milk and sour cream. Just before you mix wet and dry ingredients together, heavily grease a 10" cast iron skillet and heat until nearly smoking.

Mix dry and wet ingredients until blended into a smooth batter. Add a few drops of milk if needed. Pour batter into hot skillet, pop into the oven, and bake for 23 minutes. Serve hot with butter. Crust should be brown and crisp.

Prep. time: 10 minutes
Baking time: 23 minutes
Serves: 8

> "Everyone is rebuilding and up and down the coast people are working. I'm proud of our people. We've picked ourselves up by our bootstraps and are going on. ... It's hard to take but we're fighters."

house in Dallas while Robert stayed behind to deal with the fallout of Rita.

"Rob did a heroic thing," Kelly said of that ordeal. "He brought a lot of ice and water and we distributed it along the way to people in broken-down cars. They were standing out there with their hands out not knowing what to do."

Once back home, Kelly's priority has been getting her kitchen operational again. As of December, she had new countertops, freshly painted walls and new cabinets. Flooring was stacked up

Super Crab Sandwiches

This is a lovely dish for a party buffet or luncheon—delicious and pretty, too.

4	large fresh English muffins (split and toasted)
1	lb. lump crabmeat (blue crab if possible)
3	TB minced sweet onion
	juice of 1 lemon (divided)
¾	Cup mayonnaise
½	Cup finely chopped celery
8	thick slices of fresh ripe tomato
1	Cup shredded sharp cheddar (hand-grated)

Place 4 muffin halves in one 8"x8" microwaveable pan and the other 4 in a similar dish. In microwave-safe bowl, combine crabmeat and onion and squeeze half of the lemon over it. Cover the bowl with waxed paper or plastic wrap and microwave on high for about 2 minutes. Stir and check onions for doneness and cook another 30 seconds. In a small bowl, mix mayonnaise and celery and squeeze the other half of the lemon over it. Set aside.

Divide crab mixture among the 8 English muffin slices. Place a slice of tomato on each. Divide mayonnaise mixture and top each sandwich (If you like more mayonnaise, double amounts of mayonnaise, celery and lemon juice).

Sprinkle each sandwich liberally with cheese. Microwave each dish 2-4 minutes, depending on oven, turning dish at least once during cooking. Serve hot with plain salad.

Kelly likes her microwave and this recipe works very well using it. If you don't use one, cook the crab and onion part in a small saucepan over low heat until the onion is tender, about 8 minutes, and pop the muffins (in a baking dish) in a 375° oven for 3-5 minutes to brown the cheese.

Serves: 8 for lunch or 4 for dinner
Prep. time: 5 minutes
Cooking time: 6 minutes

Kelly and her niece.

in another room, ready to be installed.

"Just having a functioning kitchen once again is a blessing," Kelly said, as this was where she and her husband Jim spent many hours cooking together.

Little by little, things are improving for her and her neighbors. Kelly lost 20 pounds, which she blames on all those TV dinners, but she's regaining her strength and spirit.

"I'm a whole lot better now. I can see the light at the end of the tunnel. Everyone is rebuilding and up and down the coast people are working. I'm proud of our people. We've picked ourselves up by our bootstraps and are going on. As neighbors we are closer than we ever have been. It's God's will or it wouldn't have happened. It's hard to take but we're fighters."

Kelly knew things had turned the corner when she looked outside one morning. Amidst the mud and ruins of her devastated garden, there were green leaves and tiny ruby buds emerging from the rosebush Jim had planted many years ago.

"It's a message," she said.

Miriam Lewis

"We were all together. It meant a lot to me. I hated to see them leave."

Miriam and some of her family at a church supper in Milwaukee.

"I miss New Orleans but I don't want to go back," says 78-year-old Miriam Lewis. She left her hometown for the last time via helicopter from an overpass on I-10. "That wasn't my first helicopter ride. When Betsy happened we had to get on a roof on the corner until they came and got us. That was 1965. I'll never forget that." Hurricane Betsy flooded New Orleans 40 years ago, almost to the day that Katrina struck, in a very similar fashion. It was the first hurricane to top $1 billion in damages earning it the nickname "Billion Dollar Betsy."

This time Miriam left her senior apartment to ride out the storm at her grandchild's brick apartment building. "My children called and said they was coming to get me. I packed a few things. That was Saturday, then come the storm on Sunday and I got between two walls in a hall. We went through it. It was a shakin' and a tremblin' and the water coming." Miriam requires kidney dialysis three times a week. As the water rose, her health became a concern. Her son-in-law was able to get her to the overpass in his fishing boat and after two nights on the bridge, she was taken by helicopter and given medical attention. "I think about it all the time," says Miriam. "If he wouldn't have brought that boat, I don't know what we would have done."

From the second floor porch they lowered Miriam into the boat. "I was so scared. God... I kept saying don't drop me, don't drop me." She is proud of the man who saved her. "My son-in law, Raymond Carter is his name, he's to be commended for the work he did, bringing people off those porches out to the overpass." The boat ride was heartbreaking for Miriam. "People's children were on the porch shouting 'Mister, are you gonna come back and get us?' Oh, I felt so sorry. I said, 'Raymond are you going to come back and get those people?' He said, 'Yeah, if I have time I'm gonna get 'em all.'"

After dialysis, Miriam felt better but was alone at a medical shelter in Alexandria. A man there asked her if there was anyone he could contact for her. She said her daughter's name was Karen Craig but could not remember her phone number. "I told him she lives in Milwaukee, Wisconsin and she works at a health-care place, I didn't know what it was. About 45 minutes later he came back and said 'I found your daughter.' Oh I was so tickled I just cried."

She eventually reunited with her granddaughter Rochelle and they made their way to Houston. From there, much of the family traveled by train to Karen's house in Milwaukee. In all, 17 relatives made the trip. After the nightmare of the storm and flood, being with all those family members was a dream for Miriam. "We were all together. It meant a lot to me. I hated to see them leave." She paused in thought, then added, "Yeah, we had a time. It was the time of our life. Prayers brought us through."

Miriam's Gumbo

This recipe has never been written down before. Miriam just had it up in her head. We tried it two ways, with boneless chicken white meat and with chicken wings. The batch with chicken wings was incredible as long as you don't mind dodging the bones.

1	lb. shrimp, peeled, deveined, tails removed
12	blue crabs (cleaned "gumbo ready") or 1 lb. lump crab meat
2	lbs. chicken wings or chicken meat (Miriam uses chicken gizzards)
1	lb. hot sausage, raw
2	bunches green onions, minced
1	large onion, minced
2	cloves garlic, minced
¼	Cup vegetable oil
3	TB flour
5	bay leaves
1	TB dried thyme—"the more the better"
1	TB salt
2	tsp. black pepper
6-8	Cups water gumbo file powder to taste
6	Cups hot cooked rice

Remove casing from the sausage and roll into balls. You may want to fry or bake the sausage to remove some of the fat. If using chicken gizzards, simmer them for about an hour before you start. If you are using chicken wings or meat, throw them in as-is; be sure to pick out as many bones as possible and warn diners about bones. In a stock pot, start out making your roux over medium heat with the oil and flour, stirring constantly. Miriam says the roux is the most important part (see note). When it is nice and brown, add both types of onion, garlic and chicken. Cover and cook for about 15 minutes stirring occasionally. Stir in the water and add the bay leaves, thyme, and sausage. Bring to a boil then reduce heat to medium-low. Simmer for 1 to 1½ hours. Start your rice about ½ hour before you are ready to serve. Add the crab and shrimp to the pot minutes before serving. When the shrimp and crab are done, serve in a bowl "like soup" with a spoonful of rice. Miriam likes to sprinkle the file powder in her bowl.

Prep. time: 30 minutes
Cooking time: 2 hours
Serves: 12

Note: This roux is more wet than a typical roux because you are cooking the onions in it. Don't worry about over-browning the roux, as the onions prevent this from happening.

Kids, grandkids and great-grandkids all together. "Yeah, we had a time. Prayers brought us through," says Miriam.

Karen Craig

Karen Craig doesn't like to say "I told you so" but in this case she has the right. She had urged her family to get out of New Orleans before Hurricane Katrina but they were convinced they could get through the storm. "I was terrified. I couldn't get in touch with nobody. All the phones were out." She heard from her daughter Rochelle on Monday after the storm but the cell phone was working intermittently. "It would work for like five minutes and we had to talk real fast." Rochelle told her the water was rising and didn't understand where it was coming from. "I said you all better get out of there. I told you before the storm came."

Karen had moved to Milwaukee five years ago. Before the storm she had planned on moving back to New Orleans to care for her mother Miriam. Now Miriam was last seen being airlifted by a helicopter from a freeway overpass. "I was going to work, worried. My blood pressure went sky-high, I was worried to death, crying. Every time the phone would ring I was running to it hoping it was somebody in my family. Then this lady called and said she had found my mother and had a number to call. I was like, 'Praise the Lord!'" She had not waited idly. "Me and my friend from work called every dialysis center and hospital in Baton Rouge. Nobody heard of her. Then when I found her they said she was in Alexandria at a special needs shelter."

When most of the family had reunited in Houston, Karen knew exactly what to do. "They said they didn't have nowhere to go but stay in shelters. I said, 'Well you all can come up here till you all get on your feet. You know, get a house or whatever may happen. Just come up here.'" It made for some close quarters. "I think there was 17 of them plus me and my two sons. They stayed for two weeks." Asked if things were a little strained or if tempers flared, Karen said, "It was actually fun the whole while. It was real cool. Everyone got along good. You couldn't stay in the bathroom but 15 minutes. You had to hurry up and do what you had to do and get out."

Of course everyone had to be fed. "The ladies went to the grocery store. We'd make a list of what we were going to cook that day. We had to make sure we had enough supplies. We would be outside barbequing and the neighbors would bring us soda and water; they were helping out. It was actually fun when everybody got here."

Shrimp and Crawfish Pasta

Crawfish is usually available in the frozen food section. This recipe is very easy, absolutely delicious and will stick to your ribs.

1	lb.	egg noodles (we used medium width)
1	lb.	crawfish meat, thawed
1	lb.	shrimp, peeled, deveined, tails removed
16	oz.	Velveeta cheese, cubed
1		Cup half & half
1		stick butter
1		bunch green onions, minced
2		cloves garlic, minced

Cook noodles al dente, remove from water and set aside. Sauté onion and garlic in butter over medium-high heat for 3 minutes. Add shrimp and crawfish and sauté until pink, 3-4 minutes. Lower heat to medium-low and stir in half and half. Add the cheese a little at a time, stirring as you go. Then add the noodles by the kitchen spoonful until all are mixed in. Serve hot and bubbly.

Prep. time: 30 minutes
Cooking time: 20 minutes
Serves: 10-12

"It was actually fun when everybody got here."

Breakfast at Karen's house.

Raymond Carter

Raymond Carter loves to go fishing. He is the proud owner of a 17-foot Sea Swirl fishing boat, yet with Hurricane Katrina heading toward his East New Orleans home, he didn't think about taking it with him. "I wasn't even planning on taking the boat. Then my brother-in-law called up and said, 'Why don't you bring the boat because you never know what's going to happen.' And sure enough we needed it. Without the boat we wouldn't have gotten out like we did. It was just lucky."

Raymond and his wife Giselle hooked up the boat and joined others at a family member's sturdy brick apartment building. The storm came and went. It was a typical sunny, hot and humid New Orleans day. Then the water began to rise in the streets. "We realized what was going on and then everyone around us was panicking and carrying on. We all thought they were going to come out and start picking people up but it never happened. So I took my boat and just went around riding about and I started seeing things and thought man... nobody's coming out here?"

Raymond stands in front of his fishing/rescue boat.

Nobody indeed. With no power and little information it was hard to imagine the scale of the disaster unfolding around them. "We saw some folks going to the bridge (an I-10 overpass) and the choppers were picking people up from the bridge. But you had to get to the bridge in order to get picked up. So I just started picking up people, mostly the elderly, the kids, the pregnant women and all that, and bringing them to the bridge." This went on into nightfall. "That's how we got stuck sleeping on the bridge overnight. Then I got back up and got some more people. The Fire Department gave me some gas so I could continue on."

Raymond hauled out over 200 people during those two days. "As small as that boat was I was bringing in like 16 or 17 people at a time. But I was cautious, taking my time." The debris in the water made for slow going. "You could see the roofs of the cars. I pretty much knew the neighborhood but I had to watch for the cars. Some of them were floating too you know." He laughed and added, "You had to be there to see it."

Raymond prepares his boat as the waters rise.

Finally Raymond and Giselle waded out to higher ground. "When we got out we gave the boat to the Red Cross. When we went back to get it, when the water was down, the boat was gone. Then we located the boat through the Wildlife and Fishery

Department. They spotted the boat across the lake. Some tow truck was going around picking up boats. I don't know who gave them authorization." In every disaster there are opportunists and Raymond had to pay $1700 in storage fees to get his boat back. With their house flooded out, they are currently living in a trailer on his company grounds. They hope to rebuild their house soon.

"I was blessed to take and do what I did," says Raymond. "Some people say I'm a hero. I'm not a hero. You would've done the same thing I did." Only a true hero would say that.

Treacherous waters—a typical street Raymond negotiated during his rescue efforts.

Pecan Pralines

These pralines are from Raymond's wife Giselle.

- 4 Cups sugar
- 2 5 oz. cans evaporated milk
- 2 sticks butter (1 Cup)
- 1 tsp. vanilla extract
- 1½ Cups coarsely chopped pecans

In a heavy saucepan, combine the sugar, milk and butter and bring to a boil. Reduce heat and continue cooking until foam dies down, about 30 minutes. Stir constantly. Add the vanilla and nuts and cook for another 5-10 minutes. The consistency should be thick and spoonable. Working quickly, using a tablespoon, drop mixture onto a lightly-greased cookie sheet or parchment paper. Or, if preferred, pour mixture on a cookie sheet and cut into squares right away.

Prep. time: 5 minutes
Cooking time: 50 minutes
Yield: about 42

Rochelle Washington

"I never thought we were coming back home...
New Orleans is gone."

This photo was taken by Rochelle from the I-10 freeway overpass where she and her family spent 2 long days and nights.

Happier Times: Rochelle dressed in her Zulu wear at Mardi Gras 2006.

"It was a beautiful, sunny day. That was the strange thing," says Rochelle Washington of the weather after Katrina passed. She and her 12-year-old son Jinaga (everyone calls him Nookie) rode out the storm in the same apartment as her Uncle Raymond and Grandmother Miriam. "But it was so hot. Then the water started to come up and we didn't know where it was coming from."

Fortunately Uncle Raymond was there with his boat so Rochelle and Nookie joined Miriam on the overpass for a couple nights. Yet the boat ride to the overpass was harrowing and heart-breaking. "Everybody was saying come get us, please help us, we'll pay you," says Rochelle, "People were just scream-ing and panicking. I was thinking just get me to the interstate so I can get out of here. It was just crazy." Once her grandmother was safely evacuated for much needed medical attention, Rochelle decid-ed two nights on a freeway bridge was enough. It was time to head for higher ground.

To get there she and Nookie waded down I-10 through treacherous, murky waters some-times chest deep and filled with debris. Months later, driving the route the family walked seemed to take an eternity. The waterlines were still clearly visible on the sound walls along the freeway. As Rochelle waded out and eventu-ally bussed out of town, it hurt to see her city. "I never thought we were coming back home, to be honest with you. We'll never go home. New Orleans is gone."

Even though the city she once knew might be gone, life has gone on. Nookie is back in school and Rochelle is back to work at Wal-Mart. While some things have re-turned to an appearance of normal, life will never be the same. It will take many years for the city of New Orleans to get back on its feet. Yet, the smile on Rochelle's face shows the spirit of New Orleans will live on.

A photo from the Ninth Ward in New Orleans taken by Rochelle's son Nookie.

Walking Warrior from South Africa at Mardi Gras 2006.

Photo by Rochelle

Stuffed Peppers

Not your traditional stuffed peppers. Carefully slice the shrimp down the middle to make them go further.

1   lb. medium shrimp, peeled, deveined, tails removed, sliced down the middle
1   lb. diced, smoked ham
12   Cups bread cubes (from day-old bread)
3   Cups water
1   bunch green onions, minced
    1 medium white onion, minced
    1 TB seasoned salt
¼   tsp. black pepper
½   tsp. garlic powder
8-10   bell peppers
2   TB bread crumbs

Mix the spices with the water. Pour over bread cubes. Mix in the onions, ham, and shrimp. Cut the tops off the peppers. Dice the pepper tops and add to the stuffing. Bake stuffing in a casserole dish in the oven at 350° for ½ hour, stirring occasionally. Remove seeds from the peppers. Fill with stuffing mixture and place in a shallow baking dish with about 1 inch of water. Sprinkle the tops with bread crumbs. Bake at 275° for 45 minutes. Pop under the broiler to brown the tops, if desired.

Prep. time: 30 minutes
Cooking time: 1 hour 15 minutes
Serves: 8-10

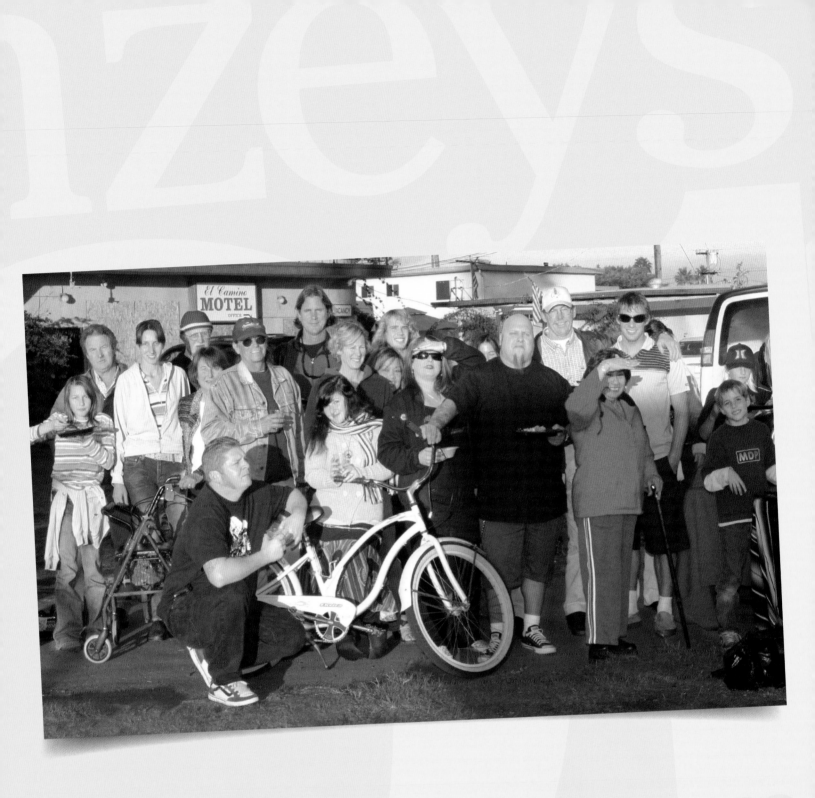

As we look to the future of *Penzeys One* I think our time spent in Imperial Beach says a lot about our way forward. Something about this article, the food, the colors, the energy: it all just worked so right. Of course without the people at the heart of it, it would not be anything. Find someone who cooks, get them talking about their life and you end up with a great read and great recipes as well. People who cook are interesting, but even better than that, people who cook are cool.

As we move forward I would love for each and every time you pick up a new issue in addition to finding the very best tasty recipes inside that you are also reminded that as someone who cooks, you belong, and what you belong to is a very wondrous and cool group of people. And as a cook yours is the best kind of cool. It is coolness without detachment, being cool without being aloof. It is coolness while making a difference. You should be very proud of who you are.

In California, three miles from Mexico, lies Imperial Beach.

It is a town on the border between North and South, East and West, Sea and Sand.

We can choose to live inside borders or on top of them.

In "IB" people choose to surf.

Rosa Adams has lived in Imperial Beach, California since 1990. "I was born in Mexico City. I was there until I was 23 years old," says Rosa. "When I was there, I liked it. But then when I came here, I loved it!" Her older brother invited her to come and live near him in San Ysidro, a city on the Mexican border just east of Imperial Beach. "That was 1975," adds Rosa. "He wanted us to come over here to live close to him."

Rosa and her husband Arthur have three sons, Albert (27), Arturo (23) and Alex (18). "Albert has three kids, two girls and one boy. Sometimes I baby-sit them," says Rosa. "The oldest grandchild is 10, the other is 7 and the youngest is 3. They call me 'Abuelita.' It means 'grandmother' in Spanish."

Rosa with son Alex

When she first married Arthur the couple moved to Baltimore, apparently at the wrong time of year. "We lived there for a little bit, like for five or six months, but I didn't like it because it was too cold!" Rosa adds, "It wasn't much fun and I told him I wanted to come back to the San Diego area. It is my favorite place."

They moved back to San Ysidro and stayed about ten years before settling in Imperial Beach in 1990. Visiting the beach became part of her routine. "The name of the beach is Silver Strand. It's a little north of Imperial Beach. I used to go four times a week. It's really nice. I'd take the bus and stay there for a while. There're a lot of people there. Sometimes they

have events and parties. They play music, people swimming in the water." Except when the rains come and wash sewage from Tijuana into the ocean. "The water comes in from Mexico to the beach over here," says Rosa. "They call it black water. It's contaminated. They try to keep people away from the beach during that time."

Rosa did not spend all her time at the beach and began selling Avon in Imperial Beach 11 years ago. "I went to the supervisor and paid $10 for the set to start selling," says Rosa. "Little by little I started to like it because it was fun. At the same time I sell things, I can buy things for myself." Selling Avon comes with some of the trappings of owning a small business. "Sometimes I don't make that much because sometimes people don't pay and I lose money and I have to pay for the merchandise myself. Sometimes I feel like I want to quit but I want to keep trying. I want to keep busy. I meet people that way."

In 2006 the HBO series "John From Cincinnati" came to Imperial Beach for filming and basically set up camp on the street in front of her house and even in her yard. "They were cooking out in the front. They would put everything right here," Rosa says pointing to her yard and the street in front of it. "They would say 'Come and eat.'"

Rosa's house where the crew was fed

She eventually became an extra in the show with a speaking part. "Mr. Milch saw me outside," says Rosa of David Milch, creator and executive producer of the show. "I was outside pruning my flowers and he asked me 'Do you want to be in the show?' I said, 'Right now?' He said, 'Yeah.' I said, 'Yeah I want to!'

"So they came and got all the information about me," Rosa continues. "I was so nervous! It's my first time on television. At the beginning I thought, maybe he's kidding. But he told me he was serious. 'I want you to be in the show,' he said. They came and took pictures of me. After that, I got ready and they put me by the window."

In the scene Rosa is pruning roses in her front yard when one of the characters asks her for directions. "I talked to the doctor, he was walking by. He said 'Oh, you have some beautiful flowers.' I said 'Thank you.' He asked me about this motel in the back. 'Is this the way?' And I said 'Yeah.' Then he came back and we tried again. It took 30 minutes.

"They were here over a year," says Rosa. "The show was done in June (2007). We went to the premiere in May. Then they came back and finished." Mr. Milch sent a limousine to pick up Rosa and bring her to

Rosa, David Milch, Alex

Rosa and her roses

Mexican Spaghetti with Shrimp

2	lbs. medium shrimp, peeled, deveined, tails removed
1	lb. spaghetti
2	Cups sour cream
2	TB lemon juice (1 lemon), divided
½	large bunch fresh cilantro, washed, tops only, roughly 1½ Cups
1	California or guajillo chile pepper or a dash of cayenne red pepper (optional)
2	cloves garlic, whole peeled
2	TB butter or olive oil, divided
1	clove garlic, minced
2	TB Parmesan cheese
¾	tsp. chicken soup base or 1 bouillon cube

Fill a large kettle with water and set it on the stove to boil. In a blender, combine the sour cream, 1 TB of the lemon juice, the cilantro, chile pepper (if using), and whole garlic cloves. Blend until smooth. In a large skillet, heat half of the butter or olive oil over low heat. Add the minced garlic, remaining lemon juice and the shrimp and cook until the shrimp are done, about 5 minutes. Remove from the pan, sprinkle with the cheese and set aside. Add the pasta and soup base to the kettle of boiling water and cook according to package directions. While the pasta is cooking, heat the remaining butter or olive oil in the skillet over medium heat. Add the sour cream mixture to the pan. Reduce the heat to low and let simmer for about 10 minutes, stirring occasionally. Drain the pasta well and add to the sour cream mixture. Stir in the shrimp, salt and pepper to taste and serve topped with extra cheese as desired.

Prep. time: 20 minutes
Cooking time: 17 minutes
Serves: 6-8

Rosa (in the hat) with her mother Petra and two nephews, Ricardo Alberto and Alexander

the premier in Los Angeles. "I liked the limousine!" she says. "It was fun. Then we went to San Diego for an interview with Channel 51. I went there with one of my sons and my three little grandchildren."

Like many of the folks around Imperial Beach, Rosa wishes the show could have continued. "I liked all the people from the show. They're very nice and friendly. I miss it. I miss everybody."

Back in Mexico, when Rosa was 3 years old, she contracted polio. "I've had a cane since then. I use a brace for my left leg because I cannot move my leg." She never let it slow her down. "It was normal for me because I don't remember when I could walk. All I remember is having polio. I don't feel it's a difference because I don't remember before it. I want to move around and go everywhere. I don't give up. I don't want to feel like I can't."

Rosa grew up near Mexico City where she and her sisters would often go to the river to do some fishing. "I would sometimes get up at 6 o'clock with my sisters and would go to the river and catch shrimp. I would fill up a big bucket. It was really fun." The real fun came when Rosa brought the shrimp home. "My mother would make shrimp soup with vegetables."

Chicken Burritos

4	bone-in, skin-on chicken breasts
1	clove garlic, whole
1	tsp. salt
1	TB olive oil
1	Cup chopped onion
1	clove garlic, minced
1	Cup chopped fresh tomatoes (2 medium)
1	tsp. black pepper
¾	tsp. chicken soup base or 1 bouillon cube
1	jalapeño or serrano pepper, chopped
	sour cream
	shredded lettuce
	tortillas

Put the chicken breasts, whole garlic clove and salt in a large kettle and cover with water. Bring to a boil and simmer until tender, about 45 minutes. Remove the chicken, reserving ½ Cup of the water. Remove and discard the chicken skin and bones as well as the garlic clove. Shred the chicken and set aside. Heat the olive oil in a skillet over medium-high heat. Add the onion and minced garlic and cook for about 5 minutes. Add the tomato, black pepper, chicken soup base and reserved water. Cover and simmer for 20 minutes. Stir in the chicken and simmer, uncovered for about 20 more minutes, until the juice is almost gone. Serve in warm tortillas with chopped pepper, sour cream and shredded lettuce.

Prep. time: 20 minutes
Cooking time: 1 hour, 30 minutes
Serves: 6-8

Mexican Chicken Soup

1	whole chicken, cut into pieces
8	Cups water
2	dry California or guajillo chile peppers, stems and seeds removed
1	garlic clove
1	TB whole cumin seeds
3	tsp. chicken soup base or 4 bouillon cubes
2	Cups cubed potatoes
1	Cup cubed carrots
1	Cup cubed zucchini
2½	Cups cooked white rice

Wash the chicken and place in a stock pot. Cover with water and bring to a boil over medium-high heat. Boil the chicken pieces in the water for about 45 minutes, skimming off the foam occasionally while cooking. You can either leave the chicken as is for a more traditional meal or remove the meat from the bones and shred it and add it back to the pot. Add the chili peppers and garlic to the water and simmer for a few minutes to soften them a bit. Remove the peppers and garlic clove and put them in a blender along with the cumin seeds and 1 Cup of cooled chicken-cooking water. Blend until smooth. Pour the pepper mix back into the pot with the chicken. Stir in the chicken soup base until dissolved. Add the potatoes and carrots and cook until tender, 10-20 minutes, depending on the size of the carrots and potatoes. Add the zucchini and cook a couple more minutes until softened. Serve over white rice.

Prep. time: 10 minutes
Cooking time: 1 hour or so
Serves: 8-10

Shrimp Soup

Rosa used to go to the river early in the morning and catch shrimp with her brothers. This is the soup her mom made with the shrimp they caught.

1	lb. raw medium shrimp
2	TB olive oil
½	medium onion, chopped
2	cloves fresh garlic, peeled and minced
3-4	ripe tomatoes, chopped
3	Cups chicken stock (or 3 cups water with 2-3 tsp. chicken soup base)
1	tsp. dried epazote or 1 TB fresh
3	Cups cooked white rice

Heat the olive oil in a stockpot over medium-high heat. Add the onion and garlic and cook until lightly browned, about 5 minutes. Add the tomatoes and cook an additional 5 minutes. We removed the skins from the tomatoes by plunging briefly in boiling water, and we discarded about half the seeds during chopping, which made for a nice, sweet-flavored soup. Pour in the chicken stock, reduce heat to low, let simmer for 15-20 minutes. Add the shrimp (we deveined our shrimp and removed all the shell but left the tail, as leaving some shell does add extra shrimp flavor to this quick-cooking soup) and epazote and cook until the shrimp are cooked through, 5-10 minutes more depending on the size of the shrimp. Serve over a small scoop of rice or stir the hot cooked rice into the soup before serving.

Prep. time: 10 minutes
Cooking time: 27-37 minutes
Serves: 6

Serge Dedina, executive director and founder of Wildcoast

WiLDCOAST COSTASALVAjE

"Our goal is not to work with environmentalists," says Serge Dedina, executive director and founder of Wildcoast, an organization dedicated to preserving and protecting coastal ecosystems. "Our goal is to work with people that don't define themselves as environmentalists." While that may seem strange, the logic is sound. "Ninety-nine percent of the population wants clean air and clean water." Serge continues, "How do you communicate with them in a way that really respects their values and their way of seeing the world? Even with our clean water campaign, we point out it's not just environmentalists that are being affected by the polluted water. It's everybody."

The Wildcoast offices are located right across the street from the base of the pier in Imperial Beach (IB), California, just three miles from the border with Mexico. "When I was

Serge's parents Josephine and Michel with Serge's son Daniel

a kid the Hell's Angels hung out here. It was a pretty heavy place. It's interesting to see how people use this space now and it's really changed the dynamic of the beach area." Serge grew up in IB and wrote a historical book about surfers called *Watermen: Tales of the Tijuana Sloughs.* Now at the base of the IB pier, where the Hell's Angels used to hang out, is a monument to surfers known as Surfhenge (pg. 318-319). "People really love it," says Serge. "They take photos of it, kids play on the rocks nearby. It's really a good example of public space."

Serge and his wife Emily share a love for the outdoors. They met in 1985 while they were both exchange students in Peru. Shortly after meeting they went on a 12-mile hike up a 15,000-foot mountain. "I thought it was 12 kilometers, not 12 miles," says Emily. "I was pretty worn out and hiding behind rocks trying to catch my breath." At the end of that semester Emily returned to school at the University of Wisconsin and Serge returned to UC-San Diego to complete his undergraduate degree in political science. Eventually they got together again and married, but certainly did not settle down.

"We lived in a small town in Mexico, and everyone would always ask us when we were going to have kids," says Serge. "They would give us this plant, Damiana, they use that to make a fertility tea. They told us if we drank it, we would have babies." Whether the plant worked or not, Israel (now 12) and Daniel (now 10) were born.

The Dedina family was living in Tucson while Serge and Emily completed their PhDs. They had moved 12 times during their marriage. Serge and Emily decided on one more move, back to Serge's hometown of Imperial Beach. "All of a sudden, we're not going anywhere," says Serge. "We're finally home."

Once he was home he started Wildcoast, an environmental concern that tackles serious issues but still keeps a sense of humor as evidenced by this press release from 2007.

Superstar Mexican lucha libre star and WiLDCOAST ocean defender, El Hijo del Santo, received the "Environmental Hero" award from the Monterey Bay Aquarium on September 9th for his work fighting the "enemies of the sea." Throughout 2007, El Santo, traveled throughout Mexico with WiLDCOAST to fight

Sour Cream Coffee Cake

According to Serge, "This cake is unbeatable. We hope you love this as much as we do. It is definitely a family favorite."

½	Cup butter (1 stick)
½	Cup shortening
1¼	Cups sugar
2	eggs, beaten
1	Cup sour cream
1	tsp. vanilla extract
2	Cups sifted cake flour or all-purpose flour (cake flour will make a more tender, fine-textured cake)
1	tsp. baking powder
½	tsp. baking soda

Topping—mix together the following:

½	Cup finely chopped nuts (we used pecans)
1	TB cinnamon sugar

for clean ocean water quality, to stop the slaughter of sea turtles and to protect marine mammals.

Serge calls Santo his "eco-warrior." "We convince people to not eat endangered wildlife," says Serge. "For example, sea turtles are an endangered species and you are prohibited by law from eating them. In Mexico, it's a cultural tradition to eat sea turtle meat in soup and in tacos, as well as sea turtle eggs for sexual potency. We campaign through the media to convince people not to eat sea turtles."

Wildcoast staffers Jessica Glanz and Jessica Robbins.

Wildcoast is also focusing on sharks because there is a big market for shark's fin soup. The sharks are killed simply for

Preheat oven to 350°. Cream together the butter, shortening and sugar, mixing well on high speed. Add the eggs, sour cream and vanilla and mix well. Switch to a spoon and gradually add the flour, baking powder and baking soda. The mixture will be thick, which is fine, but if it is mixed too long with a high-speed mixer, the cake can turn out dry or tough, so use the spoon until well blended. Spread half of the batter in a greased 9-inch tube spring-form pan, angel food pan. Sprinkle with half of the topping. Add the remaining batter and top with the remaining topping. Bake at 350° for 45- 55 minutes or until a knife inserted in the cake comes out clean. Let cool before cutting. If using a bundt pan, some of the topping can be sprinkled in first before adding the batter, so it will end up on top when the cake is turned out of the pan. That can make it tricky to get the cake out of the pan, so make sure you grease the pan thoroughly, and it might be good to flour the pan as well.

Prep. time: 20 minutes
Baking time: 45-55minutes
Serves: 20

Baja Fish Camp Tacos

According to Serge, "This recipe for fish tacos Emily learned from spending two years living with fishing families in remote fishing villages along the Pacific coast of the Baja Peninsula while we were conducting research for our doctoral dissertations. People in Mexico really don't eat fish tacos—they cook fish and use tortillas to eat them with."

1   whole fish (best to use a fresh fish that is plentiful in your
        area) or 2 lbs. fresh fish fillets

Marinade:
1   Cup mayonnaise
2   TB prepared mustard

Toppings (amounts depend on the size of the fish):
        small corn and/or flour tortillas, warmed
        fresh chopped cilantro
        sour cream
        guacamole
        shredded red cabbage
        shredded lettuce
        pico de gallo
        chopped tomatoes

If you are using a charcoal grill, get the coals nice and hot. Butterfly the fish by cutting along both sides of the dorsal fin. Mix together the mayonnaise and mustard and liberally brush on all sides of the fish. Place the fish in a grilling rack with the belly side of the fish on the bottom. Lock into the grilling rack and place on the grill over direct heat with the belly side down. If you are using fish fillets, brush all sides with the marinade and place them in a grilling rack skin side down if there is still skin on it. Use indirect heat as direct heat may burn the fish too quickly. In either case, grill until the fish is very tender and flakes easily, about 10-12 minutes, depending on the size of the fish. Do not turn over. The mustard and mayo will brown and make a soufflé-like sauce. Fill bowls with the toppings of your choice and place on the table along with the warmed tortillas. Put the fish on a serving platter and let everyone help themselves. "The key here is the simplicity of the ingredients and focusing on the fish," says Serge. "The fresher the better."

Prep. time: 10 minutes
Cooking time: 10-12 minutes
Yield: 4-6 tacos, although this really depends on the size of the fish

DANGER

CONTAMINATED WATER
AVOID WATER CONTACT
FROM THIS POINT SOUTH
TO THE
INTERNATIONAL BORDER

PELIGRO
AGUA CONTAMINADA
/ALEJESE
EVITE CONTACTO
CONEL AGUA HASTA
LA LINEA INTERNACIONAL

COUNTY OF SAN DIEGO DEPT. OF ENVIRONMENTAL HEALTH
(619)338-2073

their fins and the rest of the fish is discarded. "Shark is like second-class fish," says Serge adding, "This idea of a national consciousness in Mexico about the environment is really new.

"People in Mexico eat sea turtle eggs because they think it's like a form of organic Viagra," says Serge. "So we had an ad with a sexy model in a bikini—she's really famous in Latin America—she is saying (in Spanish) 'My man doesn't need sea turtle eggs to be more potent.' We had feminists in Mexico attack us but we worked in partnership with the Mexican government to get the message out and crack down on people poaching turtles." Wildcoast tries to get the message out and have a little fun along the way. Not to make fun of the situation but to be effective. "I think the thing with the environmental and conservation movements, it's really about giving people choices and not to be so negative. The turtle campaign is not about death and gloom. It's funny."

Serge says it's not enough to just say no or don't do it. "So we're going to work with some of the top chefs in Mexico City and do a whole event to promote sustainable seafood. Identify the slim-pickings of sustainable seafood in Mexico and bring in the fishermen so they can promote it and get people hooked on the idea that if they're going to eat seafood, it should be sustainable. Create a market for it. We don't want to stop development and we don't want to stop fishing. What we want to do is encourage people." Rather than simply tell fishermen to stop, Wildcoast tries to work with them and give them alternatives. "It really is about giving people choices and not to be so negative. Let's find ways to help ranchers manage their land and give them a cash incentive to maybe help them invest in eco-tourism or something like that."

Another major issue for Wildcoast is the sewage that washes out of Tijuana into the Tijuana River on the United States side and eventually in the ocean. "Yeah. It's sad, we all pray for a drought," Serge says while looking over the border at Tijuana. "What's interesting about it, if you're standing here in the morning, is that you're looking at a city of two million people. It doesn't seem like there are a lot of people but it goes back forever. Only a million have sewage infrastructure so when it rains, everything from

Tijuana flows into the Tijuana River. It's like a flash flood. What happens is the runoff overloads the sewage system and it starts flying up on the streets. The conditions are so awful—you can't believe it. It's not just here, it's sixty miles south of here (in Mexico). There's another canyon where thirty million gallons of sewage flows every day out on the beach." Imperial Beach is not the only place affected. "It makes its way up to Coronado," say Serge. "We have a monitoring system—we can do real-time monitoring of the plume coming out of the Tijuana River so we know at all times where that plume is and what the water is doing."

How does this get fixed? Can it be fixed? Is there hope? Serge says yes but we can't just throw money at it. "It's not money. It's having a vision and a way to frame it so that it makes sense and getting public support for doing the right thing. People that work on the border are really smart but if they're influenced by politics, they can't really do their job. Everyone on the border understands what we need to do with these programs. We want the media to scrutinize what's happening and start taking a different look at the border. You have to make people accountable and say that you can solve the problem. This is not Mars."

Politicians like big projects like treatment plants that show something is being done. Serge wants to start at the root of the problem. "You can build all the treatment plants you want; if no one has sewage pipes to their houses, it doesn't work. You have to start small and you have to start somewhere," says Serge. "I talked to a local city council person and he said, 'There's nothing you can do. It's impossible.' I say why is this guy in office? We do these tours (to the border) all of the time and that's made a big difference. Take public officials and legislators down to both sides of the border and have them see what the problems are.

"It's about quality of life on both sides of the border," Serge continues. "We've been working with a bunch of different agencies creating a master plan for infrastructure, to create a low-tech, low-cost infrastructure to reduce sewage flows and improve quality of life."

Serge and Wildcoast try to find allies in non-traditional places. "Most environmentalists wouldn't work with the Border Patrol or people in the Navy. Actually, we have a lot of supporters on the Navy SEAL Team because they have to train in this water." Another source of pollution for the Tijuana River are ranches on the U.S. side. "There's been a real effort to clean up and restore the valley and improve recreational opportunities. There's been a big split between environmentalists and the horse stables over some of the restorations in the valley but we've been trying to say we respect the rights of horse owners to have trail riders but the bigger picture is pollution. I did an interview on TV about water pollution problems with the guy who owns the ranch right here. Anytime I can get on TV, talking about cleaning up water with a cowboy, it's a good thing. You want them to be on your side."

COW-A-BUNGA

Pier Plaza Imperial Beach California

Ice Cream Coffee Smoothies

Homemade Ice Cream

Home of the DIP-A-BUNGA
DIP (Delicious Ice-Cream Portion)
Open year around
8:30 AM until Sunset

e met in France, in Paris, in a kitchen because she was a cook too at the time," says Fabrice Gaunin of his wife Nelly. "She was going to come to California and I was going to Beirut. We split apart for a little bit. In Beirut, it wasn't happening the way I thought it would so I thought okay, California was good for her—I'll go to California. It was totally different from Beirut, of course."

Fabrice and Nelly cooked at the Le Meridian Hotel on Coronado Island. "We loved Coronado but it had become too expensive. That's how we found Imperial Beach. We love it here." Fabrice and Nelly continued to commute to and from Imperial Beach and Coronado, about 20 or 30 minutes, until Nelly could not do it anymore, and for a very good reason. "Nelly was a chef until she was eight months pregnant," says Fabrice. "She was working in fine dining at a good restaurant in Le Meridian. It was one of the best restaurants in San Diego. She stopped and then she never went back to the restaurant kitchen."

After Fabrice and Nelly had their two children, Anais (10) and Mark Yves (8), Fabrice found it increasingly difficult to continue working as a chef. "I stopped because I was working too many hours and I wasn't seeing my kids grow up," says Fabrice. "I could never eat dinner with them. I never brought them to school, I never had lunch with them. I was working every weekend." Adds Nelly, "I stopped working in the kitchen when my first child was born. I understand why he stopped working."

Fabrice did not exactly stop working. "When I made the decision to stop being a chef, I tried to have an open mind," he says. "I had to extend my perception of what I want to do." Fabrice had great managerial skill but it seemed his background in the kitchen was great for getting jobs running kitchens, but not necessarily in other areas. "I thought my

best bet was to have my own business. When I looked to get my own business, I still wanted to be tied to food. And I loved IB (Imperial Beach) and I wanted to be here. I thought if I wanted to open a small restaurant, it was not going to happen because those are long hours again. I want to have something, where if I'm going to work long hours, the kids can be in it with me. This place was for sale and I got thinking about it."

Fabrice and Nelly bought the Cow-a-Bunga Ice Cream Shop right at the base of the Imperial Beach pier. "In the winter it is not so busy and we have a great family life. In the summers the kids can come in and help. Next summer my mom may come from France. We will see." They make all their own ice cream right in the shop. Fabrice also loves coffee and is very proud of the coffee he serves in his shop. So proud that he and Nelly renamed the shop Cow-a-Bunga Ice Creamery and Espresso. He loves to incorporate coffee into his ice cream.

The House Special is called "When Coffee Meets Ice Cream." It is a scoop of vanilla with a shot of espresso poured over it, some whipped cream, a bit of chocolate sauce and topped with two chocolate covered espresso beans. "It's been very popular. Some people will try it with ice cream other than vanilla but they usually go back to vanilla. It is best."

When the HBO series "John from Cincinnati" was filming in Imperial Beach, Fabrice's coffee was very popular among the crew. It inspired him to make a namesake ice cream for the show. "I tried to tie it into Cincinnati but I was

Continued on page 334

Continued on page 334

Fabrice and Nellie with daughter Anais and son Mark Yves in front of the Cow-a-bunga Ice Cream Shop

330

Ratatouille

This traditional French dish is a favorite of Nelly and Fabrice.

5   TB olive oil, divided
1   red onion, peeled and chopped
1   green bell pepper, seeded and chopped into ¾-inch cubes
1   red bell pepper, seeded and chopped into ¾-inch cubes
1   lb. eggplant, cut into ¾-inch cubes (1 large eggplant)
1   lb. zucchini, cut into ¾-inch cubes (2 medium zucchini)
3   cloves garlic, finely chopped
2   tsp. chopped, fresh thyme
2   tsp. chopped, fresh rosemary
2   bay leaves
6   vine-ripened tomatoes, peeled and chopped (3-4 cups)
3   TB shredded, fresh basil

Heat 2 TB of the oil in a large saucepan over medium heat. Add the onion and cook until softened, about 2-3 minutes. Add the bell peppers and cook an additional 2-3 minutes. Add 2 more TB of the oil along with the eggplant and zucchini and cook for another 2-3 minutes. Stir in the garlic, thyme, rosemary and bay leaves. Cook, stirring, for 2-3 minutes. Add the remaining oil and the tomato. Taste and adjust seasonings to taste. Simmer for about 20-25 minutes, stirring occasionally. Shortly before serving, stir in the basil.

Prep. time: 15 minutes
Cooking time: 35 minutes
Serves: 4-6

Healthy Cake

Each bite of this yummy cake is full of nutritious apples, walnuts, raisins and yogurt. It's good for a snack–or even for breakfast.

1½	Cups flour
1	tsp. baking soda
3	eggs
⅔	Cup brown sugar
⅓	Cup white sugar
1½	Cups plain yogurt
1	tsp. vanilla extract
1	TB olive oil
3	apples, peeled, cored and coarsely chopped
1	Cup walnuts, coarsely chopped
1	Cup raisins

Preheat oven to 350°. Sift together the flour and baking soda and set aside. In a roomy bowl, lightly beat the eggs. Add the sugars and beat until well blended. Add the yogurt, vanilla and oil and beat for an additional 1-2 minutes. Add the flour mixture gradually and beat until thoroughly combined. Fold in the apples, walnuts and raisins. Pour into a greased 9x13 pan and bake at 350° for 40-45 minutes or until a toothpick inserted in the center comes out clean.

Prep. time: 15 minutes
Baking time: 40-45 minutes
Yield: 20-24 pieces

John from Cincinnati Ice Cream

To make 2 quarts:
- ½ Cup brewed espresso, room temperature (not too dark roasted)
- 1⅓ Cups orange juice concentrate
- 2 TB + 2 tsp. Dutch cocoa powder
- 3½ Cups cream
- 1½ Cups half & half
- 1⅓ Cups sugar
- ⅛ tsp. salt
- ⅓ Cup coarsely chopped dark chocolate

To make 1 quart:
- ¼ Cup brewed espresso, room temperature
- ⅔ Cup orange juice concentrate
- 1 TB + 1 tsp. Dutch cocoa powder
- 1⅔ Cups cream
- ¾ Cup half & half
- ⅔ Cup sugar
- dash salt
- 2 TB + 2 tsp. coarsely chopped dark chocolate

Chill a large bowl in the refrigerator for a couple hours. Remove the bowl and add the espresso, orange juice concentrate, cocoa, cream, half & half, sugar and salt. Mix well. Pour into an ice cream maker and freeze according to the manufacturer's directions. Remove from the freezer, fold in the chocolate pieces and put back in the freezer until the ice cream is as firm as you like it. If you add the chocolate earlier in the process, it will break down in the ice cream instead of staying in nice little bits.

Prep. time: 12 minutes
Freezing time: depends on your ice cream maker
Yield: 1 or 2 quarts

House Special: When Ice Cream Meets Coffee

"We are an ice cream shop and a coffee shop. You don't see that very often. So we mix the coffee and the ice cream and call it 'When Ice Cream Meets Coffee.' We take one scoop of vanilla ice cream and pour a shot of espresso over it so it is like a coffee float. People love it. We top it with some whipped cream, chocolate syrup and a chocolate-covered coffee bean on top. People are welcome to change flavors of ice cream, but most go back to vanilla."

Continued from page 330

not very successful," Fabrice laughs. " I thought, 'What do I know about Cincinnati food-wise?' So I ask around and no one can really help me. So Cincinnati—I know they have the Bengals and they are orange and black and everybody in Imperial Beach has an orange tree in their backyards so I went for orange flavor. I added some chocolate chips for the black stripe (on the Bengals uniform) and coffee because people from the show liked my coffee. So we did an Orange-Mocha-Cappuccino and called it 'John from Cincinnati Ice Cream.'"

Unfortunately his unusual concoctions were not readily received at first. "The first year I tried so many things and people were not really responding. Because when they go to an ice cream shop they want to have Vanilla, Strawberry, Rocky Road, Butter Pecan and the low fat kinds. You have to give people what they want but I always try to have something different." Fabrice makes only 6 quarts per batch so the ice

cream is always freshly made. "In the summer the ice cream machine never stops," he adds.

Another popular item is "Healthy Cake," which Nelly makes every day from a recipe handed down from her mother. Nelly has made it since she was 10 years old and she makes it from memory. "I see how it mixes and how fluffy it is, you know?" says Nelly. Luckily she agreed to share her recipe, which is amazing to Fabrice. "I can't believe she is giving you the recipe because she would never give it to me. All I can do is peel the apples," he says with a laugh.

Many locals say that Cow-a-Bunga is a great place to have coffee after hitting the waves. The lines during the summer attest to the deliciousness of their ice cream. What is going on there is one of those uniquely American stories. A French family making some of the best homemade ice cream you can get anywhere, on a beach in California just a few miles from the border between the US and Mexico. All so that a dad can spend more time with his kids.

Macaroni and Cheese

2	tsp. olive oil
1	boneless, skinless chicken breast, chopped
1	Cup chopped, fresh mushrooms
2½	Cups dry elbow macaroni
1	Cup chopped broccoli florets
1	Cup chopped carrots (2 medium)
4	TB butter (½ stick)
4	TB flour
¼	tsp. salt
⅛	tsp. pepper
2	Cups milk

¾	Cup shredded sharp cheddar cheese
½	Cup grated Parmesan cheese
1	Cup diced tomatoes – canned and drained or fresh

Preheat oven to 350°. Bring a large pot of water to a boil for the macaroni. Heat the oil over medium-high heat in a frying pan. Add the chicken and mushrooms and cook until lightly browned. Remove from heat and set aside. Place the broccoli and carrots in a steamer basket and set over the boiling water until the vegetables are soft, about 3 minutes. Set aside. Add the macaroni to the boiling water and cook according to package directions. While the macaroni is cooking, melt the butter over medium-low heat in a saucepan. Whisk in the flour and cook until smooth and bubbly – about 5 minutes. Stir in the salt and pepper. Increase the heat to medium-high. Gradually add the milk, stirring constantly, and cook until thickened, which will take about 10 minutes. Add the cheddar cheese and continue to cook and stir until melted. Remove from heat and stir in the vegetables, chicken and mushrooms. In an 8x10 baking dish, alternate layers of drained macaroni and cheese sauce. Sprinkle the Parmesan and tomatoes over the top and bake at 350° for about 20 minutes.

Prep. time: 20 minutes
Cooking time: 30 minutes
Serves: 6-8

Steve and Susan in their backyard

I'm in the Navy; I drafted her about 3 years ago when we got married," laughs Steve Viola referring to his wife Susan. She adds, "Steve and I went to high school together. We just reconnected after 25 years. It's really a funny story."

It's a funny story with overtones from the bar scenes in the movie *Top Gun*. Part of Steve's job was to train medics, which took him back to their hometown of San Antonio. "On a night off, I went out with one of the guys to a bar and he was talking to some girl and it happened to be Susan's sister." Susan was there and she and Steve began to reconnect. "I was like 'Holy cow, I haven't seen you since we graduated,'" says Steve. Susan was getting together with her sisters the next night and invited Steve to meet up with them. "Susan showed up and when she walked in the room, I go, 'Hey that's the lady I'm going to marry.' Just the attitude and the sass. She's like 'Which one of you monkey boys is gonna buy me a margarita?' I said, 'Right over here.'"

Their love blossomed, particularly in the kitchen. "The funny thing is, we love to cook but I hated his prepping because when he's cooking for me, everything was huge," says Susan. "The onions were cut large, the broccoli was cut large—I called everything chunky-style. So I asked, 'Can I cut things please?' I cut them, I finely chop them and I dice them. Or he'll tell me what to do and it works out well." While Steve's chopping skills perhaps weren't to Susan's liking, she has no complaints about his cooking.

"I'm half-Italian, half-Lebanese so a lot of my influence is Mediterranean," says Steve. "I also like to venture into Asian. The difference between the Lebanese spices and Syrian is the Lebanese will use the allspice and the Syrians will use a lot of cinnamon. So if you see any traditional Mediterranean dishes, you'll look at it and say, 'Ok, there's cinnamon, there's allspice,' you can differentiate. It's almost like northern Italy versus southern Italy. Just like in Arizona and Mexico with the green chilies and the red chilies."

"He doesn't need a spice rack. He needs a spice room," Susan says. "I'm slowly taking over one of our cupboards right now," Steve admits. "I think he's in denial thinking that a cupboard will suffice," laughs Susan adding, "What's happening is because since we have a mixture of dishes— we'll go from Thai, to Japanese, to Italian, to Lebanese, back to Mexican in two weeks. There are all these spices, we have to have." Steve adds, "When we grew up in high school together, they would always have a specific lunch day.

The Violas on their wedding day

Wednesday was always Mexican food day. You could always get enchiladas and chocolate cake. Friday was the Catholic day—fish sticks, stuff like that. So that's what we try to do at the house. We'll do a different 'ethnicity' for each day. Then by the end of the week, whatever's leftover in the refrigerator—here you go, it's buffet day," he says laughing.

Steve's travels with the Navy have allowed him to experience different foods from faraway lands. "I've been throughout the South Pacific. I've been to Malaysia, Indonesia, Thailand, Korea, Guam, the Micronesian Islands.

"Killer Commando" cooking in the kitchen

Surfboards, typical of an IB backyard

week—it's like 20 guys, and I just cooked for the whole crew. I would do the meal the night before so it would be ready throughout the day. I made breakfast and lunch."

Steve is a medic or a corpsman as they call it in the Navy SEALs. "I wasn't always a corpsman. I became one in '92 after four years in the Navy and it put me on a path of adventure. It's been a good time, I cannot complain at all. I went to boot camp at Great Lakes. I really, to be honest with you, I was looking to get out in two-and-a-half years. I picked up a magazine that talked about being a Navy SEAL and so I went and tried out and became one. When I showed up at the SEAL team, they said, 'You gotta go and become a medic because we're short on corpsmen.'"

Steve has lived in Imperial Beach (IB) since 1994. "I moved away in '99 and came back. Back in the late 80s and early 90s, IB was the number one spot for U.S. Marshals to get the most wanted. So that's what it's historically known for. Why? Because you're 15 minutes from the international border, so if you got a bandito or someone on the lam, they can get through the border."

By all accounts the border situation has much improved in IB but the water pollution, particularly the "black water" coming from Tijuana, has not. "It comes out straight from the river," says Susan. "That's what shocked me; the Tijuana River dumps so much stuff into the ocean that it swims upstream, so our beaches—you can't even swim." Steve adds, "It's a shame because we have all these regulations for smog and water treatment." It has gotten so bad the Navy SEALs, some of the toughest people anywhere, stopped training near the islands off of Tijuana because swimming in the water was making them sick and giving them skin infections.

I love to go to Hong Kong and Singapore." But when you are in those foreign lands there is nothing like a home-cooked meal. "My first deployment we were in Kuwait and we met some stewardesses there. They were European and we were all away from home. We went to the market and I made Thanksgiving dinner for them that was all Lebanese-style. They had their Yorkshire pudding and a whole bunch of other stuff so it was like East meets West and the Middle East. It was fun.

"This last trip we went to Fort Knox, Kentucky for training," says Steve. "So every time I'd meet up with the guys, I'd try to make food for them. They paid me $80 for a

Lebanese Salad

Bursting with bright, tangy flavor, this salad tastes like summer.

Dressing:
2-3	tsp salt
3-4	cloves fresh garlic, peeled
4	lemons, juice of (1–1½ Cups)
4	TB olive oil
2	cucumbers, sliced
2	small heads lettuce, chopped (we used romaine)
2	tomatoes, wedge-cut into eighths
½	Cup roughly chopped fresh parsley

Put the garlic cloves and salt in the bottom of a large, sturdy salad bowl. Mash the garlic and salt together with a fork or pestle to make a paste. Whisk in the olive oil and lemon juice. Add the salad ingredients, toss to combine, and serve. Top with freshly ground black pepper to taste.

Prep. time: 15 minutes
Cooking time: none
Serves: 6-8

Lebanese Fried Cauliflower with Lamb

2	lbs. lamb stew meat, cut into bite-sized pieces
1	small head of cauliflower, cut into florets
2	TB olive oil, divided
1	medium onion, chopped
1	28 oz. can diced tomatoes
½	tsp. salt
½	tsp. black pepper
½	tsp. ground allspice
1	lemon (juice of)

Heat 1 TB of the oil in a large frying pan over medium heat. Add the cauliflower florets and cook until golden brown, about 10 minutes.

Drain on paper toweling and set aside. In the same pan, heat the remaining olive oil over medium-high heat and brown the lamb for about 5 minutes. If you are using a smaller pan the lamb may need to be browned in two batches. Add the onions to the pan, reduce heat to medium, and cook for another 5 minutes. Add the cauliflower and tomatoes to the pan. Stir in the salt, pepper and allspice, cover, and cook over medium-low for 1½ hours. Sprinkle with lemon juice right before serving.

Prep. time: 20 minutes – less if the lamb is cubed
Cooking time: 1 hour, 40 minutes total
Serves: 6

Tamale Brownies

We made these brownies by using our Happy Brownie recipe and recreating the happy accident of mixing in corn flour. So, these could also be called Feliz Brownies. By whatever name you call them, they're sure to be a hit.

1	Cup butter (2 sticks)
12	TB. (¾ Cup) cocoa, natural or Dutch process
2	Cups sugar
2	tsp. vanilla extract
4	eggs
¾	Cup all-purpose flour
¾	Cup corn flour (white will be a little finer textured than yellow)
½	Cup chopped walnuts or pecans (optional–kids don't usually like nuts)
½	Cup powdered sugar to sift on top of brownies (optional)

Preheat oven to 325°. Grease a 9x13 inch glass pan. Melt butter in a small pan over low heat, then sift in cocoa and whisk until smooth. Pour into a large mixing bowl, let cool. Add sugar and vanilla extract, mix well. Lightly whisk the eggs, then add to batter and stir to blend. Add flour and corn flour and stir until combined. Brownies should be stirred by hand, until just blended. Add nuts if desired, spoon into baking dish. Bake for 30-40 minutes, until the middle springs back when lightly pressed and the edges start to pull away from the sides of the pan. Let cool, and then sift powdered sugar over the top if desired. Let cool well, as the corn flour makes them a little harder to cut while warm, then cut into squares and serve or store in a covered container.

Prep. time: 10 minutes

Cooking time: 30-40 minutes

Yield: 16-24 squares

Back in their kitchen and safely away from the black water, the Violas have had some interesting experiences including a few mix-ups. "The first Christmas we spent together, I was making brownies and Steve was making tamales at the same time in the kitchen. So we both have mixing bowls full of stuff," says Susan. Both had to leave the house for a bit. "We had the two recipes on the counters," continues Susan. "I saw this mixture of flour or what I thought was flour. So I start mixing it up and I start making my fudge. When it came out, it looked weird. I was like 'What the hell is this?' It was tamale masa with the cinnamon, nutmeg, pecans and the brown sugar." Steve actually liked it. "It was like a tamale cookie. I took it, put it with vanilla ice cream and with chocolate on there, it was great," he laughs. Susan chimes in, "After that whole thing, I have my pink mixing bowls and he has his blue mixing bowls. That was our first cooking experience together and I was so bummed—I really wanted something sweet."

A tradition that that the Violas have started is to make 13 dozen tamales and give them away as Christmas presents. "We freeze them," says Steve. "It's fun. I'll make the masa and the meat. We just taught Susan's nephew, who's a novice, how to roll them, Spread it out, put the meat in and roll it up. Her nephew's are a little bit thicker than hers. But they still turned out good." Susan adds, "It's great. You just sit there, you drink beer and roll tamales. One time I watched 'The Sopranos' with my girlfriend and drank some wine. Steve is just handing us the stuff and putting it on the table and I'm rolling tamales." "It's mind-numbing and very stimulating at the same time," adds Steve. "To me that's how I unwind—I cook. Susan will know if I've had a bad day because I'll just go in the kitchen and start cooking. It's total stress relief." Susan concurs, "He's happiest when he's in the kitchen."

Penzeys One arranged an interview with Katy Fallon at her coffee shop for 7 a.m. Upon arrival, her co-worker told us that something had come up and she would be in later. Our photographer decided to hit the beach and photograph some surfers when one of them waved to him. It was Katy.

"It's really interesting when you meet people in the water," says Katy. "Surfers have a reputation of 'Dudes!' and 'California!' You'll go out there and there're a lot of teachers in the water. I surf with a chemical engineer. He's a professor at State. There are all kinds of people that surf.

"I started surfing when I was 40. It's never too late to start. I took my dad out last summer. He's 73 and it was his first

time." But surfing wasn't the hard part. "He said putting on the wetsuit was the tough part. He still runs and stays healthy."

Katy's son Joey got a quicker start on surfing than his mother and grandfather, starting at 4 years old. He's now a student at the City College in San Diego.

Katy was the manager at Coronado Brewing Company up until two years ago when a little coffee shop was up for sale, which became IB Coffee & Books. She had a vision for how her shop would be successful. "I decided it just needed a consistent product and a consistent staff. It needed to be redecorated. The location's good, you're at a beach, it's got a nice shape, it should work. And it did."

Shortly after the shop opened, the "John From Cincinnati" crew showed up outside the door. "From the first day they came in it was like a bulldozer hit. They came in with these squads. The next thing I know, the TV is in the bathroom, all my toilets are out the backdoor. Then I came back and everything was back to where it was before. I realized they were efficient at what they did. If they broke it, they fixed it."

Katy was sad to see the show cancelled. "I miss seeing my friend Luke Perry," she says.

Homemade Granola

2	Cups old-fashioned oats (not quick-cooking)
¼	Cup wheat germ
¼	Cup ground flaxseed (find it by the flour, nuts, pasta or in the health food aisle)
1	Cup almonds, coarsely chopped
¼	Cup sunflower seeds
2	TB brown sugar
¼	Cup honey
3	TB canola or your favorite vegetable oil
1½	tsp. vanilla extract
¼	tsp. almond extract
½	Cup nonfat milk powder (usually in the baking section)
¼	tsp. salt
1	TB water
3	oz. dried sweetened cranberries (craisins)

Preheat oven to 325°. Spray a rimmed baking sheet with cooking spray. Mix oats, wheat germ, flaxseed, almonds and sunflower seeds in a large bowl. In a separate bowl, mix together the brown sugar, honey, oil, extracts, milk powder and salt, adding the water at the end to smooth the consistency. Pour the liquid into the oat mixture, mixing until everything is coated. Using your hands may be messy, but it helps to work the liquid through all the dry ingredients.

Spread the mixture on the cookie sheet in an even layer. Bake for 20 minutes, stir, and rotate the pan so it cooks evenly. Bake another 10-20 minutes until the oats are golden brown. Do not overcook. Let cool completely in the pan, the oats will crisp as they cool. When the mixture has cooled, add the cranberries.

Prep. time: 10 minutes
Baking time: 30-40 minutes
Yield: about 4 Cups

Acai Syrup

Pronounced ah-sai-ee, this flavorful fruit is really healthy, but usually isn't found whole or as syrup in most of the country. Usually it is sold as juice, so we made our own syrup, great for topping cereal, fruit, oatmeal and yogurt.

½	Cup acai juice (does not need to be pure acai juice; may be found in the refrigerated produce section)
½	Cup orange juice
2	TB honey

Combine juices and honey in a medium saucepan. Bring to a medium boil and cook until reduced by half, about 15-20 minutes.

Prep. time: none
Cooking time: 25-30 minutes
Yield: about ½ Cup

Steve and Kim in front of dish towel curtains left by the "JFC" crew

me that the water was contaminated. We have always had some of that in the bay but because of the recent rains, the runoff makes it really bad. I caught some really nice bass but I ended up putting them back in. I wasn't that worried about it until I saw the signs that were posted."

Fortunately his garden is not affected by black water. Carl grew up with a garden in his backyard. "I would say it was at least 12-by-18. At some point in time we had a hot house. We also had watermelon and cantaloupes." His current garden is not as large as the one his family had growing up but it is plenty for him and Kimberlee. "We've been growing peas, zucchinis, tomatoes, radishes and carrots. There's a big difference between what you grow and what you get in a store," says Carl. "There's a lot more flavor with what you can grow; it's almost generic what you buy in a store."

Carl has a quick and easy-to-remember recipe for making salsa with ingredients that come out of his garden. "Have you ever seen the Mexican flag?" asks Carl. "There you go. Onions are white, you got your green with jalapeños and cilantro, and red tomatoes. I also put in lime juice. I learned that from a Mexican friend."

We found Carl and his wife Kimberlee while we were gawking at their house. Their home was used as the Yost family house in the HBO series "John From Cincinnati." Kimberlee is very friendly and she saw us. She waved us over and after

I learned cooking from my parents," says Imperial Beach resident Carl Block. "When I was younger, I would hang out in the kitchen." Growing up in nearby Chula Vista, Carl and his family didn't spend all their time in the kitchen but much of it was spent growing or pursuing food. "We always had a garden with tomatoes, vegetables, zucchinis, squash. So a lot of the meals we had, we caught or grew." Carl adds, "We would go hunting and diving, so we always had lobster, abalone, fish, a lot of seafood. My dad was the one who was certified and who did the diving. I'd go down there snorkeling. We'd go fishing and diving."

In addition to their quests on the ocean he and his father would do a little hunting on the beach. "South of here, between here and the border, we used to go clamming before it got too contaminated. You dig a little bit and you come back with piles and piles of them," says Carl. "Soak them for a couple of days, boil them, clean them; they were good."

The contamination he talks about is "black water," the sewage that washes into the ocean from Tijuana. "I was fishing here recently down in the bay and people were walking by telling

The "Yost House" from "JFC," invasion of the crew and today

10 Pepper Pork

"It's not spicy hot, but after about 5 minutes, you're sweating."

1	5 lb. bone-in pork butt
10	tomatillos, peeled
10	jalapeños, stemmed
10	yellow chile peppers, stemmed (banana peppers)
10	cloves garlic, peeled
½	Cup chopped fresh cilantro
½	tsp. ground cumin
½	tsp. salt
1	onion, chopped
20	tortillas

Place the pork in a large kettle. Fill with enough water to cover the pork by 1-2 inches. Bring to a simmer and cook until the meat is tender, about 2½-3 hours. Remove the pork from the kettle, let cool a bit, and then shred. While the pork is cooking, bring a large kettle of water to a boil and add the tomatillos (husks removed), peppers and garlic cloves and boil until easily poked with a fork, about 1 minute. Drain well and put in the blender along with the cilantro, cumin and salt and blend until smooth. The more seeds from the peppers you include, the hotter the sauce will be. Pour over the shredded pork and mix well. Roll into a tortilla with the onion and enjoy.

Prep. time: 10 minutes
Cooking time: 2½-3 hours
Serves: 10-12

Yost Stuffed Mushrooms

1½   lb. pkg. medium to large mushrooms
       (27 or so mushrooms)
8   oz. bulk breakfast sausage (we used hot)
½   tsp. seasoned salt we used 4/S
¼   tsp. black pepper
¼   tsp. rubbed sage
1   tsp. minced garlic
3   oz. pkg. cream cheese, room temperature
2   scallions, sliced
5   slices (prepackaged, burger-sized slices)
       mozzarella cheese

Preheat oven to 350°. Heat a large skillet over medium-high heat. Add the sausage, seasoned salt, pepper, sage and garlic and cook until nicely browned, about 7 minutes total. While the sausage is cooking, wash the mushrooms and leave them slightly damp. Remove the stems, dice them and add them to the sausage for the final 2 minutes cooking time. Remove from heat, place in a large bowl, draining the excess fat if there is any, it depends on the sausage you choose. Add the cream cheese and scallions and mix well. Brush the mushroom caps on the outside with olive oil, this will keep them moist during cooking and they'll turn a lovely golden brown. Fill the mushroom caps to heaping with the sausage mixture, 1½-2 teaspoons filling should do it, and place on a baking sheet. Cut the mozzarella slices into small pieces and place over each mushroom. Bake at 350° for about 20 minutes or until lightly browned.

Prep. time: 30 minutes
Cooking time: 20 minutes
Yield: about 25 mushrooms

Carl and Kim with Bruce Greenwood who played Mitch Yost on "JFC"

then back by evening. All they left was the curtains made from dishtowels that the couple decided to keep. The production crew also built a clubhouse in the backyard but it was not up to building codes so no clubhouse for Carl. Fortunately through all this they did not disturb Carl and Kimberlee's garden.

a brief chat told us her husband Carl loved to cook. Next thing we knew we were invited over. "They shot Luke Perry or whoever coming in and out of the house. This was the kitchen for the show," says Kimberlee motioning around her living room. "The rest of the interior of the house was built up near Los Angeles." "Obviously they can't film the streets and all of the other stuff there," says Carl, "so they shot that here." "We got to meet them all from the show," continues Kimberlee. "Ed O'Neill is a very sweet guy."

"We would get a call the day before they wanted to shoot and we had to vacate the house by 5:00 a.m." says Carl. Their house would be transformed into the Yost house and

Carl's Criss-Cross Rib-eye
Simple, and simply delicious.

2	rib-eye steaks, ¾-1½ inches thick
1	TB minced garlic
1	tsp. seasoned salt
½	tsp. black pepper

Score the steak with ¼-inch deep criss-cross cuts about ½ inch apart. Rub the steaks with the garlic and then sprinkle with the seasoned salt and pepper. Grill on high heat 5-7 minutes per side or until cooked to your desired level of doneness. Make sure the grill or pan is really hot when you put the steaks on; this makes the criss-cross cuts stand out and look great. Excellent with grilled corn on the cob.

For simple grilled corn, soak the corn (husk still on) in cold water for at least 30 minutes. Place on the grill and cook for about 20 minutes, turning once.

Prep. time: 5 minutes (30 minutes if soaking corn)
Cooking time: 10-14 minutes for steak, 20 for corn
Serves: 2

As much as I can get excited about this idea or that, as much as I can dream of years to come and all the things we can do as we grow our staff and gain in experience, the reality is all we really need to do is quite simple. For all my thoughts and dreams and desires, all we really need to do to be the magazine I want us to be, is to time and again show cooks, and show the richness that cooking brings to their lives. As much as we will cast a wide net and go down roads less traveled in pursuit of variety it really can come down to being as simple as a word.

In this case, the word is "Hope."

It is fitting that we end our book, end the story of our beginning at the place where we started. Hope. I hope you have enjoyed what we have been up to so far, that in our pages and in the stories of the cooks who have been gracious enough to grace our pages you have found a kindred spirit, a feeling of belonging, and maybe even the sense that what you do for those around you when you cook is something very, very special.

Thanks for reading,

Bill

Brian and Maureen Luce, New Hope, Pennsylvania

Maureen and Brian Luce met on Valentine's Day at the gym. As she says, it's a sure bet two people both working out at 8:00 pm on Valentine's Day are bound to be single. As Maureen told Brian on their first date, "I'm looking for someone who can make me laugh," and to this day, she hasn't stopped laughing.

They have built a wonderful life together in Bucks County, Pennsylvania, where Brian works as a realtor and Maureen works for the State of New Jersey Judiciary. While they started out in Holland, PA, Brian's job took him 'round and 'round the county, and one day he came home and told her about a neighborhood in New Hope he thought they'd like. Tourists plan day trips to artsy, scenic New Hope on the Delaware River, and sure enough, soon the Luces were settled in about a mile from town on a four-acre wooded hilltop. The town may be quaint and scenic, but Maureen is only an hour from Philadelphia and an hour and a half from New York City and skiing in the Poconos. They keep up their exercise by biking on the 60 mile tow canal path along the Delaware River, take "dates" to the Home Depot to deal with the many projects they've undertaken on their home, and enjoy their dogs and the wild deer and turkeys around the house. They both enjoy their separate hobbies as well—Brian tinkering with old cars and Maureen taking classes in everything from photography to real estate to cake decorating to sewing (that one she says didn't work out so well) to interior design. As Maureen says, "Years ago I heard someone say, 'If you aren't learning something new, then you are slowly dying,' and I've adopted this motto." Most of all, they enjoy each other and doing the fun, simple things in life. Maureen doesn't put much credence in expensive gifts and flowers on all occasions, as she says, "The things that count

are the little things that make me laugh."

Every day when Maureen drives home from her job in Trenton along the winding, scenic river, she feels like she's heading home to her vacation villa. She started working at the judiciary in 1995 as a budget analyst, preparing annual budgets for New Jersey's Superior Courts. Now she is supervisor of the Grants Administration Unit, where she administers all the federal funding that the judiciary receives for special projects. Maureen says, "It is a truly rewarding job in that I administer federal grant programs that give 'new hope' to many people." For instance, funds are used for such things as:

Helping those defendants struggling with substance abuse problems.

Training volunteers who handle domestic violence issues.

Providing vocational training to troubled juveniles to learn a trade.

Creating databases to notify victims of the change in status of particular criminals.

Creating a safe environment for visitation of children in troubled situations, and many more.

As Maureen sums it up, "Working in the grants field of the judiciary has also opened my eyes to the reality that there are many people in our own country, struggling to make a life for themselves and their families. These people need hope, and in an indirect way, I feel like I am helping to provide that hope."

Tomato Salad

2-3	lbs. tomatoes (6-8), chopped (a mix of colors is nice)
3	green onions, thinly sliced
1	small red onion, chopped in small slivers
1/2	Cup fresh mozzarella, cubed

Dressing:

3/4	Cup raspberry vinegar
2/3	Cup olive oil
2	garlic cloves, minced
2-3	TB sugar
1	tsp. salt
1	tsp. chopped fresh basil
	dash black pepper

Chop and slice the vegetables and cheese. Combine the tomatoes, green onions and red onion in a bowl. Put the mozzarella in a separate container. Combine the dressing ingredients in a cruet or a jar with a tight-fitting lid and shake to combine. Although this is a very tasty side dish, it doesn't look appetizing if it's left to marinate for several hours. I usually keep one container with the tomato mixture, another with the cheese and a third with the dressing. About one hour prior to serving, I mix everything together, thereby allowing the flavors to meld. When zucchini is in season, I've also thrown that into the salad.

Prep. time: 15 minutes
Cooking time: none
Marinating time: 1 hour
Serves: 6

After the Revolutionary War, Benjamin Perry, a real go-getter, started operating two very successful mills on the Delaware River, which, unfortunately, burned down in 1790. Rather than giving up, the mills were rebuilt and called the "New Hope Mills," bringing new hope to the town and the people in it.

New Hope, Pennsylvania is a tiny town of four streets—Main Street, Bridge Street, Ferry Street and Mechanic Street. It is nestled along the banks of the Delaware River and the Delaware Canal. The Delaware Canal was a tow canal, the kind where teams of mules pulled barges filled with the soft coal of the Upper Lehigh Valley to Philadelphia, New York City and the Eastern Seaboard where it went off into the world. The mules are long gone (well, actually, they do pull a tourist barge if you're interested!), but the towpath remains. In fact, the 60-mile Delaware Canal is the only remaining continuously intact canal of the early 19th century. Today it is an outstanding biking and walking path that Maureen and Brian can ride the mile into town and take for longer weekend cycling trips. As Maureen says, "What Brian and I enjoy about the towpath is that one can ride the path safely for 60 miles without the fear of interacting with auto traffic. And additionally, it doesn't have hills, which makes for a fantastic leisurely ride."

George Washington famously crossed the Delaware to fight the battle of Trenton. After the war, Benjamin Perry, a real go-getter, started operating two very successful mills on the Delaware River, which, unfortunately, burned down in 1790. Rather than giving up, the mills were rebuilt and called the "New Hope Mills," bringing new hope to the town and the people in it. That spirit continues to this day. New Hope is now a thriving little village of art galleries, restored historic inns and breathtaking scenery, but it has been hard hit by heavy storms in the past several years. Three of the last four years the town has been completely flooded out, which is particularly bad for a town that counts

Photo(s) Courtesy of Liesbeth Bisschops • www.elevated-images.com

on summer visitors. Each time, everyone in town has pulled together to help each other and gotten the streets open and the shops back up and running in a remarkably short time. To support the shopkeeps and the town, check out this year's Arts and Crafts Festival September 29-30, or how about the "Local Ghosts of New Hope Cemetery Tour" on October 27th?

The land around New Hope was originally owned by William Penn, and it changed hands several times through the period until the Revolution. Bowman's Hill, the high point of Bucks County, was used as an observation point during the war, as it offers an unobstructed view of miles of the Delaware River. It is also very close to the point where

Raspberry Cream Cheese Bars

3/4	Cup butter, softened (1¹/₂ sticks)
1	Cup brown sugar, firmly packed
1¹/₂	Cups all-purpose flour
1¹/₂	Cups quick-cooking oats
¹/₂	tsp. baking soda
¹/₂	tsp. salt
¹/₂	Cup sugar
2	8 oz. pkg. cream cheese, softened
2	large eggs
1	TB Raspberry Enlightenment (or 1 tsp. raspberry extract)
1	12 oz. jar red raspberry preserves
¹/₂	Cup chopped, slivered almonds

Preheat oven to 350°. Grease a 9x13 baking pan. In a roomy bowl, cream together the butter and brown sugar. In a separate bowl, combine the flour, oats, baking soda and salt. Add this to the creamed mixture and stir well. Press the mixture into the greased pan, reserving a generous cup for the topping. Bake the crust at 350° for 11-12 minutes. While the crust is baking, in another mixing bowl, beat the sugar and cream cheese together on low speed until well mixed. Add the eggs one at a time, mixing between each addition. Add the Raspberry Enlightenment and beat until well mixed. When the crust comes out of the oven, spread with the cream cheese mixture. Drop spoonfuls of the raspberry preserves over the cream cheese mixture and swirl with a spatula until evenly distributed. In a small bowl, combine the almonds and the reserved oat mixture. Sprinkle over the preserves. Bake for approximately 25-30 minutes or until the edges are golden brown. Cool before cutting and serving. Keep in the refrigerator until ready to serve.

Prep. time: 25 min. Baking time: 25-35 min. Serves: 28.

Bonnie Norton, Fairhope, Alabama

In the last twelve months, the things **Bonnie Norton** and her husband **Bobby** were hoping to be done with were many, serious, and adding up quickly. Last summer, Bonnie's mom was suddenly hospitalized with a severe lung infection, and just as she was turning the corner in August, Bonnie's 27-year-old daughter Lauren was diagnosed with melanoma. Two weeks later Lauren lost her job. In September Bonnie developed a painful disc problem in her neck and was booked for several painful procedures. In November her

"We are fortunate to have good friends and family nearby that we enjoy entertaining. I love to set a beautiful table with flowers, sterling flatware and pretty china and crystal. I am lucky to have many lovely pieces from my grandmother and mother-in-law. We may be wearing jeans and flip flops when we sit down, but the table will be black tie!"

mother was diagnosed with breast cancer. To top it all off, in January husband Bobby had a stroke. So, a lot of hope for a better year!

In the middle of all that agony and uncertainty, Bonnie says, "We have so much to be thankful for." With a lot of "mad cap planning, Bobby's beautiful daughter, Hallie, was married and we are so happy for her and our new son-in-law Jason."

Last year's hoping for a better future has really paid off. Daughter Lauren, whose melanoma was caught very early, has had no recurrence and her prognosis is excellent. She also found a new job she loves that is "100

times better than the one she had before." Bonnie's mom has also bounced back wonderfully and her prognosis is good as well. Bonnie's neck is great, and Bobby is back at work and minding his doctors. And, as Bonnie says, "Our very happiest news is our daughter Louise, mother of our grandson Cole, is expecting a baby girl this summer. We are truly blessed and fortunate with hearts full of love and so much to cherish in our lives."

It pays to have Hope.

Fairhope, Alabama, the home of Bobby and Bonnie Norton, is a small town on the eastern shore of Mobile Bay. As Bonnie tells it, the town was founded in 1894 by a group of visionaries who wanted to start a community where everyone had an equal opportunity to own and work the land. "When the Fairhope Colony was established, the Colony was the titleholder of all the land. Residents could lease land from the Colony. To this day, there is still Colony land, from tiny farms to million dollar homes. If you have a home on Colony land, you pay a lease every year to what is now called the Fairhope Single Tax Corporation. Leases are for 99 years but we still refer to the Colony land as 'un-deeded' property. In any event, when Fairhope was in its infancy, an original founding member of the Colony supposedly made the comment that this revolutionary idea of leasing Colony land had a 'fair hope' of being successful, hence our name."

Cheese Wafers

1	stick butter, softened ($1/2$ Cup)
1	lb. extra sharp cheddar cheese, grated (2 Cups)
$1/2$	Cup finely chopped pecans
1	Cup flour
$3/4$	tsp. salt
$1/4$	tsp. cayenne pepper (or to taste)
2-3	drops hot pepper sauce (or to taste)

Place the butter and cheese in a large bowl. With your hands, mix and cream together well. Add the salt and cayenne and continue to mix with your hands. Add the flour and pecans a bit at a time and mix with your hands. Add the pepper sauce and mix well until dough is smooth and can be rolled into a ball. Divide the dough into three portions. On a piece of waxed paper, roll each portion out into a log, about 1 inch in diameter. Wrap each log in waxed paper and refrigerate overnight. The dough will keep in the refrigerator for about 2 weeks. When ready to bake, preheat the oven to 275°. Unroll the logs from the waxed paper and, using a sharp knife, slice the dough into thin wafers, about $1/8$ inch thick. Place on aluminum foil-covered baking sheets. Bake at 275° for about 30 minutes. You will need to make sure they are good and dry—you want them to be crisp. Remove to a wire rack to cool. Store in an airtight container; good for about 1 week.

Prep. time: 10 min. plus overnight chilling. Baking time: 30 min. Yield: 15 dozen wafers.

L.A. Caviar   "L. A. is an abbreviation for Lower Alabama."

2	Cups frozen field peas or fresh sugar snap peas cut in small pieces
1	large tomato, peeled and chopped
$1/2$	Cup chopped purple onion
1	7-8 oz. can corn, drained or 1/2 lb. frozen sweet corn (shoepeg corn if available)
2	tsp. dried cilantro
1	tsp. dried parsley
$1/4$	Cup olive oil
$1/4$	Cup lime juice
1	TB red wine vinegar
$1/4$	tsp. salt
$1/4$	tsp. coarse ground black pepper

Cook the peas according to package directions, drain and let cool. If you are using snap peas, cook in boiling water for 1-2 minutes, drain and let cool. Combine all of the ingredients in a bowl and mix well. Cover and chill in the refrigerator for several hours so the flavors can blend and develop. Serve with tortilla chips.

Prep. time: 10 minutes. Cooking time: 5 minutes. Yield: 4 Cups.

Hope Groth

Hope and the gas station dinosaur.

Hope and Mac, their newest female sled dog. She's actually quite young, she went grey early!

Hope Groth and her husband Matt live in northern Minnesota—15 miles outside of Grand Marais, very close to the Canadian border. They moved there from Sheboygan, Wisconsin, because it wasn't far enough north for them. In fact, they are about as far north as you can get and still be in the United States, which suits them just fine. They are, as Matt says, "very winter-centric people."

They have 15 Alaskan Husky sled dogs. Matt competes in various dog sled races around the area and heads off into Wisconsin and Michigan for more. They called their kennel "Oomingmak Racing Kennel." Oomingmak is a native Alaskan word for musk ox, which translates into "the bearded one." Hope loves Matt's full beard, so they figured the name was a good fit.

Matt works year-round as a carpenter, while Hope spends the summers employed house-keeping in an historic lodge on the north shore of Lake Superior. In the winter though, is when they enjoy themselves most—no bugs!

That's when Hope goes to work for the neighbors, Arleigh and Odin Jorgenson, who run a sled dog touring business with over 100 dogs that need caring for. Hope helps care for them, though she does not run teams—even their own. As she says, "Way too much controlled chaos for me!" Her love of cooking comes in very handy, as she does all the lunch-making and camping trip cooking. She makes sandwiches and brownies for trail lunches

Sled dogs training for action.

Husband Matt and Yana – retired sled dog leader – is she trying to lick the camera or the photographer?

and everything from lasagna to shrimp gumbo for the camping trips. She cooks the food and bags it in food-saver bags, freezes it and sends it out on the run. The food gets heated through or cooked out on the trail by the guides. Hope had to "dig deep" to find summer recipes to send us—her mother's grilled steak marinade and her grandmother's cucumber salad—as she says, she and her husband are "winter people." The stuffed French toast recipe, on the other hand, can be used all year long, and is a big favorite for camp breakfasts.

Arleigh's French Toast

A hearty twist on a breakfast favorite—perfect for hungry campers or Sunday brunch.

1	loaf French bread (a day or two old works best)
2	oz. ricotta cheese
2	oz. cream cheese
1/4	Cup fruit preserves (apricot, strawberry, raspberry—you choose)
4	eggs
1	Cup milk
1/4	tsp. vanilla extract
1/8	tsp. ground nutmeg

Mix together the ricotta and cream cheese until well blended. Add the preserves and mix well. Slice off the ends of the bread and discard. Cut the rest of the loaf into 1¹/₂-inch thick slices. Slice a pocket into each slice of bread. Stuff with the cheese/fruit mixture, about 1 TB per pocket. In a wide, shallow bowl, beat together the eggs, milk, vanilla and nutmeg. Spray a large, heavy skillet or griddle with non-stick cooking spray and heat to medium. Dip both sides of the bread in the egg mixture and cook until golden brown, about 1-2 minutes per side.

Prep. time: 10 min. Cooking time: 2-4 min. per batch. Serves: 6-8.

Hope and her snow bunny, growing up in Sheboygan, Wisconsin. Hope has a huge, lifelong collection of rabbits, from china and plush to garden sculptures

Hope's new baby Belle, the latest in a long line of house rabbits. Sadly their beloved bunny Reginald passed on at the age of 6 last winter, but Belle has hopped right into their hearts. She is a Flemish Giant and could grow up to be 20 pounds! She is 3 months old and about half grown in this photo.

Potato Pancakes

An easy recipe for a favorite dish.

3	large russet potatoes, peeled, grated, and well drained (about 3 Cups)
1	TB Pasta Sprinkle or your favorite herb blend
2	TB all-purpose flour
1	TB Bavarian Seasoning or extra herbs
1	tsp. salt
1/4	tsp. pepper
1	egg
3	TB vegetable oil

Peel the potatoes and place in a large bowl of cold water. In a separate bowl, mix together the Pasta Sprinkle, flour, Bavarian Seasoning, salt and pepper. In a small bowl, beat the egg and set aside. Coarsely shred the potatoes by hand with a grater or with a food processor. Once you start shredding the potatoes, work quickly to prevent the potatoes from turning brown. Squeeze the shredded potatoes to remove most of the moisture. Add the flour mixture to the potatoes and mix thoroughly. Mixing with your hands works best because you want the flour to mix evenly through the potatoes. Then, add the egg and mix well with a spoon for about 30 seconds. Heat the oil in a non-stick pan over medium heat. Heat level is very important because if the potatoes brown too quickly, they will not be done in the middle, and if they brown too slowly they will soak up too much oil. It's a good idea to start with 1 pancake to get your oil the perfect temperature. Use a 1/4 Cup measuring cup to portion your pancakes. Scoop them out of the bowl, making sure to get some of the liquid that accumulates in the bottom. Drop the potatoes in the frying pan and flatten them a bit with a spatula. After 3-4 minutes, turn carefully and cook the other side an additional 3-4 minutes. Drain on a wire rack and pat with paper toweling to absorb any excess oil.

Prep. time: 12 minutes. Cooking time: 6-8 minutes per batch. Yield: about 10 pancakes

What is Hope hoping for?

"I am hoping for a very long and snowy winter (not to be confused with a dark and stormy night!)."

What is she hoping will be over?

"I will be glad when summer comes to an end so that I can say good-bye to bugs, heat and humidity!"

"P.S. My husband Matt says to remind you that we are very 'winter-centric' people!"

Mom's Marinated Flank Steak

A great grilled dish—perfect until the snow flies.

1	lb. flank steak
1/2	lemon (juice of)
1/2	Cup soy sauce
1	TB chopped fresh garlic (or 1 tsp. dried minced garlic)
1	TB (heaping) horseradish (we used horseradish powder mixed with 1 1/2 TB water)
1	TB freshly ground black pepper (or to taste)

Whisk together the lemon juice, soy sauce, garlic, horseradish and pepper. Marinate the flank steak at least 12 hours in the refrigerator for best flavor. Grill the steak over medium-high heat for about 4-5 minutes per side for medium-rare, longer if you prefer your steak more well done. If you'd like, you may bring the marinade to a boil, let the sauce reduce and serve over the flank steak. If you are not comfortable reusing marinade, simply reserve 1/4 Cup of the marinade before adding the steak. Warm the reserved marinade over low heat and pour over the grilled steak before serving.

Prep. time: 5 minutes. Marinating time: 12 hours.
Cooking time: 8-10 minutes. Serves: 3

Hope Riley

Hope Riley and her husband Bill have six daughters, three sons-in-law and four grandchildren between them (with one more on the way). Some are close to home in the Philadelphia area (Hope and Bill live in Villanova), and some have migrated to Illinois and Seattle. When everyone is together it means blueberry pancakes for all! As Hope tells it, "Four of the kids are vegetarians; it's been a challenge to meet all their needs. They always wanted us to put a cookbook together titled: *Food for Picky Vegetarian Kids Whose Parents Aren't.*"

Holly Zug, Casey and Lorin Riley

Hope and Bill Riley

Hope is a psychologist in private practice, and when she isn't working, she loves gardening, cooking and playing golf. She's an avid member of the Philadelphia unit of the Herb Society of America, and is responsible for finding herb-related items to sell at the annual Spring Herb Sale held by chapters around the country.

Jan and Tracey Tackett, and daughter Cassia – yes, Cassia, like the cinnamon.

Scott, Carson and Kendy Weller

At Marion Golf Club, Hope combines her favorite pastimes of golf, herbs and cooking by co-chairing herb-themed tournaments: "Herbal Tees," "Asian Herbal Tees," "Herbal Reme-Tees" and this summer's "Herbal Ameni-Tees." Next summer they're thinking "Herbal Par-tees." Each tee box has its own mystery herb for players to sniff and identify for prizes. What are the prizes? Well, at least some of them have been from Penzeys!

Paige, John, Tricia and Matthew Braunlich

All the kids and grandkids love the blueberry pancakes recipe. Whenever they're all together at the Shore house in Ocean City, NJ it's blueberry pancakes for breakfast!

Blueberry Pancakes

2	Cups flour
1/2	tsp. salt
2	TB sugar
4	TB baking powder (seems like a lot, but blueberries are heavy)
1/2	tsp. cinnamon
1/4	tsp. ground nutmeg
4	eggs
1 1/2	Cups milk
2 1/2	Cups blueberries

Mix together the flour, salt, sugar, baking powder, cinnamon and nutmeg in a large bowl. Beat the eggs and the milk slightly and add to the dry ingredients. You may adjust the amount of milk depending on how thick or thin you prefer your pancakes. Mix until the batter is smooth. Fold in the blueberries. Heat a greased pan or griddle over medium-high heat. Pour the batter by the 1/4 Cup onto the griddle. Flip the pancakes when bubbly, after about 3-4 minutes. Cook the other side for an additional 3-4 minutes.

Prep. time: 5 minutes
Cooking time: 6-8 minutes per batch
Yield: about 20 pancakes

Hope's hopeful wish is . . .

"Health and happiness for my family and friends."

credits

Recipe for: _____
from the kitchen of: _____

Jenna Murack

Grandma Murack
cuddles two-year-old
Jenna who's fallen
asleep in her arms.

Lasagna

*Jenna says, "My Grandma Murack (in the photo
with me) made the best bread in the world.
Sadly, she took that recipe with her, so I am
sharing this family favorite recipe, which came
from my dad's co-worker who was a cook in the
Navy. I like to make this when I have people over
for dinner because I can have everything ready
and in the oven before my friends and family
arrive so I have more time to spend with them
and less time bustling about the kitchen."*

3	lbs. ground chuck
3	TB olive oil
4	garlic cloves, minced or crushed
2	medium onions, chopped
3	15 oz. cans tomato sauce
1	18 oz. can tomato paste
1½	Cups red wine or water (I like Chianti Classico)
2-4	tsp. sugar
¾	tsp. salt
1½	tsp. garlic powder
1½	TB dried oregano or Pasta Sprinkle
½	tsp. pepper
1½	TB dried basil
12	lasagna noodles
1½	lb. ricotta cheese or small curd cottage cheese
1	egg
1	10 oz. package frozen, chopped spinach, thawed and drained (optional)
½-¾	Cup Parmesan cheese, shredded
1	lb. mozzarella cheese, shredded

Brown and drain the ground chuck and set
aside. Heat olive oil over medium-low heat in a
large stock pot. Sauté the onion and garlic until
soft and lightly browned, about 10 minutes. Stir
in the browned meat, tomato sauce, tomato
paste, and wine or water. Stir well to dissolve
the tomato paste. Add the sugar, salt, garlic
powder, oregano and pepper. Stir until well
blended. Bring the sauce to a simmer. Cover
and simmer over low heat for at least 30
minutes (I usually let the sauce simmer for a few
hours), stirring occasionally. Add the basil and
simmer for 10 more minutes.

Cook the lasagna noodles according to
package directions. Drain and rinse with cold
water. Rinse again. Toss the noodles with a bit
of olive oil to prevent sticking. While the noodles
are cooking, mix the ricotta or cottage cheese
with the egg and drained spinach. Preheat
oven to 350°. In a 9x13 pan (I use glass) spread
about 2 cups of sauce over the bottom of the
pan to prevent the noodles from sticking. Next,
put down a layer of four noodles to cover the
bottom of the pan. Then, spread out a layer
of the ricotta or cottage cheese mixture. The
easiest way to do this is to put large spoonfuls
in each corner and one in the middle and
spread the mixture out to evenly cover the
noodles. Follow this with a layer of Parmesan
cheese and a layer of mozzarella. Next, pour
on a layer of sauce followed by another layer
of noodles. Repeat this order for the next
layer. After the third layer of noodles, the order
changes a bit. Follow the noodles with a layer
of cottage cheese mixture, then a layer of
sauce, Parmesan cheese, and mozzarella (You'll
probably have a few cups of sauce leftover.
Since my gatherings usually involve children
and children are often suspect of lasagna, I
usually make the entire box of lasagna noodles,
cut up the extras and mix them with the leftover
sauce for the kids. No scary spinach!). Bake
at 350° for 45 minutes. Let cool for about 15
minutes to set before cutting.

Serves: 9-12
Prep. time: 1 hour
Cooking time: 45 minutes

Up North Sausage and Cheese Bake

Mary tells us, "This recipe has been in our family for years. I always make this when we are entertaining at our cabin up north, hence the name (I can't remember what we used to call it before I changed the name...). Just thinking about it reminds me of good times with family and friends."

1½	lbs. bulk hot/spicy sausage, cooked, drained, and crumbled
3	Cups spoon-sized shredded wheat
3	TB butter, melted
2	Cups shredded Monterey Jack cheese
2	Cups shredded Swiss cheese
12	eggs
1½	Cups milk
¼	Cup white wine*
1	medium onion, minced
1	TB hot mustard powder

While the sausage is browning, lightly butter a 9 x 13 baking dish. Spread spoon-sized shredded wheat in the dish. Drizzle with the melted butter. Sprinkle with Monterey Jack and Swiss cheeses and the sausage. In a medium bowl, beat the eggs, milk, wine, onion and mustard. Pour over the layers in the dish. Cover with foil and refrigerate at least 6 (and up to 24) hours. Let the casserole stand at room temperature for 30 minutes before baking. Preheat the oven to 325° while the casserole stands. Bake, uncovered, at 325° until set, about 75-80 minutes. Let stand for 5 minutes before slicing into squares.

*A note from Mary: "I often substitute brandy for the wine (after all, I DO live in Wisconsin) and it tastes great!"

Prep. time: 20 minutes
Baking time: 75-80 minutes
Serves: 12

All bundled up, Mary and her husband Pat enjoy a late spring snow.

Here's what's cooking:

Serves:

Recipe from the kitchen of:

Mary A. Henreman

Jack, his mother-in-law Mardelle (middle) and wife Gail are all smiles as they're about to sit down to dinner.

Mom's Brown Bread

Jack remembers, "When the brown bread appeared, we knew the holidays were right around the corner. Making the bread was easy. Keeping all eight kids out of it until the holiday was the hard part! Mom traditionally made this bread in beer cans with the tops removed. Now we use vegetable cans. It makes such nice round loaves for slicing."

1	Cup raisins
1	Cup dates, chopped
2	Cups boiling water
2	tsp. baking soda
2	TB vegetable shortening
1½	Cups sugar
2	beaten egg yolks (save the whites)
4	Cups flour
1	tsp. baking powder
⅛	tsp. salt
1	tsp. vanilla
1	Cup chopped walnuts
2	egg whites

Preheat oven to 350°. Mix together the raisins, dates, boiling water and baking soda. Set aside to let the mixture cool.

Cream together the shortening and sugar. Add the egg yolks, flour, baking powder, salt, vanilla and mix well. Fold in the walnuts.

Add all of this to the cooled first mixture. Beat the egg whites until soft peaks form, and then fold gently into the mix. Spoon batter into 5-6 greased or sprayed cans (14-15 oz.), or small individual bread pans, about ⅔ full. Bake at 350° for 35-40 minutes or until a toothpick comes out mostly clean. Let stand for 10 minutes on a rack before removing from cans by turning over and gently thumping the bottom and sides of the can. Turn right side up, let cool completely before wrapping and storing.

Serve warm or cold (both are delicious) with cream cheese, butter or just plain. Can be made ahead, wrapped and frozen for future use. Keep at least one hidden from the family for those unexpected holiday visitors! It's a nice treat with a cup of coffee!

Prep. time: 15 minutes
Baking time: 35-40 minutes
Yield: 5-6 cans of bread

360

credits

MY FAVORITE RECIPE FOR—

SERVES—

TIME TO PREPARE—

Carrie Deke

FROM THE RECIPE FILE OF—

Carrie and her mom Patricia enjoy "a girls' day" out in Madison, Wisconsin.

Porcupine Meatballs

Carrie shares, "Here's one of my favorite retro family recipes. It's easy and definitely enjoyed by both adults and children. My mom used to make these for my sister and me when we were kids—it was one of our absolute favorite dinners. Even though they are named for the rice grains resembling porcupine quills, when we were real young, we actually thought they were made out of porcupines! Now I make them for my husband, and my sister makes them for hers, and I know we'll both be making them for our children. It's definitely a fun and simple recipe that will be handed down in our family for a long time to come."

1	lb. ground beef
½	Cup uncooked rice
½	Cup milk
4	TB chopped onion
1	tsp. salt
½	tsp. celery salt
¼	tsp. garlic salt or garlic powder
⅛	tsp. pepper
2	TB shortening
2	8 oz. cans tomato sauce
1	Cup water
3	tsp. Worcestershire sauce

In a roomy bowl, mix together the beef, rice, milk, onion, salt, celery salt, garlic salt and pepper. Form into 8 meatballs. In a large skillet, heat the shortening. Add the meatballs and cook over medium, turning frequently, until they are browned on all sides. Add the tomato sauce, water and Worcestershire sauce. Mix well. Bring to a boil. Cover, reduce heat to medium-low and simmer for 45 minutes. Flip the meatballs halfway through cooking. Add a small bit of water if the liquid cooks down too much. It is important that the sauce is definitely simmering so the rice on the inside of the meatballs gets cooked all the way through. Delicious!

Prep. time: 15 minutes
Cooking time: 45 minutes
Yield: 8 meatballs

credits

Pasta Carbonara

John shares, "My kids have always loved noodles. A little butter or olive oil, some garlic salt, a sprinkle of Parmesan cheese and that was dinner in their minds. I needed to find a way to get some protein into their favorite dish when along came carbonara. Bacon, eggs and pasta. What's not to like? It has become a staple in our household and will be for a long time to come."

1	lb. dry pasta (we like penne, fusilli, or wagon wheels for holding lots of sauce)
¼-½	lb. bacon, diced (optional)
4	TB butter (½ stick) or 2 TB butter plus 2 TB olive oil
1	Cup milk
¼	tsp. garlic powder
½	tsp. Italian Herb mix
1	pinch ground cloves
2	TB white vinegar
2	eggs, beaten
⅓	Cup Parmesan or Romano cheese, shredded or grated coarsely ground black pepper and/or parsley to taste (optional)

Put a large pot of water on to boil for the pasta. Fry the bacon until crisp, drain, and set aside. Add the butter and olive oil. When the butter has melted, add the milk, garlic, Italian Herb mix, and ground cloves. Heat over medium. When milk begins to simmer, stir in the vinegar and simmer for 15 minutes. Try and time it so the noodles and sauce will be done at the same time. Cook the pasta (according to package directions) al dente and drain, but do not rinse, so it stays very hot. Quickly put the hot pasta in a large serving bowl and toss with the sauce, bacon, the beaten eggs, and the cheese. The heat of the pasta will cook the eggs, but if you are concerned about it, use the "pasteurized egg product" available in the dairy section at most grocery stores. Toss the pasta well to evenly coat with the delicious sauce. Sprinkle with pepper and/or parsley and serve.

Prep. time: 10 minutes
Cooking time: 15 minutes
Serves: 4-6

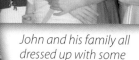

John and his family all dressed up with some place to go.

John's middle name is meat! Here he is preparing his namesake for the Penzeys Christmas party.

362

credits

Kathy and her husband Bruce take a brief break from wintry Wisconsin to vacation in Jamaica.

"My sister Laurie (right) and I were often mistaken for twins when we were growing up," says Kathy. "We were such tomboys on the farm, but on special occasions my mom would dress us up in ribbons, bows and lace."

Chocolate Oatmeal Cookies

Kathy reminisces, "These are one of the first cookies I remember 'helping' my mother make when I was a little girl. It was my job to flatten each cookie by pressing it down with a fork. But my favorite part was scraping the bowl clean. Yum!"

½	Cup butter
1	Cup sugar
1	egg, slightly beaten
2	squares unsweetened baking chocolate, melted
1	tsp. vanilla extract
1	tsp. baking powder
½	tsp. salt
1	Cup flour
1½	Cups rolled oats or quick-cooking oats

Preheat oven to 375°. Cream together the butter and sugar until fluffy. Add the egg, chocolate and vanilla and mix well. In a separate bowl, sift together the baking powder, salt and flour. Gradually add to the creamed mixture. Fold in the rolled oats and mix well. Drop by the teaspoon onto lightly greased baking sheets. Dip a fork in cold water and press the top of each cookie until slightly flat. Bake at 375° for 8-10 minutes. The cookies are soft and chewy when eaten warm from the oven. If you prefer a crisper cookie, they firm up within a day (if they last that long!).

Prep. time: 15 minutes
Baking time: 8-10 minutes
Yield: about 24-30 cookies

Banana Bread

Colin remembers, "I used to baby-sit my little brother when I was in high school and when I would come home from school, there was banana bread sitting on the stove from my mom. I can still remember that banana smell in the kitchen. My mom is a wonderful baker but the banana bread is my favorite!"

3-4	slightly over-ripe bananas
2	TB sour milk (use buttermilk or mix 1/4 tsp. vinegar + 2 TB regular milk)
1/2	Cup butter (1 stick)
1	Cup sugar
2	eggs, beaten
2	Cups flour
1	tsp. salt
1	tsp. baking powder
1/2	tsp. baking soda
1/2	Cup nuts (optional)

Preheat oven to 350°. Place the bananas in a bowl. Add the sour milk and mash the bananas vigorously with a fork. Set aside.

Here's what's cookin'
Recipe from: _____

Serves: _____

Colin Rodcliffe

In a large mixing bowl, cream together the butter and sugar. Add the eggs and mix well. In a separate bowl, sift together the flour, salt, baking powder and baking soda. Gradually add to the batter, alternating with the banana/milk mixture until well mixed. Fold in the nuts if using. Pour into a greased loaf pan and bake at 350° for 60-65 minutes, until brown and springy to the touch.

Prep. time: 15 minutes
Baking time: 60-65 minutes
Yield: 10-14 slices

Colin walks along Lake Michigan in northern Wisconsin.

Swedish Meatballs

Keith tells us, "Mom Cliffe's Swedish meatball recipe is a childhood favorite of my wife, Liz. She introduced me to this fast and easy meal soon after we started dating, and it quickly became one of my favorites also. This is certainly comfort food and really hits the spot on cold wintry days, although we like it so much we make it year round."

1	lb. ground beef
¼	Cup finely chopped onion
3	TB dry bread crumbs or cracker crumbs
½	tsp. salt
⅛	tsp. pepper
¼-½	tsp. garlic powder
⅛-¼	tsp. ground nutmeg
1	egg
2	TB oil
¼	Cup flour
2	Cups water
1	tsp. beef soup base or 2 beef bouillon cubes

In a mixing bowl, combine the ground beef, onion, bread crumbs, salt, pepper, garlic, nutmeg and egg. Mix until well blended. Shape into 1-inch balls. In a roomy frying pan, heat the oil. Add the meatballs and brown on all sides, being careful not to blacken the drippings. Remove the meatballs. Add the flour to the drippings in the pan. Cook, stirring, over low heat until the flour browns. Add the water and soup base. Cook, stirring constantly, until the mixture comes to a boil. Reduce the heat. Add the meatballs, cover, and simmer for 15-20 minutes which should give you enough time to boil some egg noodles to serve with the meatballs.

Prep. time: 20 minutes
Cooking time: 20-25 minutes
Yield: about 20 meatballs

That's Keith on a trip to Florida—always looking at life through the lens of a camera!

credits

Here's what's cookin'

Serves:

Judi Larkin

Judi with a few of her relatives at a family gathering in Utah, summer 2007. Not everyone was there, obviously.

Terese's Spinach Salad

According to Judi, "This delicious (and ginormous) salad recipe comes from my sister-in-law Terese, who is not only a wonderful cook, she's a wonderful cook for huge crowds—which is a good thing considering when we all get together we have a pretty big group...42 I think, unless someone has given birth as this goes to press."

Salad:

1	bunch fresh spinach (2 bags)
1	head iceberg or red leaf lettuce
1	lb. bacon
1	lb fresh mushrooms (your favorite), cleaned and sliced
½ ¾	lb. freshly grated Swiss cheese
1	large purple (red) onion, peeled and sliced
1	Cup large curd cottage cheese, rinsed

Dressing:

¾	Cup olive oil
½	Cup red wine vinegar
⅓	Cup sugar
½	tsp. dry mustard
¾	tsp. salt
¾	tsp. onion powder
2-3	TB poppy seeds

Wash and dry the spinach and lettuce. Rip the lettuce into pieces and place in a very large bowl with the spinach. Combine the dressing ingredients, whisk to blend, and set aside. Chop the bacon into bite-sized pieces, cook over medium heat until brown and crispy, drain on absorbent paper toweling and set aside. Just before serving, combine all the salad ingredients, pour on most of the dressing, toss, add the rest of the dressing if desired, toss again and serve.

Prep. time: 15 minutes, including bacon-cooking time
Cooking time: 0
Serves: 6-8

Butter Noodles

Judi says, "These seasoned, buttered noodles are something I hit upon after frequenting a local restaurant and seeing my sons order the same noodle dish time after time. I thought I could probably re-create it with our Sandwich Sprinkle seasoning, and I was right! Now I make it as an after school–before soccer snack for them. It's delicious, healthy and filling—perfect for two teenage boys."

½	lb. wide egg noodles
2	TB butter
2	TB olive oil
2-4	tsp. Sandwich Sprinkle or garlic salt mixed with your favorite herbs shredded or grated Asiago cheese for sprinkling, optional

Bring a large pot of water to a rolling boil. Add egg noodles, cook according to package directions, usually 7 minutes or so. Drain and rinse very briefly so they stay hot. Melt butter with oil and seasoning—start with the smaller amount, toss with hot pasta, taste, add more seasoning and Asiago cheese as desired, and serve.

Prep. time: 1 minute
Cooking time: 7 minutes
Serves: 4

credits

Recipe for: _____
from the kitchen of: _____

Jerry Boarski

You won't find a bigger camera collection than Jerry's. He has over 50. Here's another one he received for a Christmas gift a few years ago.

Jerry's daughter Beth (right) celebrates her birthday in July 1977 with her family- (left to right) Joel, Jeff, Chris and Lea.

Wacky Cake

Jerry recalls, "This was one of our favorite family recipes for years. It is called a Wacky Cake and it is not only tasty but it is easy and fun to make for young children. It is all assembled in the baking pan, so there is a minimum of mess in the kitchen. As parents all know, when their children are between the ages of 8 and 14 they get an urge to cook and help Mom in the kitchen. When our oldest son, Jeff, was that age he wanted to be a chef when he grew up. And at age 10 our daughter, Beth, was an avid baker. This recipe was her absolute favorite to make and was always welcomed by the family."

1½	Cups flour
1	Cup sugar
3	TB cocoa powder
1	tsp. baking soda
⅓	tsp. salt
1	TB vinegar
1	tsp. vanilla extract
6	TB canola oil
1	Cup cold water
	powdered sugar for dusting

Preheat oven to 350°. In an ungreased, 8-inch square metal baking pan, sift together the flour, sugar, cocoa, baking soda and salt. Level dry ingredients. With the back of a spoon, make 3 depressions. Into the first one, pour the vinegar. Into the second, pour the vanilla. Into the third, pour the oil. Pour the water over the entire cake. Stir thoroughly with a fork. Bake at 350° for 25-30 minutes. Remove from the oven and let cool. Before serving, dust the top with powdered sugar. This cake is very moist and will keep for up to 5 days, but as Jerry says, "At our house it never lasted that long."

Prep. time: 12 minutes
Baking time: 25-30 minutes
Serves: 9-12

367

MY FAVORITE RECIPE FOR—

SERVES—

TIME TO PREPARE—

Eva Erato-Rudek

FROM THE RECIPE

Cinnamon Bread

Eva remembers, "The cinnamon bread recipe that my grandmother made is one of my very favorites. It brings me back to my childhood; she was an amazing cook and baker. She made this on the weekends in the fall, so I can't think of cinnamon or fall without remembering eating this bread when it was warm, with butter, on a cool fall day."

1	package yeast
¼	Cup water
2	Cups milk
½	Cup sugar
½	Cup butter
2	tsp. salt
2	eggs, beaten
7	Cups flour, divided
1	Cup sugar +1½ TB cinnamon

Preheat oven to 375°. Mix the yeast and water in a roomy measuring cup. Gently heat the milk, sugar, and butter in a saucepan until the butter melts; DO NOT BOIL. Mix the yeast mix with the butter mix. Sift salt and 3 cups of flour into a large bowl. Add the frothy yeast/milk mixture and 2 beaten eggs. Add to the flour and mix to form a dough, adding up to 4 more cups of flour to get a springy dough. Knead for 10 minutes. Cover and leave to rise for 1 hour. Knock back and then divide into two. Roll out into two rectangles the size of a jelly roll pan, approximately 1½ inches thick. Sprinkle each roll with the cinnamon sugar, saving 2 TB for the topping, then sprinkle with water, about 2 tsp. per roll. Roll up the breads and then leave to rise about 30 minutes. Dust the tops with the remaining cinnamon sugar and bake for 35-40 minutes. If the loaves start to brown too quickly cover with foil for the remaining cooking time.

Prep. time: 2 hours
Baking time: 40 minutes
Yield: 2 large loaves

A (somewhat) younger Eva holds her birthday cake.

credits

Jack shares a meal with his mother Elizabeth and brother Volker in the early 1960s.

Jack Weissmann (signature)

Baltic-Latvian Pierogi

Jack recalls, "As the middle child it was my duty to help in the kitchen, so I learned how to cook from my mother. My mom was a phenomenal cook! She would make the pierogi and serve them with all different soups and heavy crusty breads which I still enjoy today. The pierogi was regular fare for my family who had fled their homeland of Germany to live in Latvia before the outbreak of WWII, but during the holidays she would make huge batches for my family and all our friends to share."

Dough:
³⁄₄	Cup milk
¼	Cup butter (½ stick)
2	tsp. salt
2	tsp. sugar
¼	Cup warm water
1	tsp. dry yeast
1	egg
3-3½	Cups flour

Mix the yeast in warm (not hot) water in a large bowl. Let stand for 5 minutes, watch for it to get brown froth or bubbles on top so you know it's active. If nothing happens, get fresh yeast and start over. Scald the milk by heating it in a small heavy bottomed pot over medium heat until it is just about to boil and forms a skin. Turn it off; add butter, salt and sugar, and stir, removing any skin that clings to the spoon. Let cool to lukewarm, add to the yeast mix. Lightly beat egg and add to the bowl. Add 1½ cups flour, stir until smooth. Add the rest of the flour gradually, ½ cup at a time. Stop at 3 cups and stir well, adding the rest of the flour only if needed to form a non-sticky dough. Cover with a warm damp non-fuzzy towel and let sit in a warm place by the oven for 10 minutes. Sprinkle flour on a clean surface and turn the dough out on top of it. Knead 6 minutes or so until dough is smooth and soft, sprinkling with just a bit of extra flour if needed. Pour a little oil or melted butter in a clean large bowl, and put in the ball of dough, turning it so it is greased on all sides. Cover again with a warm damp towel and let rise until nearly doubled—which can take 30-75 minutes depending on how warm it is. Don't worry if the dough doesn't totally double as there isn't a lot of yeast in it.

While the dough is rising, prepare the filling.

Filling:
1	large onion, finely chopped
³⁄₄	lb. Westphalian ham, diced about ¼-inch
½	Cup golden raisins
1	tsp. black pepper
¼-½	tsp. salt (to taste)

Don't cut all the fat off the ham, it will melt out during cooking and helps make the filling extra delicious. If there is absolutely no fat on the ham; add 2 TB. oil or butter to the filling. In a large skillet, cook ham, raisins, onions and black pepper for 20 minutes over low heat. Taste and add salt as desired.

Glaze (for brushing on top of pierogi):
1	egg
2	tsp. milk or water
¼	tsp. sugar

After the dough is done rising, preheat the oven to 400°. Grab pieces of dough about the size of golf balls and roll them out to the size of a small hand. Add about 1½ tsp. of filling and fold the dough over to make a half moon shape. Use a fork or pinch firmly to seal the edges well. Place on ungreased cookie sheets. Let rise again for 20-30 minutes. Brush with glaze, bake at 400 degrees for 13-18 minutes, until golden brown.

Prep. time: 2 hours
Baking time: 13-18 minutes
Yield: about 24

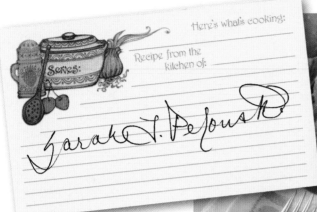

Klutska Soup

According to Sarah, "This traditional Polish soup variation has been a family favorite for generations. My great-grandmother, a Polish immigrant, began this tradition and it has since become a favorite of mine. It was traditionally made and served as an inexpensive meal alongside a loaf of homemade crusty bread or served atop a bowl of boiled potatoes. Money was tight and food was scarce but with a few common kitchen staples, Klutska Soup could be made in a short amount of time and enjoyed by everyone as a hearty inexpensive meal."

Soup Broth:

2	qts. water
2	TB chicken soup base
2	carrots, cut into 1/2 inch coins
2	celery stalks, cut into 1/2-inch slices
2	whole bay leaves
3	whole allspice berries (kubabas in Polish)
1/4	tsp. pepper
1/2	tsp. salt

Dumplings:

2	eggs, beaten
1/4	Cup milk
1 1/4	Cups flour

In a medium soup pot bring water to a boil. Once boiling, add the chicken soup base and continue boiling until dissolved, about 5 minutes. Add to the boiling water the carrots, celery, bay leaves, whole allspice, pepper and salt. Simmer, covered, over low heat for 20 minutes for the spice flavors to infuse the broth and the vegetables to soften.

While waiting for the broth, in a small bowl, mix together the dumpling ingredients with a fork until well combined. The dumpling mixture will have a thick consistency. Once the broth has finished its simmering, remove the bay leaves and allspice and discard them. Return the broth to a boil and drop dumpling mixture into the pot of boiling broth by teaspoonfuls until all the mixture is used up. Return the soup to a simmer over medium-high heat and simmer, uncovered, for 5 minutes, stirring occasionally. This will cook the dumplings throughout. The dumplings will expand in size as they cook, so don't start with too much batter.

Prep. time: 15 minutes
Cooking time: 30 minutes
Serves: 6-8

Sarah as a toddler helping her Grandma Regina in the kitchen.

credits

Stir-Fry and Yellow Rice

Pam tells us, "It's actually saffron rice, but if I was ever out of saffron, the rice was viewed with great suspicion by three pairs of small eyes with furrowed brows because it just wasn't the yellow rice they knew and loved. Now that the kids are grown, they make this however they want—from vegetarian to poultry to steak, and it always tastes great."

Stir-fry:

1	lb. sirloin steak, cut in thin bite-sized strips
1	large onion, cut in strips large enough to be eaten around by those who don't prefer them
8	oz. snap peas or pea pods, cut in half
1	8 oz. can sliced water chestnuts, drained and rinsed
4	TB soy sauce
1	TB honey
2	tsp. Chinese 5 spice powder
½	tsp. garlic
¼	tsp. ginger
dash	cayenne red pepper (more if cooking for those who like it hot)
2	TB sesame oil
2	tsp. arrowroot or cornstarch mixed in 2 TB. water

Whisk the soy sauce, honey, 5 spice, garlic, ginger and cayenne together in a bowl. Add the steak and onion, cover and refrigerate at least 30 minutes—if you can do this a day ahead, it tastes even better. In a large heavy fry pan or wok, heat the sesame oil over medium-high heat. Add the steak in three batches, browning for a few minutes and removing to a bowl. When the last batch has been removed, add peas and water chestnuts to the pan, cook 2 minutes. Add all the beef back to the pan; cook another 3 minutes, tossing frequently. Tip the pan so the liquid collects at the bottom, pushing the meat to the side. Pour in half the arrowroot/water and stir to thicken. Add the other half of the arrowroot mix to thicken further if desired. Serve immediately with saffron rice.

Prep. time: 15 minutes. **Cooking time:** 10 minutes. **Serves:** 4

Saffron Rice:
Start the rice 30 minutes before dinner.

1	Cup long grain white rice
1	pinch saffron threads
1	TB butter
2	Cups water
¼	tsp. salt

In a small heavy saucepan with a lid, melt butter over low heat. Crumble in saffron; stir briefly until the color starts coming out. Rinse the rice; add to the pan and stir to coat. Pour in the water, add the salt and bring to a boil over high heat. Cover and turn the heat to low. Cook 15-18 minutes, until rice is golden and dry. It is done when there are several significant holes visible when you take the lid off. Remove from heat and let stand until stir-fry is done – it stays hot a long time. Gently fluff with a fork before serving.

Prep. time: 1 minute. **Cooking time:** 25-30 minutes. **Serves:** 4

"A hard day for sure, but a glorious day as well. This is what you pray for from the moment they arrive."
Eva, Lucas, mom Pam and Caity together on the day Lucas leaves for his senior year of high school in France and the girls for their second year of college.

credits

My Favorite Recipe For—
SERVES—
TIME TO PREPARE—

FROM THE RECIPE FILE OF—

Bran Muffins

Kevin recalls, "Growing up in Milwaukee in the 1970s meant a lot of wonderful things: eating healthy wasn't one of them. My mom is a great cook but calorie consciousness wasn't high on her watch list back then. So imagine my family's surprise when Mom whipped up a batch of delicious and *gasp* healthy bran muffins for us to try. Imagine her surprise when I raved about how wonderful they were. Never mind the fact that we ate them warm, slathered in butter, the Murack family knew how to eat healthy! Now that I'm older I've carried on the tradition of baking bran muffins for my daughters. They enjoy them plain so that's how we eat them today. The butter only makes an occasional appearance when the girls aren't around."

1	Cup water
2	Cups "all bran" cereal
1	Cup sugar
1	stick butter (½ Cup)
2	eggs
2	Cups buttermilk
1	tsp. vanilla extract
2½	Cups flour
½	tsp. salt
2½	tsp. baking soda
1	tsp. cinnamon
1	Cup "bran buds" cereal

Boil the water. Pour into a large mixing bowl. Add the all bran cereal, stir, and set aside. In another mixing bowl, cream together the sugar and butter. Gradually add the eggs, buttermilk and vanilla and mix well. Gently stir in the flour, salt, baking soda, cinnamon and bran buds. Add the water/all bran mix and stir to combine. Cover and refrigerate for at least 1 hour.

Preheat oven to 350°. Line a muffin pan with paper liners. Pour the batter into the liners ¾ full and bake at 350° for 20 minutes. If you'd like, you can cover the batter and refrigerate up to 1 week and make a few muffins at a time. That way they're nice and warm and fresh.

Prep. time: 15 minutes
Baking time: 20 minutes
Yield: 22-24 muffins

Kevin with his family having Breakfast with Santa- (From left to right) Marin, Kevin, Isabel and Mary.

credits

Swedish Coffee Cake

Lani reminisces, "This recipe has been around as long as I can remember. My kids and my brother's kids always ask for this one and somewhere along the way it has become known as 'S' cake due to its shape. Some like it with the nuts and some without so my mom either makes two or just puts nuts on half to please us all. What a mom! On the off chance this doesn't all get eaten in one day, store the rest in the refrigerator so it won't dry out."

Top:
1	Cup water
½	Cup margarine or shortening—butter does not work as well
1	Cup flour
3	eggs
1	tsp. vanilla extract

Bottom:
1	Cup flour
½	Cup margarine or shortening—butter does not work as well here either
1	TB water

Frosting:
½	Cup butter
1½	Cups powdered sugar
1	tsp. maple syrup
	milk to spreadable consistency

Preheat oven to 400°.

Top: Make this first as it must cool. Bring the water and margarine/shortening quickly to a boil. Add the flour and mix well. Cool while preparing the bottom mixture.

Bottom: Mix the flour and margarine (as for a pie crust). Add the water and mix on low until you can roll between your hands like a rope. Lay on a greased cookie sheet in the shape of an "S". Spread about 4 inches wide by pressing with your fingers.

Top: Add the eggs, one at a time, to the cooled top mixture and mix well after each addition. Add the vanilla and mix again. Spread over the bottom all the way to the edges. Bake at 400° for 30 minutes. Don't peek.

While the cake is baking, make the frosting. Beat together the butter, powdered sugar and syrup until creamy. Add enough milk to make it the consistency you'd like, either a frosting or a drizzle. Turn the oven off and let cool in the oven for 10 minutes. Remove from the oven. Frost when cool and sprinkle with walnuts over the entire cake or on half if some do not care for the nuts.

Prep. time: 30 minutes
Baking time: 30 minutes
Serves: 8

Here's what's cookin' _____
Recipe from: _____   Serves _____

Lani Haag

The Pack did "Win it all" on this Sunday in January 1997. "I just love those handmade cheese-heads!" says Lani. Mom Yvonne, Grandma Hilda, son Tyler, son Mitch, dad Frank, Lani and her husband Doug all cheer on the Green Bay Packers to victory!

Lani's Grandma Hilda celebrates her 79th birthday with the "S" cake.

BOOK recipe index

nutritional information

Hummus Dip   36
(SERVINGS 8; SERVING SIZE 64g); CALORIES 130; CALORIES FROM FAT 70; FAT 8g; SODIUM 300mg; CARB 13g; DIETARY FIBER 2g; CHOLESTEROL 0mg

Sausage Rolls   37
(SERVINGS 8; SERVING SIZE 132g); CALORIES 390; CALORIES FROM FAT 240; FAT 27g; SODIUM 760mg; CARB 24g; DIETARY FIBER 1g; CHOLESTEROL 40mg

Cheese Scones   37
(SERVINGS 8; SERVING SIZE 70g); CALORIES 250; CALORIES FROM FAT 130; FAT 14g; SODIUM 330mg; CARB 25g; DIETARY FIBER <1g; CHOLESTEROL 40mg

Cheesy Toast Points   38
(SERVINGS 10; SERVING SIZE 49g); CALORIES 160; CALORIES FROM FAT 80; FAT 9g; SODIUM 380mg; CARB 13g; DIETARY FIBER <1g; CHOLESTEROL 20mg

Mexican Bean Dip   39
(SERVINGS 12; SERVING SIZE 63g); CALORIES 80; CALORIES FROM FAT 30; FAT 3.5g; SODIUM 280mg; CARB 8g; DIETARY FIBER 2g; CHOLESTEROL 15mg

Gingered Carrot Salad   40
(SERVINGS 4; SERVING SIZE 103g); CALORIES 110; CALORIES FROM FAT 0; FAT 0g; SODIUM 55mg; CARB 27g; DIETARY FIBER 3g; CHOLESTEROL 0mg

Chocolate Soup   40
(SERVINGS 12; SERVING SIZE 35g); CALORIES 140; CALORIES FROM FAT 80; FAT 9g; SODIUM 60mg; CARB 15g; DIETARY FIBER 0g; CHOLESTEROL 25mg

Gingered Tuna Salad   44
(SERVINGS 4; SERVING SIZE 139g); CALORIES 260; CALORIES FROM FAT 130; FAT 14g; SODIUM 670mg; CARB 12g; DIETARY FIBER 1g; CHOLESTEROL 35mg

Chicken and Salad Wraps   45
(SERVINGS 6; SERVING SIZE 260g); CALORIES 480; CALORIES FROM FAT 220; FAT 25g; SODIUM 950mg; CARB 39g; DIETARY FIBER 2g; CHOLESTEROL 70mg

Steak Tacos   46
(SERVINGS 6; SERVING SIZE 248g); CALORIES 430; CALORIES FROM FAT 150; FAT 17g; SODIUM 650mg; CARB 42g; DIETARY FIBER 3g; CHOLESTEROL 60mg

Bill's Spaghetti and Chicken   47
(SERVINGS 4; SERVING SIZE 468g); CALORIES 410; CALORIES FROM FAT 60; FAT 7g; SODIUM 410mg; CARB 62g; DIETARY FIBER 7g; CHOLESTEROL 40mg

Shrimp with Herbs, Tomato and Pasta   48
(SERVINGS 4; SERVING SIZE 165g); CALORIES 190; CALORIES FROM FAT 70; FAT 8g; SODIUM 400mg; CARB 4g; DIETARY FIBER <1g; CHOLESTEROL 180mg

Melty Portobella Sandwiches   49
(SERVINGS 2; SERVING SIZE 215g); CALORIES 380; CALORIES FROM FAT 180; FAT 20g; SODIUM 1350mg; CARB 38g; DIETARY FIBER 3g; CHOLESTEROL 20mg

Peg Anderson's Southern Pecan Pralines   53
(SERVINGS 36; SERVING SIZE 24g); CALORIES 100; CALORIES FROM FAT 50; FAT 5g; SODIUM 15mg; CARB 13g; DIETARY FIBER <1g; CHOLESTEROL 5mg

Alabama Blueberry Bread   54
(SERVINGS 20; SERVING SIZE 79g); CALORIES 190; CALORIES FROM FAT 10; FAT 1g; SODIUM 190mg; CARB 42g; DIETARY FIBER 1g; CHOLESTEROL 30mg

Roy's Minestrone   55
(SERVINGS 10; SERVING SIZE 358g); CALORIES 230; CALORIES FROM FAT 90; FAT 10g; SODIUM 520mg; CARB 27g; DIETARY FIBER 8g; CHOLESTEROL 10mg

Grandmother Rucker's Refrigerator Rolls   57
(SERVINGS 48; SERVING SIZE 34g); CALORIES 90; CALORIES FROM FAT 10; FAT 1.5g; SODIUM 55mg; CARB 17g; DIETARY FIBER <1g; CHOLESTEROL 5mg

Chocolate "Wet" Cake   57
(SERVINGS 24; SERVING SIZE 78g); CALORIES 280; CALORIES FROM FAT 110; FAT 13g; SODIUM 65mg; CARB 40g; DIETARY FIBER <1g; CHOLESTEROL 35mg

Brisket and Barbecue Sauce   58
(SERVINGS 50; SERVING SIZE 82g); CALORIES 120; CALORIES FROM FAT 50; FAT 5g; SODIUM 230mg; CARB 3g; DIETARY FIBER 0g; CHOLESTEROL 45mg

Greenlawn-Otey Eggnog   60
(SERVINGS 20; SERVING SIZE 119g); CALORIES 340; CALORIES FROM FAT 180; FAT 20g; SODIUM 55mg; CARB 24g; DIETARY FIBER 0g; CHOLESTEROL 175mg

Todd Lowe's Smoked Turkey   61
(SERVINGS 18; SERVING SIZE 172g); CALORIES 270; CALORIES FROM FAT 130; FAT 15g; SODIUM 100mg; CARB 3g; DIETARY FIBER <1g; CHOLESTEROL 120mg

Sweet Potato Soup   63
(SERVINGS 8; SERVING SIZE 193g); CALORIES 100; CALORIES FROM FAT 15; FAT 2g; SODIUM 280mg; CARB 13g; DIETARY FIBER 1g; CHOLESTEROL 20mg

Cucumber Salad   64
(SERVINGS 48; SERVING SIZE 83g); CALORIES 40; CALORIES FROM FAT 0; FAT 0g; SODIUM 115mg; CARB 8g; DIETARY FIBER <1g; CHOLESTEROL 0mg

Oatmeal Cake   66
(SERVINGS 12; SERVING SIZE 177g); CALORIES 660; CALORIES FROM FAT 290; FAT 32g; SODIUM 290mg; CARB 89g; DIETARY FIBER 3g; CHOLESTEROL 55mg

MeMe's Cream Cheese Pound Cake   68
(SERVINGS 16; SERVING SIZE 126g); CALORIES 490; CALORIES FROM FAT 210; FAT 23g; SODIUM 210mg; CARB 65g; DIETARY FIBER <1g; CHOLESTEROL 130mg

Savory Butter Beans   70
(SERVINGS 10; SERVING SIZE 245g); CALORIES 120; CALORIES FROM FAT 40; FAT 4.5g; SODIUM 540mg; CARB 16g; DIETARY FIBER 4g; CHOLESTEROL 15mg

Lamb Shanks Toulouse   71
(SERVINGS 6; SERVING SIZE 534g); CALORIES 510; CALORIES FROM FAT 150; FAT 17g; SODIUM 1270mg; CARB 31g; DIETARY FIBER 5g; CHOLESTEROL 85mg

French Toast   78
(SERVINGS 6; SERVING SIZE 70g); CALORIES 130; CALORIES FROM FAT 45; FAT 5g; SODIUM 230mg; CARB 14g; DIETARY FIBER <1g; CHOLESTEROL 185mg

Shawn's Noodles   79
(SERVINGS 4; SERVING SIZE 193g); CALORIES 130; CALORIES FROM FAT 5; FAT 0.5g; SODIUM 240mg; CARB 28g; DIETARY FIBER 3g; CHOLESTEROL 0mg

Pho (Rice Noodle and Beef Soup)   82
(SERVINGS 6; SERVING SIZE 334g); CALORIES 250; CALORIES FROM FAT 35; FAT 3.5g; SODIUM 1430mg; CARB 44g; DIETARY FIBER 1g; CHOLESTEROL 20mg

Tandoori Chicken with Spicy Red Sauce   83
(SERVINGS 10; SERVING SIZE 254g); CALORIES 330; CALORIES FROM FAT 160; FAT 18g; SODIUM 860mg; CARB 23g; DIETARY FIBER 3g; CHOLESTEROL 85mg

Monster Cookies   86
(SERVINGS 108; SERVING SIZE 61g, 2 cookies); CALORIES 270; CALORIES FROM FAT 120; FAT 13g; SODIUM 130mg; CARB 34g; DIETARY FIBER 2g; CHOLESTEROL 30mg

Spinach and Eggplant Lasagna   87
(SERVINGS 6; SERVING SIZE 437g); CALORIES 380; CALORIES FROM FAT 200; FAT 22g; SODIUM 950mg; CARB 22g; DIETARY FIBER 9g; CHOLESTEROL 105mg

Kaitlyn's Easy Chicken and Rice Stir-fry   89
(SERVINGS 4; SERVING SIZE 244g); CALORIES 320; CALORIES FROM FAT 130; FAT 14g; SODIUM 560mg; CARB 29g; DIETARY FIBER 2g; CHOLESTEROL 85mg

Empanadas with Filling 1   93
(SERVINGS 10; SERVING SIZE 174g); CALORIES 420; CALORIES FROM FAT 180; FAT 21g; SODIUM 850mg; CARB 41g; DIETARY FIBER 2g; CHOLESTEROL 100mg

Empanadas with Filling 2   93
(SERVINGS 10; SERVING SIZE 158g); CALORIES 410; CALORIES FROM FAT 180; FAT 20g; SODIUM 800mg; CARB 44g; DIETARY FIBER 2g; CHOLESTEROL 80mg

Quick and Easy Cinnamon Rolls   95
(SERVINGS 18; SERVING SIZE 77g); CALORIES 290; CALORIES FROM FAT 120; FAT 13g; SODIUM 210mg; CARB 40g; DIETARY FIBER <1g; CHOLESTEROL 50mg

Butterhorns   98
(SERVINGS 37; SERVING SIZE 50g); CALORIES 170; CALORIES FROM FAT 70; FAT 7g; SODIUM 55mg; CARB 23g; DIETARY FIBER <1g; CHOLESTEROL 30mg

Great Grandma Moog's Gingersnaps   99
(SERVINGS 30; SERVING SIZE 28g, 2 cookies); CALORIES 130; CALORIES FROM FAT 50; FAT 5g; SODIUM 105mg; CARB 19g; DIETARY FIBER 0g; CHOLESTEROL 5mg

Cocoa Snowflakes   99
(SERVINGS 30; SERVING SIZE 20g, 2 cookies); CALORIES 80; CALORIES FROM FAT 20; FAT 2.5g; SODIUM 50mg; CARB 13g; DIETARY FIBER 0g; CHOLESTEROL 15mg

Phyllo Cheese Straws   104
(SERVINGS 14; SERVING SIZE 54g); CALORIES 130; CALORIES FROM FAT 60; FAT 6g; SODIUM 490mg; CARB 11g; DIETARY FIBER 0g; CHOLESTEROL 10mg

Shredded Chicken and Walnut Sauce   104
(SERVINGS 12; SERVING SIZE 93g); CALORIES 170; CALORIES FROM FAT 100; FAT 11g; SODIUM 380mg; CARB 6g; DIETARY FIBER 1g; CHOLESTEROL 25mg

Eggplant Dip with Pita Crisps 106
(SERVINGS 16; SERVING SIZE 134g); CALORIES 130; CALORIES FROM FAT 70; FAT 8g; SODIUM 250mg; CARB 19g; DIETARY FIBER 4g; CHOLESTEROL 0mg

Stuffed Eggplant 107
(SERVINGS 4; SERVING SIZE 561g); CALORIES 400; CALORIES FROM FAT 260; FAT 29g; SODIUM 3640mg; CARB 37g; DIETARY FIBER 13g; CHOLESTEROL 0mg

Kofta (Turkish Grilled Sausages) 109
(SERVINGS 15; SERVING SIZE 41g); CALORIES 90; CALORIES FROM FAT 50; FAT 6g; SODIUM 180mg; CARB 2g; DIETARY FIBER 0g; CHOLESTEROL 30mg

Turkish Mixed Grill 109
(SERVINGS 2; SERVING SIZE 278g); CALORIES 520; CALORIES FROM FAT 270; FAT 30g; SODIUM 1030mg; CARB 5g; DIETARY FIBER 2g; CHOLESTEROL 170mg

Sautéed Rice with Leeks 109
(SERVINGS 4; SERVING SIZE 391g); CALORIES 350; CALORIES FROM FAT 130; FAT 14g; SODIUM 1760mg; CARB 51g; DIETARY FIBER 2g; CHOLESTEROL 0mg

Hazim's Chicken 110
(SERVINGS 6; SERVING SIZE 159g); CALORIES 310; CALORIES FROM FAT 160; FAT 18g; SODIUM 1390mg; CARB 7g; DIETARY FIBER 2g; CHOLESTEROL 105mg

Hazim's Pasta 110
(SERVINGS 6; SERVING SIZE 99g); CALORIES 360; CALORIES FROM FAT 90; FAT 10g; SODIUM 530mg; CARB 57g; DIETARY FIBER 3g; CHOLESTEROL 80mg

Deviled Eggs à la Sam 116
(SERVINGS 20; SERVING SIZE 55g); CALORIES 80; CALORIES FROM FAT 50; FAT 6g; SODIUM 190mg; CARB 3g; DIETARY FIBER 1g; CHOLESTEROL 105mg

Sushi Rice Eggs 120
(SERVINGS 12; SERVING SIZE 59g); CALORIES 80; CALORIES FROM FAT 10; FAT 1.5g; SODIUM 240mg; CARB 14g; DIETARY FIBER 0g; CHOLESTEROL 25mg

Lobster Chicken on a Nest 121
(SERVINGS 4; SERVING SIZE 289g); CALORIES 450; CALORIES FROM FAT 250; FAT 28g; SODIUM 870mg; CARB 7g; DIETARY FIBER 2g; CHOLESTEROL 260mg

Easy Hollandaise Sauce 121
(SERVINGS 8; SERVING SIZE 32g); CALORIES 180; CALORIES FROM FAT 170; FAT 19g; SODIUM 125mg; CARB 1g; DIETARY FIBER 0g; CHOLESTEROL 150mg

Ice Cream Egg of Delight 122
(SERVINGS 2; SERVING SIZE 175g); CALORIES 360; CALORIES FROM FAT 140; FAT 16g; SODIUM 65mg; CARB 52g; DIETARY FIBER <1g; CHOLESTEROL 130mg

Nate's Mom's Potato Soup 127
(SERVINGS 8; SERVING SIZE 376g); CALORIES 220; CALORIES FROM FAT 10; FAT 1g; SODIUM 640mg; CARB 39g; DIETARY FIBER 4g; CHOLESTEROL 10mg

Nate's Mom's Vegetable Soup 127
(SERVINGS 8; SERVING SIZE 483g); CALORIES 90; CALORIES FROM FAT 20; FAT 2g; SODIUM 1280mg; CARB 17g; DIETARY FIBER 4g; CHOLESTEROL 0mg

Cream of Broccoli Soup 129
(SERVINGS 3; SERVING SIZE 410g); CALORIES 380; CALORIES FROM FAT 240; FAT 26g; SODIUM 860mg; CARB 25g; DIETARY FIBER 2g; CHOLESTEROL 75mg

Carrot and Orange Soup 130
(SERVINGS 4; SERVING SIZE 278g); CALORIES 260; CALORIES FROM FAT 170; FAT 19g; SODIUM 400mg; CARB 22g; DIETARY FIBER 2g; CHOLESTEROL 10mg

Simple Split Pea Soup 130
(SERVINGS 4; SERVING SIZE 352g); CALORIES 370; CALORIES FROM FAT 140; FAT 16g; SODIUM 880mg; CARB 44g; DIETARY FIBER 21g; CHOLESTEROL 0mg

Gram's Goulash Soup 133
(SERVINGS 12; SERVING SIZE 227g); CALORIES 200; CALORIES FROM FAT 110; FAT 12g; SODIUM 700mg; CARB 10g; DIETARY FIBER 1g; CHOLESTEROL 45mg

Gram's Bean Soup 133
(SERVINGS 16; SERVING SIZE 326g); CALORIES 170; CALORIES FROM FAT 25; FAT 2.5g; SODIUM 35mg; CARB 23g; DIETARY FIBER 6g; CHOLESTEROL 25mg

Roast Duck with Sauerkraut Stuffing 139
(SERVINGS 4; SERVING SIZE 499g); CALORIES 990; CALORIES FROM FAT 630; FAT 71g; SODIUM 1480mg; CARB 18g; DIETARY FIBER 3g; CHOLESTEROL 190mg

Yum-Yum 141
(SERVINGS 6; SERVING SIZE 228g); CALORIES 290; CALORIES FROM FAT 160; FAT 18g; SODIUM 500mg; CARB 16g; DIETARY FIBER 2g; CHOLESTEROL 55mg

Onion Pie with Bacon 143
(SERVINGS 6; SERVING SIZE 131g); CALORIES 320; CALORIES FROM FAT 210; FAT 23g; SODIUM 480mg; CARB 22g; DIETARY FIBER 1g; CHOLESTEROL 125mg

Lamb and Cabbage Stew 145
(SERVINGS 10; SERVING SIZE 435g); CALORIES 300; CALORIES FROM FAT 130; FAT 14g; SODIUM 600mg; CARB 16g; DIETARY FIBER 5g; CHOLESTEROL 85mg

Broiled Chicken 146
(SERVINGS 4; SERVING SIZE 316g); CALORIES 650; CALORIES FROM FAT 370; FAT 42g; SODIUM 860mg; CARB 4g; DIETARY FIBER 0g; CHOLESTEROL 225mg

Shrimp in Dill Sauce 151
(SERVINGS 4; SERVING SIZE 175g); CALORIES 470; CALORIES FROM FAT 370; FAT 41g; SODIUM 340mg; CARB 2g; DIETARY FIBER 0g; CHOLESTEROL 325mg

Rare Roast Leg of Lamb 153
(SERVINGS 12; SERVING SIZE 166g); CALORIES 320; CALORIES FROM FAT 150; FAT 17g; SODIUM 670mg; CARB 2g; DIETARY FIBER 0g; CHOLESTEROL 120mg

Fried Green Cabbage 153
(SERVINGS 8; SERVING SIZE 182g); CALORIES 100; CALORIES FROM FAT 60; FAT 7g; SODIUM 660mg; CARB 10g; DIETARY FIBER 4g; CHOLESTEROL 15mg

Pork Chops with Sour Cream Sauce 155
(SERVINGS 6; SERVING SIZE 147g); CALORIES 140; CALORIES FROM FAT 140; FAT 16g; SODIUM 660mg; CARB 4g; DIETARY FIBER <1g; CHOLESTEROL 85mg

Hickory Nut Torte with Frosting 156
(SERVINGS 10; SERVING SIZE 130g); CALORIES 540; CALORIES FROM FAT 310; FAT 34g; SODIUM 410mg; CARB 56g; DIETARY FIBER 1g; CHOLESTEROL 75mg

Sour Cream Muffins (reduced fat) 158
(SERVINGS 9; SERVING SIZE 56g); CALORIES 140; CALORIES FROM FAT 60; FAT 6g; SODIUM 280mg; CARB 18g; DIETARY FIBER 0g; CHOLESTEROL 40mg

Chocolate Nut Pie 159
(SERVINGS 8; SERVING SIZE 78g); CALORIES 280; CALORIES FROM FAT 170; FAT 19g; SODIUM 55mg; CARB 25g; DIETARY FIBER 2g; CHOLESTEROL 40mg

Carrot Loaf (no nuts) 166
(SERVINGS 12; SERVING SIZE 130g); CALORIES 520; CALORIES FROM FAT 270; FAT 30g; SODIUM 360mg; CARB 59g; DIETARY FIBER 2g; CHOLESTEROL 70mg

Kourabiedes (Greek butter cookies) 167
(SERVINGS 30; SERVING SIZE 44g, 2 cookies); CALORIES 210; CALORIES FROM FAT 110; FAT 13g; SODIUM 15mg; CARB 22g; DIETARY FIBER <1g; CHOLESTEROL 40mg

Yai Yai's Chicken 167
(SERVINGS 8; SERVING SIZE 185g); CALORIES 270; CALORIES FROM FAT 150; FAT 16g; SODIUM 300mg; CARB 7g; DIETARY FIBER 1g; CHOLESTEROL 70mg

Greek Spaghetti 167
(SERVINGS 8; SERVING SIZE 123g); CALORIES 330; CALORIES FROM FAT 170; FAT 19g; SODIUM 470mg; CARB 24g; DIETARY FIBER 1g; CHOLESTEROL 60mg

Grandma Landers's Chicken 'n' Rice 168
(SERVINGS 8; SERVING SIZE 271g); CALORIES 330; CALORIES FROM FAT 140; FAT 15g; SODIUM 1440mg; CARB 23g; DIETARY FIBER <1g; CHOLESTEROL 70mg

Citrus Martini–White Chocolate Mousse 169
(SERVINGS 6; SERVING SIZE 137g); CALORIES 600; CALORIES FROM FAT 440; FAT 49g; SODIUM 90mg; CARB 34g; DIETARY FIBER 0g; CHOLESTEROL 120mg

Citrus Martini–Lemon Curd 169
(SERVINGS 6; SERVING SIZE 178g); CALORIES 640; CALORIES FROM FAT 350; FAT 39g; SODIUM 20mg; CARB 71g; DIETARY FIBER 0g; CHOLESTEROL 490mg

Risotto with Chicken and Lemon Grass 170
(SERVINGS 8; SERVING SIZE 320g); CALORIES 310; CALORIES FROM FAT 150; FAT 16g; SODIUM 1490mg; CARB 25g; DIETARY FIBER 2g; CHOLESTEROL 30mg

Lamb Chop Persillade 170
(SERVINGS 4; SERVING SIZE 135g); CALORIES 430; CALORIES FROM FAT 290; FAT 32g; SODIUM 470mg; CARB 4g; DIETARY FIBER <1g; CHOLESTEROL 120mg

Chinese Duck Pizza 171
(SERVINGS 120; SERVING SIZE 12g, 1 piece); CALORIES 25; CALORIES FROM FAT 10; FAT 1g; SODIUM 60mg; CARB 3g; DIETARY FIBER 0g; CHOLESTEROL 5mg

Spaghetti Pie (with Parmesan) 174
(SERVINGS 8; SERVING SIZE 329g); CALORIES 580; CALORIES FROM FAT 270; FAT 30g; SODIUM 1030mg; CARB 56g; DIETARY FIBER 4g; CHOLESTEROL 145mg

Hoisin Chicken — 175
(SERVINGS 4; SERVING SIZE 162g); CALORIES 230; CALORIES FROM FAT 80; FAT 9g; SODIUM 1470mg; CARB 20g; DIETARY FIBER 2g; CHOLESTEROL 20mg

Lemon Meringue Pie — 179
(SERVINGS 8; SERVING SIZE 164g); CALORIES 510; CALORIES FROM FAT 200; FAT 22g; SODIUM 320mg; CARB 72g; DIETARY FIBER <1g; CHOLESTEROL 180mg

Rogan Josh — 185
(SERVINGS 6; SERVING SIZE 372g); CALORIES 480; CALORIES FROM FAT 250; FAT 28g; SODIUM 620mg; CARB 9g; DIETARY FIBER 2g; CHOLESTEROL 150mg

Aloo Gobi — 187
(SERVINGS 4; SERVING SIZE 448g); CALORIES 340; CALORIES FROM FAT 60; FAT 7g; SODIUM 80mg; CARB 64g; DIETARY FIBER 10g; CHOLESTEROL 15mg

Simple Chicken Curry — 188
(SERVINGS 4; SERVING SIZE 342g); CALORIES 260; CALORIES FROM FAT 90; FAT 10g; SODIUM 125mg; CARB 12g; DIETARY FIBER 2g; CHOLESTEROL 70mg

Pork Vindaloo — 191
(SERVINGS 4; SERVING SIZE 526g); CALORIES 470; CALORIES FROM FAT 270; FAT 30g; SODIUM 470mg; CARB 17g; DIETARY FIBER 7g; CHOLESTEROL 100mg

Duck Vindaloo — 191
(SERVINGS 4; SERVING SIZE 562g); CALORIES 470; CALORIES FROM FAT 180; FAT 20g; SODIUM 660mg; CARB 17g; DIETARY FIBER 6g; CHOLESTEROL 60mg

Chicken Biryani — 192
(SERVINGS 6; SERVING SIZE 311g); CALORIES 310; CALORIES FROM FAT 80; FAT 9g; SODIUM 910mg; CARB 34g; DIETARY FIBER 1g; CHOLESTEROL 65mg

Tandoori Chicken Kabobs — 194
(SERVINGS 8; SERVING SIZE 117g); CALORIES 210; CALORIES FROM FAT 90; FAT 10g; SODIUM 270mg; CARB 3g; DIETARY FIBER 0g; CHOLESTEROL 85mg

Tuna with Curry Sauce — 195
(SERVINGS 6; SERVING SIZE 410g); CALORIES 900; CALORIES FROM FAT 280; FAT 31g; SODIUM 530mg; CARB 64g; DIETARY FIBER 3g; CHOLESTEROL 160mg

Tomato Salad — 195
(SERVINGS 6; SERVING SIZE 57g); CALORIES 50; CALORIES FROM FAT 40; FAT 4.5g; SODIUM 100mg; CARB 3g; DIETARY FIBER <1g; CHOLESTEROL 0mg

Sweet Summer Cornbread — 204
(SERVINGS 24; SERVING SIZE 74g); CALORIES 230; CALORIES FROM FAT 80; FAT 9g; SODIUM 240mg; CARB 32g; DIETARY FIBER 1g; CHOLESTEROL 40mg

Southern Style Baby Back Ribs — 204
(SERVINGS 20; SERVING SIZE 61g); CALORIES 120; CALORIES FROM FAT 80; FAT 9g; SODIUM 820mg; CARB 5g; DIETARY FIBER 0g; CHOLESTEROL 30mg

Southern Style Barbecue Sauce — 205
(SERVINGS 43; SERVING SIZE 30g, 2 TB); CALORIES 25; CALORIES FROM FAT 5; FAT 0.5g; SODIUM 120mg; CARB 5g; DIETARY FIBER 0g; CHOLESTEROL 0mg

Blueberry Pie — 208
(SERVINGS 12; SERVING SIZE 129g); CALORIES 330; CALORIES FROM FAT 150; FAT 17g; SODIUM 200mg; CARB 42g; DIETARY FIBER 2g; CHOLESTEROL 0mg

Pecan Pie — 210
(SERVINGS 12; SERVING SIZE 98g); CALORIES 410; CALORIES FROM FAT 240; FAT 27g; SODIUM 90mg; CARB 42g; DIETARY FIBER 2g; CHOLESTEROL 75mg

Jambalaya — 212
(SERVINGS 10; SERVING SIZE 279g); CALORIES 330; CALORIES FROM FAT 120; FAT 13g; SODIUM 380mg; CARB 32g; DIETARY FIBER 2g; CHOLESTEROL 85mg

Iron Pot Chili — 213
(SERVINGS 10; SERVING SIZE 358g); CALORIES 290; CALORIES FROM FAT 80; FAT 9g; SODIUM 580mg; CARB 24g; DIETARY FIBER 7g; CHOLESTEROL 55mg

Meatloaf — 214
(SERVINGS 6; SERVING SIZE 232g); CALORIES 210; CALORIES FROM FAT 70; FAT 7g; SODIUM 1090mg; CARB 12g; DIETARY FIBER 1g; CHOLESTEROL 130mg

Mushroom Gravy — 214
(SERVINGS 12; SERVING SIZE 226g, 1/4 cup); CALORIES 110; CALORIES FROM FAT 80; FAT 8g; SODIUM 360mg; CARB 7g; DIETARY FIBER 1g; CHOLESTEROL 10mg

Sautéed Chicken — 218
(SERVINGS 6; SERVING SIZE 150g); CALORIES 250; CALORIES FROM FAT 100; FAT 11g; SODIUM 330mg; CARB 6g; DIETARY FIBER 0g; CHOLESTEROL 85mg

Irish Soda Bread — 220
(SERVINGS 8; SERVING SIZE 93g); CALORIES 290; CALORIES FROM FAT 70; FAT 7g; SODIUM 290mg; CARB 52g; DIETARY FIBER 2g; CHOLESTEROL 40mg

Enchiladas — 222
(SERVINGS 18; SERVING SIZE 221g); CALORIES 440; CALORIES FROM FAT 270; FAT 30g; SODIUM 900mg; CARB 36g; DIETARY FIBER 7g; CHOLESTEROL 40mg

Chicken and Grape Salad — 225
(SERVINGS 4; SERVING SIZE 158g); CALORIES 320; CALORIES FROM FAT 190; FAT 21g; SODIUM 300mg; CARB 16g; DIETARY FIBER 1g; CHOLESTEROL 45mg

Mom's Meatloaf — 225
(SERVINGS 6; SERVING SIZE 209g); CALORIES 300; CALORIES FROM FAT 130; FAT 14g; SODIUM 490mg; CARB 15g; DIETARY FIBER 2g; CHOLESTEROL 145mg

Scalloped Potatoes — 226
(SERVINGS 10; SERVING SIZE 219g); CALORIES 260; CALORIES FROM FAT 160; FAT 18g; SODIUM 520mg; CARB 14g; DIETARY FIBER 4g; CHOLESTEROL 50mg

Carrot Cake — 226
(SERVINGS 16; SERVING SIZE 134g); CALORIES 550; CALORIES FROM FAT 300; FAT 34g; SODIUM 400mg; CARB 60g; DIETARY FIBER 2g; CHOLESTEROL 45mg

Scalloped Corn — 229
(SERVINGS 9; SERVING SIZE 139g); CALORIES 280; CALORIES FROM FAT 150; FAT 17g; SODIUM 290mg; CARB 32g; DIETARY FIBER 2g; CHOLESTEROL 60mg

Beef and Cornbread Bake — 232
(SERVINGS 6; SERVING SIZE 274g); CALORIES 370; CALORIES FROM FAT 140; FAT 15g; SODIUM 590mg; CARB 31g; DIETARY FIBER 4g; CHOLESTEROL 105mg

Blueberry Muffins — 234
(SERVINGS 12; SERVING SIZE 86g); CALORIES 210; CALORIES FROM FAT 45; FAT 5g; SODIUM 210mg; CARB 37g; DIETARY FIBER 1g; CHOLESTEROL 45mg

Rosemary Roasted Sweet Potatoes — 237
(SERVINGS 3; SERVING SIZE 97g); CALORIES 120; CALORIES FROM FAT 40; FAT 4.5g; SODIUM 35mg; CARB 19g; DIETARY FIBER 3g; CHOLESTEROL 0mg

Pork Chops with Apples and Onions — 237
(SERVINGS 4; SERVING SIZE 310g); CALORIES 350; CALORIES FROM FAT 150; FAT 16g; SODIUM 650mg; CARB 19g; DIETARY FIBER 2g; CHOLESTEROL 90mg

Savory Oranges — 238
(SERVINGS 3; SERVING SIZE 194g); CALORIES 170; CALORIES FROM FAT 90; FAT 10g; SODIUM 320mg; CARB 22g; DIETARY FIBER 5g; CHOLESTEROL 0mg

Ceviche-style Shrimp — 239
(SERVINGS 12; SERVING SIZE 129g); CALORIES 60; CALORIES FROM FAT 5; FAT 1g; SODIUM 640mg; CARB 6g; DIETARY FIBER <1g; CHOLESTEROL 55mg

Stuffed Steak — 241
(SERVINGS 6; SERVING SIZE 277g); CALORIES 270; CALORIES FROM FAT 100; FAT 11g; SODIUM 135mg; CARB 7g; DIETARY FIBER 2g; CHOLESTEROL 90mg

Carrot Cake without frosting — 243
(SERVINGS 24; SERVING SIZE 93g); CALORIES 340; CALORIES FROM FAT 190; FAT 21g; SODIUM 180mg; CARB 37g; DIETARY FIBER 2g; CHOLESTEROL 45mg

Carrot Cake Frosting — 243
(SERVINGS 24; SERVING SIZE 24g); CALORIES 100; CALORIES FROM FAT 45; FAT 5g; SODIUM 30mg; CARB 13g; DIETARY FIBER 0g; CHOLESTEROL 15mg

Sweet and Sour Basting Sauce — 247
(SERVINGS 4; SERVING SIZE 106g); CALORIES 190; CALORIES FROM FAT 60; FAT 7g; SODIUM 360mg; CARB 31g; DIETARY FIBER <1g; CHOLESTEROL 0mg

Chicken with White Wine Sauce — 249
(SERVINGS 4; SERVING SIZE 281g); CALORIES 550; CALORIES FROM FAT 300; FAT 33g; SODIUM 1100mg; CARB 12g; DIETARY FIBER 0g; CHOLESTEROL 175mg

Pollo en Pipian — 252
(SERVINGS 6; SERVING SIZE 244g); CALORIES 350; CALORIES FROM FAT 190; FAT 21g; SODIUM 160mg; CARB 13g; DIETARY FIBER 2g; CHOLESTEROL 65mg

Pechugas Verde (with reg. sour cream) — 253
(SERVINGS 2; SERVING SIZE 406g); CALORIES 690; CALORIES FROM FAT 440; FAT 49g; SODIUM 210mg; CARB 41g; DIETARY FIBER 10g; CHOLESTEROL 140mg

Pechugas Verde (with light sour cream) — 253
(SERVINGS 2; SERVING SIZE 406g); CALORIES 590; CALORIES FROM FAT 310; FAT 34g; SODIUM 230mg; CARB 43g; DIETARY FIBER 10g; CHOLESTEROL 130mg

Pozole   257

(SERVINGS 10; SERVING SIZE 692g); CALORIES 300; CALORIES FROM FAT 60; FAT 7g; SODIUM 480mg; CARB 34g; DIETARY FIBER 5g; CHOLESTEROL 55mg

Al's Firehouse Lasagna   260

(SERVINGS 12; SERVING SIZE 348g); CALORIES 600; CALORIES FROM FAT 290; FAT 32g; SODIUM 1570mg; CARB 34g; DIETARY FIBER 3g; CHOLESTEROL 100mg

Walnut Coffee Cake   261

(SERVINGS 12; SERVING SIZE 94g); CALORIES 350; CALORIES FROM FAT 180; FAT 19g; SODIUM 340mg; CARB 42g; DIETARY FIBER <1g; CHOLESTEROL 75mg

Cinnamon Sour Cream Coffee Cake   261

(SERVINGS 12; SERVING SIZE 85g); CALORIES 310; CALORIES FROM FAT 140; FAT 16g; SODIUM 160mg; CARB 37g; DIETARY FIBER 1g; CHOLESTEROL 65mg

Marmalade Glazed Turkey w/Stuffing   263

(SERVINGS 12; SERVING SIZE 376g); CALORIES 680; CALORIES FROM FAT 290; FAT 33g; SODIUM 950mg; CARB 35g; DIETARY FIBER 2g; CHOLESTEROL 205mg

Vegetable Beef Soup   264

(SERVINGS 8; SERVING SIZE 604g); CALORIES 230; CALORIES FROM FAT 70; FAT 7g; SODIUM 1080mg; CARB 24g; DIETARY FIBER 7g; CHOLESTEROL 35mg

Baked Ham with Spicy Sauce   264

(SERVINGS 18; SERVING SIZE 351g); CALORIES 440; CALORIES FROM FAT 100; FAT 11g; SODIUM 3150mg; CARB 29g; DIETARY FIBER 0g; CHOLESTEROL 155mg

Shrimp Kabobs   265

(SERVINGS 6; SERVING SIZE 77g); CALORIES 90; CALORIES FROM FAT 20; FAT 2g; SODIUM 230mg; CARB 1g; DIETARY FIBER 0g; CHOLESTEROL 115mg

Vegetable Kabobs   265

(SERVINGS 6; SERVING SIZE 107g); CALORIES 50; CALORIES FROM FAT 15; FAT 2g; SODIUM 360mg; CARB 7g; DIETARY FIBER 1g; CHOLESTEROL 0mg

Chris and Aunt Mary's Stromboli   267

(SERVINGS 8; SERVING SIZE 159g); CALORIES 520; CALORIES FROM FAT 310; FAT 34g; SODIUM 1380mg; CARB 28g; DIETARY FIBER 1g; CHOLESTEROL 80mg

Aunt Pat's Pizza Meat   268

(SERVINGS 6; SERVING SIZE 201g); CALORIES 280; CALORIES FROM FAT 130; FAT 14g; SODIUM 1320mg; CARB 20g; DIETARY FIBER 3g; CHOLESTEROL 50mg

Cracchiola Family Sauce   271

(SERVINGS 96; SERVING SIZE 65g, 1/4 cup); CALORIES 25; CALORIES FROM FAT 15; FAT 1.5g; SODIUM 150mg; CARB 1g; DIETARY FIBER 0g; CHOLESTEROL 5mg

Chris's Baked Ziti   271

(SERVINGS 12; SERVING SIZE 159g); CALORIES 260; CALORIES FROM FAT 80; FAT 9g; SODIUM 470mg; CARB 29g; DIETARY FIBER 1g; CHOLESTEROL 20mg

Aunt Eleanor's Spedini   272

(SERVINGS 10; SERVING SIZE 90g); CALORIES 210; CALORIES FROM FAT 110; FAT 12g; SODIUM 580mg; CARB 14g; DIETARY FIBER 1g; CHOLESTEROL 40mg

Roasted Sweet Potatoes   275

(SERVINGS 12; SERVING SIZE 101g); CALORIES 150; CALORIES FROM FAT 70; FAT 7g; SODIUM 330mg; CARB 20g; DIETARY FIBER 3g; CHOLESTEROL 0mg

No Bowl Cake with Frosting   277

(SERVINGS 16; SERVING SIZE 62g); CALORIES 200; CALORIES FROM FAT 60; FAT 6g; SODIUM 150mg; CARB 36g; DIETARY FIBER 0g; CHOLESTEROL 15mg

Salmon Mousse   281

(SERVINGS 12; SERVING SIZE 84g); CALORIES 160; CALORIES FROM FAT 110; FAT 12g; SODIUM 320mg; CARB 2g; DIETARY FIBER 0g; CHOLESTEROL 55mg

Gram's Banana Birthday Cake   285

(SERVINGS 12; SERVING SIZE 258g); CALORIES 830; CALORIES FROM FAT 260; FAT 29g; SODIUM 420mg; CARB 139g; DIETARY FIBER 3g; CHOLESTEROL 140mg

Bananas Foster Bread Pudding   290

(SERVINGS 20; SERVING SIZE 228g); CALORIES 440; CALORIES FROM FAT 140; FAT 15g; SODIUM 230mg; CARB 62g; DIETARY FIBER 2g; CHOLESTEROL 100mg

George's World Famous Bloody Marys   291

(SERVINGS 4; SERVING SIZE 506g); CALORIES 290; CALORIES FROM FAT 0; FAT 0g; SODIUM 2020mg; CARB 25g; DIETARY FIBER 3g; CHOLESTEROL 0mg

Daddy's Sauce Piquant   292

(SERVINGS 8; SERVING SIZE 522g); CALORIES 540; CALORIES FROM FAT 290; FAT 32g; SODIUM 1330mg; CARB 31g; DIETARY FIBER 5g; CHOLESTEROL 60mg

Garlic Cheese Grits   292

(SERVINGS 8; SERVING SIZE 212g); CALORIES 260; CALORIES FROM FAT 200; FAT 22g; SODIUM 280mg; CARB 5g; DIETARY FIBER 0g; CHOLESTEROL 115mg

Cool Cuke and Tomato Salad   294

(SERVINGS 6; SERVING SIZE 117g); CALORIES 100; CALORIES FROM FAT 90; FAT 10g; SODIUM 10mg; CARB 6g; DIETARY FIBER 1g; CHOLESTEROL 0mg

Simple Sautéed Greens   294

(SERVINGS 4; SERVING SIZE 139g); CALORIES 140; CALORIES FROM FAT 90; FAT 10g; SODIUM 45mg; CARB 14g; DIETARY FIBER 2g; CHOLESTEROL 0mg

Perdido Key Fish   295

(SERVINGS 6; SERVING SIZE 280g); CALORIES 280; CALORIES FROM FAT 140; FAT 15g; SODIUM 320mg; CARB 11g; DIETARY FIBER 3g; CHOLESTEROL 80mg

Louisiana Stuffed Eggplant   296

(SERVINGS 2; SERVING SIZE 915g); CALORIES 600; CALORIES FROM FAT 190; FAT 21g; SODIUM 1480mg; CARB 48g; DIETARY FIBER 16g; CHOLESTEROL 240mg

Dorothy's Jambalaya   298

(SERVINGS 12; SERVING SIZE 349g); CALORIES 720; CALORIES FROM FAT 340; FAT 38g; SODIUM 740mg; CARB 59g; DIETARY FIBER 3g; CHOLESTEROL 120mg

Bar-B-Cue Shrimp   298

(SERVINGS 8; SERVING SIZE 235g); CALORIES 860; CALORIES FROM FAT 770; FAT 85g; SODIUM 840mg; CARB 6g; DIETARY FIBER 0g; CHOLESTEROL 295mg

George's Chicken Salad   299

(SERVINGS 6; SERVING SIZE 125g); CALORIES 170; CALORIES FROM FAT 50; FAT 5g; SODIUM 160mg; CARB 16g; DIETARY FIBER 2g; CHOLESTEROL 40mg

Mrs. B's Royal Cajun-Swiss Pot Roast   300

(SERVINGS 8; SERVING SIZE 320g); CALORIES 510; CALORIES FROM FAT 260; FAT 29g; SODIUM 1250mg; CARB 8g; DIETARY FIBER <1g; CHOLESTEROL 130mg

Red Rice and Beans   302

(SERVINGS 6; SERVING SIZE 291g); CALORIES 560; CALORIES FROM FAT 240; FAT 26g; SODIUM 1540mg; CARB 45g; DIETARY FIBER 17g; CHOLESTEROL 60mg

Crawfish Étouffée   303

(SERVINGS 6; SERVING SIZE 185g); CALORIES 220; CALORIES FROM FAT 150; FAT 17g; SODIUM 230mg; CARB 6g; DIETARY FIBER 1g; CHOLESTEROL 125mg

Shrimp Creole   303

(SERVINGS 4; SERVING SIZE 159g); CALORIES 160; CALORIES FROM FAT 60; FAT 7g; SODIUM 250mg; CARB 7g; DIETARY FIBER 1g; CHOLESTEROL 180mg

Jim's Skillet Cornbread   306

(SERVINGS 8; SERVING SIZE 93g); CALORIES 250; CALORIES FROM FAT 110; FAT 12g; SODIUM 440mg; CARB 28g; DIETARY FIBER 2g; CHOLESTEROL 75mg

Super Crab Sandwiches   307

(SERVINGS 8; SERVING SIZE 323g); CALORIES 290; CALORIES FROM FAT 120; FAT 14g; SODIUM 590mg; CARB 23g; DIETARY FIBER 2g; CHOLESTEROL 65mg

Miriam's Gumbo   309

(SERVINGS 12; SERVING SIZE 472g); CALORIES 450; CALORIES FROM FAT 170; FAT 19g; SODIUM 1070mg; CARB 28g; DIETARY FIBER 2g; CHOLESTEROL 155mg

Shrimp and Crawfish Pasta   311

(SERVINGS 12; SERVING SIZE 285g); CALORIES 450; CALORIES FROM FAT 200; FAT 22g; SODIUM 710mg; CARB 38g; DIETARY FIBER 2g; CHOLESTEROL 185mg

Pecan Pralines   313

(SERVINGS 21; SERVING SIZE 71g, 2 pralines); CALORIES 300; CALORIES FROM FAT 140; FAT 16g; SODIUM 75mg; CARB 40g; DIETARY FIBER <1g; CHOLESTEROL 25mg

Stuffed Peppers   315

(SERVINGS 10; SERVING SIZE 381g); CALORIES 280; CALORIES FROM FAT 50; FAT 6g; SODIUM 1230mg; CARB 32g; DIETARY FIBER 4g; CHOLESTEROL 95mg

Mexican Spaghetti with Shrimp   321

(SERVINGS 8; SERVING SIZE 241g); CALORIES 460; CALORIES FROM FAT 140; FAT 16g; SODIUM 350mg; CARB 47g; DIETARY FIBER 2g; CHOLESTEROL 210mg

Chicken Burritos   322

(SERVINGS 8; SERVING SIZE 204g); CALORIES 340; CALORIES FROM FAT 160; FAT 18g; SODIUM 760mg; CARB 26g; DIETARY FIBER <1g; CHOLESTEROL 60mg

Mexican Chicken Soup   323

(SERVINGS 10; SERVING SIZE 382g); CALORIES 390; CALORIES FROM FAT 190; FAT 21g; SODIUM 350mg; CARB 22g; DIETARY FIBER 2g; CHOLESTEROL 100mg

Shrimp Soup — 324

(SERVINGS 6; SERVING SIZE 365g); CALORIES 300; CALORIES FROM FAT 70; FAT 8g; SODIUM 290mg; CARB 35g; DIETARY FIBER 1g; CHOLESTEROL 120mg

Sour Cream Coffee Cake — 326

(SERVINGS 20; SERVING SIZE 57g); CALORIES 230; CALORIES FROM FAT 130; FAT 14g; SODIUM 105mg; CARB 25g; DIETARY FIBER <1g; CHOLESTEROL 35mg

Baja Fish Camp Tacos — 327

(SERVINGS 6; SERVING SIZE 276g); CALORIES 350; CALORIES FROM FAT 130; FAT 14g; SODIUM 540mg; CARB 23g; DIETARY FIBER 2g; CHOLESTEROL 125mg

Ratatouille — 331

(SERVINGS 6; SERVING SIZE 314g); CALORIES 170; CALORIES FROM FAT 110; FAT 12g; SODIUM 15mg; CARB 15g; DIETARY FIBER 6g; CHOLESTEROL 0mg

Healthy Cake — 332

(SERVINGS 24; SERVING SIZE 64g); CALORIES 140; CALORIES FROM FAT 45; FAT 5g; SODIUM 70mg; CARB 21g; DIETARY FIBER <1g; CHOLESTEROL 25mg

"John from Cincinnati" Ice Cream — 333

(SERVINGS 16; SERVING SIZE 125g); CALORIES 340; CALORIES FROM FAT 230; FAT 25g; SODIUM 30mg; CARB 35g; DIETARY FIBER <1g; CHOLESTEROL 80mg

Macaroni and Cheese — 334

(SERVINGS 8; SERVING SIZE 233g); CALORIES 450; CALORIES FROM FAT 120; FAT 13g; SODIUM 310mg; CARB 63g; DIETARY FIBER 4g; CHOLESTEROL 40mg

Lebanese Salad — 336

(SERVINGS 8; SERVING SIZE 278g); CALORIES 100; CALORIES FROM FAT 70; FAT 7g; SODIUM 890mg; CARB 9g; DIETARY FIBER 3g; CHOLESTEROL 0mg

Lebanese Fried Cauliflower with Lamb — 337

(SERVINGS 6; SERVING SIZE 360g); CALORIES 290; CALORIES FROM FAT 110; FAT 13g; SODIUM 470mg; CARB 12g; DIETARY FIBER 4g; CHOLESTEROL 100mg

Tamale Brownies — 338

(SERVINGS 24; SERVING SIZE 51g); CALORIES 200; CALORIES FROM FAT 80; FAT 9g; SODIUM 70mg; CARB 29g; DIETARY FIBER 4g; CHOLESTEROL 50mg

Homemade Granola — 339

(SERVINGS 16; SERVING SIZE 46g); CALORIES 200; CALORIES FROM FAT 80; FAT 9g; SODIUM 80mg; CARB 24g; DIETARY FIBER 4g; CHOLESTEROL 0mg

Acai Syrup — 339

(SERVINGS 8; SERVING SIZE 36g); CALORIES 30; CALORIES FROM FAT 0; FAT 0g; SODIUM 0mg; CARB 8g; DIETARY FIBER 0g; CHOLESTEROL 0mg

10 Pepper Pork — 341

(SERVINGS 12; SERVING SIZE 235g); CALORIES 410; CALORIES FROM FAT 170; FAT 19g; SODIUM 540mg; CARB 32g; DIETARY FIBER 2g; CHOLESTEROL 85mg

Yost Stuffed Mushrooms — 342

(SERVINGS 20; SERVING SIZE 53g); CALORIES 90; CALORIES FROM FAT 70; FAT 7g; SODIUM 190mg; CARB 2g; DIETARY FIBER 0g; CHOLESTEROL 20mg

Carl's Criss-Cross Rib-eye — 343

(SERVINGS 2; SERVING SIZE 301g); CALORIES 500; CALORIES FROM FAT 230; FAT 25g; SODIUM 960mg; CARB 3g; DIETARY FIBER 0g; CHOLESTEROL 165mg

Tomato Salad — 347

(SERVINGS 6; SERVING SIZE 218g); CALORIES 200; CALORIES FROM FAT 140; FAT 16g; SODIUM 240mg; CARB 10g; DIETARY FIBER 2g; CHOLESTEROL 15mg

Raspberry Cream Cheese Bars — 349

(SERVINGS 28; SERVING SIZE 63g); CALORIES 230; CALORIES FROM FAT 110; FAT 12g; SODIUM 150mg; CARB 28g; DIETARY FIBER <1g; CHOLESTEROL 45mg

Cheese Wafers — 351

(SERVINGS 25; SERVING SIZE 30g); CALORIES 140; CALORIES FROM FAT 100; FAT 11g; SODIUM 210mg; CARB 5g; DIETARY FIBER 0g; CHOLESTEROL 30mg

L.A. Caviar — 351

(SERVINGS 30; SERVING SIZE 30g); CALORIES 35; CALORIES FROM FAT 20; FAT 2g; SODIUM 50mg; CARB 4g; DIETARY FIBER <1g; CHOLESTEROL 0mg

Arleigh's French Toast — 353

(SERVINGS 8; SERVING SIZE 143g); CALORIES 360; CALORIES FROM FAT 70; FAT 8g; SODIUM 690mg; CARB 58g; DIETARY FIBER 3g; CHOLESTEROL 115mg

Potato Pancakes — 354

(SERVINGS 10; SERVING SIZE 114g); CALORIES 130; CALORIES FROM FAT 40; FAT 4.5g; SODIUM 340mg; CARB 20g; DIETARY FIBER 1g; CHOLESTEROL 20mg

Mom's Marinated Flank Steak — 355

(SERVINGS 3; SERVING SIZE 170g); CALORIES 250; CALORIES FROM FAT 100; FAT 11g; SODIUM 860mg; CARB 2g; DIETARY FIBER 0g; CHOLESTEROL 55mg

Blueberry Pancakes — 357

(SERVINGS 8; SERVING SIZE 154g); CALORIES 200; CALORIES FROM FAT 35; FAT 3.5g; SODIUM 530mg; CARB 36g; DIETARY FIBER 3g; CHOLESTEROL 110mg

Lasagna — 358

(SERVINGS 12; SERVING SIZE 384g); CALORIES 540; CALORIES FROM FAT 210; FAT 23g; SODIUM 910mg; CARB 37g; DIETARY FIBER 4g; CHOLESTEROL 120mg

Up North Sausage and Cheese Bake — 359

(SERVINGS 12; SERVING SIZE 198g); CALORIES 480; CALORIES FROM FAT 320; FAT 35g; SODIUM 790mg; CARB 18g; DIETARY FIBER 2g; CHOLESTEROL 270mg

Mom's Brown Bread — 360

(SERVINGS 24; SERVING SIZE 77g); CALORIES 220; CALORIES FROM FAT 45; FAT 5g; SODIUM 135mg; CARB 41g; DIETARY FIBER 2g; CHOLESTEROL 25mg

Porcupine Meatballs — 361

(SERVINGS 8; SERVING SIZE 163g); CALORIES 190; CALORIES FROM FAT 70; FAT 8g; SODIUM 740mg; CARB 15g; DIETARY FIBER 1g; CHOLESTEROL 35mg

Pasta Carbonara — 362

(SERVINGS 6; SERVING SIZE 154g); CALORIES 410; CALORIES FROM FAT 100; FAT 11g; SODIUM 290mg; CARB 59g; DIETARY FIBER 2g; CHOLESTEROL 95mg

Chocolate Oatmeal Cookies — 363

(SERVINGS 12; SERVING SIZE 58g); CALORIES 250; CALORIES FROM FAT 100; FAT 11g; SODIUM 190mg; CARB 35g; DIETARY FIBER 2g; CHOLESTEROL 35mg

Banana Bread — 364

(SERVINGS 10; SERVING SIZE 108g); CALORIES 310; CALORIES FROM FAT 90; FAT 10g; SODIUM 410mg; CARB 50g; DIETARY FIBER 2g; CHOLESTEROL 60mg

Swedish Meatballs — 365

(SERVINGS 5; SERVING SIZE 191g); CALORIES 250; CALORIES FROM FAT 130; FAT 14g; SODIUM 480mg; CARB 9g; DIETARY FIBER <1g; CHOLESTEROL 90mg

Terese's Spinach Salad — 366

(SERVINGS 8; SERVING SIZE 309g); CALORIES 500; CALORIES FROM FAT 340; FAT 38g; SODIUM 850mg; CARB 20g; DIETARY FIBER 3g; CHOLESTEROL 50mg

Buttered Noodles — 366

(SERVINGS 4; SERVING SIZE 72g); CALORIES 330; CALORIES FROM FAT 130; FAT 15g; SODIUM 320mg; CARB 40g; DIETARY FIBER 2g; CHOLESTEROL 75mg

Wacky Cake — 367

(SERVINGS 12; SERVING SIZE 64g); CALORIES 200; CALORIES FROM FAT 70; FAT 7g; SODIUM 170mg; CARB 31g; DIETARY FIBER <1g; CHOLESTEROL 0mg

Cinnamon Bread — 368

(SERVINGS 32; SERVING SIZE 62g); CALORIES 180; CALORIES FROM FAT 30; FAT 3.5g; SODIUM 180mg; CARB 33g; DIETARY FIBER <1g; CHOLESTEROL 20mg

Baltic-Latvian Pierogi — 369

(SERVINGS 24; SERVING SIZE 58g); CALORIES 130; CALORIES FROM FAT 35; FAT 4g; SODIUM 250mg; CARB 16g; DIETARY FIBER <1g; CHOLESTEROL 35mg

Klutska Soup — 370

(SERVINGS 8; SERVING SIZE 309g); CALORIES 110; CALORIES FROM FAT 15; FAT 1.5g; SODIUM 790mg; CARB 20g; DIETARY FIBER 1g; CHOLESTEROL 45mg

Stir-Fry and Yellow Rice — 371

(SERVINGS 4; SERVING SIZE 474g); CALORIES 590; CALORIES FROM FAT 180; FAT 20g; SODIUM 1260mg; CARB 60g; DIETARY FIBER 4g; CHOLESTEROL 110mg

Bran Muffins — 372

(SERVINGS 18; SERVING SIZE 95g); CALORIES 210; CALORIES FROM FAT 60; FAT 6g; SODIUM 360mg; CARB 37g; DIETARY FIBER 5g; CHOLESTEROL 35mg

Swedish Coffee Cake — 373

(SERVINGS 8; SERVING SIZE 159g); CALORIES 630; CALORIES FROM FAT 420; FAT 46g; SODIUM 420mg; CARB 47g; DIETARY FIBER <1g; CHOLESTEROL 100mg

ALL-INCLUSIVE recipe index

ALL-INCLUSIVE recipe index

384